Defending Frenemies

Defending Frenemies

Alliances, Politics, and Nuclear Nonproliferation in US Foreign Policy

JEFFREY W. TALIAFERRO

OXFORD
UNIVERSITY PRESS

Oxford University Press is a department of the University of Oxford. It furthers
the University's objective of excellence in research, scholarship, and education
by publishing worldwide. Oxford is a registered trade mark of Oxford University
Press in the UK and certain other countries.

Published in the United States of America by Oxford University Press
198 Madison Avenue, New York, NY 10016, United States of America.

© Oxford University Press 2019

All rights reserved. No part of this publication may be reproduced, stored in
a retrieval system, or transmitted, in any form or by any means, without the
prior permission in writing of Oxford University Press, or as expressly permitted
by law, by license, or under terms agreed with the appropriate reproduction
rights organization. Inquiries concerning reproduction outside the scope of the
above should be sent to the Rights Department, Oxford University Press, at the
address above.

You must not circulate this work in any other form
and you must impose this same condition on any acquirer.

Library of Congress Cataloging-in-Publication Data
Names: Taliaferro, Jeffrey W., author.
Title: Defending Frenemies : Alliances, Politics, and Nuclear Nonproliferation
in US Foreign Policy / Jeffrey W. Taliaferro.
Description: New York, NY : Oxford University Press, 2019. |
Includes bibliographical references.
Identifiers: LCCN 2018058357 | ISBN 9780190939304 (hardcover : alk. paper) |
ISBN 9780190939311 (pbk. : alk. paper) |
ISBN 9780190939342 (oxford scholarship online)
Subjects: LCSH: Nuclear nonproliferation—Government
policy—United States—History. | Nuclear arms control—Government
policy—United States—History. |
United States—Foreign relations—1945–1989. | Alliances.
Classification: LCC JZ5665 .T365 2019 | DDC 327.1/7470973—dc23
LC record available at https://lccn.loc.gov/2018058357

3 5 7 9 8 6 4 2

Paperback printed by Marquis, Canada
Hardback printed by Bridgeport National Bindery, Inc., United States of America

CONTENTS

List of Figures and Tables vii
Acknowledgments ix
List of Abbreviations and Acronyms Used in the Texts and Notes xiii

1. Introduction 1

2. Neoclassical Realist Theory, Alliance Politics, and Nonproliferation 36

3. The United States and Israel's Nuclear Weapons Program, 1961–1973 64

4. The United States and Pakistan's Nuclear Weapons Program, 1975–1990 112

5. The United States and South Korea's Nuclear Weapons Program, 1970–1981 160

6. The United States and Taiwan's Nuclear Weapons Program, 1967–1978 211

7. Conclusions 259

Index 277

FIGURES AND TABLES

Figures

1.1 Neoclassical Realist Theory   15
1.2 Spectrum of (Bilateral) Asymmetric Alliances   19

Tables

1.1 States with Active and Abandoned Nuclear Weapons Programs, 1941–2016   24
2.1 Possible Combination of Values on the IVs and the DV   48
2.2 Possible Combination of Values on the IVs, the IVV, and the DV   55
2.3 Alternative Theories, IVs, and Testable Hypotheses   61
2.4 Cross-Case Comparisons of Alternative Theories   63
7.1 Empirical Support for Alternative Hypotheses   263

ACKNOWLEDGMENTS

I have been interested in great power politics, nuclear weapons, and the United States' relationships with strategically vulnerable (and often, obstreperous) allies for as long I can remember. By the time I started my graduate studies in Harvard University's Government Department in the early 1990s, however, the Cold War had ended, the Soviet Union dissolved, and both nuclear weapons and great power competition appeared relegated to the dustbin of history. The international relations subfield of political science, especially its security studies wing, appeared to be in existential crisis. Now, twenty-five years later, great power competition, nuclear weapons and proliferation, and the United States' relations with vulnerable allies are back in the news, on the minds of policymakers, and at the forefront of scholarly research agendas.

I simply could not have completed this book without the support of many mentors, research institutions, colleagues, friends (not frenemies), and family.

Throughout my career, I have admired international relations scholars whose works transcend different schools of theories (realism, liberalism, and constructivism) and different levels of analysis, who ask big and important questions, and who combine a commitment to theory construction with detailed historical research. I am supremely fortunate to have three such scholars as mentors and friends: Tony Smith, Benjamin Miller, and T. V. Paul.

Tony was my colleague, mentor, and trusted confidante in the Tufts University Political Science Department until his retirement in 2016. He is a brilliant and prolific scholar of comparative politics, international relations, and US foreign policy. He and I rarely see "eye to eye" on theoretical matters—he is a proponent of Wilsonian liberalism and I am a (neoclassical) realist. We do share an interest in the cross-fertilization of international relation and international history. We also share a certain bemusement (and sometimes bewilderment) at recurrent patterns in US foreign policy. Over the years, Tony has been one of my strongest supporters. I owe him a tremendous debt.

Ben Frankel, the founding editor of the journal *Security Studies*, introduced me to Benny Miller in the early 2000s. I had read Benny's first book as a PhD student. I was impressed by his willingness to step beyond the confines of Kenneth Waltz's structural realism and to develop a theory to explain the integrative dynamics between the superpower rivalry and the rivalry between his native Israel and its Arab adversaries during the Cold War. Over the years, Benny has become a dear friend and mentor.

Finally, T. V. Paul has been a source of inspiration and support for many years. It would be an understatement to call him an accomplished, influential, and prolific international relations scholar. He is also an extremely generous scholar and superb mentor of graduate students and younger scholars. Much of my thinking about regions and regional power dynamics originated with a chapter that he asked to me contribute to volume he edited on *International Relations Theory and Regional Transformation*. I benefited from his scholarship on the India-Pakistan conflict, status hierarchies in world politics, and nuclear proliferation. Finally, T. V. provided extensive written comments on several chapters, offering insightful criticisms and suggestions to improve the book manuscript.

I first began to conceive of this project while on sabbatical in spring semester 2013. T. V. invited me to spend the month of April 2013 as a faculty fellow at the Université de Montreal–McGill University Centre for International Politics and Security Studies. The Associate Professor Research Fellowship awarded by the Office of the Dean of the School of Arts and Sciences at Tufts University in spring semester 2015 enabled me to do some preliminary research toward this book.

In May and June 2016, I had held a research fellowship at the Norwegian Nobel Institute in Oslo, Norway. I am grateful to Asle Toje, the research director of the Norwegian Nobel Institute, for his hospitality and his interest in my scholarship. I had the good fortune to present very early versions of chapters 1 and 3 at the Institute and at the Nobel Symposium on "The Causes of Peace" held at Solstad Hotel and Bad in Øs Commune, Norway.

I revised the earlier chapters and wrote the final two empirical chapters during my fellowship at the Woodrow Wilson International Center for Scholars in Washington, DC, between September 2017 and May 2018. I could not have imagined a more supportive, collegial, and intellectual stimulating environment.

I am especially grateful to Robert V. Litwak, the Wilson Center's senior vice president and director of the International Security Studies Program, for his support, encouragement, and insightful comments on my work. Kim Conner, Arlyn Charles, Lindsay Collins, and Beverly Thomas in the Office of Scholar and Academic Relations were wonderfully supportive. Janet Spikes, the director of the Wilson Center Library, and Michele Kamalich and Katherine Wahler, research librarians, were extremely helpful in obtaining books from the Library of

Congress and from various university research libraries in the Washington, DC, area. I thank Charles Kraus, a program associate in the Wilson Center's History and Public Policy Program, for sharing the declassified documents he obtained from the Gerald R. Ford Presidential Library and Jimmy Carter Presidential Library. I am grateful to the AY 2017–2018 class of Wilson Center scholars for their feedback on my work, especially Michael Gordon, Amy Holmes, Stephen Kaplan, Aynne Kokas, Akira Kurosaki, Patrick McEachern, Neeti Nair, Elizabeth Stanley, and Irene Wu.

Many colleagues and friends provided written comments and suggestions on various parts of this manuscript. I would like to thank Stephen Brooks, Timothy Crawford, Jeffrey Friedman, Ronan Tsemin Fu, Brendan Rittenhouse Green, Patrick James, Igor Kovic, Alexander Lanoszka, Jennifer Lind, Mary McKinney, Jonathan Markowitz, Nicholas Miller, Evan Bradon Montgomery, Nuno Monteiro, Daryl Press, Brain Rathbun, Evan Resnick, Randall Schweller, Joshua Shifrinson, Benjamin Valentino, and William Wohlforth. Alex Lanoszka generously gave me access to declassified documents he obtained through the Remote Archives Capture Program (RAC) at the Ford and Carter Presidential Libraries, as well as at the National Archives II in College Park.

I am especially grateful to Norrin Ripsman and Steven Lobell, my collaborators on several previous projects, for their support, wisdom, and friendship over the years. Our scholarly collaboration has deeply shaped how I think about international politics and international relations theory. Our friendship is one of the most rewarding aspects of my academic career.

In addition to the Nobel Institute and the Wilson Center, I presented parts of this manuscript at the Dartmouth College's Dicky Center for International Understanding; the Department of Political Science at the University of Cincinnati; the Science, Technology, and Society (STS) Program Faculty Seminar at Tufts University; the Center for International Studies at the University of Southern California; and the International Studies Association Annual Convention. I thank the participants and the discussants at those seminars and conference panels.

I have had superb research assistance at Tufts University and at the Wilson Center. At Tufts, my research assistants included David Wallsh and Prashanth Parmeswaran, both PhD students at the Fletcher School, and Zachary Shapiro, Patrick Hamon, Jason Peluso, Austin Brush, and Jameson Moore, who were, at the time, undergraduates majoring in international relations. At the Wilson Center, my "scholar interns" were Salman Ameri, Alexander Roberts, and Jeffrey Hunter Johnson. Their assistance was invaluable.

Three other people at Tufts University deserve mention. Elizabeth Remick and Ioannis (Yannis) Evrigenis have been loyal friends and valued colleagues for many years, as has our department administrator, Paula Driscoll. I thank them each for their encouragement, support, and friendship.

I am particularly grateful to Oxford University Press. I would like to thank my editor, David McBride, for this enthusiasm for this project, as well as his patience in awaiting the delivery of the final manuscript. I thank Emily Mackenzie for shepherding this book through the production process.

Finally, I would like to thank my family, specifically my family of choice. Paul R. Fisher has lived with this book project longer than anyone else, aside from my two "research" cats—Micah and Biff. I thank him from the bottom of my heart.

Jeffrey W. Taliaferro
Boston
November 2018

ABBREVIATIONS AND ACRONYMS USED IN THE TEXTS AND NOTES

ABM	Antiballistic missile
ACADA	Arms Control and Disarmament Agency, United States
ADD	Agency for Defense Development, South Korea
AEC	Atomic Energy Commission, United States
AECA	Arms Export Control Act of 1976, United States
AID	Agency for International Development, United States
APC	Armored Personnel Carrier
AWACS	Airborne Warning and Control System
BJP	Bharatiya Janata Party, India
CAEC	Chinese Atomic Energy Council, Taiwan
CANDU	Canada Deuterium Uranium
CBMs	Confidence Building Measures
CCP	Chinese Communist Party
CENTCOM	Central Command, United States
CIA	Central Intelligence Agency, United States
CINCPAC	Commander-in-Chief, Pacific Command, United States
CINCUSFK	Commander-in-Chief, United States Forces in Korea
CINUNC	Commander-in-Chief, United Nations Command, Korea
CIST	Chungshan Institute of Science and Technology, Taiwan
CPSU	Communist Party of the Soviet Union
CTBT	Comprehensive Test Ban Treaty
CWIHP	Cold War International History Project, Woodrow Wilson International Center for Scholars
D	Democratic Party, United States
DCI	Director of Central Intelligence, United States
DEFCON	Defense Condition
DIA	Defense Intelligence Agency, United States

DMZ	Demilitarized Zone, Korea
DNSA	Digital National Security Archives
DoD	Department of Defense, United States
DoE	Department of Energy, United States
DoS	Department of State, United States
DPRK	Democratic People's Republic of Korea, commonly known as North Korea
DRA	Democratic Republic of Afghanistan
DSAA	Defense Security Assistance Agency, United States
EA	Bureau of East Asia and Pacific Affairs, Department of State
ERDA	Energy Research and Development Administration, United States
ESF	Executive Secretariat File
EUCOM	European Command, United States
EUR	Bureau of European and Eurasian Affairs, Department of State
EURATOM	European Atomic Energy Community
EXCOM	Executive Committee, National Security Council, Kennedy administration (1961–1963)
EXDIS	Exclusive Distribution
EXIM	Export Import Bank, United States
FAA	Foreign Assistance Act of 1961, United States
FMET	Foreign military education and training
FMS	Foreign military sales
FOIA	Freedom of Information Act, United States
FRG	Federal Republic of Germany, commonly known as West Germany, 1949–1990
FRUS	*Foreign Relations of the United States*
FY	Fiscal Year
GBL	George Bush Presidential Library
GFL	Gerald R. Ford Presidential Library
GOI	Government of Israel
GOJ	Government of Japan
GOP	Government of Pakistan
GROC	Government of the Republic of China (Taiwan)
HAK	Henry A. Kissinger
HEU	Highly Enriched Uranium
HFAC	House Foreign Affairs Committee
HSTL	Harry S. Truman Presidential Library
IAEA	International Atomic Energy Agency
IAEC	Israeli Atomic Energy Commission

IDAF	Israel Defense Air Force
IDF	Israel Defense Forces
INER	Institute of Nuclear Energy Research, Taiwan
INR	Bureau of Intelligence and Research, Department of State
ISA	Office of International Security Affairs, Department of Defense
ISI	Inter Services Intelligence, Pakistan
JCL	Jimmy Carter Presidential Library
JCS	Joint Chiefs of Staff, United States
JFKL	John F. Kennedy Library
KAERI	Korea Atomic Energy Research Institute, South Korea
KANUPP	Karachi Nuclear Power Plant, Pakistan
KCIA	Korea Central Intelligence Agency
KMT	Kuomintang (Chinese Nationalist Party), Taiwan
KNFDI	Korea Nuclear Fuel Development Institute, South Korea
KPA	Korean People's Army, North Korea
LBJL	Lyndon B. Johnson President Library
LEU	Low Enriched Uranium
LWR	Light Water Reactor
MAC	Military Assistance Command
MAP	Military Assistance Program
Memcon	Memorandum of Conversation
MND	Ministry of National Defense, South Korea or Taiwan
MOFA	Ministry of Foreign Affairs, various countries
MOST	Ministry of Science and Technology, South Korea
MOU	Memorandum of Understanding
NAC	North Atlantic Council
NARA	National Archives and Records Administration
NATO	North Atlantic Treaty Organization
NEA	Bureau of Near Eastern Affairs, Department of State
NIC	National Intelligence Council
NIE	National Intelligence Estimate
NIO	National Intelligence Officer
NNPA	Nuclear Nonproliferation Act of 1978, United States
NNWS	Non-Nuclear Weapons State
NODIS	No Distribution Without Permission
NPIHT	Nuclear Proliferation International History Project, Woodrow Wilson International Center for Scholars
NPL	Richard M. Nixon Presidential Library
NPT	Treaty on the Nonproliferation of Nuclear Weapons of 1968, commonly known as the Nuclear Nonproliferation Treaty

NRX	National Research Experimental
NSA	National Security Agency, United States
NSA	National Security Archive, George Washington University
NSA EBB	*National Security Archive Electronic Briefing Book*
NSC	National Security Council, United States
NSDM	National Security Decision Memorandum
NSPG	National Security Planning Group, National Security Council, Reagan administration (1981–1989)
NWS	Nuclear Weapons State
OES	Bureau of Oceans and International Environmental and Scientific Affairs, Department of State
OMB	Office of Management and Budget, United States
OPEC	Organization of Petroleum Exporting Countries
OSD	Office of the Secretary of Defense, United States
PACOM	Pacific Command, United States
PD	Presidential Decision
PDPA	People's Democratic Party of Afghanistan
PPP	Pakistan People's Party
PRC	People's Republic of China, commonly known as China
PRC	Policy Review Committee, National Security Council, Carter administration (1977–1981)
PRM	Presidential Review Memorandum
PSF	President's Secretary's File
PTBT	Partial Test Ban Treaty
R	Republican Party, United States
RG	Record Group, National Archives
ROC	Republic of China on Taiwan, commonly known as Taiwan
ROK	Republic of Korea, commonly known as South Korea
ROKG	Republic of Korea Government
RRL	Ronald Reagan Presidential Library
SACEUR	Supreme Allied Commander–Europe
SALT	Strategic Arms Limitation Treaty
SAM	Surface-to-air missile
SCI	Bureau of International Scientific and Technological Affairs, Department of State
SEA	Southeast Asia
SecDef	Secretary of Defense, United States
SecState	Secretary of State, United States
SF	Subject File
SFRC	Senate Foreign Relations Committee
SLOC	Sea Lanes of Communication

SNIE	Special National Intelligence Estimate
S/P	Policy Planning Staff, Department of State
SRC	Senior Review Committee, National Security Council, Carter administration (1977–1981)
SSA	Security Supporting Assistance
TelCon	Telephone Conversation
TRA	Taiwan Relations Act of 1979, United States
TRR	Taiwan Research Reactor
UN	United Nations
UNC	United Nations Command (Korea)
UNSC	United Nations Security Council
UNSCR	United Nations Security Council Resolution
USAID	United States Agency for International Development
USDDO	US Declassified Documents Online
USG	United States Government
USSR	Union of Soviet Socialist Republics, commonly known as the Soviet Union
WEC	Weapons Exploration Committee, South Korea
WHORM	White House Office Record Management
WMD	Weapons of mass destruction
WSAG	Washington Special Actions Group, National Security Council, Nixon and Ford administrations (1969–1977)

Defending Frenemies

1

Introduction

When has the United States employed coercive strategies, such as intrusive inspections of nuclear facilities, economic sanctions, or the withdrawal of US military personnel, toward a strategically vulnerable ally in an effort to restrain or even halt that ally's nuclear ambitions? When is the United States more likely to offer a strategically vulnerable ally tangible inducements, such as conventional arms transfers and explicit security guarantees, to accomplish the same nonproliferation objectives? And when is the United States likely to acquiesce in an ally's development of nuclear capabilities?

These questions arise in part because US hegemony underpins the global nuclear nonproliferation regime. Much of that regime originated in the 1960s and the 1970s, although unilateral efforts by Washington policymakers to control the spread of fissile materials and nuclear technology date back to the Baruch Plan in 1945. Historian Francis J. Gavin contends that nuclear nonproliferation, the containment of great power adversaries, and the promotion of economic openness have been the three key pillars of US grand strategy for the past seventy years: all three are means to preserve the United States' power preponderance and its hegemonic role in the international system since World War II.[1]

I beg to differ. As the succeeding chapters explain, the strategies the United States pursued in support of one pillar—containment—sometimes undercut the strategies it pursued in support of a second pillar—nonproliferation. In some circumstances, US policymakers were so concerned with preventing the Soviet Union from increasing its military, economic, or political involvement in a region, that they pursued accommodative nonproliferation strategies to vulnerable allies, up to and including the provision of generous US military

---

[1] Francis J. Gavin, "Strategies of Inhibition: U.S. Grand Strategy, the Nuclear Revolution, and Nonproliferation," *International Security*, Vol. 40, No. 1 (2015), pp. 9–46. For an analysis of how the maintenance of power preponderance became a core objective of US grand strategy after World War II, see Melvyn P. Leffler, *A Preponderance of Power: National Security, the Truman Administration, and the Cold War* (Stanford, CA: Stanford University Press, 1992).

assistance packages in exchange for allies' pledges to abide by nuclear "red lines." Yet, in other circumstances, US policymakers concluded that thwarting the nuclear programs of weaker allies was necessary for the achievement of other geostrategic objectives in a region, whether that objective was containing growth of the Soviet Union's military, economic, or diplomatic involvement or later enlisting China as an "ally of convenience" against the Soviet Union.

These questions also arise because for seven decades the United States has exercised hegemony through its military alliances. These include multilateral treaty alliances such as North Atlantic Treaty Organization (NATO); bilateral defense pacts with Japan, the Republic of Korea, and the Philippines; and non-treaty security partnerships with states such as Saudi Arabia, Egypt, Pakistan, and Israel. Currently, the United States maintains defense ties, in one form or another, with some sixty other countries. These alliances not only enable the US armed forces to maintain command of the global commons and to project kinetic force into distant regions, but also enable Washington to exert a certain amount of leverage over allies' foreign policies and military strategies.[2] Yet the United States also has actively tried to thwart the nuclear weapons ambitions of its own allies, in addition to the nuclear ambitions of the Soviet Union and China. Over the past quarter century, the United States has also tried to thwart the nuclear weapons and long-missile development programs of regional adversaries like Libya, Iraq, Iran, and North Korea.

This book examines how the United States has bargained with four strategically vulnerable and occasionally obstreperous allies in three volatile regions from the early 1960s to the early 1990s. The book presents a historical and comparative analysis of how successive US presidential administrations employed both inducements and coercive diplomacy in their dealings with Israel, Pakistan, the Republic of Korea, and Taiwan over nuclear proliferation.

The nonproliferation strategies the United States has undertaken toward these allies resulted from the interplay of international (systemic) forces and domestic politics. In assessing the consequences of an ally's nuclear ambitions, presidents and their advisers made initial calculations about the current distribution of power in the region where the ally was located, as well as the time horizons for threats to US interests in that region. Yet the type of strategies the United States ultimately pursued, which ranged from overt coercion to accommodation, were also shaped by American domestic politics. The height of the domestic mobilization hurdles the administration had to overcome, specifically the degree of opposition or support in Congress, played an intervening role. As

---

[2] Michael Beckley, "The Myth of Entangling Alliances: Reassessing the Security Risks of U.S. Defense Pacts," *International Security*, Vol. 39, No. 4 (2015), pp. 7–48.

a consequence, the United States sometimes pursued overtly coercive strategies to thwart the nuclear ambitions of some allies, but far more accommodating strategies toward the nuclear weapons programs of other allies. Occasionally, high domestic mobilization hurdles led presidential administrations to pursue what I term hybrid strategies toward nuclear-aspiring allies—that is, strategies that combined elements of coercion and accommodation.

Drawing upon neoclassical realism, I propose that presidents and their administrations will pursue coercive nonproliferation strategies toward an ally, when they perceive the United States as facing a favorable regional power distribution and long time horizons for threats to US interests in that region. However, this presumes the domestic mobilization hurdles to pursuing a coercive strategy are low. Conversely, presidents and their administrations will likely offer inducements toward a nuclear-aspiring ally or even acquiesce in an ally's maintenance of a latent nuclear capability, when they perceive the United States as facing an unfavorable regional power distribution and short time horizons for threats to US interests in that region. This also presumes, however, that the domestic mobilization hurdles to pursuing such an accommodative strategy are low.

The succeeding chapters test hypotheses derived from this neoclassical realist theory against four historical nonproliferation disputes between the United States and an ally (or quasi-ally). Chapter 3 examines the strategies employed by the administrations of Presidents John F. Kennedy and Lyndon B. Johnson to halt Israel's secret nuclear weapons program between 1960 and 1969 and then the President Richard M. Nixon administration's accommodation to a nuclear-armed Israel in exchange for certain guarantees between 1969 and 1973. The strategies employed by the administrations of Presidents Gerald R. Ford, Jimmy Carter, and Ronald Reagan to thwart Pakistan's efforts to develop a nuclear weapon between 1975 and 1990 are examined in chapter 4. Chapter 5 and 6 examine the strategies employed by the Nixon, Ford, and Carter administrations to halt the nuclear weapons and missile programs of South Korea and Taiwan, between 1970 and 1981 and between 1967 and 1978, respectively.

All four cases are of interest for scholars of international politics, nuclear proliferation, and the history of US foreign relations more broadly. For example, the "special understanding" that Nixon negotiated with Israeli prime minister Golda Meir in autumn 1969 and the nuclear "red lines" that Reagan and his surrogates established with the Pakistani military dictator General Muhammad Zia-ul-Haq between 1982 and 1985 had implications for the balance of power in the Middle East and South Asia. These nonproliferation arrangements, as well as the accompanying transfers of advanced weapons to Israel and Pakistan, would also shape the United States' later efforts to diffuse the Arab-Israeli and India-Pakistan conflicts. Likewise, the efforts by the Ford and the Carter administrations to coerce ROK President Park Chung-hee and ROC premier (later president) Chiang Ching-kuo into ending their respective nuclear weapons programs had implications for the United States' security commitments in East Asia.

Although this book focuses on historical cases of nuclear proliferation, the neoclassical realist theory developed herein is relevant to other key challenges facing the United States and various allies in the coming years. Thus, far being a purely academic exercise, the book seeks to offer insights for the Washington policy community in managing the fraught relationships with various allies in East Asia, South Asia, and the Middle East on issues of nuclear proliferation, crisis management, the resolution of long-standing territorial disputes, counter-terrorism strategies, and defense spending.

US Hegemony and the Problem of Nuclear Proliferation

Broadly speaking, hegemony connotes both a state's preponderance of material power—in terms of both economic and military capabilities—and its leadership role in the international system. There are multiple and competing definitions of "hegemony" among different schools of international relations theories. Some theories emphasize the politico-military aspects of the hegemon's role and others focus on the institutional, economic, and normative underpinnings of that role and the resulting benefits for other states.[3] Most definitions, however, acknowledge the hegemon's relative power advantage and its provision of "public goods" in the realms of security and international political economy. In short, hegemons create and enforce international rules.

I adopt Steven E. Lobell's definition of a global hegemon as a state with sufficient material capabilities to simultaneously exert military and/or economic dominance across several regions of the globe. Global hegemons may be great powers with vast formal empires, such as the Spanish Empire in the sixteenth and seventeenth centuries or the British Empire in the nineteenth and early twentieth centuries. They may also be great powers with far-flung spheres of

---

[3] Charles P. Kindleberger, *The World in Depression, 1929–1939* (Berkeley: University of California Press, 1973); Robert Gilpin, *War and Change in World Politics* (Cambridge: Cambridge University Press, 1981); Robert O. Keohane, *After Hegemony: Cooperation and Discord in the World Political Economy* (Princeton: Princeton University Press, 1984); Paul M. Kennedy, *The Rise and Fall of the Great Powers: Economic Change and Military Conflict from 1500 to 2000* (New York: Random House, 1987); A. F. K. Organski, *World Politics* (New York: Knopf, 1958); A. F. K. Organski and Jacek Kugler, *The War Ledger* (Chicago: University of Chicago Press, 1980); and David A. Lake, *Hierarchy in International Relations* (Ithaca, NY: Cornell University Press, 2009).

influence or regions of strategic concern such as the Soviet Union and the United States during the Cold War and continuing to the present day.[4] In the aftermath of World War II, the United States created and maintained a network of international institutions, alliances, and forward military bases that provided public goods, namely, economic openness and military security. Military alliances enabled Washington to exercise some measure of influence over regional powers and weaker states.[5]

Lobell's regionally differentiated framework highlights two dynamics relevant for the present book. First, global hegemons often face different challengers across geographic space due to the loss-of-strength gradient—the erosion of the ability to project military capabilities over long distances due to logistics, command, control, communications, and intelligence (C^3I) difficulties, morale problems, and the degree of local resistance to foreign forces—and due to the differentiated nature of power.[6] Second, since hegemons rarely have the requisite human or financial resources to simultaneously dominate all categories of military capabilities (e.g., land, sea, and air forces), they will tend to favor one over the other. "This differential characteristic of power reduces the probability that a single actor can dominate all regions of the globe simultaneously," which, in turn, limits the number of regions a hegemon could effectively dominate.[7] In other words, since hegemons have finite resources, leaders have to make trade-offs in redressing emerging threats in different regions.

The terms "dominance" and "regions" require a bit of explanation. Dominance is not synonymous with control over international outcomes. Hegemons do not always "get their way" in international politics, despite having a relative power advantage over rival great powers and local actors. Dominance is also not synonymous with territorial control or military occupation of the states within a

---

[4] See Steven E. Lobell, *The Challenge of Hegemony: Grand Strategy, Trade, and Domestic Politics* (Ann Arbor: The University of Michigan Press, 2003), p. 8.

[5] See Keohane, *After Hegemony*; G. John Ikenberry, *After Victory: Institutions, Strategic Restraint, and the Rebuilding of Order after Major Wars* (Princeton, NJ: Princeton University Press, 2001); Ikenberry, *Liberal Leviathan: The Origins, Crisis, and Transformation of the American World Order* (Princeton, NJ: Princeton University Press, 2011); Robert Gilpin, *War and Change in World Politics* (Cambridge: Cambridge University Press, 1981); Stephen D. Krasner, *Defending the National Interest: Raw Materials Investments and U.S. Foreign Policy* (Princeton, NJ: Princeton University Press, 1978); Robert Gilpin and Jean M. Gilpin, *The Political Economy of International Relations* (Princeton, NJ: Princeton University Press, 1987); Stephen G. Brooks and William C. Wohlforth, *World out of Balance: International Relations and the Challenge of American Primacy* (Princeton, NJ: Princeton University Press, 2008); and Brooks and Wohlforth, *America Abroad: The United States' Global Role in the 21st Century* (New York: Oxford University Press, 2016).

[6] On the loss-of-strength gradient see Kenneth E. Boulding, *Conflict and Defense: A General Theory* (New York: Harper, 1962), pp. 260–262 and 268–269.

[7] Ibid., p. 11.

region. Instead, I use the term "dominance" to mean that the hegemon state could, if necessary, extract and mobilize sufficient material and human resources from its society to project sustained military force, economic investment, or diplomatic engagement into a region.

I define a "region" as a cluster of geographically proximate states that constitute a defined subsystem within a global international system due to the regularity and intensity of the interactions and interconnections among those constituent states.[8] The geographic boundaries of those regions can sometimes be ambiguous and can also change over time. Because of this, I chose to focus on how policymakers in Washington defined the geographic parameters of distant regions (namely, East Asia, the Middle East, and South Asia) at the time. Likewise, distribution of capabilities within a regional subsystem can and does change over time, as can the patterns of amity and enmity between the local states.[9] Great powers may try to alter regional power distributions through alliances, arms transfers, economic assistance, or territorial conquest.

Structural Realist Baselines for the United States and Nuclear Proliferation

Two strands of structural realism provide competing baselines or sets of predictions for how the United States, as a hegemon, would respond to the proliferation of nuclear weapons to adversaries and allies in various regions during the Cold War and afterward. For ease of exposition, I refer to these two strands as "nuclear proliferation optimism" and "nuclear domino theory," even though both positions subsume a number of different empirical theories.

Nuclear proliferation optimism questions why the United States would oppose the diffusion of nuclear capabilities to allies.[10] Kenneth N. Waltz, the father

---

[8] My definition of a region builds upon "regional security complexes" (RSCs) in Barry Buzan and Ole Wæver, *Regions and Powers: The Structure of International Security* (Cambridge: Cambridge University Press, 2003), p. 46. Also see the conceptions of regions in David A. Lake and Patrick M. Morgan, "The New Regionalism in Security Affairs," in David A. Lake and Patrick M. Morgan, eds., *Regional Orders: Building Security in a New World* (University Park: Pennsylvania State University Press, 1997), pp. 3–19; T. V. Paul, "Regional Transformation in International Relations," in T. V. Paul, ed., *International Relations Theory and Regional Transformation* (New York: Cambridge University Press, 2012), pp. 3–21; and Norrin M. Ripsman, *Peacemaking from Above, Peace from Below: Ending Conflict between Regional Rivals* (Ithaca, NY: Cornell University Press, 2016), pp. 5–7.

[9] See Ripsman, *Peacemaking from Above, Peace from Below*, pp. 18–33.

[10] Much of the modern proliferation optimism literature builds upon nuclear deterrence theory and to a lesser extent structural realist balance-of-power theory. For critical reviews see Jeffrey W. Knopf, "Recasting the Proliferation Optimism-Pessimism Debate," *Security Studies*, Vol. 12, No. 1 (2002), pp. 41–96; and Matthew Kroenig, "The History of Proliferation Optimism: Does It Have a Future?," *Journal of Strategic Studies*, Vol. 38, No. 1–2 (2015), pp. 1–28.

of structural realism, argues that neither the United States nor the Soviet Union should have been entrapped by their respective allies, since the addition or the defection of weaker states could not shift the overall distribution of power within a bipolar international system.[11] Moreover, Waltz argues nuclear weapons had a stabilizing effect on superpower competition by rendering each one's homeland effectively unconquerable and that over time, both superpowers learned to tread cautiously in brandishing nuclear threats. There is every reason to believe that second- and third-generation nuclear states would learn the same lessons.[12]

Since even a rudimentary nuclear weapon capability might serve as a strategic deterrent, nuclear proliferation optimism might expect the United States to have been indifferent or perhaps even mildly supportive of a weaker ally's effort to cross the nuclear threshold. Nuclear-armed or at least nuclear-threshold frontline allies might have deterred possible attacks by the Soviet Union and other proximate adversaries at a far lower cost to the American taxpayer than the maintenance of overseas bases and the forward deployment of conventional and strategic (nuclear) forces.[13] However, as Gavin notes, if the United States' overriding grand strategic objective during the Cold War had been to contain the Soviet Union by freezing the post-1945 territorial status quo in Europe and East Asia, then the efforts by successive US administrations to inhibit the spread of nuclear weapons to vulnerable allies is puzzling.[14]

A second strand of structural realism, hegemonic or power preponderance theories, offers a different baseline exception for how the United States would respond to nuclear proliferation by adversaries and allies. Unlike the equilibrium or balance-of-power theories, hegemonic theories begin with the supposition that the United States should strive to maintain the preponderant power position it has enjoyed since World War II. To achieve this objective, Washington would not only need to maintain conventional military forces capable of dominating what Barry Posen terms the "global commons" (defined as the high seas, airspace above fifteen thousand feet, and outer space), but also a network of standing military alliances and forward-basing arrangements intended to simultaneously contain great power adversaries and to exercise a certain amount

---

[11] Kenneth N. Waltz, *Theory of International Politics* (Reading, MA: Addison-Wesley 1979), pp. 169–179.

[12] See, for example, Kenneth N. Waltz, "The Spread of Nuclear Weapons: More May Be Better," *Adelphi Papers No. 171* (London: International Institute for Strategic Studies, 1981); and Scott D. Sagan and Kenneth N. Waltz, *The Spread of Nuclear Weapons: A Debate Renewed* (New York: W. W. Norton & Co., 2003).

[13] For an argument in favor of controlled nuclear proliferation in Europe, after the drawdown of US and Soviet strategic forces in the early 1990s, see John J. Mearsheimer, "Back to the Future: Instability in Europe after the Cold War," *International Security*, Vol. 15, No. 1 (1990), pp. 5–56.

[14] Gavin, "Strategies of Inhibition," pp. 15–16.

of restraint over local allies.[15] If the United States could best advance its security through a strategy of deep engagement (or primacy) outside the Western Hemisphere, then US policymakers should try to inhibit the diffusion of nuclear weapons to those regions in order to minimize the risks of access denial or containment failure.[16]

Access denial, according to Evan Bradon Montgomery, refers to the risk of a local actor withholding critical resources or restricting the access of the hegemon (or another outside great power) to its region. A local actor might do this by "withholding indigenous resources or restricting the presence of outside powers within its neighborhood, in particular, by refusing to export commodities, impeding passage through the area, charging higher rents to host foreign troops, or even evicting those forces and barring their return."[17]

Containment failure, according to Montgomery, refers to the risk of a rival great power conquering a geographic region in whole or in part.[18] I broaden the definition of "containment failure" to include scenarios in which a rival great power increases it economic, political, and/or military penetration of a geographic region through alliance formation, arms sales, and economic aid to local states. In other words, containment failure does not need to be synonymous with a rival great power actually occupying all or part of a region. It is sufficient for that great power to increase its political or military penetration of that region.

Why should the United States be so resistant to the proliferation of nuclear weapons and long-range missiles, as opposed to the proliferation of conventional weapons? Nicholas Miller uses the term "nuclear domino theory" in reference to a set of beliefs and propositions held by policymakers about the adverse consequences of nuclear proliferation for international stability, as well as for national security.[19]

---

[15] For a discussion of US command of the commons see Barry R. Posen, "Command of the Commons: The Military Foundation of U.S. Hegemony," *International Security*, Vol. 28, No. 1 (2003), pp. 5–46. For a discussion of the conclusion of bilateral alliances with Japan, South Korea, and Taiwan as mechanisms for US control, see Victor D. Cha, "Powerplay: Origins of the U.S. Alliance System in Asia," *International Security*, Vol. 34, No. 3 (2010), pp. 158–196.

[16] On the strategy of deep engagement see Stephen G. Brooks, G. John Ikenberry, and William C. Wohlforth, "Don't Come Home, America: The Case against Retrenchment," *International Security*, Vol. 37, No. 3 (2012), pp. 7–51; and Stephen G. Brooks and William C. Wohlforth, *America Abroad: The United States' Global Role in the 21st Century* (New York: Oxford University Press, 2016), pp. 88–102.

[17] Evan Braden Montgomery, *In the Hegemon's Shadow: Leading States and the Rise of Regional Powers* (Ithaca, NY: Cornell University Press, 2016), p. 12.

[18] Ibid., pp. 12–13.

[19] Nicholas L. Miller, "Nuclear Dominoes: A Self-Defeating Prophecy?" *Security Studies*, Vol. 23, No. 1 (2014), pp. 33–73.

Nuclear domino effects, also known as reactive nuclear proliferation, increase the risk of regional arms races and may prompt states to initiate preventive military actions against nuclear-aspiring neighbors. Nuclear-armed states, or even nuclear threshold states, would be less reliant on the United States for protection.[20] Reactive proliferation by an ally could also increase the risk of containment failure. During the Cold War, the Soviet Union could respond to the nuclear proliferation behavior of a US ally by increasing conventional arms transfers to its own allies or by deploying Soviet conventional forces to the region. Reactive proliferation would also undermine the credibility of the United States' nonproliferation efforts worldwide. This last concern became increasingly salient after the Nuclear Nonproliferation Treaty (NPT) went into effect in 1971, which became the centerpiece of the US-led nuclear nonproliferation regime.[21]

As T. V. Paul observes, the five nuclear weapons states (NWS) recognized by the NPT (the United States, the Soviet Union/Russia, the United Kingdom, France, and the People's Republic of China) were "driven by the fear that [nuclear weapons] diffusion would blur the line between major and minor powers, as one of the attributes of major power status has been the ability to intervene in the affairs of minor powers without fear of punishment to their home territory in return."[22] Once a state possesses nuclear warheads and a viable delivery system, it

---

[20] See Matthew Kroenig, "Force or Friendship? Explaining Great Power Nonproliferation Policy," *Security Studies*, Vol. 23, No. 1 (2014), pp. 1–32.

[21] See James Cameron and Or Rabinowitz, "Eight Lost Years? Nixon, Ford, Kissinger, and the Non-Proliferation Regime, 1969–1977," *Journal of Strategic Studies*, Vol. 40, No. 6 (2016), pp. 1–31; Roland Popp, "Introduction: Global Order, Cooperation between the Superpowers, and Alliance Politics in the Making of the Nuclear Non-Proliferation Regime," *The International History Review*, Vol. 36, No. 2 (2014), pp. 195–209; Dane Swango, "The United States and the Role of Nuclear Co-Operation and Assistance in the Design of the Non-Proliferation Treaty," *The International History Review*, Vol. 36, No. 2 (2014), pp. 210–229; and William Burr, "A Scheme of 'Control': The United States and the Origins of the Nuclear Suppliers' Group, 1974–1976," *The International History Review* Vol. 36, No. 2 (2014), pp. 252–276. In this book I am less concerned about the United States' role in crafting and maintaining the nonproliferation regime than I am with addressing the narrower research questions introduced at the outset of chapter 1. For an argument that the establishment and perseverance of the nonproliferation regime poses anomalies for both hegemonic stability theory and the functional theory of regimes (i.e., institutionalist theory), see Roger K. Smith, "Explaining the Non-Proliferation Regime: Anomalies for Contemporary International Relations Theory," *International Organization*, Vol. 41, No. 2 (1987), pp. 253–281.

[22] T. V. Paul, "Great Equalizers or Agents of Chaos? Weapons of Mass Destruction and the Emerging International Order," in T. V. Paul and John A. Hall, eds., *International Order and the Future of World Politics* (Cambridge: Cambridge University Press, 1999), p. 373. Also see Joseph S. Nye, "NPT: The Logic of Inequality," *Foreign Policy*, No. 59 (1985), pp. 123–131. Article IX, Section 3 of the NPT defines a nuclear weapons state (NWS) as "one which has manufactured and exploded a nuclear weapon or other nuclear explosive device before 1 January 1967." See "Treaty on the

acquires the ability to challenge US hegemony in its region. A nuclear-armed ally would depend neither on the United States' nuclear umbrella nor on US conventional forces to defend its territory. Additionally, nuclear weapons development threatens the international status hierarchy, which favors the United States, the Soviet Union (now Russia), and the other three NWS under the NPT.[23] Nuclear weapons afford a state a higher status in international politics.[24] The majority of states in the international system simply lack the means to even contemplate nuclear weapons development.[25]

Nuclear weapons proliferation increases the risk of access denial for the United States. This could happen through several pathways. First, an adversary's development of even a rudimentary nuclear capability and delivery system might increase its ability to threaten non-nuclear US allies in the region and inhibit the United States from defending those allies. Specifically, the prospect of unacceptable damage to an ally's homeland might deter policymakers in Washington from undertaking any form of military intervention in the region. Second, reactive proliferation may increase the risk of access denial by sparking the types of arms races, arms transfers from outside powers, and extensions of security commitments by outside powers described above. Third, a nuclear weapons capability may embolden some states to engage in limited aggression or crisis initiation.[26] For example, a rival great power or the neighboring states may have an incentive to launch preventive military strikes against suspected nuclear facilities before that target state achieves nuclear breakout or an arsenal of nuclear warheads and viable delivery systems.[27]

Non-Proliferation of Nuclear Weapons (NPT)," United Nations Office for Disarmament Affairs, http://www.un.org/disarmament/wmd/nuclear/npt/text (accessed 11 March 2018).

[23] On the role of nuclear weapons as psychological markers of higher international status among so-called oppositional nationalist leaders, see Jacques E. C. Hymans, *The Psychology of Nuclear Proliferation: Identity, Emotions, and Foreign Policy* (Cambridge: Cambridge University Press, 2006), pp. 35–39.

[24] On status hierarchies in international politics, see T. V. Paul, Deborah Welch Larson, and William Curti Wohlforth, eds., *Status in World Politics* (New York: Cambridge University Press, 2014).

[25] I am agnostic about the impact of the so-called nuclear taboo. On that taboo see Nina Tannenwald, *The Nuclear Taboo: The United States and the Non-Use of Nuclear Weapons since 1945* (Cambridge: Cambridge University Press, 2007). My point here is a narrower one: since 1945, the vast majority of states in the international system have lacked the wherewithal to mount a nuclear weapons program in the first place.

[26] Mark S. Bell, "Beyond Emboldenment: How Acquiring Nuclear Weapons Can Change Foreign Policy," *International Security*, Vol. 40, No. 1 (2015), pp. 87–119, esp. pp. 91–92. Also see S. Paul Kapur, *Dangerous Deterrent: Nuclear Weapons Proliferation and Conflict in South Asia* (Stanford, CA: Stanford University Press, 2007).

[27] Two quantitative studies of the prevalence and the efficacy of preventive military strikes on states' nuclear weapons programs are: Sarah E. Kreps and Matthew Fuhrmann, "Attacking the Atom: Does Bombing Nuclear Facilities Affect Proliferation," *Journal of Strategic Studies*, Vol. 34, No.

Matthew Kroenig writes: "Leaders in power-projecting states are concerned that nuclear proliferation might deter [US policymakers] from using military force to secure their interests, reduce the effectiveness of their coercive diplomacy, trigger regional instability that could engulf them in conventional conflict, weaken the integrity of their alliance structures, dissipate strategic attention, and set off further nuclear proliferation within their spheres of influence."[28] This statement encapsulates the logic of nuclear domino theory. The prospects of access denial and containment failure led the United States to oppose nuclear proliferation in most regions during the Cold War and afterward. These are certainly not the only rationales given by US policymakers for opposing nuclear proliferation. For example, the remote possibility that Iraqi dictator Saddam Hussein might transfer fissile materials or even an assembled nuclear weapon to terrorist groups was one of the stated justifications for the George W. Bush administration's invasion of Iraq in spring 2003.[29]

Nuclear domino theory might explain why US policymakers did not actively thwart the British and the French nuclear weapons programs in the 1950s and early 1960s. The United States actively assisted the British nuclear program in the 1950s.[30] The French and the British nuclear programs developed during a period when the US commitment to maintaining a permanent military presence in Western Europe was unclear. Senior officials, including President Dwight

---

2 (2011), pp. 161–187; and Matthew Fuhrmann and Sarah E. Kreps, "Targeting Nuclear Programs in War and Peace: A Quantitative Empirical Analysis, 1941–2000," *Journal of Conflict Resolution*, Vol. 54, No. 6 (2010), pp. 831–859. For the argument that preventive military strikes on states' nuclear facilities are actually rare, see Michael D. Cohen, "How Nuclear Proliferation Causes Conflict: The Case for Optimistic Pessimism," *The Nonproliferation Review*, Vol. 23, No. 3–4 (2016), pp. 425–442. Also see Michael D. Cohen and Mark S. Bell, "Correspondence: The Effects of Acquiring Nuclear Weapons," *International Security*, Vol. 41, No. 1 (2016), pp. 186–190. For an analysis of how the United States actively retrained Israel from launching a preventive strike on Iran's nuclear facilities, see Daniel Sobelman, "Restraining an Ally: Israel, the United States, and Iran's Nuclear Program, 2010–2012," *Texas National Security Review*, Vol. 1, No. 4 (2018), at https://tnsr.org/2018/08/restraining-an-ally-israel-the-united-states-and-irans-nuclear-program-2011-2012/.

[28] Matthew Kroenig, *Exporting the Bomb: Technology Transfer and the Spread of Nuclear Weapons* (Ithaca, NY: Cornell University Press, 2010), p. 3.

[29] For an examination of the plausibility of the claim that states might give nuclear weapons to terrorist organizations, see Keir A. Lieber and Daryl G. Press, "Why States Won't Give Nuclear Weapons to Terrorists," *International Security*, Vol. 38, No. 1 (2013), pp. 80–104. For a re-examination of Saddam Hussein's rationale for obstructing UN inspectors after the 1991 Gulf War, see Gregory D. Koblentz, "Saddam Versus the Inspectors: The Impact of Regime Security on the Verification of Iraq's WMD Disarmament," *Journal of Strategic Studies*, Vol. 41, No. 3 (2018), pp. 372–409.

[30] Jan Melissen, "The Restoration of the Nuclear Alliance: Great Britain and Atomic Negotiations with the United States, 1957–58," *Contemporary Record*, Vol. 6, No. 1 (1992), pp. 72–106; and John Baylis, "The 1958 Anglo-American Mutual Defence Agreement: The Search for Nuclear Interdependence," *Journal of Strategic Studies*, Vol. 31, No. 3 (2008), pp. 425–466.

D. Eisenhower and Secretary of State John Foster Dulles, did not favor the permanent stationing of US troops in Western Europe, but instead saw this a temporary measure until NATO's European members could defend themselves against the Soviet Union.[31] Nonetheless, Washington could exercise a measure of control through the tight integration of US and British nuclear forces and through France's membership in NATO, even after the French withdrawal from the alliance's integrated military command in 1966.[32]

The United States, however, opposed the Federal Republic of Germany's nascent nuclear ambitions because of that country's front-line position in Central Europe, as well as fears that an indigenous German nuclear weapons program would provoke the Soviet Union. The Kennedy and Johnson administrations employed a variety of coercive strategies, including allegedly the threat of military abandonment, to dissuade the governments of chancellors Konrad Adenauer and Ludwig Erhard from developing an independent nuclear deterrent in the 1960s.[33]

Nuclear domino theory, however, is arguably less able to explain variation in the US responses to the nuclear programs of other vulnerable allies outside of Western Europe. For example, why was the Kennedy administration so adamant that Israel open its nuclear reactor complex at Dimona to inspections by US scientists in the early 1960s, but equally opposed to selling Israel advanced conventional weapons to defend itself? How and why did the Nixon administration learn to "live with" a nuclear-armed Israel in early 1970s? Yet why did the Ford and the Carter administrations actively thwart the nuclear ambitions of South Korea and Taiwan, two long-standing treaty allies, just a few years later? Why did the United States' stance toward Pakistan's clandestine nuclear weapons program oscillate from the Carter administration's imposition of economic sanctions in 1979, to the Reagan administration's provision of military and economic aid to Pakistan between 1981 and 1988, and to the Bush administration's reimposition of sanctions in 1990?

---

[31] See Marc Trachtenberg, *A Constructed Peace: The Making of the European Settlement, 1945–1963* (Princeton, NJ: Princeton University Press, 1999), pp. 146–200.

[32] See Andreas Wenger, "Crisis and Opportunity: NATO's Transformation and the Multilateralization of Détente, 1966–1968," *Journal of Cold War Studies*, Vol. 6, No. 1 (2004), pp. 22–74. On the French nuclear weapons program, see Debs and Monteiro, *Nuclear Politics*, pp. 418–435; Colette Barbier, "The French Decision to Develop a Military Nuclear Programme in the 1950s," *Diplomacy & Statecraft*, Vol. 4, No. 1 (1993), pp. 103–113; Mervyn O'Driscoll, "Missing the Nuclear Boat? British Policy and French Military Nuclear Ambitions During the EURATOM Foundation Negotiations, 1955–56," *Diplomacy & Statecraft*, Vol. 9, No. 1 (1998), pp. 135–162; and O'Driscoll, "Explosive Challenge: Diplomatic Triangles, the United Nations, and the Problem of French Nuclear Testing, 1959–1960," *Journal of Cold War Studies*, Vol. 11, No. 1 (2009), pp. 28–56.

[33] See Gerzhoy, "Alliance Coercion and Nuclear Restraint," pp. 111–124; Debs and Monteiro, *Nuclear Politics*, pp. 403–417; and Alexander Lanoszka, *Atomic Assurance: The Alliance Politics of Nuclear Proliferation* (Ithaca, NY: Cornell University Press, 2018), pp. 48–78.

Neoclassical Realist Theory

The theory I develop draws upon neoclassical realism. Rather than merely being the logical extension of Waltz's structural realism to explain anomalous foreign policy behavior or grand strategic maladjustment, neoclassical realism is a broad research program. Neoclassical realism encompasses various theories that can explain and predict phenomena ranging from individual states' strategies in international crises up to longer-term patterns of international outcomes.[34]

Global hegemons have strategic interests in several regions around the globe in addition to their homelands and home regions ("near abroad"). Consequently, they encounter different power distributions in different regions. It is entirely possible for a global hegemon to simultaneously confront a favorable distribution of power in one region and an unfavorable power distribution in another. Likewise, global hegemons confront different time horizons regarding emerging threats to their interests in those regions. The hegemon might simultaneously confront short time horizons for threats in one region, but long time horizons for threats in another. In deciding how to respond to an ally's nuclear proliferation activities, presidents and their national security teams make assessments about the regional power distribution and the time horizon for emerging threats.

The threats to the United States' interests in a region do not directly arise from the nuclear weapons program of an ally, per se. Instead, the threats arise from the heightened risk of containment failure or access denial resulting from the reactions of neighboring states or a rival great power to the ally's nuclear weapons development. For example, an ally's efforts to develop nuclear weapons may exacerbate threats to US interests in the region by increasing the risk of a counterproliferation attack by a neighboring state or a great power. Such an attack might obligate Washington to respond. Similarly, a rival great power might respond to a US ally's nuclear proliferation by increasing conventional arms transfers and economic assistance to its own ally in that region.

The strategies that the United States ultimately pursues toward a nuclear aspiring ally, however, are not solely a function of these systemic variables. Neoclassical realism assumes that domestic-level intervening variables condition how states respond to international stimuli. Since nuclear proliferation disputes are likely to unfold over a number of months and years, presidents and

---

[34] See Norrin M. Ripsman, Jeffrey W. Taliaferro, and Steven E. Lobell, *Neoclassical Realist Theory of International Politics* (New York: Oxford University Press, 2016), pp. 1–15. For a concise overview of the different schools of realism (especially structural realism, neoclassical realism, and classical realism) and a discussion of the areas of divergence and convergence among them, see Adam Quinn, "Realisms," in Alexandra Gheciu and William C. Wohlforth, eds., *Oxford Handbook of International Security* (New York: Oxford University Press, 2018), pp. 71–85.

other administration officials must mobilize support for, or at least diffuse opposition to, their preferred foreign and security policies toward that ally. The height of the domestic mobilization hurdles the presidential administration must overcome is the intervening variable. High mobilization hurdles, in turn, may make it more difficult for an administration to pursue its preferred strategy toward the ally at any given time.

The tools that a presidential administration might employ to influence the nuclear behavior of a dependent ally include: conventional arms transfers, the extension of explicit US security guarantees, long-term basing arrangements and troop deployments, economic assistance, export controls, and diplomatic support in international organizations, especially in the United Nations (UN) Security Council. The executive branch, however, seldom has complete autonomy in using many of these policy tools. Several of them, such as arms transfers and forward-basing decisions, require some level of notification of Congress. Some of them require explicit legislative authorization and appropriations.

Variation in the types of nonproliferation strategies the United States ultimately pursue toward a given ally is the dependent variable, or outcome, the theory purports to explain.[35] The dependent variable exists along a continuum from coercion to accommodation. A coercive strategy might be defined as one that, if implemented, might diminish the military or economic capabilities of the target state (the ally). An accommodative strategy, by contrast, is one that, if implemented, might augment the military and/or economic capabilities of the target state. A hybrid strategy, which chapter 2 discusses at greater length, is one that combines elements of coercion and accommodation. Alliance coercion can be defined as the conditional use of threats or inducements by one ally (in this case the hegemon) in order to alter the cost-benefit calculations and behavior of the other ally (the client). There are two necessary conditions. First, the client must have some level of military or diplomatic dependence upon the hegemon. Second, the hegemon's threatened sanction or promised inducement must be conditional on the client's behavior.[36]

Figure 1.1 depicts the basic causal scheme of the theory.

---

[35] Neoclassical realist theory falls into what Ripsman, Taliaferro, and Lobell call "type II neoclassical realism," pp. 81–90.

[36] See Gerzhoy, "Alliance Coercion and Nuclear Restraint," pp. 92–93.

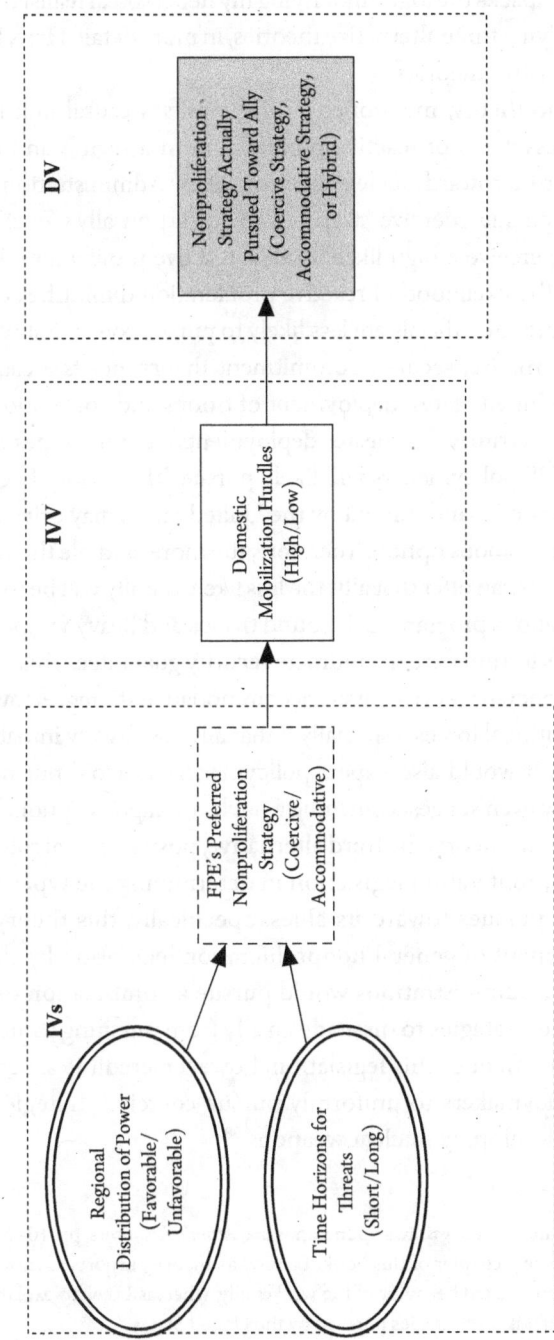

Figure 1.1 Neoclassical Realist Theory

Alternative Theories

The next chapter unpacks the logic underlying my neoclassical realist theory, as well as that logic underlying three alternative theories, in more detail. Here, I merely outline the three alternative theories.

Nuclear domino theory, mentioned earlier, posits a causal link between US policymakers' assessments of reactive proliferation in a region and the types of strategies they pursue toward nuclear-aspiring allies. Administration officials are more inclined to pursue coercive strategies to thwart an ally's nuclear activities if and when they perceive a high likelihood of reactive proliferation by that ally's neighbors. When the likelihood of reactive proliferation diminishes or is not present at all, administration officials are less likely to pursue coercive strategies.

The second alternative, security commitment theory, posits a causal relationship between the United States' deployment of troops and conventional weapons on or near an ally's territory (in-theater deployments) and the types of nonproliferation strategies US policymakers will likely pursue. This theory begins with the supposition that fear of abandonment by the United States may drive certain allies to pursue a nuclear weapons option. Therefore, the more credible the security guarantee that US officials can offer that ally, the less likely the ally will be to start or continue a nuclear weapons program. US ground troops and heavy weapons deployed on or near the ally's territory are the ultimate security guarantee. This theory, therefore, expects US policymakers to pursue accommodative strategies toward any ally hosting US conventional forces, especially if that ally has already initiated a nuclear weapons program. It would also expect policymakers to avoid pursuing coercive strategies if that ally even suggests pursuing a nuclear weapons option.[37]

Credible sanctions theory, the third alternative, posits a causal role for binding and universal nonproliferation legislation in determining the types of strategies the United States pursues toward its allies. Specifically, this theory holds that prior to the enactment of general nonproliferation legislation by the Congress beginning in 1976, administrations would pursue a combination of accommodative and coercive strategies to dissuade an ally from pursuing a nuclear option. Following the enactment of this legislation, however, credible sanctions theory would expect policymakers to uniformly pursue coercive strategies toward an ally suspected of developing nuclear weapons.[38]

---

[37] Security commitment theory draws upon Lanoszka, *Atomic Assurance*, pp. 10–22. As discussed at greater length in the next chapter of this book, Lanoszka's theory purports to explain variation in the nuclear proliferation–related behavior of the weaker ally, whereas I seek to explain the variation in the nuclear nonproliferation strategies pursued by the United States.

[38] As discussed at greater length in the next chapter, what I call credible sanctions theory is derivative of the first theory developed in Nicholas L. Miller, *Stopping the Bomb: The Sources and Effectiveness of US Nonproliferation Policy* (Ithaca, NY: Cornell University Press, 2018), pp. 69–94.

Frenemies

I seek to explain why the United States pursued overtly coercive strategies to thwart the nuclear weapons programs of some vulnerable allies, but occasionally pursued more accommodative strategies in response to others. I also seek to explain variation in the types of strategies that US policymakers pursued toward the same ally over time.

For the purposes of this book, I define an alliance as a formal or informal relationship of security cooperation between two or more states, which assumes some level of commitment and exchange of benefits between the contracting parties.[39] That definition includes alliances governed by formal multilateral or bilateral security treaties, as well as more informal types of security arrangements between the United States and another country. These informal partnerships may be governed by executive agreements (e.g., memoranda of understanding) regarding arms transfers, basing rights, intelligence cooperation, and other security-related matters.[40] The United States has forged alliances with other states for a variety of strategic objectives, many of which are not mutually exclusive. These include: deterring aggression from rival great powers or regional adversaries, signaling ex ante commitments, and exercising some measure of control over an ally's foreign and security strategies.[41]

My focus is on explaining these dynamics between the United States and a subcategory of bilateral allies that I call "frenemies" (alternatively spelled "frienemies"). According to *The Oxford English Dictionary*, the first recorded

---

The dependent variable for Miller's second theory pertains to the nuclear proliferation related behavior of the target state.

[39] Stephen M. Walt, *The Origins of Alliances* (Ithaca, NY: Cornell University Press, 1987), p. 1, fn. 1. Also see Roger V. Dingman, "Theories of, and Approaches to Alliance Politics," in Paul Gordon Lauren, ed., *Diplomacy: New Approaches in Theory, History, and Policy* (New York: Free Press, 1979), pp. 245–250.

[40] For the argument that conventional arms transfers and security guarantees (specifically mutual defense pacts) were alternative strategies that the United States pursued toward various clients, see Keren Yarhi-Milo, Alexander Lanoszka, and Zack Cooper, "To Arm or to Ally? The Patron's Dilemma and the Strategic Logic of Arms Transfers and Alliances," *International Security*, Vol. 41, No. 2 (2016), pp. 90–139. I contend that US policymakers across several administrations did not see conventional arms transfers and the extension of security guarantees (whether in the form of mutual defense pacts or executive agreements) as mutually exclusive.

[41] See, for example, Victor D. Cha, "Powerplay: Origins of the U.S. Alliance System in Asia," *International Security*, Vol. 34, No. 3 (2010), pp. 158–196; Cha, *Powerplay: The Origins of the American Alliance System in Asia* (Princeton, NJ: Princeton University Press, 2016); Glenn H. Snyder, *Alliance Politics* (Ithaca, NY: Cornell University Press, 1997); and James D. Morrow, "Arms Versus Allies: Trade-Offs in the Search for Security," *International Organization*, Vol. 47, No. 2 (1993), pp. 207–233.

appearance of this neologism is a column by Walter Winchell in the 4 April 1953 issue of *The Nevada State Journal*, "Howz about calling the Russians our Frienemies?" That dictionary defines a frenemy as: "A person with whom one is friendly, despite a fundamental dislike or rivalry; a person who combines the characteristics of a friend and an enemy."

In the realm of international politics, I use the term "frenemy" to denote a state located in a volatile region that has an ongoing bilateral security relationship with the United States, despite the existence of divergent security interests and political objectives between the parties. In order to be a frenemy, the ally must display a pattern of deception, manipulation, evasion, or obstruction of the expressed interests of its superpower patron. The ties between the United States and its frenemies are asymmetric in several respects, including: the sheer imbalance in military and economic capabilities; the anticipated domestic political costs for leaders on both sides in initiating, renegotiating, or terminating the relationship; and the scope conditions for Washington to provide military assistance to the ally. Allied leaders' fears of "abandonment" by the United States, along with US policymakers' fears of entanglement in undesired conflicts, are a recurrent dynamic. The weaker allies have their own security interests in the region. An ally's interests do not necessarily coincide with the broader security interests of the United States.

What I term "frenemies" are just one among several categories of asymmetric alliances the United States (and other great powers) have contracted with other states across history.[42] Figure 1.2 displays the full spectrum of such alliances. Evan Resnick defines an "alliance of convenience" as a temporary security partnership between "two states that are ideological and geopolitical adversaries, in an effort to balance the growing threat posed by a third party that each of the partners views as a greater immediate danger to its security than is posed by the other partner."[43]

Alliances of convenience generally entail short-term and largely transactional cooperation largely directed toward mitigating the common threat posed by a third party. Two examples of such transactional partnerships were the United States' alliances with the Soviet Union during World War II and with Iraq during the 1980s. Following the military defeat or the successful containment of the shared adversary, Germany and Iran, respectively, competing strategic interests, often exacerbated by pre-existing ideological differences,

---

[42] Frenemies and other categories of bilateral alliances are "ideal types." No single alliance is likely to display all of the elements associated with each one at any given time.

[43] Evan N. Resnick, "Strange Bedfellows: U.S. Bargaining Behavior with Allies of Convenience," *International Security*, Vol. 35, No. 3 (2010), pp. 144–184, at p. 147.

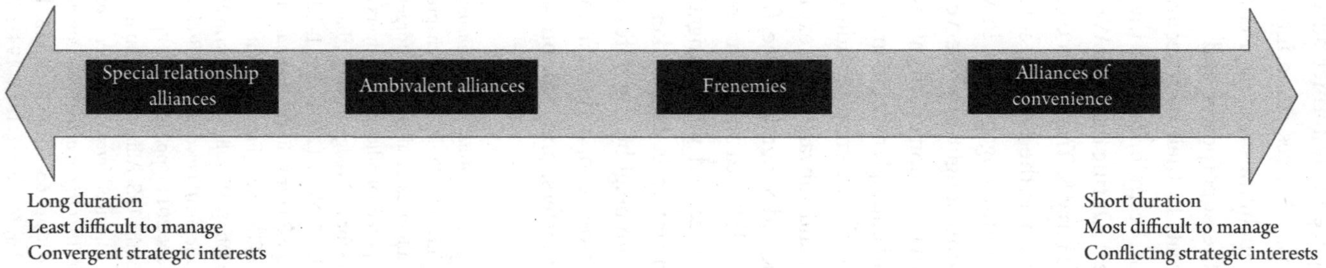

Special relationship alliances — Ambivalent alliances — Frenemies — Alliances of convenience

Long duration
Least difficult to manage
Convergent strategic interests

Short duration
Most difficult to manage
Conflicting strategic interests

Figure 1.2 Spectrum of (Bilateral) Asymmetric Alliances

drove these former allies of convenience into open conflict with each other.[44]

While frenemies are not necessarily former adversaries, they do have divergent security interests. Most alliances come into being for the purpose of aggregating their members' capabilities against a common adversary.[45] In the case of frenemies, however, the superpower and its weaker partner not only identify different primary threats to their own security and interests, but may also actively work to undercut, restrain, or limit the other partner's efforts to deal with its own primary threat. During the Cold War, US policymakers in nine presidential administrations (Harry S. Truman to George H. W. Bush) consistently identified the Soviet Union as the primary adversary. The United States' military, diplomatic, and economic engagement in various regions, and with particular states in those regions, sought to preserve its own access and/or to contain the influence of the Soviet Union and its allies. US policymakers forged other alliances in order to avoid entanglement in unwanted wars with secondary adversaries. In the early 1950s, the Eisenhower administration contracted alliance treaties with South Korea and Taiwan for the express purpose of preventing their leaders, Chiang Kai-shek and Syngman Rhee, from unilaterally launching military operations against North Korea and China, respectively.[46]

Frenemies are primarily concerned with mitigating immediate threats to their own survival and strategic interests. For weaker allies of the United States, those threats generally arise from neighboring states or other local actors in the region. Extra regional great powers can, and often do, exacerbate those threats through alliance ties, arms transfers, and economic assistance. Nonetheless,

---

[44] Ibid., p. 150. Also see Evan N. Resnick, *Allies of Convenience: A Theory of Bargaining in US Foreign Policy* (New York: Columbia University Press, 2019), chapter 1.

[45] An exception to this would be alliances or alignments forged by one party with the express purpose of denying or "peeling off" potential allies to an adversary. On wedge strategies in alliance formation, see Timothy W. Crawford, "Wedge Strategy, Balancing, and the Deviant Case of Spain, 1940–41," *Security Studies*, Vol. 17, No. 1 (2008), pp. 1–38; Crawford, "Preventing Enemy Coalitions: How Wedge Strategies Shape Power Politics," *International Security*, Vol. 35, No. 4 (2011), pp. 155–189; and Crawford, "Powers of Division: From the Anti-Cominterm to the Nazi-Soviet and Japanese Soviet Pacts, 1936–1941," in Jeffrey W. Taliaferro, Norrin M. Ripsman and Steven E. Lobell, eds., *The Challenge of Grand Strategy: The Great Powers and the Broken Balance between the World Wars* (New York: Cambridge University Press, 2011), pp. 246–278.

[46] See Cha, "Powerplay: Origins of the U.S. Alliance System in Asia," pp. 168–181; Cha, "Rhee-Straint: The Origins of the U.S.-ROK Alliance," *International Journal of Korean Studies*, Vol. 15, No. 1 (2011), pp. 1–15; and Cha, *Powerplay: The Origins of the American Alliance System in Asia* (Princeton, NJ: Princeton University Press, 2016), pp. 65–93 and 94–115. For a discussion of alliances as tools of restraint see Paul W. Schroeder, "Alliances, 1815–1945: Weapons of Power and Tools of Management," in Paul W. Schroeder, David Wetzel, Robert Jervis, and Jack S. Levy, eds., *Systems, Stability, and Statecraft: Essays on the International History of Modern Europe* (New York: Palgrave Macmillan, 2004), pp. 195–222.

from the standpoint of the weaker ally's leadership, the local adversary (or adversaries) will be the primary concern. Forging and maintaining alliance ties with the United States, for the stated purpose of countering a common adversary, is largely a means for the weaker ally to obtain security guarantees and material assistance against its local adversary.

Frenemies and other weaker allies are not passive actors in their relationships with the United States. When the United States tries to reshape the dynamics of an ally's region by, for example, pursuing rapprochement with a great power or another state, a frenemy may attempt to disrupt those efforts. Efforts by Washington to "reset" bilateral relations with another great power or another local state may be seen as threatening to the frenemy. This is especially prevalent in situations where the frenemy has an ongoing rivalry with a neighbor. Instead of risking an open breach with the United States, however, the ally may employ "passive-aggressive" tactics designed to undermine US strategic objectives.

Allied leaders may claim to support US objectives in their public pronouncements or in private meetings with US officials, while working behind the scenes to sabotage those efforts. They may do this through outright deception or through obfuscation and partial compliance. Leaders may initially agree to certain terms, but then backtrack on the agreement. They might plead that domestic politics constrains their ability to meet the United States' demands. Some officials might warn about the unintended consequences of complying with those demands. Another tactic involves the mobilization of supporters in the United States, such as sympathetic members of Congress, lobbyists, and members of their diaspora communities, to modify, slow, or even thwart an administration's policies.[47] The leaders of each of the allies examined in subsequent chapters employed some combination of these tactics.[48]

In some regards, frenemies are similar to what Resnick calls "ambivalent alliances." These are partnerships characterized by some degree of preexisting geopolitical conflict and ideological conflict between the parties.[49] Ideological

---

[47] Stephen M. Walt refers to this as domestic political penetration. See Walt, *Taming American Power: The Global Response to US Primacy* (New York: W. W. Norton & Company, 2005), pp. 194–217. Also see John J. Mearsheimer and Stephen M. Walt, *The Israel Lobby and US Foreign Policy* (London: Allen Lane, 2007); and Tony Smith, *Foreign Attachments: The Power of Ethnic Groups in the Making of American Foreign Policy* (Cambridge: Harvard University Press, 2000).

[48] For the list of tactics, see Robert M. Hathaway, *The Leverage Paradox: Pakistan and the United States* (Washington, DC: Woodrow Wilson International Center for Scholars, 2017), p. 4, https://www.wilsoncenter.org/sites/default/files/hathaway_leverage_paradox.pdf. Also see Howard B. Schaffer and Teresita C. Schaffer, *How Pakistan Negotiates with the United States: Riding the Roller Coaster* (Washington, DC: United States Institute of Peace, 2011). The use of these various tactics, however, is not unique to Pakistan.

[49] Resnick, "Strange Bedfellows," pp. 149–150. A classic example of an ambivalent alliance between a superpower and a regional client would be the Sino-Soviet alliance of 1949–1962. See

disharmony, however, is not a necessary condition for the United States and a weaker ally to be frenemies. In the historical cases examined, the main issues of contention between senior officials in Washington and their counterparts in other capitals stemmed from conflicting strategic interests, rather than conflicting ideology.

At the other end of the spectrum are so-called special relationship alliances. These are long-standing partnerships between the United States and other states characterized by a high degree of convergence in strategic interests and ideology. They also entail some level of institutionalized cooperation, especially in defense and intelligence matters, and a sense of collective identity or sentimental attachment between their governments, as well as powerful interest groups within each state.[50]

The United States' alliances with Britain and Israel are often cited as the archetypical special relationships. Both alliances came into existence due to shared security concerns.[51] Over time, however, institutional linkages between military and intelligence establishments made cooperation path-dependent. Additionally, a shared collective identity formed, based upon a combination of liberal democratic governance; ethnic, cultural, and religious affinity; and ideology. Institutionalization, collective identity, and reciprocal cooperation advance the strategic interests of both parties and are mutually reinforcing. The US-British and the US-Israeli special relationships have endured over time, despite occasional divergence in their strategic interests or a lack of rapport between their leaders, as illustrated by the contentious relationship between former US President Barack Obama and Israeli Prime Minister Benjamin Netanyahu.[52] It is conceivable that frenemies might evolve into ambivalent alliances or even special relationships over time. Explaining when, why, and under what circumstances such an evolution might occur, however, lies outside the scope of this book.

Thomas J. Christensen, *Worse Than a Monolith: Alliance Politics and Problems of Coercive Diplomacy in Asia* (Princeton, NJ: Princeton University Press, 2011).

[50] See Ruike Xu and Wyn Rees, "Comparing the Anglo-American and Israeli-American Special Relationships in the Obama Era: An Alliance Persistence Perspective," *Journal of Strategic Studies*, Vol. 41, No. 4 (2018), pp. 1–25. On "special relationship" alliances also see Charles Kupchan, *How Enemies Become Friends: The Sources of Stable Peace* (Princeton, NJ: Princeton University Press, 2010).

[51] David Reynolds, *The Creation of the Anglo-American Alliance, 1937–41: A Study in Competitive Co-Operation* (Chapel Hill: University of North Carolina Press, 1982); Mark A. Stoler, *Allies and Adversaries: The Joint Chiefs of Staff, the Grand Alliance, and U.S. Strategy in World War II* (Chapel Hill: University of North Carolina Press, 2000); and Yaacov Bar-Siman-Tov, "The United States and Israel since 1948: A 'Special Relationship'?," *Diplomatic History*, Vol. 22, No. 2 (1998), pp. 231–262.

[52] Xu and Rees, "Comparing the Anglo-American and Israeli-American Special Relationships," pp. 4–6.

Case Selection

The universe of potential cases is quite small. It comprises states that have (or had) nuclear weapons programs and that were concurrently allies or quasi-allies of the United States during all or part of the time their nuclear weapons programs operated.[53] Figure 1.2 lists eighteen states (including the United States) that had active nuclear weapons programs in the period between 1945 and 2016. Only eight of those eighteen states—Britain, France, West Germany, Israel, Pakistan, South Korea, Taiwan, and South Africa—were allies of the United States during all or part of the period when their nuclear weapons programs were active.

Within that subpopulation of seven cases, I submit that four states fall into the category of frenemies: Israel, Pakistan, South Korea, and Taiwan. Successive governments in all four states displayed the requisite patterns of deception, evasion, and obstruction with respect to their clandestine nuclear weapons programs and other areas. Likewise, successive presidential administrations in Washington made highly conditional security guarantees to these allies to minimize the risk of the United States being dragged into unwanted conflicts.[54]

Several additional reasons have led me to focus on Washington's sometimes quarrelsome relationships with Israel, Pakistan, Taiwan, and South Korea. Each state is located in a strategically important and volatile region where the United States has long-standing interests in containing rival great powers and preserving its own access. All four have been major receipts of conventional arms transfers and economic assistance packages. In turn, all four were (or became) dependent on the United States for security against their respective local adversaries. Overall, the United States came to depend upon these states to preserve its influence and to serve as a regional bulwark against expansion by the Soviet Union and/or China, albeit in different time periods. Thus, Israel, Pakistan, South Korea, and Taiwan's respective nuclear weapons programs, as well as the efforts of successive US presidential administrations to halt (or at least slow) those programs, were inextricably linked to broader Cold War dynamics.

---

[53] See Matthew Fuhrmann and Benjamin Tkach, "Almost Nuclear: Introducing the Nuclear Latency Dataset," *Conflict Management and Peace Science*, Vol. 32, No. 4 (2015), 443–461. Fuhrmann and Tkach's nuclear latency dataset codes thirty-one states between 1939 and 2012 that possessed the uranium enrichment or reprocessing capabilities to produce fissile material for nuclear energy or nuclear weapons. Christopher Way's database lists twenty-nine states that explored, pursued, or actually acquired nuclear weapons since 1945. Christopher Way, 12 June 2012 "Nuclear Proliferation Dates." Cornell University, http://falcon.arts.cornell.edu/crw12documentsNuclear%20Proliferation%20Dates.pdf (accessed 11 February 2017). Also see Christopher Way and Jessica L. P. Weeks, "Making It Personal: Regime Type and Nuclear Proliferation," *American Journal of Political Science*, Vol. 58, No. 3 (2014), pp. 705–719.

[54] See Tongfi Kim, "Why Alliances Entangle but Seldom Entrap States," *Security Studies*, Vol. 20, No. 3 (2011), pp. 350–377.

Table 1.1 **States with Active and Abandoned Nuclear Weapons Programs, 1941–2016**

State	Duration of Nuclear Weapons Program	Disposition of Program
Germany (Nazi)	1941–1945	End of World War II
United States	1941–present	Nuclear test in 1945
Soviet Union (Russia)	1943–present	Nuclear test in 1949
United Kingdom	1941–present	Nuclear test in 1951
France	1954–present	Nuclear test in 1960
People's Republic of China	1955–present	Nuclear test in 1964
India	1958–present	PNE in 1974; nuclear test in 1998
Israel	1955–present	Nixon-Meir understanding, Sept. 1969
Pakistan	1972–present	Nuclear test in 1998
Germany, Federal Republic of	1957–1967	End of program
Taiwan	1967–1979 (1987)	End of program
South Korea	1971–1979	End of program
South Africa	1971–1990	End of program
Libya	1970–2003	End of program
Argentina	1976–1990	End of program
Brazil	1978–1990	End of program
North Korea	1982–present	Nuclear test in 2006
Iran	1984–present	2015 JCOPA
Iraq	1973–1991	End of 1991 Persian Gulf War

Adapted from Alexander H. Montgomery and Adam Mount, "Misestimation: Explaining US Failures to Predict Nuclear Weapons Programs," *Intelligence and National Security*, Vol. 29, No. 3 (2014), pp. 357–386, Table 1 at p. 360.

There is variation in the eventual outcomes of the proliferation disputes. Two of the allies examined, Israel and Pakistan, are currently nuclear-armed states. Two others, South Korea and Taiwan, abandoned their nuclear weapons programs in response to Washington's coercive diplomacy in the late 1970s and early 1980s.[55] There is variation in the independent variables of the neoclassical realist theory within each case. There is also variation in the independent variables posited by the alternative theories (nuclear domino theory, security commitment theory, and credible sanctions theory) within each case, as well as across the cases.[56] Finally, the values of the dependent variable change within each case, as well as across the several cases.

During the period studied, from roughly 1960 to 1990, South Korea, Taiwan, Israel, and Pakistan each faced existential threats from their more powerful and threatening neighbors: North Korea, China, Egypt and Syria, and India, respectively.[57] As the succeeding chapters illustrate, their governments had good reason to doubt the credibility of US security guarantees. Israel, for example, embarked on its nuclear program in the mid-1950s, a period when the United States sought to avoid becoming enmeshed in the Arab-Israeli conflict. During the nascent years of the Israeli nuclear program (roughly 1957 to 1961), the Eisenhower administration refused to sell advanced conventional weapons to the Israelis for fear of antagonizing the Arab states. The Kennedy administration sold the HAWK antimissile batteries to Israel with great reluctance in 1962 and rebuffed Israeli Prime Minister David Ben-Gurion's request for a mutual defense treaty the following year.

As explained below, as a founding member of the Central Treaty Organization (CENTO) or Baghdad Pact, Pakistan was a treaty ally of the United States. The purpose of CENTO, however, was to deter a possible attack by the Soviet Union on the states of the Middle East and South Asia.[58] The United States had no

---

[55] See Eugene B. Kogan, "Coercing Allies: Why Friends Abandon Nuclear Plans" (PhD diss., Brandeis University, 2013), p. 302. Kogan's dissertation seeks to explain the uneven record of the United States' nonproliferation efforts vis-à-vis Israel, Pakistan, South Korea, and Taiwan. He finds that the type of coercion attempted and the type of inducement offered, as well as the target state's degree of security dependence on the United States, shaped the outcome of the proliferation dispute. By contrast, I am interested in explaining the variation in the types of nonproliferation strategies US policymakers pursued toward these allies, in the first place.

[56] As I explain in greater detail in chapter 2, security commitment theory and credible sanctions theory have narrower scope conditions that nuclear domino theory and neoclassical realist alliance theory. Hence, the security commitment theory is only applicable to the US-Taiwan and the US–South Korea proliferation disputes. Credible sanctions theory is not applicable to the US-Israeli proliferation dispute. See Figure 2.4: Cross Case Comparisons.

[57] The four nuclear-aspiring allies studied were situated in what T. V. Paul refers as "high conflict zones." See T. V. Paul, *Power Versus Prudence: Why Nations Forgo Nuclear Weapons* (Montreal: McGill–Queens University Press, 2003), pp. 14–36.

[58] Pakistan was also a founding member of the South East Asia Treaty Organization (SEATO), along with the United States, the United Kingdom, Australia, New Zealand, Philippines, and Thailand.

treaty obligation to come to Pakistan's assistance in the event of hostilities with its more powerful (and non-aligned) neighbor India.

Fear of "abandonment" by the United States in the late 1960s and early 1970s prompted Taiwan and South Korea to embark on their respective nuclear weapons and missile programs. Specifically, the Nixon administration's efforts to seek rapprochement with the People's Republic of China, coupled with the drawdown of the US military presence throughout East Asia and Southeast Asia (in accordance with the Nixon Doctrine), led officials in Taipei and Seoul to pursue a nuclear weapons option.

The neoclassical realist theory developed in the next chapter does not purport to explain *why* these states embarked upon nuclear weapons programs and then ultimately chose nuclear weapons acquisition or nuclear forbearance.[59] Thus it does not address the debates among proponents of various security-driven, political economy, supply-side, and psychological theories of nuclear proliferation.[60] Nor does this theory purport to explain why these states chose particular

---

[59] T. V. Paul writes, "Nuclear forbearance is the result of a conscious effort by technologically capable states not to create an intense negative security externality for other significant actors that will most be affected." See Paul, *Power Versus Prudence*, p. 15. Nuclear forbearance can subsume a range of activities—from the complete dismantlement of infrastructure and surrender of fissile material to the maintenance of a latent nuclear capability. For recent works on the strategic value of nuclear latency, see Tristan A. Volpe, "Atomic Leverage: Compellence with Nuclear Latency," *Security Studies*, Vol. 26, No. 3 (2017), pp. 517–544; Rupal N. Mehta and Rachel Elizabeth Whitlark, "Unpacking the Iranian Nuclear Deal: Nuclear Latency and US Foreign Policy," *The Washington Quarterly*, Vol. 39, No. 4 (2016), pp. 45–61; and Matthew Fuhrmann and Benjamin Tkach, "Almost Nuclear: Introducing the Nuclear Latency Dataset," *Conflict Management and Peace Science*, Vol. 32, No. 4 (2015), pp. 443–461. On the strategy of nuclear hedging, see Ariel E. Levite, "Never Say Never Again: Nuclear Reversal Revisited," *International Security*, Vol. 27, No. 3 (2002), pp. 59–88.

[60] For recent overviews and critical evaluations of the nuclear proliferation literature, see Alexandre Debs and Nuno P. Monteiro, "Conflict and Cooperation on Nuclear Nonproliferation," *Annual Review of Political Science*, Vol. 20 (2017), pp. 331–349; Mark S. Bell, "Examining Explanations for Nuclear Proliferation," *International Studies Quarterly*, Vol. 60, No. 3 (2016), pp. 520–529; and Scott D. Sagan, "Two Renaissances in Nuclear Security Studies," H-Diplo/ISSF Forum: What we talk about when we talk about nuclear weapons (Ann Arbor, MI: H-Diplo/ISSF Forum, 2014), pp. 2–10, http://issforum.org/ISSF/PDF/ISSF-Forum-2.pdf. Examples of security-driven, political economy, supply-side, and psychological theories of nuclear proliferation include: Paul, *Power Versus Prudence*; Alexandre Debs and Nuno P. Monteiro, *Nuclear Politics: The Strategic Causes of Proliferation* (New York: Cambridge University Press, 2016); Etel Solingen, *Nuclear Logics: Contrasting Paths in East Asia and the Middle East* (Princeton, NJ: Princeton University Press, 2007); Matthew Fuhrmann, *Atomic Assistance: How "Atoms for Peace" Programs Cause Nuclear Insecurity* (Ithaca, NY: Cornell University Press, 2012); Matthew Kroenig, *Exporting the Bomb: Technology Transfer, and the Spread of Nuclear Weapons* (Ithaca, NY: Cornell University Press, 2010); and Jacques E. C. Hymans, *The Psychology of Nuclear Proliferation: Identity, Emotions, and Foreign Policy* (Cambridge: Cambridge University Press, 2006).

strategies of nuclear proliferation.⁶¹ Rather, the theory purports to explain the variation in the types of coercive diplomacy and inducements the United States pursued toward them.⁶²

The sample cases includes two formal treaty allies and two non-treaty allies of the United States. The Republic of Korea (ROK) and the Republic of China (ROC) on Taiwan had bilateral alliance treaties with Washington when their respective nuclear weapons programs were active.⁶³ The 1953 US-ROK Mutual Defense Treaty remains in effect.⁶⁴ The United States terminated its Mutual Defense Treaty with Taiwan effective 1 January 1980, as part of the process of normalizing diplomatic relations with China. In April 1979, Congress passed the Taiwan Relations Act, which obligates the United States "to resist any resort to force or other forms of coercion that would jeopardize the security" of Taiwan and "to provide Taiwan with arms of defensive character."⁶⁵

Pakistan was a member of the CENTO from its inception in 1955, until that organization's dissolution in 1979. A series of agreements, signed between 1954 and 1959, governed the bilateral alliance ties between the United States and Pakistan during the period under study. Israel has never had a formal mutual defense treaty with the United States. Instead, a de facto US-Israeli alliance evolved through various memoranda of understanding on the transfer of US-made conventional weapons systems that entered into force between 1965 and 1971.⁶⁶

The exclusion of South Africa, which had a nuclear weapons program from 1974 to 1979, and which possessed a rudimentary nuclear arsenal in the 1980s, requires some explanation. South Africa has the distinction of being the first target of nonproliferation-related US economic sanctions, in 1975, as well as the

---

⁶¹ For a typology of different nuclear proliferation strategies and a neoclassical realist theory to explain when and why states pursue one strategy over others, see Vipin Narang, "Strategies of Nuclear Proliferation: How States Pursue the Bomb," *International Security*, Vol. 41, No. 3 (2017), pp. 110–150.

⁶² For a formal theory on when nonproliferation deals between the United States and would-be proliferators are likely to obtain, see Muhammet A. Bas and Andrew J. Coe, "Give Peace a (Second) Chance: A Theory of Nonproliferation Deals," *International Studies Quarterly*, Vol. 62, No. 3 (2018), pp. 606–617.

⁶³ US Congress Senate Foreign Relations Committee and US Department of State Historical Office, eds., *American Foreign Policy, 1950–1955, Vol 1: Basic Documents* (Washington, DC: GPO, 1957), https://hdl.handle.net/2027/mdp.39015017671572.

⁶⁴ Mutual Treaty of Defense between the United States and the Republic of Korea, http://avalon.law.yale.edu/20th_century/kor001.asp.

⁶⁵ Taiwan Relations Act, Public Law 96-8, 96th Congress, 1st session (10 April 1979), at https://www.gpo.gov/fdsys/pkg/STATUTE-93/pdf/STATUTE-93-Pg14.pdf.

⁶⁶ Office of the Legal Adviser Treaty Affairs Staff, US Department of State, ed., *Treaties in Force: A List of Treaties and Other Agreements of the United States in Force as of 1 January 2016* (Washington, DC: GPO, 2016), https://www.state.gov/documents/organization/264509.pdf.

only state to voluntarily dismantle its nuclear arsenal, in 1993.[67] Furthermore, the Ford, Carter, and Reagan administrations employed a variety of inducements and coercive strategies intended to dissuade the South African government, under Prime Minister Balthazar Johannes ("John") Vorster and later President P. W. Botha, from continuing with uranium enrichment and conducting a nuclear weapons detonation.[68] Yet I exclude South Africa for three reasons.

South Africa enjoyed overwhelming military and economic advantages over its immediate neighbors. That is not to dismiss the perceived threat to the white minority government in Pretoria posed by Soviet and Cuban support for the leftist government of Mozambique and the People's Movement for the Liberation of Angola (MPLA). Nonetheless, South Africa had a gross domestic product (GDP) over ten times that of Angola in 1975. As Alexandre Debs and Nuno Monteiro observe, there was a low likelihood of a counterproliferation strike on South Africa's nuclear facilities by one of its regional adversaries.[69]

Compared to other regions, the likelihood of the United States suffering containment failure or access denial in southern Africa was quite low. South Africa was an important source of natural uranium, especially during the early years of the Cold War. Successive National Party governments in Pretoria were vehemently anti-Communist. The risk of increased Soviet penetration of southern Africa through conventional arms transfers, economic assistance, or explicit security guarantees to local actors was low in comparison to other regions.

Even though South Africa might be considered a "loose" ally of the United States during the early decades of the Cold War, by the time the nuclear proliferation dispute between Pretoria and Washington began in earnest in the mid-1970s that alliance was largely defunct.[70] The revelation of covert US assistance

---

[67] See Peter Liberman, "The Rise and Fall of the South African Bomb," *International Security*, Vol. 26, No. 2 (2001), pp. 45–86; Helen E. Purkitt, Stephen F. Burgess, and Peter Liberman, "South Africa's Nuclear Decisions," *International Security*, Vol. 27, No. 1 (2002), pp. 186–194; and Vipin Narang, *Nuclear Strategy in the Modern Era: Regional Powers and International Conflict* (Princeton, NJ: Princeton University Press, 2014), pp. 207–221.

[68] See Or Rabinowitz and Nicholas L. Miller, "Keeping the Bombs in the Basement: U.S. Nonproliferation Policy toward Israel, South Africa, and Pakistan," *International Security*, Vol. 40, No. 1 (2015), pp. 47–86, at pp. 60–70; Rabinowitz, *Bargaining on Nuclear Tests: Washington and Its Cold War Deals* (Oxford: Oxford University Press, 2014), pp. 106–136; Martha S. van Wyk, "Ally or Critic? The United States' Response to South African Nuclear Development, 1949–1980," *Cold War History*, Vol. 7, No. 2 (2007), pp. 195–225; and Eugene Gerzhoy, "Coercive Nonproliferation: Security, Leverage, and Nuclear Reversals" (PhD diss., University of Chicago, 2014), pp. 166–217.

[69] Debs and Monteiro cite United Nations data from 2013 suggesting that Angola's GDP in 1975 was approximately $3.1 billion compared to South Africa's, which was $36.9 billion (in current US dollars). See Debs and Monteiro, *Nuclear Politics*, p. 267, fn. 461.

[70] Debs and Monteiro code South Africa as a "loose" ally of the United States. Debs and Monteiro, *Nuclear Politics*, pp. 84–85. Also see Stephen F. Burgess, "South Africa's Nuclear Weapons Policies," *The Nonproliferation Review*, Vol. 13, No. 3 (2006), pp. 519–526; and Martha van Wyk, "Sunset over

to the South African forces fighting in Angola in 1975 prompted Congress to pass an amendment sponsored by Senator Dick Clark (D-Iowa) to the Arms Export Control Act (AECA) in February 1976. The Clark Amendment prohibited covert assistance and conventional arms transfers to states and non-state actors involved in military and paramilitary activities in Angola.[71] The brutal suppression of riots in Soweto and other townships the following year turned the apartheid government in Pretoria into an international pariah. The Reagan administration pursued a strategy of "constructive engagement" toward South Africa, aimed, in part, to end the regime's international isolation. Notwithstanding, by the late 1970s, South Africa and the United States were not exactly allies.

Lastly, the exclusion of India also merits some discussion. India started a civil nuclear energy program in 1948, with the creation of the Indian Atomic Energy Commission (IAEC). The country became a major recipient of Atoms for Peace in the 1950s. US firms exported civilian nuclear equipment to India. Indian nuclear scientists and engineers participated in Atoms for Peace training programs.[72] The Central Intelligence Agency (CIA), the National Security Agency (NSA), and other US intelligence agencies identified India as a potential nuclear weapons proliferator beginning in the early 1960s.[73] In the aftermath of China's first nuclear weapons test at Lop Nor in October 1964, Prime Minister Lal Bahadur Shastri authorized a program to develop an underground nuclear explosive device for civilian purposes.[74]

Atomic Apartheid: United States–South African Nuclear Relations, 1981–93," *Cold War History*, Vol. 10, No. 1 (2010), pp. 51–79.

[71] For contemporary assessments of the Clark Amendment's impact on the Angola civil war, see "24. Summary of Conclusions of Special Coordination Committee Meeting, Re: Horn of Africa, 15 May 1978, 3:30–4:23 PM," *FRUS, 1977–1980, Vol. XVI: Southern Africa* (Washington, DC: GPO, 2016), https://history.state.gov/historicaldocuments/frus1977-80v16/d24; and "Note from Robert M. Gates, Deputy Director for Intelligence to Tom Cormack, Executive Secretary, Re: Angola-Effect of the Clark Amendment, 14 April 1983 [Sanitized Copy]," *CIA Electronic Reading Room* (Washington, DC: Central Intelligence Agency, 2010), https://www.cia.gov/library/readingroom/docs/CIA-RDP85T00287R000400320001-4.pdf.

[72] India's civil nuclear program also benefited from early collaboration with France. See Jayita Sarkar, "'Wean Them Away from French Tutelage': Franco-Indian Nuclear Relations and Anglo-American Anxieties During the Early Cold War, 1948–1952," *Cold War History*, Vol. 15, No. 3 (2015), pp. 375–394.

[73] For an examination of the US Intelligence Community's efforts to track India's nuclear weapons program up to the May 1974 PNE see Richelson, *Spying on the Bomb*, pp. 218–232. For declassified US intelligence estimates of the Indian nuclear program, see Jeffrey Richelson, ed., *National Security Archive Electronic Briefing Book No. 187: US Intelligence and the Indian Bomb* (Washington, DC: National Security Archive, 2006), https://nsarchive2.gwu.edu/NSAEBB/NSAEBB187/index.htm.

[74] For a detailed history of India's nuclear weapons program up to the 1990s, see George Perkovich, *India's Nuclear Bomb: The Impact on Global Proliferation* (Berkeley: University of California Press, 1999).

India's peaceful nuclear explosion (PNE) in the Thar Desert in Rajasthan on 8 May 1974 prompted the US Congress to enact comprehensive nonproliferation legislation, most notably the 1976 Symington Amendment to the Foreign Assistance Act and the 1978 Nuclear Nonproliferation Act.[75] Other US nonproliferation initiatives, including the Nuclear Suppliers' Group (NSG) and later the Missile Technology Control Regime (MTCR), emerged in the aftermath of India's PNE.[76]

The Kennedy, Johnson, and Nixon administrations attempted to dissuade India from developing a nuclear explosive device.[77] After the PNE of May 1974, the Ford, Carter, and Reagan administrations all attempted to dissuade India from weaponizing its nuclear option.[78] When India resumed nuclear testing in May 1998, after a twenty-four-year moratorium, the Clinton administration imposed economic sanctions.[79] The bilateral relationship changed in the 2000s, however, when President George W. Bush and his advisers concluded India might be a useful partner against a rising China.[80] In the nuclear cooperation agreement that Bush and Prime Minister Manmohan Singh signed in July 2005, the United States essentially recognized India—a non-signatory of the NPT—as a nuclear-armed state.[81]

---

[75] For the argument that India's PNE and the Nixon administration's muted reaction to it, along with the Ford administration's subsequent decision to provide fuel for India's nuclear power reactor, prompted Congress to pass the Symington Amendment, see Miller, *Stopping the Bomb*, pp. 74–81.

[76] See William Burr, "A Scheme of 'Control': The United States and the Origins of the Nuclear Suppliers' Group, 1974–1976," *The International History Review*, Vol. 36, No. 2 (2014), pp. 252–276; and Cameron and Rabinowitz, "Eight Lost Years?" pp. 16–19.

[77] See Thomas P. Cavanna, "Geopolitics over Proliferation: The Origins of US Grand Strategy and Their Implications for the Spread of Nuclear Weapons in South Asia," *Journal of Strategic Studies*, Vol. 41, No. 4 (2018), pp. 1–28, esp. pp. 5–13. Cavanna's analysis overlaps with the argument I develop in this book. We both agree that regional power dynamics in South Asia largely drove the types of nonproliferation strategies that United States pursued toward Pakistan and India.

[78] Cavanna contends that the shift in US foreign policies toward South Asia had the unintended consequence of encouraging nuclear proliferation through three interconnected levels: security, technology, and national identity. See Ibid., esp. pp. 7–8 and pp. 1–15.

[79] William J. Clinton, "Message to the Congress Reporting the Detonation of a Nuclear Device by India, 13 May 1998," *Public Papers of the Presidents of the United States: William J. Clinton, 1998* (Washington, DC: GPO, 1999), p. 798; and William J. Clinton, "Presidential Determination No. 98-22 of 13 May 1998: Sanctions against India for Detonation of a Nuclear Explosive Device," *Federal Register*, Vol. 63, No. 97 (1999), p. 27665.

[80] See T. V. Paul and Mahesh Shankar, "Why the US-India Nuclear Accord Is a Good Deal," *Survival*, Vol. 49, No. 4 (2007), pp. 111–122; Harsh V. Pant, "The US-India Nuclear Pact: Policy, Process, and Great Power Politics," *Asian Security* Vol. 5, No. 3 (2009), pp. 273–295; and Gerald Felix Warburg, "Nonproliferation Policy Crossroads: Lessons Learned from the US-India Nuclear Cooperation Agreement," *The Nonproliferation Review*, Vol. 19, No. 3 (2012), pp. 451–471.

[81] Joint Statement between President George W. Bush and Prime Minister Manmohan Singh, 18 July 2005, Office of the Press Secretary, The White House, https://georgewbush-whitehouse.archives.gov/news/releases/2005/07/20050718-6.html (accessed 1 March 2018); and the United

Nonetheless, I exclude the US-India proliferation case for a simple reason: India was not an ally of the United States during the Cold War. India became the leader of the Non-Alignment Movement in the 1950s, eschewing overt alliances with either superpower. Sensing an opportunity after the 1962 Sino-Indian War, however, the Kennedy administration attempted to enlist India as an ally in order to forestall China's threat to South Asia, but without abandoning the existing alliance with Pakistan. The United States and Britain even granted Indian Prime Minister Jawaharlal Nehru's request for small arms, military equipment, and joint training exercises for British, US, and Indian forces.[82]

This US-India rapprochement faltered after Kennedy's assassination in November 1963.[83] India continued to buy weapons from the Soviet Union. Officials in the Johnson administration grew frustrated by the inability of Pakistan and India to reach a negotiated settlement over Kashmir. They also saw that forging closer ties with India had the unintended consequence of driving Pakistan closer to China.[84] While some scholars contend that the United States extended an implicit security guarantee to India in the wake of China's October 1964 nuclear weapons test, other scholars note that the Johnson administration rebuffed multiple requests from Shastri to put India under the US nuclear umbrella.[85] Repeated attempts by Shastri and later his successor, Indira Gandhi, to secure a multilateral guarantee from the United States, Britain, and the Soviet Union against a potential Chinese attack also faltered.[86]

During the 1965 Kashmir War, President Johnson imposed an arms embargo on India and Pakistan, even though the latter initiated the war. This embargo

---

States–India Nuclear Cooperation Approval and Nonproliferation Enhancement Act, Public Law 110-369 (8 October 2008), 110th Congress, 2nd session, https://www.congress.gov/110/plaws/publ369/PLAW-110publ369.pdf.

[82] See Montgomery, *In the Hegemon's Shadow*, pp. 104–109; and R. Devereux David, "The Sino-Indian War of 1962 in Anglo-American Relations," *Journal of Contemporary History*, Vol. 44, No. 1 (2009), pp. 71–87.

[83] Dennis Kux, *India and the United States: Estranged Democracies, 1941–1991* (Washington, DC: National Defense University Press, 1992), pp. 209–213.

[84] For analysis of the Kennedy and Johnson administrations' unsuccessful efforts to broker a negotiated settlement to the Kashmir dispute between 1962 and 1965, see Timothy W. Crawford, *Pivotal Deterrence: Third-Party Statecraft and the Pursuit of Peace* (Ithaca, NY: Cornell University Press, 2003), pp. 135–168.

[85] See Andrew B. Kennedy, "India's Nuclear Odyssey: Implicit Umbrellas, Diplomatic Disappointments, and the Bomb," *International Security*, Vol. 36, No. 2 (2011), pp. 120–153, esp. pp. 129–132; and Šumit Ganguly, "India's Pathway to Pokhran II: The Prospects and Sources of New Delhi's Nuclear Weapons Program," *International Security*, Vol. 23, No. 4 (1999), pp. 148–177, esp. 153–155.

[86] Ganguly, "India's Pathway to Pokhran II," pp. 157–158.

remained in place until 1975.[87] The efforts by President Nixon and Assistant to the President for National Security Affairs Henry A. Kissinger to seek a rapprochement with China in summer 1971, followed by their "tilt toward Pakistan" during the South Asia Crisis later that year, further strained US-India relations.[88] As Robert Jervis observes, "While Nixon and Kissinger did not create the crisis between India and Pakistan in 1971, they did realize that resulting friction between the US and India would increase the common interests between the US and China."[89]

Methodology

The book employs qualitative methods, specifically comparative case studies of the United States' efforts to stem the nuclear aspirations of Israel, Pakistan, South Korea, and Taiwan over a period of approximately thirty years, from 1961 to 1990. Each case is divisible into a number of discrete observation periods. In each period, I employ process tracing to discern whether the causal mechanisms posited by my theory of alliance coercion are present. I also employ the congruence procedure to discern whether the strategies actually undertaken by each presidential administration vis-à-vis the allied state are in the predicted direction.[90]

Recently declassified documents make it possible to trace the deliberations of senior and mid-level officials across seven presidential administrations. I draw upon documents obtained from the Kennedy, Johnson, Nixon, Ford, Carter, Reagan, and George (H. W.) Bush presidential libraries; the National Archives and Records Administration (NARA) II at College Park, Maryland; the various *National Security Archive (NSA) Electronic Briefing Books* and other document collections compiled by the National Security Archive at George Washington

---

[87] "185. Telegram from the Department of State to the Embassy in Pakistan, Washington, 5 September 1965, 3:57 PM," and "194. Telegram from the Department of State to the Embassy in India, Washington, 8 September 1965, 7:12 PM," *FRUS, 1964–1968, Vol. XXV: South Asia* (Washington, DC: GPO, 2000); "193. National Security Decision Memorandum 289, Washington, 24 March 1975," *FRUS, 1969–1976, Vol. E-8: Documents on South Asia, 1973–1976* (Washington, DC: GPO, 2007).

[88] See Perkovich, *India's Nuclear Bomb*, pp. 166–170; and Montgomery, *In the Hegemon's Shadow*, pp. 124–125.

[89] See Robert Jervis, *System Effects: Complexity in Political and Social Life* (Princeton, NJ: Princeton University Press, 1997), pp. 216. On the general problem of trying to simultaneously befriend two long-term adversaries, see pp. 234–237.

[90] Alexander L. George and Andrew Bennett, *Case Studies and Theory Development in the Social Sciences* (Cambridge: MIT Press, 2005), pp. 205–233; James Mahoney, "Process Tracing and Historical Explanation," *Security Studies*, Vol. 24, No. 2 (2015), pp. 200–218.

University; the digital archives and various conference books compiled by the History and Public Policy Program (HAPP) at the Woodrow Wilson International Center for Scholars; subscription databases such as the Digital National Security Archives (DNSA) and US Declassified Documents Online (USDDO); and the documents published in *The Foreign Relations of the United States* (*FRUS*) series. Whenever possible, I rely on primary sources, although I do supplement them with secondary works.

I limit the analysis to members of the foreign policy executive (or FPE), the senior officials who are charged with the formulation of grand strategy and foreign and security policies.[91] These officials stand at the intersection of the international system and the domestic political arenas. They possessed privileged information about the capabilities and intentions of other actors in the international system by virtue of their access to intelligence assessments, policy papers, diplomatic cables, and their meetings with foreign leaders. These officials stand atop bureaucratic organizations charged with supporting and implementing different elements of a state's foreign and security policies. At the same time, the FPE members cannot be divorced from domestic politics.

In the United States in the late twentieth and early twenty-first centuries, the FPE always includes the president, the vice president, the secretary of state, the secretary of defense, the president's national security adviser and deputy national security adviser,[92] and the deputy secretaries and the relevant undersecretaries in the Department of State and the Department of Defense (DoD).[93] I include the two statutory advisers to the National Security Council (NSC)—the director of

---

[91] On the necessity of identifying the scope and members of the FPE, see Ripsman, Taliaferro, and Lobell, *Neoclassical Realist Theory*, pp. 123–129.

[92] McGeorge Bundy and his successor Walt W. Rostow were formerly titled "special assistant to the president" or "special assistant to the president for national security affairs" during the Kennedy and the Johnson administrations (January 1961 to January 1969). From Henry Kissinger's appointment in January 1969 to the present day, the formal title of the position has been "the assistant to the president for national security affairs." It was during Kissinger's tenure in the post (20 January 1969 to 3 November 1975) that the more informal title "national security adviser" or "national security advisor" came into widespread use. Throughout the text, I generally use informal designation "national security adviser."

[93] The relevant subcabinet officials in the State Department were the undersecretary of state (the department's second ranking officer until 1972), the deputy secretary of state (the second ranking officer after 1972), the undersecretary of state for political affairs (the department's third-ranking officer who oversees the various regional bureaus), and the undersecretary of state for security assistance (which was retitled undersecretary of state for international security and arms control in 1994). The relevant subcabinet officials in the Defense Department were the deputy secretary of defense and the assistant secretary of defense for international security affairs. See "Principal Officers of the Department of State," https://history.state.gov/departmenthistory/people/principalofficers (accessed 8 May 2017); and *Department of Defense Key Officials: September 1947–September 2016* (Washington, DC: Historical Office, Office of the Secretary of Defense, 2016).

central intelligence (DCI) and the chairman of the Joint Chiefs of Staff (JCS)—where appropriate.[94] Where appropriate, I also examine the assessments of the assistant secretaries overseeing the relevant functional and regional bureaus (or offices) in the State and Defense Departments, since those officials were heavily involved in the formulation of nonproliferation and arms transfer policies.[95]

The Plan of the Book

The remainder of the book is organized as follows. Chapter 2 lays out my neoclassical realist theory. I explicate how the two independent variables—the distribution of power in the region where the ally is located and the time horizons in which threats for US interests in that region—can create incentives of US presidential administrations to favor coercive or accommodative strategies toward an ally seeking nuclear weapons. The likelihood of the United States actually pursuing a coercive or an accommodative strategy, however, is shaped by the height of the domestic mobilization hurdles—namely, the degree of support or opposition in Congress—the administration must garner or overcome. The chapter discusses the measurement of the variables, and the types of evidence that might confirm or disconfirm the hypotheses. It also explicates three alternative explanations, nuclear domino theory, security commitment theory, and credible sanctions theory, and evidence that confirms or disconfirms hypotheses from them.

Chapters 3 through 6 comprise case studies of the United States' confrontations with Israel, Pakistan, South Korea, and Taiwan over their respective nuclear weapons programs in the period spanning from 1961 to 1990. In each chapter, I delineate the current distribution of power the United States confronted in the relevant regions and the time horizons for threats to US interests in those regions perceived by senior officials in the Kennedy, Johnson, Nixon, Ford, Reagan, and Bush administrations. I show how the height of the domestic mobilization hurdles that each administration needed to overcome

---

[94] The director of central intelligence (DCI), often incorrectly referred to as the "CIA director," was concurrently the head of the Central Intelligence Agency, the statutory intelligence adviser to the president and the National Security Council, and the titular head of the entire US Intelligence Community, most of which resided in the Department of Defense. The Intelligence Reform and Terrorism Prevention Act of 2004 (Public Law 108-458 of 17 December 2004; 118 STAT. 3638) abolished the DCI, created a director of national intelligence (DNI) to serve as overall head of the US Intelligence Community and statutory intelligence adviser to the president, and created the separate post of director of the Central Intelligence Agency (D/CIA).

[95] These midlevel officials are the assistant secretaries of state for Near Eastern Affairs, East Asian and Pacific Affairs, and Politico-Military Affairs and the above-mentioned assistant secretary of defense for International Security Affairs (ISA).

sometimes skewed the types of strategies ultimately pursued toward the ally. I evaluate the explanatory power of the hypotheses derived from neoclassical realist theory against a structural realist baseline derived from nuclear domino theory and alternative hypotheses derived from credible sanctions theory and/or security commitment theory.[96] Chapter 7 summarizes the results of the case studies, discusses the theoretical implications, and outlines the implications of my analysis for policy.

---

[96] Nicholas L. Miller, "The Secret Success of Nonproliferation Sanctions," *International Organization*, Vol. 68, No. 4 (2014), pp. 913–944; Miller, *Stopping the Bomb: The Sources and Effectiveness of US Nonproliferation Policy* (Ithaca, NY: Cornell University Press, 2018); and Alexander Lanoszka, *Atomic Assurance: The Politics of Extended Deterrence* (Ithaca, NY: Cornell University Press, 2018).

2

Neoclassical Realist Theory, Alliance Politics, and Nonproliferation

If limiting the spread of nuclear capabilities, even to its own strategically vulnerable allies, has been a core objective of the United States since 1945, then what might account for variation in the types of nonproliferation strategies Washington actually pursued toward those allies? Why did US policymakers pursue overtly coercive strategies to thwart the nuclear ambitions of certain vulnerable allies, but far more accommodating strategies toward the nuclear weapons programs of other equally vulnerable allies? The purpose of this chapter is to begin to answer those questions.

The main hypotheses of neoclassical realist theory are as follows: When presidents and their national security teams perceive the United States as facing an unfavorable distribution of power in the ally's geographic region and short time horizons for threats to US interests in that region, they will be inclined to pursue accommodative nonproliferation strategies toward an ally. Conversely, when they perceive the United States as facing a favorable distribution of power in the region and long time horizons for threats to US interests in that region, they will be inclined to pursue coercive strategies to prevent proliferation. The strategies that the United States ultimately pursues toward a nuclear aspiring ally, however, are not solely a function of these systemic-level variables.

Since nonproliferation disputes are likely to unfold over a number of years, presidents and other administration officials must often mobilize congressional support for their preferred nonproliferation strategies. At the very least, administration officials may need to diffuse or circumvent the congressional opposition to pursuing their preferred policies. These domestic mobilization hurdles the administration must overcome constitute the intervening variable. High mobilization hurdles may make it more difficult to pursue a coercive or an accommodative strategy toward the ally at any given time. In these circumstances, the administration may end up pursuing a hybrid strategy toward a nuclear proliferating ally.

The remainder of this chapter unpacks the logic behind those hypotheses and the types of evidence that might confirm or disconfirm them. I will discuss the logic of nuclear domino theory (which serves as the structural realist baseline), as well as security commitment theory and credible sanctions theory. These theories posit alternative explanations for the United States' nonproliferation strategies toward its frenemies during the late Cold War.

A Differentiated Conception of the International System

Structural realism and neoclassical realism begin with the supposition that the international system, chiefly the relative distribution of material capabilities among states, sets the parameters of international bargaining outcomes and the likely strategic behavior of individual states. However, they diverge in their conception of the international system and the relevance of particular types of systemic-level variables.

Structural realism, especially Kenneth Waltz's reformulation of balance-of-power theory, emphasizes how the structure of the international system—the anarchic ordering principle among the constituent units (states) and the relative distribution of capabilities among them—creates pervasive uncertainty and incentives for states to engage in self-help behavior. However, structure does not dictate exactly how states ought to react to systemic stimuli. Over time, through the mechanisms of socialization and competition, states "learn" which types of external behavior are consistent (or inconsistent) with the incentives of the system. States that respond to the incentives provided by the international system will be rewarded, but states that consistently fail to respond to those incentives put their very survival at risk.[1]

The structure of the international system is important. Neoclassical realism, however, holds that a range of systemic variables have a more consequential effect on international outcomes and on states' external behavior. Two of these variables are the current distribution of power in particular regions and the time horizons in which policymakers expect threats to their states' interests to materialize.[2]

---

[1] Kenneth N. Waltz, *Theory of International Politics* (Reading, MA: Addison-Wesley 1979), pp. 71, 81–82, 88–99, and 104.

[2] See Norrin M. Ripsman, Jeffrey W. Taliaferro, and Steven E. Lobell, *Neoclassical Realist Theory of International Politics* (New York: Oxford University Press, 2016), pp. 33–57.

Current Distribution of Power in a Region

Neoclassical realism suggests that a state's strategic environment (or security environment), defined as the magnitude of the external threats and opportunities it confronts at any given time, will have a more consequential impact on that state's foreign and security policies than the polarity of the international system.[3] All else equal, the more dangerous the external threats, or the more enticing the external opportunity that a state confronts, the more restrictive its strategic environment will be. Conversely, the smaller the external threat, or the less enticing the external opportunity, the more permissive its strategic environment will be.[4] I argue that the magnitude of the external threats and opportunities that any state confronts is a function of the current power distribution within the specific region where that state is located or in regions where it has major strategic interests.

Global hegemons, by definition, have strategic interests in different geographic regions, in addition to their homelands and home regions. They are concerned about not only the current distribution of power in the international system as a whole, but also the current power distribution in distant regions where they have strategic interests. Moreover, a hegemon can simultaneously encounter different power distributions across several regions.

The current distribution of power within a region (or regional power distribution for short) refers to the distribution of military and economic capabilities among the actors operating within a region. This includes the power distribution between the hegemon's ally (or allies) and its local adversaries. The involvement of extra-regional great powers can shift the regional power distribution. The main point here is that a regional power distribution is not solely a function of the indigenous capabilities of the local states.

Consider two hegemons of the past 150 years, the United Kingdom and the United States. While Britain was first among equals among several great powers in a Eurocentric multipolar system during the nineteenth and early twentieth centuries, it also ruled over an empire that spanned several continents. The United States was one of two superpowers in a global bipolar system during the Cold War. It has been the lone superpower (or unipole) for the past two decades.[5] Averting the twin outcomes of containment failure and access denial

---

[3] Ibid., pp. 53–54. See also Jeffrey W. Taliaferro, Norrin M. Ripsman, and Steven E. Lobell, eds., *The Challenge of Grand Strategy: The Great Powers and the Broken Balance Between the Wars* (Cambridge: Cambridge University Press, 2012). Vipin Narang uses the term "security environment." See Narang, *Nuclear Strategy in the Modern Era: Regional Powers and International Conflict* (Princeton, NJ: Princeton University Press, 2014), pp. 31–36.

[4] Ripsman, Taliaferro, and Lobell, *Neoclassical Realism*, pp. 53–54.

[5] It is worth reiterating that hegemony and polarity are two different concepts. Polarity refers to the relative distribution of material capabilities among the states within an international system.

in regions of interest were core objectives for both. Specifically, senior officials in London and Washington sought to prevent a rival great power from not just conquering those regions, but also increasing its regional influence. British and US policymakers also sought to maintain their own access to those regions. They sought to prevent local actors from imposing embargoes on raw materials, or charging high rents for military bases, or obstructing the passage of troops and naval forces through the region, or evicting those forces and preventing their return.[6]

In the early 1850s, Britain arguably faced a favorable distribution of power in North America. The Royal Navy dominated the North Atlantic and the antebellum United States lacked the military and economic capabilities to pose a sustained threat to the British colonies of Canada, New Brunswick, and Nova Scotia. Britain also faced a favorable distribution of power on the European continent, especially in the decades following the Napoleonic Wars. France was in no position to make a renewed bid for continental expansion. Austria and Prussia continued to vie for influence within the weak German Confederation of 1815. British leaders, however, confronted an increasingly unfavorable distribution of power in the eastern Mediterranean and the Balkans, where Russia's encroachments on the Ottoman Empire led to the outbreak of the Crimean War in 1854.[7]

With the notable exception of the 1962 Cuban Missile Crisis, the United States has generally faced favorable power distributions in the Western Hemisphere in the twentieth and now the twenty-first centuries. This is due to geographic proximity, the loss-of-strength gradient, and the sheer imbalance in material capabilities between the United States and its hemispheric neighbors. However, in other parts of the globe, such as Western Europe, the Middle East, East Asia, South Asia, and Southeast Asia, the United States encountered (and still encounters) more variability in regional power distributions. The advantages

---

Hegemony is the result of a powerful state's concerted efforts to create and maintain a set of international rules. As Christopher J. Fettweis puts it, "Power, whether potential or kinetic, creates structure, while grand strategy, or the choices about what to do with that power, creates (or does not create) hegemony." See Fettweis, "Unipolarity, Hegemony, and the New Peace," *Security Studies*, Vol. 26, No. 3 (2017), pp. 423–451, at pp. 432–433. Also see David Wilkinson, "Unipolarity without Hegemony," *International Studies Review*, Vol. 1, No. 2 (1999), pp. 141–172.

[6] See Evan Braden Montgomery, *In the Hegemon's Shadow: Leading States and the Rise of Regional Powers* (Ithaca, NY: Cornell University Press, 2016), pp. 12–13. Like Montgomery, I do not restrict the term "containment" to the specific set of strategies that the United States pursued toward the Soviet Union between 1947 and 1989.

[7] Paul M. Kennedy, *The Rise and Fall of British Naval Mastery* (London; Atlantic Highlands, NJ: Ashfield Press, 1986), 149–177.

the United States enjoyed in the Western Hemisphere were not present in these other regions.

During the first years of the Cold War, the Truman administration confronted unfavorable power distributions in Western Europe and in East Asia. Although the United States emerged from World War II with an overwhelming preponderance in economic and technological capabilities, as well as a short-lived monopoly on atomic weapons and transoceanic bombers, the Soviet Union had a conventional force advantage in Europe. As the drafters of NSC-68 observed, "If war breaks out in 1950 or in the next few years, the United States and its [Western European] allies, apart from a powerful atomic blow, will be compelled to conduct delaying actions, while building up their strength for a general offensive."[8]

President Harry S. Truman and senior officials in his administration also confronted an unfavorable power balance in East Asia, especially after the Communist victory in the Chinese Civil War in September 1949. Indeed, Secretary of State Dean Acheson's speech at the National Press Club in January 1950, in which he excluded Korea from the US defense perimeter in East Asia, was simply an articulation of long-established policy. Given the near-term shortage of US military personnel and its strategic commitments in Europe, the Truman administration decided to confine the US military presence in East Asia to island chains capable of defense by sea or air—the Ryukyus, the Philippines, and Japan.[9]

During the late 1980s and early 1990s, in comparison, the United States faced an increasingly favorable power distribution in Western Europe, as the economic capabilities of the Soviet Union went into steep, and ultimately terminal, relative decline. The collapse of Soviet bloc in Eastern-Central Europe following the revolutions of autumn 1989 led President George H. W. Bush, Secretary of State James A. Baker III, and other administration officials to push for the inclusion of a reunified Germany in NATO.[10]

Several factors might shift a regional power distribution from favorable to unfavorable (or vice versa) from the United States' perspective. First, shifts in

---

[8] "85. A Report to the National Security Council by the Executive Secretary (Lay), Enclosing NSC-68, United States Objectives and Programs for National Security, 14 April 1950," *FRUS 1950, Vol. I: National Security Affairs and Foreign Economic Policy* (Washington, DC: GPO, 1976), pp. 205–211.

[9] See "Memorandum by the Executive Secretary of the National Security Council (Souers) to the National Security Council, Enclosing NSC 48/2 Position of the United States with Respect to Asia, 30 December 1949," *FRUS, 1949, Vol. VII, Part 2: The Far East and Australasia* (Washington, DC: GPO, 1976), pp. 1215–1220. Also see Jeffrey W. Taliaferro, *Balancing Risks: Great Power Intervention in the Periphery* (Ithaca, NY: Cornell University Press, 2004), pp. 141–142.

[10] See Joshua R. Itzkowitz Shifrinson, *Rising Titans, Falling Giants: Rising States and the Fate of Declining Great Powers* (Ithaca, NY: Cornell University Press, 2018), chapter 5.

the conventional military and economic capabilities between an ally (or allies) and its local adversary (or adversaries), as well as an increase or a decrease in a rival great power's economic, political, or military penetration of that region, would shift the regional power distribution. Additionally, the acquisition or the defection of an ally or client would shift the power distribution in a region, if it involves the gain or loss of forward basing rights; access to critical resources and to sea lanes of communication (SLOCs); or if an ally is in a geographic position to deny a rival great power access to that region.[11]

Nuclear proliferation by allies or clients of the United States has implications for several of the dynamics mentioned above. Efforts to develop autonomous nuclear capabilities may increase the risks of preventive military actions or reactive proliferation by their regional adversaries, conventional arms transfers, or an extension of security guarantees by rival great powers to those adversaries in an effort to offset the perceived nuclear advantage of the ally. The acquisition of a nuclear weapon capability would make an ally less reliant on US security guarantees. Lastly, there is the possibility that a nuclear armed ally may even feel emboldened to engage in limited aggression or initiate crises. Each of these dynamics can make the power distribution within that region less favorable to the United States by increasing the risks of containment failure or access denial.

In making assessments of regional power distributions, one might expect that intelligence analysts, military strategists, and ultimately senior policymakers in Washington will focus on the military and economic capabilities of the local states. They should also be attuned to the degree of involvement of a rival great power in the region. Specifically, one might expect policymakers to ask the following: (1) Does the regional power distribution appear favorable or unfavorable to the United States' strategic interests at any given time? (2) Is the current regional power distribution stable and presumably conducive to US interests? (3) Alternatively, is the current regional power distribution unstable, and presumably shifting in a direction contrary to US interests?

Senior policymakers' contemporary assessments of regional power distributions have a hypothesized effect on a great power's foreign policy, rather than the "objective" and post-hoc measurements of power. "Power cannot be tested; different elements of power possess different utilities at different times," Aaron L. Friedberg observed, adding that "the relationship of perceived power to material resources can be capricious."[12] Those statements equally describe the dilemmas confronted by US policymakers, as well as the intelligence analysts,

---

[11] See Michael C. Desch, "Why Realists Disagree About the Third World (and Why They Shouldn't)," *Security Studies*, Vol. 5, No. 3 (1996), pp. 358–384.

[12] Aaron L. Friedberg, *The Weary Titan: Britain and the Experience of Relative Decline, 1895–1905* (Princeton, NJ: Princeton University Press, 1988), p. 308.

military strategists, and others who supported them, during the historical period examined in chapters 3 through 6 and beyond.

Time Horizons for Emerging Threats

The time horizons for emerging threats to the hegemon's interests in the region constitute the second independent variable. In microeconomic theory, a "time horizon" refers to a value an actor places on present payoffs, as opposed to future payoffs; in other words, the rate of temporal discounting. I use the term "time horizon" to connote the temporal context for leaders' threat assessments: Are the threats to the hegemon's strategic interests in a region likely to emerge in the near future? Or are the threats more likely to emerge over a longer period of time?[13]

How might one distinguish between long-term time horizons and short-term time horizons? Generally speaking, when policymakers focus on threats they think will emerge or become acute over the span of weeks, months, or a year they are operating with a short-term time horizon. However, when policymakers focus on threats they think will emerge or become acute over the span of years or a decade or more, they are operating within a long-term time horizon. As David Edelstein observes, policymakers confront a "now-or-later" dilemma, where the choice is between some immediate action or deferring any action until later. On the one hand, redressing the threat in the present entails paying certain costs in the short term. Yet, on the other hand, not acting, in order to conserve resources or to obtain better intelligence about an adversary's capabilities and intentions in the short term, may entail having to pay dramatically higher costs to redress the threat over the long term.[14]

During the Cuban Missile Crisis, President John F. Kennedy and the members of the Executive Committee of the National Security Council (EXCOM) confronted a very short time horizon for an emerging threat. The Soviet deployment of medium-range ballistic missiles, strategic nuclear weapons, and military personnel to Cuba constituted an immediate and existential threat to

---

[13] For definitions see David M. Edelstein, *Over the Horizon: Time, Uncertainty, and the Rise of Great Powers* (Ithaca, NY: Cornell University Press, 2017), pp. 5–7; and Mark Brawley, *Political Economy and Grand Strategy: A Neoclassical Realist View* (New York: Routledge, 2009), pp. 5–7. Also see Edelstein, "Managing Uncertainty: Beliefs About Intentions and the Rise of Great Powers," *Security Studies*, Vol. 12, No. 1 (2002), pp. 1–40; and Brawley, "Neoclassical Realism and Strategic Calculations: Explaining Divergent British, French, and Soviet Strategies Toward Germany Between the World Wars (1919–1939)," in Steven E. Lobell, Norrin M. Ripsman, and Jeffrey W. Taliaferro, eds., *Neoclassical Realism, the State, and Foreign Policy* (New York: Cambridge University Press, 2009), pp. 75–98.

[14] Edelstein, *Over the Horizon*, p. 17.

the physical survival of the continental United States. Once the missile site in Cuba became operational, most of North America would have been vulnerable to a Soviet nuclear first strike. The EXCOM members perceived the time frame for redressing this threat to be a matter of days, since the Central Intelligence Agency (CIA) estimated the installations would be complete before the end of the month.[15]

Iraq's invasion of Kuwait in August 1990 is illustrative of how the leaders of a middle power and a global hegemon faced a short time horizon.[16] Iraqi President Saddam Hussein concluded, following a meeting with Ambassador April Glaspie, that the United States was unlikely to oppose an Iraqi incursion into Kuwait. Declining oil revenues, due to Kuwait's overproduction of oil, and the exorbitant war debt payments to Kuwait (which financed the 1980–1988 Iran-Iraq War), convinced Saddam that he had a short time horizon to move against the emirate.[17] Despite months of saber-rattling by Saddam, the actual invasion of Kuwait on 2 August 1990 surprised Washington policymakers. Bush, Baker, and other senior officials quickly concluded the Iraqi occupation of Kuwait was an immediate threat to the stability of world oil markets and the physical security of neighboring Saudi Arabia, both of which had long been core US interests in the Middle East. The longer Iraqi forces occupied Kuwait, the more difficult they would be to dislodge.[18]

Lastly, Russia's seizure of Crimea from Ukraine in March 2014, as well as the backing of pro-Russian separatists in the Donbass region, is illustrative of how a twenty-first-century great power may react to redress a perceived short-term threat. The ouster of Ukrainian President Viktor Yanukovych in February 2014, following the Eurumaiden protests sparked by Yanukovych's rejection of an association agreement with the European Union (EU) in December, created a power vacuum. Wary of closer economic ties between Ukraine and the EU, but also recognizing that the United States and its NATO allies could not come to Ukraine's defense, Russian President Vladimir Putin moved to annex Crimea,

---

[15] See the transcripts of the secret recordings of the Executive Committee of the National Security Council (ExCom) meetings in Sheldon M. Stern, *Averting "the Final Failure": John F. Kennedy and the Secret Cuban Missile Crisis Meetings* (Stanford, CA: Stanford University Press, 2003).

[16] On windows of opportunity and windows of vulnerability, see Stephen Van Evera, *Causes of War: Power and the Roots of Conflict* (Ithaca, NY: Cornell University Press, 1999), pp. 74–75.

[17] Ripsman, Taliaferro, and Lobell, *Neoclassical Realist Theory*, p. 47. See also Charles A. Duelfer and Stephen Benedict Dyson, "Chronic Misperception and International Conflict: The U.S.-Iraq Experience," *International Security*, Vol. 36, No. 1 (2011), pp. 73–100.

[18] See Duelfer and Dyson, "Chronic Misperception and International Conflict," pp. 73–100. See also Gregory D. Koblentz, "Saddam Versus the Inspectors: The Impact of Regime Security on the Verification of Iraq's WMD Disarmament," *Journal of Strategic Studies*, Vol. 41, No. 3 (2018), pp. 372–409.

and deployed Russian army troops wearing uniforms shorn of insignia ("little green men") to further destabilize eastern Ukraine.[19]

There is an inverse relationship between the time horizons for threats and the degree of uncertainty that senior policymakers confront. If threats are expected to materialize or become acute over the course of several years, then policymakers face greater uncertainty.[20] Such threats may not actually materialize because of changes in the relative capabilities or the intentions of the relevant actors. Exogenous factors and unforeseen contingencies may diffuse long-term threats. Conversely, threats expected to materialize or become acute over the course of several weeks, months, or a year entail less uncertainty for policymakers in Washington. There is simply less time for the relative capabilities of local actors or rival great powers to change. As Stephen Brooks and William Wohlforth observe, the ability of states to create new military capabilities in the short run, say a year or two, is quite limited. If the time frame stretches over years or decades, then the development of a military capability become matters of choice, assuming the state has the necessary economic and technological resources.[21] This does not mean, however, that when time horizons are short, policymakers have certainty about threats. Rather, policymakers face less uncertainty regarding threats that will emerge in the short term, than with threats that are more temporally distant.[22]

Unlike the international crises or invasions cited above, however, nuclear weapons proliferation typically unfolds over a number of years. The initial deliberations over whether to pursue nuclear energy research, let alone to

---

[19] See Michael E. Becker, Matthew S. Cohen, Sidita Kushi, and Ian P. McManus, "Reviving the Russian Empire: The Crimean Intervention Through a Neoclassical Realist Lens," *European Security*, Vol. 25, No. 1 (2016), pp. 112–133; and Tor Bukkvoll, "Why Putin Went to War: Ideology, Interests, and Decision-Making in the Russian Use of Force in Crimea and Donbas," *Contemporary Politics*, Vol. 22, No. 3 (2016), pp. 267–282.

[20] Edelstein retrains the traditional distinction between risk and uncertainty found in microeconomic theory. He contends that when policymakers anticipate that an outcome (threat) might materialize in the next several months, then they are dealing with risk. Conversely, if they anticipate an outcome may not materialize for several years, then they are dealing with uncertainty. See Edelstein, *Over the Horizon*, pp. 10–37. Here I part company with Edelstein. Elsewhere, I argued the risk-uncertainty distinction is simply untenable in the study of international politics and foreign policy. Policymakers rarely assign numerical probabilities to outcomes, which is the definition of risk in microeconomic theory. See Jeffrey W. Taliaferro, *Balancing Risks: Great Power Intervention in the Periphery* (Ithaca, NY: Cornell University Press, 2004), pp. 22–26.

[21] Stephen G. Brooks and William C. Wohlforth, "The Rise and Fall of the Great Powers in the Twenty-First Century: China's Rise and the Fate of America's Global Position," *International Security*, Vol. 40, No. 3 (2016), p. 18.

[22] This may lead to the problem of false certainty. See Jennifer Mitzen and Randall L. Schweller, "Knowing the Unknown Unknowns: Misplaced Certainty and the Onset of War," *Security Studies*, Vol. 20, No. 1 (2011), pp. 2–35.

pursue an actual nuclear weapons program, may vary from a few months to several years.²³ Likewise, it generally takes a number of years to develop or acquire the technical expertise, build the physical infrastructure, and acquire the dual-use technologies to have a plausible path toward a nuclear weapon capability.²⁴ Once a state's program has achieved nuclear breakout, defined as the possession of a sufficient amount of high enriched uranium (HEU) or plutonium (PU) to fuel a nuclear explosive device, there are still the problems of testing (hot or cold) that device, warhead design and miniaturization, and the design and manufacture of delivery systems.

Nuclear-aspiring states have strong incentives to conceal their intentions, to safeguard their nuclear infrastructure, to obscure their relationships with foreign suppliers of fissile material or technical components, and to obfuscate when questioned by officials from the United States and the International Atomic Energy Agency (IAEA). Such states will also engage in denial and deception (D&D) to inhibit collection by US intelligence agencies. In principle, the nuclear proliferation–related behavior of most states will eventually be detected by the US Intelligence Community. I write "in principle" because of the inherent uncertainties in estimates of another state's nuclear intentions.²⁵ Aerial and satellite reconnaissance, as well as human and signals intelligence, will eventually uncover evidence of a state's clandestine nuclear weapons program, as well as evidence of neighboring states' or rival great powers' reactions to that program. These reactions include conventional military buildups, sudden force postures, arms transfers, or the extension of new guarantees to neighboring states.

This is not to dismiss the problem of intelligence failure, whether resulting from collection priorities, analytical error, or policymakers' lack of receptivity to finished intelligence.²⁶ For example, ambiguous or contradictory guidance from policymakers about nuclear proliferation concerns in particular states or

---

[23] Even then, not all nuclear energy research may lead to a nuclear weapons program. For the argument that nuclear energy programs are generally not precursors to nuclear weapons programs, see Nicholas L. Miller, "Why Nuclear Energy Programs Rarely Lead to Proliferation," *International Security*, Vol. 42, No. 2 (2017), pp. 40–77.

[24] For analyses of these dynamics and the technical barriers to nuclear weapons development, see Jacques E. C. Hymans, *Achieving Nuclear Ambitions: Scientists, Politicians, and Proliferation* (New York: Cambridge University Press, 2012); and Målfrid Braut-Hegghammer, *Unclear Physics: Why Iraq and Libya Failed to Build Nuclear Weapons* (Ithaca, NY: Cornell University Press, 2016).

[25] See Alexander H. Montgomery and Adam Mount, "Misestimation: Explaining US Failures to Predict Nuclear Weapons Programs," *Intelligence and National Security*, Vol. 29, No. 3 (2014), pp. 357–386.

[26] On the limits of intelligence on foreign policy, see Stephen Marrin, "Why Strategic Intelligence Analysis Has Limited Influence on American Foreign Policy," *Intelligence and National Security*, Vol. 32, No. 2 (2017), pp. 1–18.

regions will shape the collection priorities of intelligence agencies.[27] A lack of human or technical collection, or sporadic intelligence collection on a target's nuclear activities will impact analysis, as well as the amount and quality of finished intelligence produced. Incomplete or missing intelligence about another state's nuclear proliferation–related behavior in the hands of policymakers at time t can influence the types of policy options under consideration at time $t + 1$. This, in turn, can delimit subsequent intelligence collection and analysis, as well as the policy options at time $t + X$.[28] Policymakers may receive strategic intelligence about an ally's nuclear proliferation behavior but the window of opportunity to halt that ally's "race to the bomb" may have closed. At that late stage, mitigating the impact of an ally's nuclear breakout will become the priority for policymakers.[29]

An ally's pursuit of a nuclear weapons capability, in and of itself, would not directly threaten the physical security of the United States. Instead, its behavior may threaten US strategic interests in the region. The range of possible adverse developments include, but are not limited to, the following: preventive military strikes or covert operations launched by neighboring states or even a rival great power;[30] reactive proliferation by neighboring states; efforts by neighboring states to obtain security guarantees from rival great powers; and efforts by rival great powers to redress the impending power imbalance by initiating or augmenting conventional arms transfers, troop deployments, basing rights, and economic assistance to one or more of those neighboring states. Any of these

---

[27] For a discussion of the Intelligence Community's divided attention, see Richard K. Betts, "Fixing Intelligence," *Foreign Affairs*, Vol. 81, No. 1 (2002), pp. 43–59.

[28] For example, a vicious cycle among policymaking and intelligence collection and analysis arguably stymied the ability of the Eisenhower and Kennedy administrations to thwart Israel's nuclear program in the early stages (1959–1963). See Austin G. Long and Joshua R. Shifrinson, "How Long Until Midnight? Intelligence-Policy Relations and the United States Response to the Israeli Nuclear Program, 1959–1985," *Journal of Strategic Studies* (2018), pp. 1–36.

[29] Here I am treating the phrase "race for the bomb" as synonymous with achieving "nuclear breakout," defined as the possession of sufficient HEU or PU to fuel a nuclear explosive device. Having a nuclear weapon capability is not synonymous with having a deliverable nuclear weapon. Furthermore, possession of a nuclear weapon capability is not synonymous with achieving strategic breakout. Strategic breakout refers to both a *quantitative* increase in the number of nuclear warheads and a *qualitative* increase in warhead design and delivery systems (i.e., warhead miniaturization and ballistic missile development), such that a state can credibly hold another state's vital interests at risk. See Robert S. Litwak, *Preventing North Korea's Nuclear Breakout* (Washington, DC: Woodrow Wilson International Center for Scholars, 2017).

[30] For example, Isabella Ginor and Gideon Remez argue that the Soviet-piloted MiG 21s (Foxbats) conducted reconnaissance sorties over the Dimona nuclear reactor complex on 17 and 26 May 1967, in preparation for a possible preventive strike. See Ginor and Remez, *Foxbats over Dimona: The Soviets' Nuclear Gamble in the Six-Day War* (New Haven, CT: Yale University Press, 2007), pp. 121–127.

adverse developments increases the risk of access denial or containment failure for the United States.

In assessing time horizons, one might expect intelligence analysts, military strategists, and ultimately senior policymakers in Washington to be attuned to intelligence about anticipated shifts in relative capabilities and the intentions of regional states and rival great powers over time.[31] Specifically, one might expect policymakers to ask the following: (1) Is the threat to US strategic interests in a region likely to materialize or become acute within the next several days, weeks, or months? (2) Is the threat likely to materialize or become acute within the next year? (3) Alternatively, is the threat likely to materialize or become acute over the course of several years?

Just as there is an inverse relationship between time horizons and the degree of uncertainty senior policymakers face, there should also be an inverse relationship between time horizons and policymakers' disposition to pursue a coercive nonproliferation strategy. Recall that threats to the United States' two core interests in a region—the containment of rival great powers and the preservation of its own access—arise directly from actions of local states or a rival great power, rather than the nuclear proliferation of an ally per se. When policymakers have short time horizons, the risk of containment failure or access denial in the region should loom larger than thwarting the nuclear proliferation of an ally. On the other hand, when policymakers have longer time horizons, then the risk of containment failure or access denial are more remote.

Combinations of Values on the Independent Variables

The relative power distribution the United States faces in a region and the time horizons for threats to US interests therein are the two independent variables in the theory. The first can vary along a continuum from favorable to unfavorable. The second can vary along a continuum from short term to long term. These two variables can take on four ideal combinations of values as illustrated in Table 2.1.[32]

In cell 1, the president and other administration officials should be more inclined to offer inducements to secure an ally's nuclear forbearance. Remember, in this cell the regional power distribution is unfavorable to US interests and

---

[31] For an attempt to theorize about policymakers' receptivity to strategic intelligence about an adversary intention, see Keren Yarhi-Milo, *Knowing the Adversary: Leaders, Intelligence, and Assessment of Intentions in International Relations* (Princeton, NJ: Princeton University Press, 2014).

[32] Table 2.1 presents an explanatory typology of the theory's two independent variables. See Colin Elman, "Explanatory Typologies in Qualitative Studies of International Politics," *International Organization*, Vol. 59, No. 2 (2005), pp. 293–326.

Table 2.1 **Possible Combination of Values on the IVs and the DV**

		Current Regional Power Distribution vis-à-vis US Interests (Unfavorable to Favorable)	
		Unfavorable Power Distribution	*Favorable Power Distribution*
Time Horizon for Threats to US Interests in Region (Short to Long)	Short	1 Accommodative Strategy	2 Coercive Strategy
	Long	3 Hybrid Strategy	4 Coercive strategy

the time horizons for threats is relatively short. Policymakers will subordinate nonproliferation vis-à-vis an ally to the more immediate need to shore up the United States' overall strategic position in the region. Here one should expect a presidential administration to offer the ally inducements, such as conventional arms sales and economic assistance, in exchange for guarantees not to cross certain "red lines" in the development of nuclear weapons. At the same time, there is the risk that an ally may take advantage of Washington's preoccupation with looming threats in the region and attempt to evade those "red lines."[33]

In cell 2, policymakers should be more included to pursue coercive strategies to thwart an ally's nuclear weapons program. In this cell, the regional power distribution is favorable to US interests, but the time horizons for threats to materialize are also short. Remember, the threats to the United States' interests in the region may not directly arise from the ally's nuclear proliferation, but rather from the reactions of neighboring states or a rival great power to that ally's behavior. To ensure access to the region, as well as contain rival great powers, Washington policymakers should favor a coercive strategy toward the ally, in order to foreclose any conceivable linkages between the ally's nuclear weapons activities and threats to US interests.

In cell 3, policymakers should be inclined to pursue a hybrid strategy—that is, one the blends elements of coercion and accommodation—toward a nuclear-aspiring ally. In this cell, the regional power distribution is not favorable to the United States' interests, but there are also long time horizons. Due to these long

---

[33] Vipin Narang, "Strategies of Nuclear Proliferation: How States Pursue the Bomb," *International Security*, Vol. 41, No. 3 (2017), pp. 110–150, esp. pp. 122–123.

time horizons in which those serious threats to those interests might arise, administration officials may have difficulty prioritizing between nonproliferation and longer-term objectives in the region. A coercive strategy might thwart an ally's race to the bomb, but at the risk of diverting the administration's attention from redressing other threats to US interests. An accommodative strategy, however, runs the risk of allowing the ally to take advantage of US military or economic aid to continue its nuclear weapons pursuit. Hence, policymakers will gravitate toward a hybrid strategy. For example, they might be inclined to offer tangible inducements, such as conventional arms transfers, civil nuclear cooperation, and enhanced security guarantees, but with the implicit threat those inducements will be withdrawn if nuclear proliferation continues. In favoring a hybrid strategy, policymakers attempt to hedge their bets.

Lastly, in cell 4, policymakers should be more inclined to pursue a coercive strategy toward a nuclear aspiring ally. Here, the threats to US interests in the region posed by rival great powers or by the local adversaries are temporally distant. Moreover, from the standpoint of officials in Washington, the regional power distribution appears favorable to US interests. Since the risk of containment failure is low, the president and other administration officials should act forcefully to slow or halt an ally's nuclear weapons program.

Table 2.1 merely shows different ideal combinations of the values on the independent variables and the dependent variable. The following section considers how the intervening variable—the height of domestic mobilization hurdles—moderates the effect of the independent variables on the dependent variable, namely the type of nonproliferation strategies the United States actually pursues toward its allies.

The Intervening Variable: The Height of Domestic Mobilization Hurdles

One of the main claims of neoclassical realism is that domestic-level processes can obstruct, amplify, or distort systemic pressures. "Those intervening variables condition whether, how, and when states respond to the international systemic pressures that all variants of realism assume underlie crisis behavior, 'ordinary' foreign policy and security policies, longer-term patterns of grand strategy adjustment, and international political outcomes."[34]

---

[34] Ripsman, Taliaferro, and Lobell, *Neoclassical Realist Theory*, p. 117. Ripsman, Taliaferro, and Lobell reorganize the hereunto eclectic list of intervening variables posited by neoclassical realist theories into four broad categories: (1) leaders' images; (2) strategic culture; (3) state-society relations; and (4) domestic institutions. Ripsman, Taliaferro, and Lobell, pp. 51–79.

A recurrent theme in the neoclassical realist literature is the observation that the foreign policy executive (FPE) of any state, especially liberal democracies, rarely has automatic and immediate access to the human and material resources necessary to pursue novel and expensive foreign and defense policies.[35] Since those human and material resources reside in society and not in the state, the FPE has to bargain with a variety of domestic actors. "Key questions relate to the degree of harmony between the state and society, the degree to which society defers to state leaders on foreign policy matters in the event of disagreements, distributional completion among societal coalitions to capture the state and its associated spoils, the level of policy and social cohesion within the state, and public support for general foreign policy and national security objectives."[36]

In nuclear proliferation disputes, however, presidents and administration officials are less likely to have to bargain with key societal interests or the public-at-large, in order to pursue their preferred nonproliferation strategies toward an ally. Nuclear proliferation involves highly technical issues, which are unlikely to have a visible impact on the US electorate. For example, the resolution of a proliferation dispute with an ally would not depend upon changes in taxation, increases in the number of active-duty military personnel, or the mobilization of the National Guard and the Army Reserves. Nor would these types of intra-alliance disputes have the potential for distributional conflicts among differential societal coalitions.[37] That said, the specific policy tools at the disposal of any presidential administration are seldom ones that could be employed unilaterally or in complete secrecy. These tools generally include conventional arms transfers, the extension of an explicit US security guarantee, the deployment of US troops to the ally's territory, economic assistance, export controls, and diplomatic support in international organizations. The administration will generally have to notify Congress, if not seek explicit approval, before employing them. Again, administration officials will have to bargain with members of Congress rather than the electorate-at-large.

The intervening variable is the height of the domestic mobilization hurdle. I define those mobilization hurdles as the anticipated degree of congressional

---

[35] See, for example, Thomas J. Christensen, *Useful Adversaries: Grand Strategy, Domestic Mobilization, and Sino-American Conflict, 1947–1958* (Princeton, NJ: Princeton University Press, 1996), pp. 16–25; Fareed Zakaria, *From Wealth to Power: The Unusual Origins of America's World Role* (Princeton, NJ: Princeton University Press, 1998), pp. 35–41; Aaron L. Friedberg, *In the Shadow of the Garrison State: America's Anti-Statism and Its Cold War Grand Strategy* (Princeton, NJ: Princeton University Press, 2000), pp. 63–80; and Randall L. Schweller, *Unanswered Threats: Political Constraints on the Balance of Power* (Princeton, NJ: Princeton University Press, 2006).

[36] Ripsman, Taliaferro, and Lobell, *Neoclassical Realist Theory*, pp. 71.

[37] Hence, the manner in which I operationalize and measure the height of the domestic mobilization hurdles discussed below differs from Christensen, *Useful Adversaries*, pp. 25–28.

opposition or support for the administration's proposed policies toward the ally. Vocal congressional opposition to the administration's preferred strategies toward an ally would be indicative of a high domestic mobilization hurdle, whereas congressional support for (or at least indifference toward) the administration's proposed strategies would be indicative of a low hurdle. High domestic mobilization hurdles can take several forms, including: existing statutes, pending legislation (e.g., appropriations bills and authorization bills), congressional committee hearings, and private warnings to administration officials by influential senators and members of the House.

The height of these hurdles cannot be specified a priori. Mobilization hurdles are contextual. In the United States, Congress has always had some leverage over an administration's foreign policies through its oversight committees, control of appropriations, the passage of legislation, and routine reporting requirements for executive departments and agencies. The actual leverage, however, will vary across issue areas, the time frame, the degree to which the dispute between the United States and the ally is public knowledge, and, to some extent, the parochial and idiosyncratic concerns of influential senators and representatives.[38]

The members of Congress most interested in and knowledgeable about these issues will be members of the Foreign Relations Committee and the Armed Services Committee in the Senate, and the Foreign Affairs (or International Relations) Committee and the Armed Services Committee in the House of Representatives.[39] These committees have oversight of the executive departments and independent agencies engaged in the implementation of foreign and defense policy. The chairmen and the ranking members of the minority party on each of these four committees can be quite influential; hence, administration officials have an incentive to cultivate their support, or to at least defuse their opposition. While these four standing committees are quite important, sometimes it becomes necessary for administration officials to deal with subcommittees of these panels or to more specialized standing committees.

Laws governing the United States' security cooperation and security assistance programs, economic aid, and nuclear nonproliferation policies are the most tangible domestic mobilization hurdles a presidential administration must overcome. The 1961 Foreign Assistance Act (FAA), as amended, and the 1976 Arms Export Control Act (ACEA), as amended, govern the United States' security

---

[38] The classic treatment of how the weak American state constrains the ability of the executive branch in the realm of foreign policy is Stephen D. Krasner, *Defending the National Interest: Raw Materials Investments and U.S. Foreign Policy* (Princeton, NJ: Princeton University Press, 1978), esp. pp. 55–92.

[39] From 1975 to 1978 and again from 1995 to 2007, the House Committee on Foreign Affairs was called the House Committee on International Relations.

cooperation and security assistance programs. Under the ACEA, the secretary of state decides which countries will receive arms transfers and financing, and the secretary of defense executes the transfers. The president must formally determine that providing arms and financing to another country "will strengthen the security of the United States and promote world peace."[40] However, annual appropriations and authorization legislation governing export financing, national defense, and related programs may impose additional restrictions on the executive branch.

These domestic mobilization hurdles are not completely endogenous. Some hurdles may be the residue of prior international stimuli and prior domestic political dynamics.[41] Consider, for example, the 1976 Symington Amendment, which prohibited US economic and military assistance, as well as export credits, to countries that acquire, receive, or transfer nuclear enrichment technology not in compliance with IAEA regulations and inspections. This amendment was an effort to strengthen enforcement of the Nuclear Nonproliferation Treaty (NPT). It was also a reaction to the Nixon administration's muted response to India's nuclear test in May 1974, and the Nixon and the Ford administrations' subsequent increased economic assistance to New Delhi and continued nuclear fuel shipments to India's Tarapur reactor.[42]

Nicholas L. Miller contends the Symington Amendment and subsequent nonproliferation legislation made the threat of US sanctions credible to would-be proliferators and may have deterred some states from initiating nuclear weapons programs.[43] The Symington Amendment and the Glenn Amendment, passed the following year, however, became domestic mobilization hurdles to the Carter and Reagan administrations' preferred strategies toward Pakistan in the late 1970s and the 1980s.

Just as the AECA and the Symington Amendment reflected prior systemic conditions and domestic political dynamics, other nonproliferation

---

[40] Defense Security Cooperation Agency, 2017. Chapter 1: Security Cooperation Overview and Relationships. In *Security Assistance Management Manual*, Defense Security Cooperation Agency, http://samm.dsca.mil/chapter/chapter-1#C1.2 (accessed 10 January 2017).

[41] On this point see Jennifer Sterling-Folker, "Realist Environment, Liberal Process, and Domestic-Level Variables," *International Studies Quarterly*, Vol. 41, No. 1 (1997), pp. 1–25, esp. pp. 18–19. For a more general discussion of path dependence, see Andrew Bennett and Colin Elman, "Complex Causal Relations and Case Study Methods: The Example of Path Dependence," *Political Analysis*, Vol. 14, No. 3 (2006), pp. 250–267.

[42] George Perkovich, *India's Nuclear Bomb: The Impact on Global Proliferation* (Berkeley: University of California Press, 1999), p. 184; and Mitchell Reiss, *Without the Bomb: The Politics of Nuclear Nonproliferation* (New York: Columbia University Press, 1988), 232.

[43] See Nicholas L. Miller, "The Secret Success of Nonproliferation Sanctions," *International Organization*, Vol. 68, No. 4 (2014), pp. 913–944.

legislation was the outgrowth of previous battles between the Congress and successive administrations over nonproliferation policies. For example, the Solarz Amendment to the FAA, which Congress passed in August 1985, provided that absent a presidential waiver, the United States would terminate military and economic aid to any country that "exports illegally (or attempts to export illegally) any material, equipment, or technology which could significantly contribute to the ability of such country to manufacture a nuclear explosive device, if the president determines" that the export "was to be used to by such country in the manufacture a nuclear explosive device." As discussed in chapter 4, the Congress passed this law in reaction to a plea deal in a Pakistani nuclear smuggling case.[44]

Some of the domestic mobilization hurdles that an administration must overcome at t were the result of policies it, or previous administrations, pursued at $t - 1$. There is a degree of path dependence in legislation and congressional interest in Washington's relationships with particular allies. This, in turn, further restricts the types of accommodative or coercive strategies an administration could pursue toward an ally at $t + 1$.

Consider for example, the Johnson administration's decisions to sell A-4 Skyhawks and M-48 tanks to Israel in spring 1965. Although chapter 3 analyzes the decision in greater detail, I will briefly note that this transfer had the unintended consequence of limiting the United States' subsequent freedom of maneuver regarding future Israeli request for arms transfers. By saying he would consider Prime Minister Levi Eshkol's request to purchase fifty supersonic F-4 Phantoms in January 1968, President Lyndon B. Johnson created an expectation of future US arms transfers.[45] Threatening to withhold or delay the transfer of the F-4s became politically difficult for the Nixon administration in 1969, given the precedent of the Skyhawk sale and the Israeli government's expectation of future US arms transfers, as well as the growing importance of the Arab-Israeli conflict as a proxy struggle between the superpowers. As Keren Yarhi-Milo, Alexander Lanoszka, and Zack Cooper observe, "With institutionalization, the patron is more likely to suffer reputation costs if its client is defeated. At stake is not the patron's reputation for resolve, but rather the patron's desire to be seen as being on the winning side."[46]

---

[44] Department of State, "Classified Congressional Briefing on Pakistani Clandestine Nuclear-Related Procurement, "Circa 26 July 1987, Secret," in William Burr, ed., *NSA Electronic Briefing Book no. 446* (Washington, DC: National Security Archive, 2013), http://nsarchive.gwu.edu/nukevault/ebb446/docs/12.pdf.

[45] Douglas Little, "The Making of a Special Relationship: The United States and Israel, 1957–68," *International Journal of Middle East Studies*, Vol. 25, No. 4 (1993), pp. 563–585.

[46] Keren Yarhi-Milo, Alexander Lanoszka, and Zack Cooper, "To Arm or to Ally?: The Patron's Dilemma and the Strategic Logic of Arms Transfers and Alliances," *International Security*, Vol. 41, No. 2 (2016), p. 96.

The need to secure support or at least defuse congressional opposition can skew the types of the strategies that the United States ultimately pursues. The president and administration officials, for example, may be inclined to pursue an overtly coercive strategy toward a nuclear aspiring ally based on their assessments of the regional power distribution and time horizons for threats. High mobilization hurdles in the form of congressional opposition to sanctioning the ally, however, may limit the administration's ability to actually pursue coercive strategies. Similarly, based on their assessment of regional power distributions and time horizons, the president and other administration officials may be inclined to pursue an accommodative strategy toward an ally, despite lingering suspicions about an ally's nuclear proliferation behavior. Stringent nonproliferation legislation and strong congressional interest in the issue, however, may limit officials' freedom of maneuver.

Low domestic mobilization hurdles in the form of less stringent proliferation legislation (or nonexistent legislation, prior to the passage of the AECA and the Symington Amendment in 1976), along with congressional inattention, may give administration officials greater freedom of maneuver. Here one would expect the United States to pursue strategies toward an ally purely based on policymakers' assessments of regional power distributions and time horizons for threats.

Neoclassical realist theory suggests various causal paths linking the two independent variables and the intervening variable to the dependent variable—the types of nonproliferation strategies the United States ultimately pursues. Table 2.2 illustrates how the intervening variable—high or low domestic mobilization hurdles—might moderate the hypothesized causal effect of the two systemic independent variables.

Note that Table 2.2 contains eight cells, instead of the four cells in Table 2.2. In cells 1, 2, 3, and 4, the administration faces low domestic mobilization hurdles. It faces little or no congressional opposition to its preferred strategies to deal with an ally's nuclear proliferation behavior. Additionally, nonproliferation legislation might be nonexistent or very easily waived by the president. Therefore, in cells 1, 2, and 4 in Table 2.2, the value on the dependent variable—the type of nonproliferation strategies an administration ultimately pursues toward the ally—will be in the directions posited above.

Recall that in cell 3 of Table 2.1, policymakers should favor a hybrid strategy. They should try to hedge their bets regarding an ally's nuclear proliferation–related behavior: they want to provide inducements in the forms of arms sales, economic aid, security guarantees, and nuclear cooperation agreements (if that ally has a nuclear energy program), but with the tacit threat of withdrawing those inducements if nuclear forbearance is not forthcoming. In cell 3 of Table 2.2, the administration faces low mobilization hurdles to its preferred hybrid

Table 2.2 **Possible Combination of Values on the IVs, the IVV, and the DV**

		Current Regional Power Distribution vis-à-vis US Interests	
		Unfavorable Power Distribution	Favorable Power Distribution
Time Horizons for Threats to US Interests in Region	Short	Low Domestic Hurdle *Accommodative strategy* 1	Low Domestic Hurdle *Coercive strategy* 2
	Long	Low Domestic Hurdle *Accommodative strategy* 3	Low Domestic Hurdle *Coercive strategy* 4
		Current Regional Power Distribution vis-à-vis US Interests	
		Unfavorable Power Distribution	Favorable Power Distribution
Time Horizons for Threats to US Interests in Region	Short	High Domestic Hurdle *Accommodative strategy* 5	High Domestic Hurdle *Hybrid strategy* 6
	Long	High Domestic Hurdle *Hybrid strategy* 7	High Domestic Hurdle *Hybrid strategy* 8

nonproliferation strategy. Therefore, it ought to be able to implement such a strategy.

How would a high value on the intervening variable distort this? In cells 5, 6, 7, and 8, the administration will encounter greater resistance to the pursuit of its preferred strategies. In cell 5, US policymakers perceive an unfavorable regional power distribution, but short time horizons for emerging threats to US interests in this region. Absent the intervening variable, they should favor an accommodative strategy and be able to implement it (as in cell 3 of Table 2.1). However, administration officials also face high domestic mobilization hurdles in cell 5. This seems to suggest that when the stakes in the region for US strategic interests are dire enough, an administration should be able to overcome a high domestic mobilization hurdle and pursue its preferred nonproliferation strategy toward the ally, namely accommodation.

In cell 7 of Table 2.2, however, the dynamic changes. In this particular cell, US policymakers again perceive an unfavorable regional power distribution, but they also perceive long time horizons for emerging threats. While policymakers might prefer to pursue an accommodative nonproliferation strategy toward the ally, they have to overcome high domestic mobilization hurdles. Hence, the administration might wind up pursuing a hybrid nonproliferation strategy, which mixes inducements with implicit coercive threats. By offering the ally tangible inducements for nuclear forbearance, the administration seeks to hedge its bets. Yet, by also making the provision of inducements conditional on the ally's nuclear proliferation–related behavior, along with the implicit threat of sanctions, the administration seeks to diffuse congressional criticism and avoid actually invoking sanctions.

In cell 6 of Table 2.2, US policymakers perceive a favorable regional power distribution, but they also perceive short time horizons for emerging threats. In other words, from US policymaker's perspective, the current threat environment in the region is good, but there are storm clouds on the horizon. Back in cell 2 of Table 2.1, policymakers will opt for a coercive nonproliferation strategy toward the ally. While they might like to pursue a coercive nonproliferation strategy, the presence of high domestic mobilization hurdles makes doing so difficult (if not impossible). Therefore, the administration winds up pursuing a hybrid nonproliferation strategy. Finally, in cell 8 of Table 2.2, US policymakers perceive a favorable regional power distribution. They should prefer a coercive nonproliferation strategy. However, high domestic mobilization hurdles make doing so difficult. Here also, policymakers will wind up pursuing a hybrid strategy toward the ally.

Alternative Explanations

The next four chapters test the hypotheses derived from my neoclassical realist theory against the historical record, analyzing the United States' nonproliferation strategies toward Israel, Pakistan, South Korea, and Taiwan. I juxtapose these hypotheses against three alternative explanations: nuclear domino theory, security commitment theory, and credible sanctions theory.

Nuclear Domino Theory

Nuclear domino theory proceeds from the supposition that nuclear weapons proliferation almost always has adverse consequences for international and regional stability, as well as for US national security. According to this theory, nuclear proliferation activities by a US ally might increase the risk of reactive proliferation by its neighbors, or greater involvement by a rival great power in support of those neighbors. This, in turn, increases the risk of containment failure or access denial for the United States. As explained in chapter 1, nuclear domino theory may be considered a corollary of power preponderance theories. This theory serves as the structural realist baseline for neoclassical realist theory.[47]

Nuclear domino theory is primarily concerned with explaining the likely behavior of would-be nuclear proliferators. The theory, however, also generates hypotheses for how the United States might respond to nuclear proliferation by allies, as well as adversaries.[48] The main driver of US policy should be the perceived risk of reactive proliferation by neighboring states. Specifically, nuclear domino theory expects US policymakers to pursue coercive strategies toward an ally, if they perceive a high likelihood of reactive proliferation. Conversely, policymakers should be less inclined to pursue coercive strategies, and perhaps more inclined toward accommodative strategies, toward a nuclear-aspiring ally when there is a low likelihood of reactive proliferation in the region.

Whereas neoclassical realist theory suggests US policymakers will respond to the overall regional power distribution and the time horizon for threats to US interests in the region, nuclear domino theory suggests those policymakers will myopically focus on the likelihood of reactive proliferation in the region. Nuclear domino theory expects US officials to continue coercive strategies toward an ally, even if a rival great power concurrently increases its penetration of the region.

Security Commitment Theory

Security commitment theory refers to a set of propositions about the impact of the United States' security guarantees on the nuclear proliferation behavior of its treaty allies. An alliance treaty with a nuclear-armed superpower by itself is unlikely to dissuade a technologically capable state in a volatile region from

---

[47] See Ripsman, Taliaferro, and Lobell, *Neoclassical Realist Theory*, pp. 114–117.

[48] For discussions of nuclear domino theory, see Nicholas L. Miller, "Nuclear Dominoes: A Self-Defeating Prophecy?" *Security Studies*, Vol. 23, No. 1 (2014), pp. 33–73; Francis J. Gavin, "Same As It Ever Was: Nuclear Alarmism, Proliferation, and the Cold War," *International Security*, Vol. 34, No. 3 (2009), pp. 7–37; and Moeed Yusuf, "Predicting Proliferation: The History of the Future of Nuclear Weapons," *Brookings Institution Foreign Policy Paper Series*, Vol. 11, No. 31 (Washington, DC: Brookings Institution, 2009), https://www.brookings.edu/research/predicting-proliferation-the-history-of-the-future-of-nuclear-weapons/. Also see "64. Report by the Committee on Nuclear Proliferation, 21 January 1965," *FRUS, 1964–1968, Vol. XI: Arms Control and Disarmament* (Washington, DC: GPO, 1997).

pursuing a nuclear option.[49] However, a weaker ally's initiation or continuation of a nuclear weapons program becomes less likely if its superpower patron is willing and able to provide a credible security guarantee against potential adversaries (whether neighboring states or other great powers).[50]

Alexander Lanoszka argues that the tangible security guarantees the United States provides, such as in-theater deployments of troops and military equipment, might dissuade a weaker ally from developing a nuclear weapon capability.[51] Extended nuclear deterrent commitments by the United States or even the forward deployment of US nuclear weapons will be insufficient to dissuade a vulnerable and technologically capable ally from considering a nuclear weapon option. The US nuclear umbrella, in and of itself, according to Lanoszka, is simply not credible to allied states. Instead, in-theater deployments of US conventional troops and military equipment are more likely to be seen as credible by the treaty ally, as well as by its adversaries, because such deployments bolster deterrence-by-denial.[52] Any planned withdrawal of US conventional forces from the theater increases the ally's abandonment fears. The ally may begin to doubt the superpower's commitment enough to embark upon nuclear proliferation behavior that can range from nuclear hedging to the actual development of a nuclear weapons capability.[53] Lastly, the theory suggests it would be difficult for the United States to persuade an ally to abandon an existing nuclear weapons program. Instead, it would be far easier for the United States to dissuade an ally from pursuing a nuclear option in the first place.[54]

---

[49] To reiterate a point made in chapter 1, the vast majority of vulnerable states in the post-1945 international system simply lacked the wherewithal to even consider mounting a nuclear weapons program.

[50] See, for example, T. V. Paul, *Power Versus Prudence: Why Nations Forgo Nuclear Weapons* (Montreal: McGill–Queen's University Press, 2000), pp. 13–36 and pp. 153–154; Jeffrey W. Knopf, "Security Assurances: Initial Hypotheses," in Jeffrey W. Knopf, ed., *Security Assurances and Nuclear Nonproliferation* (Stanford, CA: Stanford University Press, 2012), pp. 13–38; and Knopf, "Varieties of Assurance," *Journal of Strategic Studies*, Vol. 35, No. 3 (2012), pp. 375–399, esp. pp. 387–394.

[51] See Alexander Lanoszka, *Atomic Assurance: The Alliance Politics of Nuclear Proliferation* (Ithaca, NY: Cornell University Press, 2018), pp. 14–22.

[52] Ibid., pp. 15–16. For an analysis of the impact of nuclear weapons stationing on allied territory and the credibility of great power security guarantees, see Matthew Fuhrmann and Todd S. Sechser, "Signaling Alliance Commitments: Hand-Tying and Sunk Costs in Extended Nuclear Deterrence," *American Journal of Political Science*, Vol. 58, No. 4 (2014), pp. 919–935. For analysis of various types of security guarantees on states' propensity to start or continue nuclear weapons programs, see Jeffrey W. Knopf, ed., *Security Assurances and Nuclear Nonproliferation* (Stanford, CA: Stanford University Press, 2012).

[53] On the concept of nuclear hedging, see Ariel E. Levite, "Never Say Never Again: Nuclear Reversal Revisited," *International Security*, Vol. 27, No. 3 (2002), pp. 59–88. For an analysis of the coercive efficacy of nuclear latency, see Tristan A. Volpe, "Atomic Leverage: Compellence with Nuclear Latency," *Security Studies*, Vol. 26, No. 3 (2017), pp. 517–544.

[54] See Lanoszka, *Atomic Assurance*, pp. 19–22.

Security commitment theory holds that when a treaty ally, fearing possible abandonment by the United States, makes a bona fide effort to obtain components for a nuclear weapons program, then it becomes incumbent upon US policymakers to take concrete steps to reassure that ally. The pursuit of overtly coercive strategies, such as broad-based sanctions or withholding arms transfers, would be counterproductive. Instead, US policymakers should offer a tangible commitment to restore or even increase troop levels deployed on the ally's territory. Under some circumstances, however, the United States might be able to leverage the ally's technological and economic dependence, in order to either halt a nuclear weapons program or redirect such a program toward peaceful purposes.

Like nuclear domino theory, security commitment theory is primarily concerned with explaining the likely nuclear behavior of the dependent ally. Nonetheless, it does suggest hypotheses for the types of strategies the United States will pursue. In general, policymakers will pursue accommodative strategies toward an ally that hosts US troops on its territory. Furthermore, policymakers will generally avoid coercive strategies toward an ally hosting US troops, if that ally has taken steps toward developing a nuclear option.

Credible Sanctions Theory

The third alternative explanation, credible sanctions theory, posits a causal relationship between the threat of legislatively mandated economic sanctions and the behavior of would-be nuclear proliferators. Specifically, the enactment of the 1976 Symington Amendment, as well as more-robust export controls, made the threat the United States would impose sanctions on suspected nuclear proliferators credible by limiting the autonomy of the executive branch. Whereas the Kennedy, Johnson, Nixon, and Ford administrations issued threats of sanctions and abandonment to would-be proliferators on a case-by-case basis, after 1977, the imposition of sanctions became automatic. Hence, the Carter, Reagan, and George H. W. Bush administrations were better able to dissuade allies from undertaking or continuing with nuclear weapons programs. Sanctions would automatically go into effect if the target state did not comply with IAEA safeguards.[55]

---

[55] See Miller, *Stopping the Bomb*, p. 29. Miller's theory builds on the various tying-hands, credibility, and audience costs theories within the broader deterrence and coercive diplomacy literature. Major works he cites include: Thomas C. Schelling, *Arms and Influence* (New Haven, CT: Yale University Press, 1966); Alexander L. George, David Kent Hall, and William E. Simons, *The Limits of Coercive Diplomacy: Laos, Cuba, Vietnam* (Boston: Little, 1971); Alexander L. George and Richard Smoke, *Deterrence in American Foreign Policy: Theory and Practice* (New York: Columbia University Press, 1974); Robert Powell, *Nuclear Deterrence Theory: The Search for Credibility* (Cambridge: Cambridge

Miller argues that the first nuclear weapons tests of China in October 1964 and India in May 1974 had three catalytic effects in the United States: (1) increased expectations of nuclear domino effects in East Asia, South Asia, and elsewhere; (2) increased government attention to the problem of nuclear proliferation around the world; and (3) a political opening for advocates to press for new nonproliferation legislation and for tighter export regulations. Congress did exactly that, passing stringent and universal nonproliferation legislation, which made the threat of US sanction more credible to would-be nuclear proliferators. One implication of this theory is that after adopting such universal nonproliferation policies, the United States would consistently oppose nuclear proliferation, even by friendly states, and work to prevent first nuclear weapons tests by those states that have already achieved a nuclear weapons capability.[56]

Like security commitment theory, credible sanctions theory is primarily concerned with explaining the likely nuclear behavior of the dependent ally. The core hypothesis is that the credible threat of US nonproliferation sanctions decreases the likelihood that other states, especially allies, will embark upon nuclear weapons programs in the first place. Nonetheless, this theory also purports to explain broad temporal changes in the United States' nonproliferation policies towards allies and adversaries. The theory suggests that, after the passage of the Symington Amendment and related nonproliferation legislation, US policymakers would consistently pursue coercive nonproliferation strategies toward allies.[57]

Table 2.3 summarizes the four alternative theories, their independent variables, and their testable hypotheses:

University Press, 1990); James D. Fearon, "Domestic Political Audiences and the Escalation of International Disputes," *American Political Science Review*, Vol. 88, No. 3 (1994), pp. 577–592; Daryl G. Press, *Calculating Credibility: How Leaders Evaluate Military Threats* (Ithaca, NY: Cornell University Press, 2005); and Branislav L. Slantchev, *Military Threats: The Costs of Coercion and the Price of Peace* (Cambridge: Cambridge University Press, 2011).

[56] See Miller, *Stopping the Bomb*, pp. 20–28. Miller develops two theories: the first to explain the evolution of US nonproliferation policies from the early 1960s to the 1980s and the second to explain the effectiveness of strengthened US nonproliferation policies on the behavior of allies and adversaries. What I call "credible sanctions theory" draws more from the first theory Miller develops, rather than second theory.

[57] Ibid., pp. 20–28. Miller's second theory suggest that the likelihood of the United States successfully dissuading an ally from continuing a nuclear weapons program is a function of two variables: (1) the credibility of US sanction threats; and (2) the target state's degree of security dependence on the United States.

Table 2.3 **Alternative Theories, IVs, and Testable Hypotheses**

Theory	IVs	Testable Hypothesis
Neoclassical realist theory	Regional power distribution time horizon for threats to US interests in region	US policymakers will pursue accommodative strategies toward an ally when they perceive unfavorable regional power distribution and short time horizons for threats, provided domestic mobilization hurdles are low.
		US policymakers will pursue coercive strategies toward an ally when they perceive favorable regional power distribution and long time horizons for threats, provided domestic mobilization hurdles are low.
Nuclear domino theory	Likelihood of nuclear domino effects (reactive proliferation)	US policymakers will be more inclined to pursue coercive strategies toward an ally if they perceive a high likelihood of reactive proliferation.
		US policymakers will be less inclined to pursue coercive strategies toward an ally if they perceive a low likelihood of reactive proliferation.
Security commitment theory	In-theater conventional military deployments	US policymakers will pursue accommodative strategies toward an ally hosting US conventional forces, if that ally has already begun to acquire the components for a nuclear weapons program.
		US policymakers will generally avoid pursuing coercive strategies toward an ally hosting US conventional forces, if that ally has hinted at a nuclear weapons option.
Credible sanctions theory	Credibility of US sanctions threats	US policymakers will pursue a combination of coercive and accommodative strategies toward an ally before the passage of nonproliferation legislation in 1976.
		US policymakers will be inclined to pursue coercive strategies toward an ally after passage of nonproliferation legislation in 1976.

Non-Exclusivity of the Alternative Explanations

Nuclear domino theory, security commitment theory, and credible sanctions theory are three alternative explanations for what I seek to explain in this book: the variation in the types of nonproliferation strategies that the United

States (or more properly, presidents and their administrations) pursued toward its vulnerable and often obstreperous allies in the Middle East, South Asia, and East Asia. As stated in the previous chapter, I do not seek to explain why those allies embarked on the path of nuclear weapons development in the first place. Furthermore, neoclassical realist theory does not purport to explain the effectiveness or the ineffectiveness of the United States' strategies on the nuclear proliferation behavior of the targeted states.[58]

It is important to note that the four theories all start from the supposition that the United States has some strategic interest in controlling the spread of nuclear weapon capabilities. The theories, however, are not mutually exclusive. Nuclear domino theory and neoclassical realist theory yield predictions for all four cases. The other two theories have narrower scope conditions and do not yield predictions for some of the cases.

Security commitment theory, or at least the hypotheses I derive from it, only purports to explain nonproliferation disputes with treaty allies that host US military bases and conventional force. Two of the cases, South Korea and Taiwan in the 1970s, fall within those parameters. Neither Israel nor Pakistan hosted US military bases or large numbers of US troops during the periods studied, 1960–1973 and 1975–1990, respectively.[59] Neither was a bilateral treaty of the United States.[60] Since the independent variable of security commitment theory is simply not present in the latter two cases, I exclude them from the cross-case comparison summarized in Table 2.4.

Credible sanctions theory seeks to account for the broad temporal variation in the types of nonproliferation strategies the United States pursued toward its allies. One of the four cases, the nonproliferation dispute between the United States and Israel, preceded the former's nonproliferation legislation entirely. The nonproliferation disputes with Pakistan, Taiwan, and South Korea straddled the enactment of US nonproliferation legislation.[61] Therefore, we might expect to see a marked shift toward coercive nonproliferation strategies, such as explicit threats of economic sanctions, after June 1976. Prior to that point, we might

---

[58] Again, this is a distinction between neoclassical realist theory and the recent theories developed by Miller, Lanoszka, as well as by Alexandre Debs and Nuno P. Monteiro. See Debs and Monteiro, *Nuclear Politics: The Strategic Causes of Proliferation* (New York: Cambridge University Press, 2016).

[59] Lanoszka examines the United States' nonproliferation dispute with South Korea (1968–1980) in depth. He briefly discusses the nonproliferation dispute between the United States and Taiwan (1967–1978). See Lanoszka, *Atomic Assurance*, pp. 110–131 and pp. 143–147.

[60] Pakistan, however, was a multilateral treaty ally of the United States a member of the Central Treaty Organization (CENTO) and the South East Asia Treaty Organization (SEATO).

[61] Miller examines the United States' nonproliferation disputes with Taiwan (1964–1978) and with Pakistan (1972–1987). He does not examine the nonproliferation dispute with South Korea. See Miller, *Stopping the Bomb*, pp. 171–192 and pp. 193–214.

Table 2.4 **Cross-Case Comparisons of Alternative Theories**

Neoclassical Realist Theory	Nuclear Domino Theory	Security Commitment Theory	Credible Sanctions Theory
US and Israeli nuclear program (1960–1973)	US and Israeli nuclear program (1960–1973)	NA	NA
US and Pakistani nuclear program (1975–1990)	US and Pakistani nuclear program (1975–1990)	NA	US and Pakistani nuclear program (1975–1990)
US and Taiwanese nuclear program (1967–1978)	US and Taiwanese nuclear program (1967–1978)	US and Taiwanese nuclear program (1967–1978)	US and Taiwanese nuclear program (1967–1978)
US and South Korean nuclear program (1970–1982)	US and South Korean nuclear program (1970–1982)	US and South Korean nuclear program (1970–1982)	US and South Korean nuclear program (1970–1982)

NA = not applicable

expect to see more variation in the nonproliferation strategies pursued toward allies.

In this chapter, I offered a neoclassical realist theory to explain when the United States is more likely to pursue coercive or accommodating nonproliferation strategies toward vulnerable allies in volatile regions. In the next four chapters, I test the hypotheses from that theory, as well as from nuclear domino theory and, where appropriate, from credible sanctions and security commitment theories, against the historical record of the United States' proliferation disputes with Israel, Pakistan, South Korea, and Taiwan. The next chapter examines the dispute between the United States and Israel.

3

The United States and Israel's Nuclear Weapons Program, 1961–1973

The confrontation between the United States and Israel in the 1960s marked the first time Washington undertook a concerted campaign to halt the nuclear weapons program of a "friendly" state. Israel's founding prime minister, David Ben-Gurion, authorized a secret nuclear program in 1955 ostensibly to meet civilian energy needs and agricultural purposes, but also with the option of eventually developing nuclear weapons. By 1958, the Israelis had a three-pronged strategy to obtain nuclear components from abroad, while concealing the true extent of the project from their suppliers. France would supply reactor technology designed for plutonium production. Norway would supply heavy water and the United States would supply a small "swimming pool" nuclear reactor at Nachal Soreq under President Dwight D. Eisenhower's "Atoms for Peace" program. The Nachal Soreq reactor would serve as camouflage for efforts to build a large reactor capable of producing weapons-grade plutonium at Dimona, near Beersheba in the Negev Desert.[1]

US diplomats in Oslo, Paris, and Tel Aviv learned about Israeli contracts to purchase Norwegian heavy water and French reactor technology in 1959. The Central Intelligence Agency (CIA), the State Department's Bureau of Intelligence and Research (INR), and the Atomic Energy Commission (AEC), however, did not deliver this intelligence to policymakers until late summer 1960. Had Eisenhower and other senior officials received this intelligence in 1958 or 1959, it is conceivable that they could have pressured France or Norway to cancel those contracts.[2] As Austin Long and Joshua Shifrinson

---

[1] Avner Cohen, *Israel and the Bomb* (New York: Columbia University Press, 1998), pp. 57–98.

[2] On this point, see Avner Cohen and William Burr, "The Eisenhower Administration and the Discovery of Dimona: March 1958–January 1961," in Avner Cohen and William Burr, eds., *NSA Electronic Briefing Book no. 510* (Washington, DC: National Security Archives, 2015), http://nsarchive.gwu.edu/nukevault/ebb510/.

contend, this intelligence failure was symptomatic of a dysfunctional cycle in policy-intelligence relations. Ambiguous guidance from Eisenhower and other senior officials about nuclear proliferation outside the Soviet bloc affected collection priorities. Lack of resources for intelligence collection in the Middle East resulted in little useful information on the activities at the Dimona complex. The paucity of timely intelligence shaped the subsequent monitoring of the Israeli nuclear program.[3]

The Eisenhower administration's belated discovery of the Dimona complex in autumn 1960 exposed interrelated dilemmas that the administrations of Presidents John F. Kennedy, Lyndon B. Johnson, and Richard M. Nixon would struggle to resolve for the next thirteen years.

First, senior officials in all three administrations were convinced that, if left unchecked, Israel's nuclear activities would increase the Soviet Union's influence in the Middle East, thus undermining what had been a key US strategic objective since the late 1940s. Second, Israel's clandestine nuclear activities challenged the credibility of US nonproliferation efforts worldwide. If the United States were unable to dissuade a "friendly country" like Israel from going down the path of nuclear weapons acquisition, then how could it convince unfriendly countries from doing so? Third, although US-Israeli relations were friendly, senior officials in the Kennedy and Johnson administrations did not seek to forge an alliance with Israel, for fear of embroiling the United States in the Arab-Israeli conflict and driving Egypt and Syria even closer to the Soviet Union. Fourth, these officials also recognized that extreme vulnerability and the lack of a credible security guarantee prompted Israel's nuclear weapons program. Yet by autumn 1969, the United States had not only forged a de facto alliance with Israel, becoming its principal arms supplier, but had also acquiesced to Israeli possession of nuclear weapons and delivery systems. How and why did this happen?

This chapter examines the confrontation between the United States and Israel over the latter's nuclear weapons program from 1961 to 1973. The overriding strategic objective of the Kennedy, Johnson, and Nixon administrations was always to avoid containment failure in the Middle East. Thwarting, or at least slowing, the Israeli nuclear weapons program was a secondary objective. When the pursuit of these two objectives came into conflict with each other, which I contend they did from the mid-1960s onward, the Johnson and Nixon administrations favored the former, even if that meant "learning to live with" a nuclear-armed Israel.

---

[3] Austin G. Long and Joshua R. Shifrinson, "How Long Until Midnight? Intelligence-Policy Relations and the United States Response to the Israeli Nuclear Program, 1959–1985," *Journal of Strategic Studies* (2018), pp. 1–36, especially pp. 9–14.

Nuclear domino theory would expect the United States to have consistently pursued coercive strategies to halt, or at least to slow, Israel's pursuit of a nuclear weapons capability in the 1960s, if US policymakers saw a risk of reactive proliferation by Arab states. Neoclassical realist theory, by contrast, would expect greater variation in the types of strategies the United States pursued toward Israel. I contend that assessments about the power distribution in the Middle East and the time horizons for emerging threats to American interests in that region shaped that types of nonproliferation strategies the Kennedy, Johnson, and Nixon administrations sought to pursue toward Israel.

A clear pattern emerges: In the early 1960s, officials in the Kennedy administration perceived a favorable regional power distribution in the Middle East and long time horizons for threats to US interests in the region. Kennedy and his subordinates pressured Ben-Gurion into allowing US scientists to conduct periodic inspections of the Dimona complex. As the regional power distribution grew more unfavorable and as time horizons for threats grew shorter in the mid-1960s, officials in Washington became less inclined to pursue coercive strategies to halt Israel's pursuit of a nuclear weapon capability. Instead, the Johnson administration, and later the Nixon administration, acquiesced to the Israeli nuclear weapons program and offered inducements in the form of arms sales and conditional security guarantees to bolster Israel as a bulwark against further Soviet penetration in the region. However, high domestic mobilization hurdles, namely increased congressional support for arms sales to Israel, made it difficult for the Johnson and the Nixon administrations to credibly threaten abandonment or to link arms sales to Israeli concessions on the nuclear issue.

The special understanding that Nixon and Israeli prime minister Golda Meir reached in September 1969 was a quid pro quo: The United States would accept Israel's opaque nuclear status. In exchange, Israel would become the United States' regional ally and a major receipt of US arms transfers, albeit without a mutual defense treaty. This special understanding, however, exposed two other dilemmas: How could Washington support this embattled and nuclear-armed ally without falling prey to entanglement? How could the United States strike a balance between selling Israel conventional weapons for self-defense without also exacerbating Arab-Israeli conflict, thus prompting even more Soviet involvement in the region?

The remainder of the chapter is organized chronologically beginning with the Kennedy administration's use of veiled threats to coerce Ben-Gurion into allowing inspections of the Dimona complex in 1961. It ends with the October 1973 War and Secretary of State Henry Kissinger's efforts to restrain a nuclear-armed Israel from destroying the encircled Egyptian Third Army.

The Kennedy Administration: Dimona Visits and Hawk Missiles (1961–1963)

Kennedy viewed nuclear proliferation as a threat to US hegemony and to international security more broadly. In addition to considering various strategies to thwart China's nuclear weapons program, Kennedy and his advisers were privately critical of the efforts by NATO allies France and the Federal Republic of Germany (FRG) to establish a Multilateral Nuclear Force (MLF).[4] From their earliest days in office, Kennedy and his advisers also worried about the efforts by friendly and unaligned states to develop a nuclear weapon capability, especially states located in volatile regions. Kennedy and other officials repeatedly pressed Ben-Gurion and his successor, Levi Eshkol, to invite AEC scientists to inspect Dimona complex and to share their findings with other states.

On 30 January 1961, Kennedy met with Ogden Reid, the outgoing US ambassador to Israel, about Ben-Gurion's interest in purchasing US anti-aircraft missiles, as well as the Dimona reactor project. In advance of that meeting, Secretary of State Dean Rusk delivered a comprehensive assessment of what was known about Israeli nuclear activities, including a record of exchanges between the Eisenhower administration and the Ben-Gurion government, as well as the list of "cover stories" Israeli officials gave to US diplomats over the past year about the purpose of the Dimona facility.[5] While Reid did not doubt the veracity of Ben-Gurion's assurances, he also told Kennedy that inspections by US scientists of the Dimona site were possible if they were arranged with the Israelis on a secret basis.[6]

---

[4] For analyses of the Kennedy administration's efforts to slow China's nuclear weapons program, including consideration of preventive military strikes and covert operations, see Jeffrey Richelson, *Spying on the Bomb: American Nuclear Intelligence from Nazi Germany to Iran and North Korea* (New York: Norton, 2006), pp. 154–156; and William Burr and Jeffrey T. Richelson, "Whether to 'Strangle the Baby in the Cradle': The United States and the Chinese Nuclear Program, 1960–64," *International Security*, Vol. 25, No. 3 (2000), pp. 54–99. On Kennedy's private reservations about the MNF see "169. Summary Record of NSC Executive Committee Meeting No. 38 (Part II), 25 January 1963, 4 P.M.," and "173. Summary Record of NSC Executive Committee Meeting No. 41, Re: The Multilateral Nuclear Force, 12 February 1963, 10 A.M.," *FRUS, 1961–1963, Vol. XIII: Western Europe and Canada* (Washington, DC: GPO, 1994).

[5] "Secretary of State Rusk to President Kennedy, 'Your Appointment with Ogden R. Reid, Recently Ambassador to Israel,' 30 January 1961, with Memorandum and Chronology Attached, Secret, Excised Copy," in Avner Cohen and William Burr, eds., *NSA Electronic Briefing Book no. 547* (Washington, DC: National Security Archive, 2016), https://assets.documentcloud.org/documents/2806668/Document-1A-Secretary-of-State-Rusk-to-President.pdf.

[6] "Memorandum of Conversation, 'Ambassador Reid's Review of His Conversation with President Kennedy,' 31 January 1961, Secret," in Avner Cohen and William Burr, eds., *NSA Electronic Briefing Book no. 547* (Washington, DC: National Security Archive, 2016), https://assets.documentcloud.org/documents/2806669/Document-1B-Memorandum-of-Conversation.pdf.

Assistant Secretary of State for Near Eastern Affairs Lewis Jones met with Israeli ambassador Avraham Harman on 3 February and raised Ben-Gurion's promise to invite qualified US scientists to "visit" Dimona. Jones warned Harman that "The idea of the proliferation of nuclear weapons was absolutely anathema to the United States and, although rightly or wrongly, the suspicion of obtaining such a capability has fallen on Israel." He added, that since the United States and Israel were such good friends, "It was simply good common sense for the visit to take place quietly and without publicity at an arranged date."[7] Rusk reiterated the president's strong interest in having US scientists visit Dimona in a meeting with Harman and Mordecai Gazit, the minister of the Israeli Embassy in Washington, on 13 February. Harman said that Ben-Gurion was aware of Kennedy's interest and that he was in favor of having scientists from a "friendly power" visit the facility. Rusk "intimated that Israel's complete candor ... would be of great importance to the future relationships of the two governments."[8] Harman assured Rusk that the Dimona reactor was at least two years away from completion.[9]

Harman and Gazit met with McGeorge Bundy, the special assistant to the president for national security affairs, two days later to discuss Egypt's acquisition of Soviet-built MIG-19 fighters and the Israeli government's interest in purchasing US-made Hawk anti-aircraft missile batteries. When Bundy raised the Dimona issue, Harman assured him, "Israel has no intention of manufacturing the [nuclear] bomb and the reactor itself is three or four years away from completion."[10] Bundy said he had no reason to doubt Ben-Gurion's assurances, but he pressed Harman to address the legitimacy of Arab states' concerns about Israeli nuclear research.[11]

By April 1961, Ben-Gurion realized that he could no longer delay inviting US scientists to visit Dimona. Harman met with Jones and Philip Farley, Rusk's special assistant for disarmament issues, and delivered an official invitation for

---

[7] "Memorandum of Conversation, 'Israeli Reactor,' 3 February 1961. Confidential," in Avner Cohen and William Burr, eds., *NSA Electronic Briefing Book no. 547* (Washington, DC: National Security Archive, 2016), https://assets.documentcloud.org/documents/2806671/Document-2B-Memorandum-of-Conversation-Israeli.pdf.

[8] "Memorandum of Conversation, 'Inspection of Israel's New Atomic Reactor,' 13 February 1961, Secret," in Avner Cohen and William Burr, eds., *NSA Electronic Briefing Book no. 547* (Washington, DC: National Security Archive, 2016), https://assets.documentcloud.org/documents/2806673/Document-2D-Memorandum-of-Conversation.pdf.

[9] Ibid.

[10] "Memorandum of Conversation, 'Israel's Security and Other Problems,' 16 February 1961, Secret," in Avner Cohen and William Burr, eds., *NSA Electronic Briefing Book no. 547* (Washington, DC: National Security Archive, 2016) https://assets.documentcloud.org/documents/2806674/Document-2E-Memorandum-of-Conversation-Israel-s.pdf.

[11] Ibid.

the visit during the week of 15 May.[12] Farley told Gazit, "While the assurances given by Ben-Gurion," as well as those of the Kennedy administration, "has done a good deal to take the pressure off the Arabs to achieve a balancing atomic capability, there would be a lingering doubt because of the secrecy of the project."[13] On the eve of the scheduled visit to Dimona, Kennedy told the new US ambassador to Tel Aviv, Walworth Barbour, that it would be in Israel's long-term interests to allay Arab suspicions about their nuclear program by opening facilities to international inspections.[14]

Ulysses Staebler, the assistant director of AEC Reactor Development Division, and Jesse Croach, a heavy-water expert from Dupont Chemicals, toured the Dimona complex on 20 May 1961. In their report to the AEC, Staebler and Croach wrote that the reactor appeared to be "non-military" and therefore, a second visit would not be necessary for at least a year. They observed the Israelis' "obsession with secrecy is regrettable, but understandable in view of Israel's physical and geopolitical circumstances."[15] Finally, they reported the Dimona reactor would be able to produce small amounts of plutonium suitable for weapons use, but there was no indication at present the Israelis planned to use the plutonium for that purpose.[16]

During their first face-to-face meeting in New York City on 30 May 1961, Kennedy told Ben-Gurion, "It is to our common interests that no one thinks that Israel is involved in the proliferation of atomic weapons. Obviously [Egypt]

---

[12] "Memorandum of Conversation, 'U.S. Visit to Dimona Reactor Site,' 10 April 1961, Secret," in Avner Cohen and William Burr, eds., *NSA Electronic Briefing Book no. 547* (Washington, DC: National Security Archive, 2016), https://assets.documentcloud.org/documents/2806681/Document-4A-Memorandum-of-Conversation-U-S-Visit.pdf.

[13] "Memorandum of Conversation, 'Israeli Atomic Energy Program,' 16 May 1961, Secret," in Avner Cohen and William Burr, eds., *NSA Electronic Briefing Book no. 547* (Washington, DC: National Security Archive, 2016), https://assets.documentcloud.org/documents/2806689/Document-6-A-Private-Debate-Memorandum-of.pdf.

[14] "Memorandum, by L. D. Battle, Executive Secretary, to McGeorge Bundy, Special Assistant to the President for National Security Affairs, 'American Scientists' Visit to Israel's Dimona Reactor,' 18 May 1961, Secret," in Avner Cohen and William Burr, eds., *NSA Electronic Briefing Book no. 547* (Washington, DC: National Security Archive, 2016), https://assets.documentcloud.org/documents/2806690/Document-7-President-Kennedy-s-Concerns.pdf.

[15] "Memorandum from Executive Secretary L. D. Battle to McGeorge Bundy, 'U.S. Scientists Visit to Israel's Nuclear Reactor,' 26 May 1961, Secret," in Avner Cohen and William Burr, eds., *NSA Electronic Briefing Book no. 547* (Washington, DC: National Security Archive, 2016), https://assets.documentcloud.org/documents/2806691/Document-8A-Memorandum-from-Executive-Secretary.pdf.

[16] "Atomic Energy Commission AEC 928/1, 'Visit to Israel by U. M. Staebler and J. W. Croach, Jr.,' 7 June 1961, Confidential," in Avner Cohen and William Burr, eds., *NSA Electronic Briefing Book no. 547* (Washington, DC: National Security Archive, 2016), https://assets.documentcloud.org/documents/2806781/8Bo.pdf.

would not permit Israel to go ahead in this field without getting into itself." Ben-Gurion replied that Dimona's purpose was desalination and that, eventually, the reactor might be used for electricity production. He added, "Israel might also want to develop a pilot program for plutonium separation . . ., but there is no intention to develop weapons capacity now." The Israeli prime minister then asked to purchase Raytheon's MIM 23 Hawk surface-to-air missiles. Kennedy said he was reluctant to sell Israel the Hawk missiles but promised "we will keep the matter continually under review."[17]

Ben-Gurion agreed to Kennedy's request for US scientists to "visit" Dimona again and to share their findings with other states, including Egypt, in May 1961. A second visit occurred on 26 September 1962, but only after months of wrangling between the two sides.[18] Moreover, the visit took place thirteen months after Kennedy secretly sent Myer "Mike" Feldman, the deputy counsel to the president, to craft an agreement with Ben-Gurion and Foreign Minister Golda Meir for the Hawk missiles transfer, ostensibly in exchange for Israeli concessions on Palestinian refugees.[19]

Kennedy signed National Security Action Memorandum (NSAM) 231 on 23 March 1963, directing the CIA, the AEC, and the State Department to improve intelligence collection and analysis of the Israeli nuclear program. NSAM-231 also tasked the State Department with developing proposals to halt the Israeli and Egyptian nuclear and missile programs.[20] Kennedy's 18 May letter

---

[17] "Memorandum of Conversation, 'President Kennedy, Prime Minister Ben-Gurion, Ambassador Avraham Harman of Israel, Myer Feldman of the White House Staff, and Philips Talbot, Assistant Secretary, Near East and South Asian Affairs, at the Waldorf Astoria, New York, 4:45 P.M. To 6:15 P.M.,' 30 May 1961, Secret, Draft," in Avner Cohen and William Burr, eds., *NSA Electronic Briefing Book no. 547* (Washington, DC: National Security Archive, 2016), https://assets.documentcloud.org/documents/2806694/Document-9B-Memorandum-of-Conversation-President.pdf.

[18] "William Brubeck, Executive Secretary, to McGeorge Bundy, 'Second Visit by U.S. Scientists to the Dimona Reactor,' 18 September 1962, Secret," in Avner Cohen and William Burr, eds., *NSA Electronic Briefing Book no. 547* (Washington, DC: National Security Archive, 2016), https://assets.documentcloud.org/documents/2806731/Document-15E-William-Brubeck-Executive-Secretary.pdf.

[19] In addition to his formal role on the White House Staff, Myer "Mike" Feldman served as Kennedy's unofficial liaison to the American Jewish community. See Cohen, *Israel and the Bomb*, p. 111. Also see "2. Memorandum from the Assistant Secretary of State for Near Eastern and South Asian Affairs (Philip Talbot) to the Secretary of State (Dean Rusk), 9 July 1962," *FRUS, 1961–1963, Vol. XVIII: Near East, 1962–1963* (Washington, DC: GPO, 1995); "3. Letter from the Deputy Assistant Secretary of Defense (William Bundy) to the Deputy Assistant Secretary of State for Near Eastern and South Asian Affairs (James P. Grant), 16 July 1962," Ibid., https://history.state.gov/historicaldocuments/frus1961-63v18/d3.

[20] "199. National Security Action Memorandum No. 231, 26 March 1963," *FRUS, 1961–1963, Vol. XVIII: Near East, 1962–1963* (Washington, DC: GPO, 1995), https://history.state.gov/historicaldocuments/frus1961-63v18/d199.

to Ben-Gurion conveyed a thinly veiled threat: US support for Israel "would be seriously jeopardized ... if it should be thought this Government was unable to obtain reliable information on ... Israel's efforts in the nuclear field." The president warned, "It is difficult to imagine that the Arabs would refrain from turning to the Soviet Union if Israel were to develop nuclear weapons capability," but he added that US intelligence saw "no present or imminent nuclear threat to Israel."[21]

Ben-Gurion resigned as prime minister on 16 June, before Barbour could deliver another letter from Kennedy. Barbour delivered a nearly identical presidential letter to the new Israeli prime minister, Levi Eshkol, on 5 July 1963.[22] Kennedy not only reiterated the abandonment threat, but also demanded Eshkol agree to twice-yearly inspections of Dimona beginning in June 1964. He further stipulated, "our scientists [must] have access to all areas of the Dimona site and to any related part of the complex, such as fuel fabrication facilities or plutonium separation plant, and that sufficient time be allotted for a thorough examination."[23] Balfour delivered an oral message to Eshkol that the next visit had to occur before the reactor went "critical" so AEC scientists could determine whether the reactor was for peaceful purposes or the production of plutonium.[24] In his reply, Eshkol agreed the next visit would occur before the reactor went critical, but he did not mention the president's other conditions. Undersecretary of State George Ball wrote that Eshkol's reply was probably as "much of a compromise as we can expect on Dimona, save on the important question of dissemination of results."[25]

The historian Avner Cohen argues that Eshkol's agreement to continue the Dimona "visits" diminished Kennedy's sense of urgency about the Israeli nuclear program.[26] Other developments, however, shaped the parameters of the US-Israel nuclear proliferation conflict for the rest of the decade. In early October, Kennedy rejected Ben-Gurion's 12 May request for a mutual defense

---

[21] "252. Telegram from the Department of State to the Embassy in Israel, 18 May 1963," *FRUS, 1961–1963, Vol. XVIII: Near East, 1962–1963* (Washington, DC: GPO, 1995). Also see Cohen, *Israel and the Bomb*, pp. 128–129.

[22] Kennedy sent a letter to Ben-Gurion dated 15 June 1963, but Ben-Gurion announced his resignation as prime minister before Balfour could deliver it. See "274. Telegram from the Department of State to the Embassy in Israel, 15 June 1963," *FRUS, 1961–1963, Vol. XVIII: Near East, 1962–1963* (Washington, DC: GPO, 1995).

[23] "289. Telegram from the Department of State to the Embassy in Israel, 4 July 1963," *FRUS, 1961–1963, Vol. XVIII: Near East, 1962–1963* (Washington, DC: GPO, 1995).

[24] "274. Telegram from the Department of State to the Embassy in Israel, 15 June 1963," *FRUS, 1961–1963, Vol. XVIII: Near East, 1962–1963* (Washington, DC: GPO, 1995).

[25] "317. Memorandum from Acting Secretary of State George Ball to President John F. Kennedy, 23 August 1963," *FRUS 1961–1963, Vol. XVIII: Near East, 1962–1963* (Washington, DC: GPO, 1995).

[26] Cohen, *Israel and Bomb*, p. 12.

treaty. He wrote to Eshkol, "I know you need no reassurance as to the constant and special United States concern for the security and independence of Israel."[27] In the same letter, Kennedy wrote if the Arab military threat to Israel increased, "I can assure you that, as in the case of the Hawk missile, we will most carefully consider with you the best ways and means of coping with it."[28] Opening the door to arms sales gave the Kennedy administration and its successors a potential inducement for Israeli nuclear restraint. Arms sales, however, would have the paradoxical effect of raising the domestic mobilization hurdles for the Johnson and the Nixon administrations.

Neoclassical realist theory and nuclear domino theory both predict that the Kennedy administration would pursue coercive nonproliferation strategies toward Israel. That coercion took the form of the administration's insistence on US scientists "visiting" Dimona, backed by the threat of diplomatic abandonment, if Israeli compliance were not forthcoming. According to nuclear domino theory, administration officials would pursue coercive strategies toward Israel if they perceived a high likelihood of reactive proliferation by Arab states. Kennedy warned Ben-Gurion during their first meeting in May 1961, and in writing, that suspicion of Israeli efforts to develop a nuclear weapon capability might prompt Egypt to follow suit. At the working level, Farley delivered a similar message to Gazit. NSAM-231 tasked the State Department with developing proposals to halt the Egyptian and Israeli missile programs, as well as the Israeli nuclear program. Still, there is slight evidence that fear of Egyptian reactive proliferation, per se, drove the Kennedy administration's hard line on the Dimona inspections, as well as its reluctance to sell Israel the Hawk missile batteries.

Instead, Kennedy administration officials' main concerns were that the Dimona project might prompt Egypt and Syria to seek additional conventional arms and stronger security guarantees from the Soviet Union. During the 1961–1963 period, the distribution of power in the Middle East was relatively stable, at least from the United States' vantage. Administration officials were concerned about Soviet arms sales to Egypt and Syria, but they did not expect the current rate of arms transfers to shift the regional power balance in the immediate future. The stable regional power distribution and the long time horizons predisposed senior officials to pursue a coercive strategy toward Israel.

Low domestic mobilization hurdles permitted the Kennedy administration to implement a coercive strategy. US officials privately communicated threats of abandonment to Israeli officials. The first two "visits" by AEC scientists to

---

[27] "332. Telegram from the Department of State to the Embassy in Israel, 2 October 1963, Re: Text of President Kennedy's Letter to Israeli Prime Minister Eshkol," FRUS, 1961–1963, Vol. XVIII: Near East, 1962–1963 (Washington, DC: GPO, 1995).

[28] Ibid.

Dimona were kept low-key, ostensibly to assuage Israeli concerns about an Arab boycott of nuclear suppliers. Finally, in the early 1960s, there was not as yet strong congressional support for US arms transfers to Israel. However, over the next four years, the regional power distribution and the time horizons for threats to US interests would shift.

The Johnson Administration: A-4 Skyhawk and F-4 Phantom Sales (1964–1968)

The third "visit" of AEC scientists to Dimona occurred on 17 and 18 January 1964. As with the two previous visits, the scientists found no evidence of weapons-related activities, noting the absence of a plutonium reprocessing plant.[29] Despite this, US intelligence analysts could never rule out the possibility the Israelis were developing the capacity to produce a nuclear weapon.[30]

CIA analysts reported in early 1964 that President Gamal Abdel Nasser of Egypt indicated "that acquisition of a nuclear weapons capability by Israel would be cause for war no matter how suicidal for the Arabs."[31] Meanwhile, Egypt continued to purchase Soviet tanks, surface-to-surface missiles, and MIG fighter jets. US and Israeli defense officials and intelligence analysts disagreed over whether Egyptian air and ground capabilities surpassed Israel's in late 1963.[32] In January 1964, the Eshkol government asked to purchase 500 M-48 and M-60 tanks, in an effort to offset the Soviet transfer of the T-54 tanks to Egypt.[33]

Johnson met with Eshkol at the White House on 1 June 1964 and urged him to put Israeli nuclear facilities under International Atomic Energy Agency

---

[29] "12. Memorandum from the Department of State's Executive Secretary (Read) to the President's Special Assistant for National Security Affairs (Bundy), 11 February 1964," *FRUS, 1964–1968, Vol. XVIII: Arab-Israeli Dispute, 1963–1967* (Washington, DC: GPO, 1995).

[30] "136. Memorandum from the Department of State's Executive Secretary (Read) to the President's Special Assistant for National Security Affairs (Bundy), 5 February 1965," *FRUS, 1964–1968, Vol. XVIII: Arab-Israeli Dispute, 1964–1967* (Washington, DC: GPO, 1995).

[31] "12. Memorandum from the Department of State's Executive Secretary (Read) to the President's Special Assistant for National Security Affairs (Bundy), 11 February 1964," *FRUS, 1964–1968, Vol. XVIII: Arab-Israeli Dispute, 1963–1967* (Washington, DC: GPO, 1995).

[32] "359. Circular Telegram from the Department of State to Certain Posts, 13 November 1963," *FRUS, 1961–1963, Vol. XVIII: Near East, 1962–1963*(Washington: GPO, 1995); and "360. Memorandum for the Record, 14 November 1963," Ibid.

[33] "8. Memorandum of Conversation between Harman and Feldman, 15 January 1964," *FRUS, 1964–1968, Vol. XVIII: Arab-Israeli Dispute, 1964–1967* (Washington, DC: GPO, 2000); "9. Memorandum from Secretary of State Rusk to President Johnson, 16 January 1964," Ibid; and "10. Memorandum from the Joint Chiefs of Staff to Secretary of Defense McNamara, JCSM-40-64, 18 January 1964," Ibid.

(IAEA) safeguards. He warned Eshkol the United States was "violently against nuclear proliferation," but he added, "we are not being naive about Nasser. What we want to do is to try and prevent him from leaning over too far towards the Russians."[34] In May 1964, the Soviets offered to sell Jordan, via Egypt, modern tanks and armored personnel carriers (APCs) on favorable credit terms.[35] The desire to preclude Soviet influence in Jordan led Johnson to reluctantly approve the sale of forty-six M48 tanks to Amman in late 1964, a move the Eshkol government and Israel's supporters in Congress strongly opposed.[36]

By January 1965, the Johnson administration sought a way to achieve several interrelated objectives in the Middle East: (1) to compensate Israel for sale of tanks, APCs, and aircraft to Jordan; (2) to redress the Arab-Israeli conventional imbalance by selling modern tanks to Israel; (3) to use those arms sales as leverage to get the Eshkol government's acceptance of IAEA controls; and thus, (4) to avoid offering Israel a mutual defense treaty.[37] The administration arranged for Israel to purchase 250 Centurion tanks from the United Kingdom and to secretly purchase 150 US-made M-48 tanks from West Germany. News of the arrangement leaked to the press, however, forcing Chancellor Ludwig Erhard to terminate the contract. In late February, Johnson sent Robert Komer, a member of the National Security Council (NSC) staff, and W. Averell Harriman, the undersecretary of state for political affairs, to Tel Aviv to negotiate a memorandum of understanding (MOU), linking future US arms sales to Israel's nuclear restraint and acquiescence to the Jordanian arms deal.[38]

Rusk instructed Harriman to make it clear to Eshkol and Meir that since the United States "cannot support any Israeli flirtation with nuclear weapons," it would "resist with every resource at our command the dissemination of nuclear weapons into the Near East."[39] Similarly, Bundy warned Israeli deputy prime minister Abba Eban, "The one thing that might upset this increasingly close relationship would be US belief that Israel was moving in the direction of a nuclear

---

[34] "65. Memorandum of Conversation, Re: Johnson/Eshkol Exchange of Views, 1 June 1964," *FRUS, 1964–1968, Vol. XVIII: Arab-Israeli Dispute* (Washington, DC: GPO, 2000).

[35] "78. Information Memorandum from Talbot to Secretary of State Rusk, 22 July 1964," *FRUS, 1964–1968, Vol. XVIII: Arab-Israeli Conflict, 1964–1967* (Washington, DC: GPO, 2000).

[36] "138. Memorandum from Komer to President Johnson, 6 February 1965," *FRUS, 1964–1968, Vol. XVIII: Arab-Israeli Conflict, 1964–1967* (Washington, DC: GPO, 2000).

[37] See Zach Levey, "The United States' Skyhawk Sale to Israel, 1966: Strategic Exigencies of an Arms Deal," *Diplomatic History*, Vol. 28, No. 2 (2004), pp. 255–276.

[38] "157. Memorandum from President Johnson to Harriman and Komer, 21 February 1965," *FRUS, 1964–1968, Vol. XVIII: Arab-Israeli Dispute, 1964–1967* (Washington, DC: GPO, 2000).

[39] "169. Telegram from the Department of State to the Embassy in Israel, 1 March 1965, 12:02 A.M.," *FRUS, 1964–1968, Vol. XVIII: Arab-Israeli Dispute, 1964–1967* (Washington, DC: GPO, 2000).

deterrent."[40] As Komer wrote to Johnson a few weeks later, "Eshkol's negative [response to sharing the Dimona visit findings with Nasser] and Mike Feldman's inability to move him on missiles further strengthen our suspicions that Israel is heading for a nuclear deterrent."[41]

On 10 March 1965, Eshkol signed an MOU that stated Israel "would not be the first to introduce nuclear weapons into the Arab-Israeli area." He also acquiesced to US arms sales to Jordan. In return, the Johnson administration said it recognized that an "effective Israeli deterrence [w]as a major factor in preventing aggression" and agreed to supply Israel 90 tanks by 1966 and an additional 100 M-48 tanks superior to those sold to Jordan. Lastly, the MOU stipulated the United States would only sell Israel combat aircraft if the Israelis were unable to identify suitable aircraft from a Western European supplier.[42] Komer confided to Bundy in cable a few days earlier that the "developing situation in [the] Middle East [would] compel us to sell tanks and probably planes to Israel sooner or later anyway, as [the] only alternative to [a] binding alliance."[43]

Despite the "no introduction" pledge, Johnson, Rusk and others continued to worry about Israeli nuclear activities. "Our efforts to slow down [Egypt's] sophisticated weapons program—as well as potential nuclear weapons programs in India and elsewhere—will be influenced by the example we set in dealing with Israel," Rusk wrote Johnson in early May. Furthermore, he argued, "So long as the Dimona reactor operates without publicly recognized safeguards, the credibility of our worldwide efforts to prevent proliferation is in doubt."[44] On 21 May, Johnson wrote to Eshkol that "A preferable alternative to these bilateral arrangements would be for Israel to place the Dimona reactor and all other nuclear facilities under IAEA controls, as you have already agreed to do for the Nahal Soreq reactor."[45] Eshkol declined Johnson's request, saying that it would politically impossible for him to agree to IAEA inspections before the Israeli general elections scheduled for November 1965. In July 1965, Rusk told

---

[40] "26. Memorandum for Record, 5 March 1964," *FRUS, 1964–1968, Vol. XVIII: Arab-Israeli Dispute, 1964–1967* (Washington, DC: GPO, 2000).

[41] "43. Memorandum from Robert W. Komer of the National Security Council Staff to President Johnson, 6 April 1964," *FRUS, 1964–1968, Vol. XVIII: Arab-Israeli Dispute, 1964–1967* (Washington, DC: GPO, 2000).

[42] "185. Telegram from the Embassy in Israel to the Department of State, Re: Text of Signed Memorandum of Understanding, 11 March 1965, 2 A.M.," *FRUS, 1964–1968, Vol. XVIII: Arab-Israeli Dispute, 1964–1967* (Washington, DC: GPO, 2000).

[43] "180. Message Komer to Bundy, 5 March 1965," *FRUS, 1964–1968, Vol. XVIII: Arab-Israeli Conflict, 1964–1967* (Washington, DC: GPO, 2000).

[44] "214. Memorandum from Rusk to President Johnson, 10 May 1965," *FRUS, 1964–1968, Vol. XVIII: Arab-Israeli Dispute, 1964–1967* (Washington, DC: GPO, 2000).

[45] "218. Letter from President Johnson to Prime Minister Eshkol, 21 May 1965," *FRUS, 1964–1968, Vol. XVIII: Arab-Israel Dispute, 1964–1967* (Washington, DC: GPO, 2000).

Barbour, "[Eshkol] should understand USG and US people feel deeply about non-proliferation and this could become point of issue between us later if no progress made."[46]

In May 1965, the Eshkol government asked to purchase 75 combat aircraft from the United States. General Earle Wheeler, the chairman of the Joint Chiefs of Staff (JCS), advised Secretary of Defense Robert S. McNamara that the sale "cannot be justified on military grounds" and "every attempt should be made to avoid a polarization in the Middle East whereby the United States becomes increasingly identified with Israel and the USSR with the Arab World."[47] Likewise, Rusk and State Department officials were reluctant to sell the Israelis combat aircraft, in particular the A-4 Skyhawk, which could be modified to deliver nuclear weapons.[48] In a meeting with the Israeli foreign minister, Abba Eban, on 9 February 1966, Rusk warned "the only major question that could have a disastrous effect on US-Israeli relations was Israel's attitude on proliferation," adding, "Israel should expect the US to be extremely clear and utterly harsh on the matter of non-proliferation."[49]

Two days later, McNamara told Eban that the United States sought assurances Israel would not use any US-supplied aircraft to deliver nuclear weapons. Eban replied that Israel had no intention of building nuclear weapons "so we will not use your aircraft to carry weapons we haven't got and hope we will never have."[50] The Johnson administration, however, also faced intense opposition from Israel's supporters in Congress to the proposed sale of additional tanks and APCs to Jordan. During a meeting in the Oval Office on 9 February, Johnson asked Eban to restrain "well-meaning friends of Israel" and to get them "to stop coming in the back door, or writing, or sending telegrams, or talking to the newspapers."[51]

---

[46] "231. Telegram from the Department of State to the Embassy in Israel, 30 July 1965," *FRUS, 1964–1968, Vol. XVIII: Arab-Israeli Dispute, 1964–1967* (Washington, DC: GPO, 2000).

[47] "211. Memorandum from the Joint Chiefs of Staff to Secretary of Defense McNamara, 6 May 1965," *FRUS, 1964–1968, Vol. XVIII: Arab-Israeli Conflict, 1964–1967* (Washington, DC: GPO, 2000).

[48] "222. Telegram from the Department of State to the Embassy in Israel, 5 June 1965," *FRUS, 1964–1968, Vol. XVIII: Arab-Israeli Dispute, 1964–1967* (Washington, DC: GPO, 2000).

[49] "269. Memorandum of Conversation, Secretary of State Rusk and Israel Foreign Minister Abba Eban, 9 February 1966," *FRUS, 1964–1968, Vol. XVIII: Arab-Israeli Conflict, 1964–1967* (Washington, DC: GPO, 2000).

[50] "271. Memorandum of Conversation between Secretary McNamara and Israeli Foreign Minister Eban, 12 February 1966," *FRUS, 1964–1968, Vol. XVIII: Arab-Israeli Conflict, 1964–1967* (Washington, DC: GPO, 2000).

[51] "268. Memorandum for the Record, President's Talk with Israeli Foreign Minister Eban, 9 February 1966," *FRUS, 1964–1968, Vol. XVIII: Arab-Israeli Conflict, 1964–1967* (Washington, DC: GPO, 2000).

In March 1966, Johnson approved the sale of 48 A-4s Skyhawks to Israel in an effort to simultaneously achieve three goals: (1) to mollify Israel's supporters in Congress over the tank sale to Jordan; (2) to redress the perceived imbalance in Arab-Israeli air capabilities; and (3) to exert leverage over the Israeli nuclear weapons program.[52] In exchange, the Eshkol government reaffirmed the "no introduction of nuclear weapons" pledge, recognized the sale did not create a precedent for future US action, and agreed not to consider the United States its principal arms supplier. Finally, Eshkol agreed to continue to seek Western European suppliers for the bulk of Israel's military requirements.[53]

In summer 1966, two developments prompted the administration to intensify efforts for Israeli acceptance of IAEA safeguards. First, the Nuclear Nonproliferation Treaty (NPT) negotiations in Geneva reached a delicate stage as the non-aligned states demanded concessions on the treaty's disarmament provisions.[54] Second, the Israeli nuclear program achieved the capacity to produce weapons-grade plutonium.[55] The report from the April 1966 Dimona visit found no evidence of plutonium production but acknowledged "a possibility that the team may have been deliberately deceived by the Israelis."[56] In late July, Rusk told Gideon Rafael, the Israeli ambassador to the United Nations (UN), "If Israel is holding open the nuclear option, it should forget US support."[57] In September, Eban complained to Barbour that Rusk's threat of sanctions "was not in accord with the atmosphere of trust and good will that should prevail between good friends."[58]

After months of delay, AEC scientists paid another "visit" to Dimona on 27 April 1967.[59] Noting the reactor was now capable of producing enough

---

[52] Zach Levey, "The United States' Skyhawk Sale to Israel, 1966: Strategic Exigencies of an Arms Deal," *Diplomatic History*, Vol. 28, No. 2 (2004), pp. 255–276.

[53] "283. Memorandum from the Assistant Secretary of Defense for International Security Affairs (McNaughton) to Secretary of Defense McNamara, 31 March 1966," *FRUS, 1964–1968, Vol. XVIII: Arab-Israeli Conflict, 1964–1967* (Washington, DC: GPO, 2000).

[54] Dimitris Bourantonis, "The Negotiation of the Non-Proliferation Treaty, 1965–1968: A Note," *The International History Review*, Vol. 19, No. 2 (1997), pp. 347–357.

[55] Cohen, *Israel and the Bomb*, p. 231. See also Avner Cohen, "Crossing the Threshold: The Untold Nuclear Dimension of the 1967 Arab-Israeli War and Its Contemporary Lessons," *Arms Control Today*, Vol. 37, No. 5 (2007), pp. 12–16.

[56] "289. Memorandum from the Director of the Defense Intelligence Agency (Carroll) to Secretary of Defense McNamara, (S/NFD), 4 May 1966," *FRUS, 1964–1968, Vol. XVIII: Arab-Israeli Dispute, 1964–1967* (Washington, DC: GPO, 2000).

[57] "312. Telegram from the Department of State to the Embassy in Israel, 28 July 1966," *FRUS, 1964–1968, Vol. XVIII: Arab-Israeli Dispute, 1964–1967* (Washington, DC: GPO, 2000).

[58] "322. Telegram from the Embassy in Israel to the Department of State, 14 September 1966," *FRUS, 1964–1968, Vol. XVIII: Arab-Israeli Conflict, 1964–1967* (Washington, DC: GPO, 2000).

[59] Cohen, *Israel and the Bomb*, p. 187.

plutonium to fuel one or two bombs per year, Undersecretary of State Nicholas Katzenbach told Johnson on 2 May: "We have no evidence that Israel is actually making a bomb, but we believe Israel intends to keep itself in a position to do so at reasonably short notice should the need arise."[60]

As the crisis between Egypt and Israel escalated in late May 1967, the Israelis assembled two deliverable nuclear explosive devices.[61] Just before the Six Day War broke out, Eshkol apparently rejected a proposal to conduct an underground nuclear detonation to deter an Egyptian attack.[62] The Israel Air Force (IAF) launched preemptive air strikes on Egyptian forces massed in the Sinai and on Syrian forces in the Golan Heights on 5 June.[63] Over the next five days, the Israel Defense Forces (IDF) captured the Gaza Strip and the Sinai peninsula from Egypt, the West Bank and the eastern half of Jerusalem from Jordan, and the Golan Heights from Syria.

The Eshkol government requested purchasing 50 F-4 Phantoms and 28 additional A-4 Skyhawks in November 1967 to recover the planes destroyed in the Six Day War and to replace the Mirage V jets that France embargoed.[64] Eban gave Barbour an aide memoire on the increased Soviet military presence in the Middle East since the war, claiming that the Soviets had replenished 80 percent of the Arab losses. At the present rate of resupply, Eban warned, the Egyptian armed forces would regain their prewar strength in five months and with equipment superior to the equipment destroyed in June 1967. Eban argued that it would be in the United States' interests to quickly approve the Israeli request for advanced military aircraft in order to redress the military and political gains from Soviet resupply efforts, thereby deterring Egypt from launching another

---

[60] "415. Memorandum from the Undersecretary of State (Katzenbach) to President Johnson, Re: The Arab-Israel Arms Race and Status of U.S. Arms Control Efforts, 1 May 1967," *FRUS, 1964–1968, Vol. XVIII: Arab-Israeli Dispute, 1964–1967* (Washington, DC: GPO, 2000).

[61] Cohen, *Israel and the Bomb*, p. 274.

[62] Avner Cohen, "Cairo, Dimona, and the June 1967 War," *Middle East Journal*, Vol. 50, No. 2 (1996), pp. 190–210.

[63] For the argument that Johnson tacitly approved of the Israeli plan to launch a preemptive attack in May and early June 1967, see William B. Quandt, "Lyndon Johnson and the June 1967 War: What Color Was the Light?," *Middle East Journal*, Vol. 46, No. 2 (1992), pp. 198–228; William B. Quandt, *Peace Process: American Diplomacy and the Arab-Israeli Conflict Since 1967* (Washington, DC: Brookings Institution Press, 2005), pp. 25–41, 49, and 52. For the argument that the Johnson administration attempted and failed to restrain Israel from launching a preemptive attack in June 1967, see Jeremy Pressman, *Warring Friends: Alliance Restraint in International Politics* (Ithaca, NY: Cornell University Press, 2008), pp. 91–99.

[64] "3. Telegram from the Embassy in Israel to the Department of State, 27 November 1967," *FRUS, 1964–1968, Vol. XX: Arab-Israeli Dispute, 1967–1968* (Washington, DC: GPO, 2001).

aerial assault on Israel and demonstrating the United States' resolve to maintain a favorable balance-of-power in the region.[65]

"The military balance is in Israel's favor and should remain so for at least a year," Katzenbach wrote to Johnson on 11 December, but added, "I believe there is a legitimate Israeli concern about their continued air superiority beyond 1968."[66] Walt Rostow, Johnson's national security adviser, agreed with this assessment of the Arab-Israeli conventional balance, but told the president, "The question is how quickly we must act to keep pace with Soviet resupply [of Egypt and Syria]."[67] Rostow recommended Johnson secretly approve the transfer of 27 A-4s, in addition to the 48 A-4s already scheduled for delivery, but hold off any decision regarding the supersonic F-4s, which would give the IAF clear air superiority over Egypt and Syria.[68]

Johnson invited Eshkol to a two-day summit at his ranch in central Texas in early January 1968. The day before the prime minister's scheduled arrival, Rostow wrote to Johnson that "More than just seeking a specific number of aircraft, Eshkol may be looking for a firmer commitment to Israel's security. He must understand that security guarantees and treaties are out, but he may seek a guaranteed source of arms."[69] Later that day, Rostow conferred with Rusk, McNamara, and Clark Clifford (Johnson's nominee to succeed McNamara as secretary of defense) regarding the arms transfer. Clifford opined that the overriding priority should be avoiding the polarization of the Middle East "in which a small Israel, backed by a US with an ambiguous commitment, faces the Arabs, led by extremists and backed by a determined USSR."[70]

Rostow forwarded to Johnson a memorandum from Rusk outlining the areas of agreement between the State and Defense Departments, which read in part, "The United States should continue to avoid being cast in the role of principal supplier of arms to any country in the area." Regarding combat aircraft sales to Israel, he added, "Until such time as an understanding with respect to arms

---

[65] "18. Telegram from the Embassy in Israel to the Department of State, 12 December 1967," *FRUS, 1964–1968, Vol. XX: Arab-Israeli Dispute, 1967–1968* (Washington, DC: GPO, 2001).

[66] "15. Memorandum from Acting Secretary of State Katzenbach to President Johnson, Re: Arms for Jordan and Israel, 11 December 1967," *FRUS, 1964–1968, Vol. XX: Arab-Israeli Conflict, 1967–1968* (Washington, DC: GPO, 2001).

[67] "20. Memorandum from the President's Special Assistant (Rostow) to President Johnson, Re: Arms for Israel and Jordan, 15 December 1967," *FRUS, 1964–1968, Vol. XX: Arab-Israeli Conflict, 1967–1968* (Washington, DC: GPO, 2001).

[68] Ibid.

[69] "35. Telegram from Rostow to President Johnson in Texas, 6 January 1968," *FRUS, 1964–1968, Vol. XX: Arab-Israeli Dispute, 1967–1968* (Washington, DC: GPO, 2001).

[70] "36. Telegram from Rostow to President Johnson in Texas, 6 January 1968," *FRUS, 1964–1968, Vol. XX: Arab-Israel Dispute, 1967–1968* (Washington, DC: GPO, 2001).

limitations in the area is reached, we consider it essential [that] there [should] be . . . a diversity of suppliers."[71] McNamara recommended approving selling 27 of the slower A-4s (preferably on a cash basis), but warned against making any commitment to sell long-lead-time items, in anticipation of a future sale of F-4s. If the military balance between the Arab states and Israel shifted against the latter, the outgoing defense secretary said Johnson could revisit the decision and then promptly deliver the F-4s to Israel.[72]

Eshkol, accompanied by Harman, Ephraim Evron, the minister in the Israeli Embassy in Washington, and Brig. Gen. Mordechai Hod, commander of the IAF, arrived at the LBJ Ranch on 7 January 1968. Eshkol told Johnson, Rusk, McNamara, Rostow, and Wheeler that Egyptian air capabilities had improved since the devastating defeat in June 1967, thanks to Soviet replacements. In addition to Soviet tanks and aircraft, Eshkol reported the presence of over 2,500 Soviet military advisers in Egypt. Johnson reminded Eshkol that when the MOU to transfer the 48 A-4s was signed in March 1965, both governments agreed Israel would look elsewhere for weapons systems beyond those covered in the agreement. Eshkol replied that his government would be delighted to look elsewhere, if Johnson "would give them an address."[73]

During a subsequent session, Wheeler stated the JCS believed that, at least for the next eighteen months, the IAF would maintain superiority over any combination of Arab adversaries, but that several contingencies might change that assessment, including: France reneging on the contract to supply Israel with Mirage V jets, a French decision to supply high-performance aircraft to Arab states, or the Soviet Union's enlarging its military assistance package to Egypt. McNamara reiterated that the 1965 MOU proceeded from the assumption that the United States would not become Israel's principal military supplier. Regarding the specific question of an F-4 transfer to Israel, he noted, "Actions on the plane request could have a bearing on this situation by bringing further Russian support. There is no reason for the Israelis to say that Israel is abandoned."[74]

Ultimately, Johnson told Eshkol that he would consider allowing Israel to purchase the F-4s on an accelerated delivery schedule, with the first planes expected

---

[71] Ibid.

[72] "38. Telegram from Rostow to Johnson in Texas, Re: Aircraft for Israel, 7 January 1968," *FRUS, 1964–1968, Vol. XX: Arab-Israeli Dispute, 1967–1968* (Washington, DC: GPO, 2001).

[73] "39. Memorandum of Conversation," *FRUS, 1964–1968, Vol. XX: Arab-Israeli Dispute, 1967–1968* (Washington, DC: GPO, 2001), https://history.state.gov/historicaldocuments/frus1964-68v20/d39.

[74] "40. Memorandum of Conversation, re: US-Israel Talks, 8 January 1968, Session 2," *FRUS, 1964–1968, Vol. XX: Arab-Israeli Dispute, 1967–1968* (Washington, DC: GPO, 2001).

in January 1970.⁷⁵ He also agreed to add 27 to 30 A-4s to the present agreement, and a further 10, if needed. Notably, the president did not make a firm commitment to transfer a specific number of F-4s. Instead, as Rostow reminded Evron a few days later, Johnson said the current and future balance between Israel and Egypt in air capabilities was a matter for Wheeler and Hod to resolve. He also said he would wait to hear from McNamara and the Defense Department about production schedules and the availability of the F-4s before making a commitment to Eshkol on a delivery schedule.⁷⁶ Meanwhile, the Defense Department and the Israeli Ministry of Defense signed an agreement on 30 January for the transfer of an additional 40 A-4s on a cash basis.⁷⁷

Throughout 1968, the Johnson administration urged Israel to sign the NPT. In late April, Rusk wrote to Eban, "Because we do not expect any Arab nuclear capability in the foreseeable future, Israel's objective must be to prevent . . . the transfer of such weapons to its neighbors."⁷⁸ In this reply, Eban wrote that Rusk "rightly and frankly placed the question of Israel adherence to the treaty in the context of our national security," but added, "We learnt last year with special incisiveness that Israel cannot realistically count on external military aid if she is attacked."⁷⁹ Rusk raised the NPT with Israeli deputy prime minister Yigal Allon, who later complained to his cabinet colleagues that "For Dean Rusk, the NPT is matter of personal obsession."⁸⁰

By October 1968, US intelligence reported Israel purchased 12 MD-620 missiles from France, capable of carrying nuclear payloads, and had taken steps "to reduce substantially the time needed to develop a deliverable nuclear weapon."⁸¹ The Johnson administration tried to link the F-4 sale to a pledge by

---

⁷⁵ "41. Memorandum of Conversation, re: US-Israel Talks, 8 January 1968, Session 3," *FRUS, 1964–1968, Vol. XX: Arab-Israeli Dispute, 1967–1968* (Washington, DC: GPO, 2001).

⁷⁶ "53. Memorandum of Conversation Between Rostow and Evron, 19 January 1968," *FRUS, 1964–1968, Vol. XX: Arab-Israeli Dispute, 1967–1968* (Washington, DC: GPO, 2001).

⁷⁷ "70. Information Memorandum from Rostow to President Johnson, Re: Aircraft Sale to Israel, 6 February 1968," *FRUS, 1964–1968, Vol. XX: Arab-Israeli Dispute, 1967–1968* (Washington, DC: GPO, 2001).

⁷⁸ "155. Telegram from the Department of State to the Embassy in Israel, Re: Letter from Secretary of State Rusk to Israeli Foreign Minister Eban, 28 April 1968," *FRUS, 1964–1968, Vol. XX: Arab-Israeli Dispute, 1967–1968* (Washington, DC: GPO, 2001).

⁷⁹ "205. Telegram from the Embassy in Israel to the Department of State, re: Foreign Minister Eban's Reply to Secretary of State Rusk's Letter of 6 April, 2 July 1968," *FRUS, 1964–1968, Vol. XX: Arab-Israeli Dispute, 1967–1968* (Washington, DC: GPO, 2001).

⁸⁰ Quoted in Cohen, *Israel and the Bomb*, p. 304.

⁸¹ Parker T. Hart to Secretary Dean Rusk, "Issues to Be Considered in Connection with Negotiations with Israel for F-4 Phantom Aircraft, 15 October 1968, Top Secret/No Dis," in William Burr and Avner Cohen, eds., *NSA Electronic Briefing Book no. 189* (Washington, DC: National Security Archive, 2006), http://nsarchive.gwu.edu/NSAEBB/NSAEBB189/IN-02.pdf.

the Eshkol government to sign the NPT. Johnson wrote to Eshkol on 23 October urging him to sign. "I understand how strongly some of your colleagues feel that Israel's future can best be guaranteed by military means and expanded borders alone," Johnson wrote, adding, "But our own experience has [proven] that real peace is not found alone on the walls of a fortress—or under the umbrella of air power—or behind a nuclear shield."[82]

Johnson remained reluctant to transfer the F-4s to Israel, telling congressional leaders in September 1968 that "We don't want to be in a position of just being arms merchants and starting an arms race with the Russians there."[83] The following month, however, the Congress passed the Foreign Assistance Act of 1968, which included a provision (Section 651) urging the president to begin negotiations with the Israeli government for the sale of "supersonic planes as may be necessary to provide Israel with an adequate deterrent force capable of preventing future Arab aggression by offsetting sophisticated weapons received by the Arab States and to replace losses suffered by Israel in the 1967 conflict."[84] Johnson signed the bill into law on 9 October and immediately directed Rusk and the State Department to begin negotiations with the Israelis on the F-4 transfer.[85]

The Johnson administration debated whether to use the F-4 negotiations to secure concessions from the Eshkol government on the nuclear issue, in particular a commitment to sign the NPT as a non–nuclear weapons state (NNWS).[86] Assistant Secretary of State for Near Eastern Affairs Parker T. Hart wrote to Rusk on 15 October that although intelligence on the Israeli nuclear program was ambiguous, there were indications the Israelis had taken a number of steps to drastically reduce the development time for a nuclear weapon. Since the United States could not get "ultimate assurances" that Israel would never produce a nuclear weapon or deploy strategic missiles, Hart argued the proposed F-4 sale represented Washington's "last best chance" to get commitments from the Eshkol government that would make it more difficult for Israel to take the critical decision "to go nuclear" in a short time frame.[87] Rusk and Clifford proposed

---

[82] "285. Letter from President Johnson to Prime Minister Eshkol, 23 October 1968," *FRUS, 1964–1968, Vol. XX: Arab-Israeli Dispute, 1967–1968* (Washington, DC: GPO, 2001).

[83] "248. Notes on President Johnson's Meeting with Congressional Leaders, 8 September 1968," *FRUS, 1964–1968, Vol. XX: Arab-Israeli Dispute, 1967–1968* (Washington, DC: GPO, 2001).

[84] "275. Telegram from the Department of State to Selected Posts, 9 October 1968," *FRUS, 1964–1968, Vol. XX: Arab-Israeli Dispute, 1967–1968* (Washington, DC: GPO, 2001).

[85] PL 90-554, 82 Stat. 960.

[86] "279. Memorandum from Harold H. Saunders to Rostow, Re: Negotiations on Phantoms, 14 October 1968," *FRUS, 1964–1968, Vol. XX: Arab-Israeli Dispute, 1967–1968* (Washington, DC: GPO, 2001).

[87] Parker T. Hart to Secretary Dean Rusk, "Issues to Be Considered in Connection with Negotiations with Israel for F-4 Phantom Aircraft, 15 October 1968, Top Secret/No Dis," in William

making the F-4 sale contingent on Israel's agreement to sign the NPT, a reaffirmation of the "no introduction" pledge, and a pledge to suspend the development of surface-to-surface missiles.[88]

Johnson met with Eban at the White House on 22 October and reiterated he only agreed "in principle" to sell the F-4s to Israel. His final decision would be contingent on the pace of Soviet arms transfers to the Arab states, and whether or not the Kremlin was receptive to US-sponsored arms control negotiations. The president further said that he would make Israel's signature on the NPT a formal condition for the F-4 sale and that Eban should be aware of the US government's strong feelings on the matter.[89] Two days later, Rusk told Eban that the nuclear and missile issues were fundamental to the US-Israeli relationship, to which Eban replied that Israel had not made the decision to become a nuclear-armed power and the deployment of strategic missiles was not imminent.[90]

In their respective meetings with Eban, Johnson and Rusk stopped just short of explicitly linking the F-4 sales to an Israeli pledge to sign the NPT. Other State Department and Defense Department officials, however, did try to make an explicit link. Rostow wrote to Johnson on 25 October that Abe Feinberg reported that Israelis were "up in arms" because Hart apparently tried to link the F-4s to the NPT in preliminary talks on "certain political questions" with Israeli diplomats. The new Israeli ambassador, Lt. Gen. Yitzhak Rabin, insisted the NPT and the F-4 sale were two separate issues. Rostow told Feinberg that although neither the president nor the secretary of state made Israel's signature on the NPT an explicit condition for the F-4 sale, both considered the NPT greatly important.[91]

Paul Warnke, the assistant secretary of defense for international security affairs, wrote to Clifford on 28 October that the "possession of a nuclear missile by Israel would be of no value to that country unless the fact were known to its Arab neighbors." Warnke warned that "If this fact were to become known,

---

Burr and Avner Cohen, eds., *NSA Electronic Briefing Book no. 189* (Washington, DC: National Security Archive, 2006), http://nsarchive.gwu.edu/NSAEBB/NSAEBB189/IN-02.pdf.

[88] "279. Memorandum from Harold H. Saunders to Rostow, Re: Negotiations on Phantoms, 14 October 1968," *FRUS, 1964–1968, Vol. XX: Arab-Israeli Dispute, 1967–1968* (Washington, DC: GPO, 2001).

[89] "284. Memorandum of Conversation Between President Johnson and Foreign Minister Eban, 22 October 1968," *FRUS, 1964–1968, Vol. XX: Arab-Israeli Dispute, 1967–1968* (Washington, DC: GPO, 2001).

[90] "288. Telegram from the Department of State to the Embassy in Israel, 24 October 1968," *FRUS, 1964–1968, Vol. XX: Arab-Israeli Dispute, 1967–1968* (Washington, DC: GPO, 2001).

[91] "290. Action Memorandum Rostow to President Johnson, re: Strong Israeli Reaction to Eban Talks Here, 25 October 1968, 2:20 P.M.," *FRUS, 1964–1968, Vol. XX: Arab-Israeli Conflict, 1967–1968* (Washington, DC: GPO, 2001).

there is every likelihood that the UAR [United Arab Republic of Egypt] and possibly other Arab countries would request and receive Soviet nuclear missiles stationed on their soil under Soviet control."[92] He recommended explicitly making the F-4 sale contingent on the Eshkol government's agreement to sign and ratify the NPT, to refrain from testing or deploying strategic missiles, to refrain from seeking or manufacturing nuclear weapons, and to continue the semi-annual inspections of the Dimona complex and other Israeli nuclear sites.[93]

In two acrimonious meetings in Warnke's Pentagon office on 4 and 5 November, Rabin rebuffed those conditions.[94] A third meeting between Warnke and Rabin occurred on 8 November, two days after the 1968 presidential election. Rabin read from a prepared text: "We have come here for the purpose of purchasing 50 Phantoms. We have not come here in order to mortgage the sovereignty of the State of Israel, not even for 50 Phantoms." Rabin said he was authorized to reaffirm Israel's long-standing pledge not to introduce nuclear weapons into the Middle East and that "Israel agrees not to use any aircrafts supplied by the US as a nuclear weapons carrier."[95] The following day, Rusk and Clifford met with Johnson at the White House. Clifford subsequently told Warnke that President Johnson was not inclined to seek additional assurances as a precondition for the sale of 50 F-4s.[96]

Rabin and Warnke signed the draft MOU on 27 November based on the following formula: The United States would sell the 50 F-4s in exchange for Israel's reaffirmation of its pledge "not to be the first power in the Middle East to introduce nuclear weapons" and not to use any US-supplied aircraft "as a nuclear weapons carrier."[97] Despite the MOU, the dispute over the precise meaning of

---

[92] "295. Memorandum from the Assistant Secretary of Defense for International Security Affairs (Warnke) to Secretary of Defense Clifford, Re: F-4 Negotiations with Israel, 28 October 1968," *FRUS, 1964–1968, Vol. XX: Arab-Israeli Dispute, 1967–1968* (Washington, DC: GPO, 2001).

[93] Ibid.

[94] "306. Memorandum of Conversation, Re: Negotiations with Israel F-4 and Advanced Weapons, 4 November 1968, 2–2:45 P.M.," *FRUS, 1964–1968, Vol. XX: Arab-Israeli Conflict, 1967–1968* (Washington, DC: GPO, 2001); and "308. Memorandum of Conversation, 5 November 1968, 2:10–2:40 P.M.," Ibid.

[95] "Memorandum of Conversation, 'Negotiations with Israel—F-4 and Advanced Weapons,' 8 November 1968. Top Secret," in William Burr and Avner Cohen, eds., *NSA Electronic Briefing Book no. 189* (Washington, DC: National Security Archive, 2006), http://www2.gwu.edu/~nsarchiv/NSAEBB/NSAEBB189/IN-03b.pdf.

[96] "311. Draft Memorandum for the Record by Harry Schwartz, Re: F-4 Negotiations with the Israelis, 9 November 1969," *FRUS, 1964–1968, Vol. XX: Arab-Israeli Dispute, 1967–1968* (Washington, DC: GPO, 2001).

[97] "Paul C. Warnke to Ambassador Yitzhak Rabin, 27 November 1968. Secret," in William Burr and Avner Cohen, eds., *NSA Electronic Briefing Book no. 189* (Washington, DC: National Security Archive, 2006), http://www2.gwu.edu/~nsarchiv/NSAEBB/NSAEBB189/IN-03d.pdf.

the "no introduction" pledge and over Israel signing the NPT carried over into the Nixon administration.

Nuclear domino theory and neoclassical realist theory would both expect the Johnson administration to be less insistent than the Kennedy administration had been on Eshkol government's compliance with the Dimona complex "visit" agreement. The two theories, however, offer different explanations. Nuclear domino theory attributes the lack of urgency with which Johnson and most of his advisers approached the Dimona inspections to the diminished risk of reaction proliferation by Egypt. There is certainly something to this, but it is an incomplete explanation for the dramatic shifts in the Johnson administration's nonproliferation and arms transfer policies toward Israel between winter 1964 and late autumn 1968.

In the mid-1960s, Johnson and his advisers were not simply concerned about reactive proliferation, but rather the overall distribution of power in the Middle East and the shorter time horizons for growing Soviet influence in the region. The Johnson administration's objective of forestalling Israel's nuclear weapon capability conflicted with its objective of averting containment failure in the region.

The Nixon Administration: F-4 Sales to the Nixon-Meir Understanding (1969–1972)

Like their predecessors, senior officials in the Nixon administration feared that revelations about Israel's nuclear and ballistic missile programs would accelerate Soviet conventional arms sales to Egypt and Syria, thus increasing Soviet influence in the region. Yet, unlike their predecessors, the new administration had to confront an Israel that likely already had workable nuclear explosives and delivery systems. There was also the unresolved matter of the NPT. President Richard M. Nixon and Henry A. Kissinger, then the assistant to the president for national security affairs, were privately skeptical of the NPT, fearing it could harm the United States' relations with key allies. Nonetheless, they knew that they could not repudiate a major treaty championed signed by the previous administration.[98]

---

[98] "Summary of Intelligence Information Gained Concerning Israel's Nuclear Capability, and Its Impact Upon U.S.-Israeli Relations, Top Secret, Department of State, 19 July 1969," *U.S. Declassified Documents Online* (Farmington Hills, MI: Gale, 2007); On Nixon and Kissinger's ambivalence about the NPT, see James Cameron and Or Rabinowitz, "Eight Lost Years? Nixon, Ford, Kissinger, and the Non-Proliferation Regime, 1969–1977," *Journal of Strategic Studies*, Vol. 36, No. 1 (2016), pp. 1–31.

Israel's continuing refusal to sign the NPT, however, posed a challenge to the credibility of US nonproliferation efforts. Henry Owen, the director of the Policy Planning Staff, told Secretary of State William P. Rogers on 7 February, "Israel is rapidly developing a capability to produce and deploy nuclear weapons, and to deliver them by surface-to-surface missile or by plane." Owen further noted that public knowledge of Israeli nuclear capabilities would have far-reaching negative consequences including: the refusal of other nuclear-capable states to sign to the NPT; increased Arab resentment of the United States; and a heightened risk that another Arab-Israeli war might escalate into a superpower confrontation.[99]

Another complication was the transformed US-Israel relationship, which began under Kennedy, who approved the one-time sale of Hawk anti-aircraft missile batteries in 1962.[100] The Johnson administration initially tried to limit US security guarantees to Israel in 1963 and 1964. However, through the transfer of the MC-48 tanks, the A-4 Skyhawks, and the promised transfer of the F-4s, the Johnson administration had effectively forged a de facto alliance with Israel. In a reversal of almost two decades of US foreign policy in the Middle East, by the end of 1968 the United States stood poised to become Israel's principal arms supplier.[101]

Lastly, there were the domestic mobilization hurdles with which the Johnson and Nixon administrations had to contend. The Eshkol government became adept at press leaks and mobilizing sympathetic individuals, organizations, and members of Congress. It used those contacts to frustrate the sale of tanks and APCs to Jordan and later to lobby for the sale of the A-4s and later the F-4s to Israel.[102] The Johnson administration tried to link the F-4 sale to an Israeli signature on the NPT, but eventually agreed to compromise language in the November 1968 MOU on the F-4 sale, in part due to the intervention of the pro-Israel members of Congress.[103] This meant the Nixon administration would have to overcome higher domestic mobilization hurdles in order to pursue any

---

[99] "Henry Owen to the Secretary, 'Impact on U.S. Policies of an Israeli Nuclear Weapons Capability,' 7 February 1969. Secret/Nodis/Noforn," in William Burr and Avner Cohen, eds., *NSA Electronic Briefing Book no. 189* (Washington, DC: National Security Archive, 2006), http://www2.gwu.edu/~nsarchiv/NSAEBB/NSAEBB189/IN-05.pdf.

[100] Abraham Ben-Zvi, *John F. Kennedy and the Politics of Arms Sales to Israel* (London: Frank Cass, 2002).

[101] See "Report to the President by the National Security Council, United States Policy Toward Arms Shipments to the Near East, NSC 65-3, Top Secret, 17 May 1950," *DNSA Collection: Presidential Directives* (Ann Arbor, MI: ProQuest, 2015).

[102] Douglas Little, "The Making of a Special Relationship: The United States and Israel, 1957–68," *International Journal of Middle East Studies*, Vol. 25, No. 4 (1993), pp. 563–585.

[103] "290. Action Memorandum from Walt Rostow to President Johnson, re: Strong Israeli Reaction to Eban Talks Here, 25 October 1968, 2:20 P.M.," *FRUS, 1964–1968, Vol. XX: Arab-Israeli Conflict, 1967–1968* (Washington, DC: GPO, 2001).

type of coercive strategy toward Israel in 1969 than did the Kennedy administration just seven years earlier.

Warnke, a holdover appointee from the Johnson administration, reintroduced the idea of linking the F-4 sale to an Israeli commitment to sign the NPT. He urged Secretary of Defense Melvin P. Laird to "consider another serious, concerted, and sustained effort to persuade Israel to halt its work on strategic missiles and nuclear weapons."[104] Laird and Deputy Secretary of Defense David Packard recommend that Nixon deliver an ultimatum to Israel's new prime minister, Golda Meir, to "cease and desist" from the "development or acquisition" of nuclear weapons and strategic missiles and to provide private assurances that Israel would sign the NPT. The delivery of the F-4s could be used as leverage. In exchange, Laird and Packard suggested offering Israel "steady military assistance," but not a mutual defense treaty.[105] Assistant Secretary of State for Near Eastern Affairs Joseph J. Sisto wrote to Rogers on 4 March that in order to make a credible threat, the administration should be "prepared to have the issue become public and to defend [its] position in the face of domestic pressure." Short of that, Sisto argued, "It would be futile and probably counterproductive for the US . . . to use Israeli requests for conventional weapons as leverage on this issue."[106]

National Security Study Memorandum 40 (NSSM 40), issued 11 April 1969, tasked Laird, Rogers, and Director of Central Intelligence (DCI) Richard Helms with preparing a report on the latest intelligence on Israeli nuclear activities,

---

[104] "Assistant Secretary of Defense for International Security Affairs [ISA] Paul Warnke to Secretary of Defense [Melvin Laird], 'Stopping the Introduction of Nuclear Weapons into the Middle East,' 15 February 1969, with Attached Record of Rabin-Warnke Conversations, October-November 1968, Top Secret, Excised Copy," in William Burr and Avner Cohen, eds., *NSA Electronic Briefing Book no. 485* (Washington, DC: Digital National Security Archive, 2014), http://www2.gwu.edu/~nsarchiv/nukevault/ebb485/docs/Doc%201%202-15-69%20Warnke%20report.pdf.

[105] "A. Routing Slip to 'Col P' [Robert E. Pursley], with Table of Contents Attached, Listing Five Documents: B. Secretary of Defense Memo to Secretary of State et al., 17 March 1969, Top Secret, Excised Copy C. Deputy Secretary of Defense Memorandum to Laird, 14 March 1969, Top Secret, Excised Copy D. Secretary Rogers Letter to SECDEF, 28 March 1969, Top Secret E. Joint Chiefs of Staff Memorandum on 'Nuclear Missile Capability in Israel,' 26 March 1969, Top Secret, Excised Copy F. International Security Affairs/Ralph Earle Memorandum, 'Stopping the Introduction of Nuclear Weapons into the Middle East,' 29 March 1969, Top Secret, Excised Copy," in William Burr and Avner Cohen, eds., *NSA Electronic Briefing Book no. 485* (Washington, DC: National Security Archive, 2014), http://www2.gwu.edu/~nsarchiv/nukevault/ebb485/docs/Doc%204A%205-5-69%20stash%20re%20Feb%201969.pdf.

[106] "Joseph J. Sisto to the Secretary, 'Israel's Nuclear Policy and Implications for the United States,' 3 April 1969. Secret/Nodis," in William Burr and Avner Cohen, eds., *NSA Electronic Briefing Book no. 189* (Washington, DC: National Security Archives, 2006), http://www2.gwu.edu/~nsarchiv/NSAEBB/NSAEBB189/IN-07.pdf.

and laying out a set of recommendations.[107] The report, submitted in late May, concluded, "The disadvantages of US global interests are such that a major US effort to induce Israel not to produce nuclear weapons is justified." The United States "should make it clear to Israel that if it elects to pursue a [nuclear] weapons program, it will be imposing a major strain on US-Israel relations, with serious risks to the US ability to continue to meet Israel's conventional arms requirements." If, on the other hand, Israel "were to sign the NPT, while maintaining the technical option to produce nuclear weapons, the US would see to it that Israel received military equipment to maintain its conventional superiority over Arab forces."[108] The only area of disagreement was over *how* to get Israel to sign the NPT with the Office of the Secretary of Defense (OSD) and the JCS favoring a threat to withhold the F-4s and other equipment, and the State Department favoring a more moderate approach.[109]

In late June 1969, Kissinger chaired two NSC Senior Review Group (SRG) meetings—consisting of Packard, Richardson, Helms, and Wheeler—to discuss how to persuade the Israeli government to both sign the NPT and refrain from testing a nuclear weapon.[110] Wheeler observed that if the Israelis were to deploy

---

[107] "National Security Study Memorandum [NSSM] No. 40, Memorandum from Henry Kissinger to Secretary of State, Secretary of Defense, and Director of Central Intelligence, 'Israeli Nuclear Weapons Program,' [Excerpted from Document 7 Below], 11 April 1969, Top Secret," in William Burr and Avner Cohen, eds., *NSA Electronic Briefing Book no. 485* (Washington, DC: National Security Archive, 2014), http://www2.gwu.edu/~nsarchiv/nukevault/ebb485/docs/Doc%205%20%20NSSM%2040.pdf.

[108] John P. Walsh, State Department Executive Secretary to Assistant to the President for National Security Affairs et al., "Israeli Nuclear Weapons Program—NSSM 40," 30 May 1969, Enclosing Report from Rodger Davies to Henry Kissinger: "Memorandum of Issues and 'Basic Study,'" Top Secret, Excised Copy," in William Burr and Avner Cohen, eds., *NSA Electronic Briefing Book no. 485* (Washington, DC: Digital National Security Archive, 2014), http://www2.gwu.edu/~nsarchiv/nukevault/ebb485/docs/Doc%206%205-30-69%20NSSM%2040%20report.pdf.

[109] "Undated Table of Contents Listing: 1. Deputy Secretary of Defense Memo, 'Israeli Nuclear Program,' 14 July 1969, with 'Scenario for Discussions with Israelis on Their Nuclear Program, and NSSM 40,' Attached, Top Secret; 2. Harry Schwartz Memorandum to Deputy Secretary of Defense, 27 June 1969; Director of Central Intelligence Agency Memorandum on "Israeli Nuclear Weapons Program—NSSM 40," 11 July 1969 [Either Not Declassified or Not in File], Top Secret," in William Burr and Avner Cohen, eds., *NSA Electronic Briefing Book no. 485* (Washington, DC: National Security Archive, 2014), http://nsarchive.gwu.edu/nukevault/ebb485/docs/Doc%209%20July%201969%20%20misc%20docs.pdf; "Unsigned Memorandum from Office of the Secretary, with Enclosed Announcement of Meeting of Ad Hoc Committee on NSSM 40, and 'Talking Paper for the Deputy Secretary of Defense and the Chairman, Joint Chiefs of Staff,' 18 June 1969," in William Burr and Avner Cohen, eds., *History and Public Policy Program Digital Archive* (Washington, DC: Wilson Center, 2017), http://digitalarchive.wilsoncenter.org/document/121097.

[110] "Rodger Davies to Mr. Austin et al., 'Review Group Consideration of Response to NSSM-40 29 June 1969,' 30 June 1969. Top Secret/Nodis," in William Burr and Avner Cohen, eds., *NSA Electronic Briefing Book no. 189* (Washington, DC: National Security Archive, 2006), http://nsarchive.gwu.edu/NSAEBB/NSAEBB189/IN-09.pdf.

surface-to-surface missiles, the Arab states might infer those missiles were nuclear-armed. Kissinger observed, "even if they suspected strongly the Israelis had nuclear warheads, they might decide to live with that fact as long as it did not become an announced fact of international life."[111]

On 16 July, Kissinger told Richardson that he was "very leery" of threatening to cut off the F-4 sale.[112] Three days later, he sent a six-page memorandum to Nixon arguing that "Israel's secret possession of nuclear weapons would increase the potential danger in the Middle East, and we do not desire complicity in it." He went on to make an important distinction, "In this case, public knowledge is almost as the possession itself," since the former "might spark a Soviet nuclear guarantee for the Arabs, tighten the Soviet hold on the Arabs, and increase the danger of our involvement."[113]

Public confirmation of Israeli nuclear capabilities, whether in the form of an underground nuclear test or a public declaration, would increase the likelihood of containment failure in the Middle East. He added that it was also possible the Kremlin recognized that disclosure might increase the risk of a superpower confrontation and therefore "the Soviets might have an incentive not to know."[114] The SRG agreed on three broad objectives: (1) persuade Israel to sign the NPT; (2) get written assurances that Israel would not introduce nuclear weapons into the Middle East, specifying "introduction" meant the possession of a nuclear explosive device; and (3) obtain written assurances that Israel would not produce or deploy the Jericho missile or any other nuclear-capable missile.[115]

The Meir government would likely not take the US position seriously, Kissinger reasoned, unless the Nixon administration was prepared to withhold something of value, such as the F-4s. If the administration withheld that F-4s and the Israelis made that decision public, then the administration would face enormous domestic pressure. "We will be in an indefensible position if we cannot explain why we are withholding the planes," Kissinger observed, adding, "Yet if we

---

[111] "35. Memorandum for the Record, Re: NSC Ad Hoc Review Group Meeting on NSSM 40—Israeli Nuclear Program, 20 June 1969," *FRUS, 1969–1976, Vol. XXIII: Arab-Israeli Dispute, 1969–1973* (Washington, DC: GPO, 2015), p. 118.

[112] "Telcon, Elliott Richardson with Mr. Kissinger, 16 July 1969, 5:55 P.M.," in William Burr and Avner Cohen, eds., *NSA Electronic Briefing Book no. 189* (Washington, DC: National Security Archive, 2006), http://www2.gwu.edu/~nsarchiv/NSAEBB/NSAEBB189/IN-12.pdf.

[113] "38. Memorandum from the President's Assistant for National Security Affairs (Kissinger) to President Nixon, Re: Israel's Nuclear Program, 19 July 1969," *FRUS, 1969–1976, Vol. XXIII: Arab-Israeli Dispute, 1969–1972* (Washington, DC: GPO, 2015), pp. 131–135.

[114] Ibid.

[115] "Memorandum from Henry Kissinger to President Nixon, 'Israeli Nuclear Program,' N.D., with Enclosures Dated 19 July 1969, Top Secret, Excised Copy," in William Burr and Avner Cohen, eds., *NSA Electronic Briefing Book no. 485* (Washington, DC: National Security Archive, 2014), http://www2.gwu.edu/~nsarchiv/nukevault/ebb485/docs/Doc%2010%207-19-69%20circa.pdf.

explain our position publicly, we will be the ones to make Israel's possession of nuclear weapons public with all the international consequences this entails."[116] Therefore, he recommended Richardson and Packard avoid any explicit linkage in the first phase of negotiations. If, however, Rabin did not agree to restraining the Israeli nuclear program, Kissinger would summon him to the White House and make the linkage explicit.[117]

Richardson met with Rabin on 29 July. He asked if the Meir government would sign the NPT, interpret the "no introduction" pledge to mean non-possession of a nuclear weapon, and not produce or deploy the Jericho strategic missile. Richardson did not make any link between Israel's responses and the Nixon administration's approval of the F-4 transfers. Rabin merely reiterated the "no introduction" pledge. He added that the Meir government was still studying the NPT and that he was not in a position to make commitments on the Jericho missiles.[118] A second meeting on 28 August between Richardson and Rabin also made little progress.[119]

On 29 September 1969, Meir met privately with Nixon in the Oval Office, while Kissinger and Rogers met separately with Rabin and other Israel Embassy officials in the Cabinet Room.[120] Although there is no actual record of this meeting, it is understood that Nixon and Meir reached the following understanding:[121] Israel would neither confirm nor deny it possessed nuclear weapons and delivery systems. Israel would also refrain from detonating a nuclear device

---

[116] Ibid.

[117] Ibid.

[118] "Acting Secretary of State Elliot Richardson to the President, 'Israel's Nuclear Program,' with Memorandum of Conversation Attached, 1 August 1969, Top Secret/Nodis," in William Burr and Avner Cohen, eds., *NSA Electronic Briefing Book no. 189* (Washington, DC: National Security Archives, 2006), http://nsarchive.gwu.edu/NSAEBB/NSAEBB189/IN-15.pdf.

[119] "Elliot Richardson to the President, 'Israel's Nuclear Program,' 28 August 1969. Top Secret/Nodis," in William Burr and Avner Cohen, eds., *NSA Electronic Briefing Book no. 189* (Washington, DC: National Security Archive, 2006), http://www2.gwu.edu/~nsarchiv/NSAEBB/NSAEBB189/IN-18.pdf.

[120] "Secretary of State William Rogers to President Nixon, 'Suggested Position for You to Take with Israeli Prime Minister Meir During Her Forthcoming Visit,' 18 September 1969, with Excerpt from Briefing Paper Attached. Top Secret/Nodis," in William Burr and Avner Cohen, eds., *NSA Electronic Briefing Book no. 189* (Washington, DC: National Security Archive, 2006), http://www2.gwu.edu/~nsarchiv/NSAEBB/NSAEBB189/IN-20.pdf. On Roger and Kissinger's concurrent meeting with Rabin, see "52. Memorandum of Conversation, Secretary Rogers, Dr. Henry A. Kissinger, et al., with Ambassador Yitzhak Rabin, et al., 25 September 1969," *FRUS, 1969–1976, Vol. XXIII: Arab-Israeli Conflict, 1969–1972* (Washington, DC: GPO, 2015), pp. 178–184.

[121] "Harold H. Saunders to Kissinger, 8 December 1969, with Barbour Letter to Sisco, 19 November 1969. Secret/Nodis," in William Burr and Avner Cohen, eds., *NSA Electronic Briefing Book no. 189* (Washington, DC: National Security Archive, 2006), http://www2.gwu.edu/~nsarchiv/NSAEBB/NSAEBB189/IN-26.pdf.

or using any US-made aircraft to carry a nuclear weapon. In exchange, the United States would no longer press Israel to sign the NPT and the annual "visits" of Dimona would end. Furthermore, the United States would become Israel's principal arms supplier.[122]

Subsequent communication between Kissinger and Rabin confirmed the administration's willingness to accept the following: (1) Israel would not become a "nuclear power," which the NPT defined as a state that detonated a nuclear explosive device prior to 1 January 1967; (2) Israel would not deploy strategic missiles until at least 1972; and (3) that, after the general election on 28 October 1969, the new Israeli government would consider signing the nonproliferation treaty.[123] On the third point, Rabin informed Kissinger on 23 February 1970, "He wanted the President to know in light of the conversation between the President and Golda Meir [in September 1969] that Israel had no intention of signing the NPT."[124]

What might explain the Nixon administration's reversal on linking the sale of the F-4s to Israeli concessions on signing the NPT, ceasing production and deployment of the strategic missiles, and acceptance of the US interpretation of the "non-introduction of nuclear weapons" pledge? Cohen contends that the decision not to link the F-4 sale to Israel signing the NPT was indicative of Nixon's toleration of Israeli proliferation and consistent with the Nixon Doctrine (or Guam Doctrine), which called upon allies to assume a greater share of responsibility for containing the Soviet Union's influence and maintaining stability in their respective regions.[125] Or Rabinowitz and Nicholas Miller take issue with Cohen's explanation, noting that like the three previous administrations, the Nixon administration saw the Israeli nuclear program as detrimental to US interests. They contend that when Nixon and Kissinger realized they could not forestall Israeli nuclear proliferation, they sought to limit the negative

---

[122] Avner Cohen and William Burr, "Israel Crosses the Threshold," *Bulletin of the Atomic Scientists*, Vol. 62, No. 3 (2006), pp. 22–30.

[123] "55. Memorandum from the President's Assistant for National Security Affairs (Kissinger) to President Nixon, Re: Rabin's Proposed Assurances on Israeli Nuclear Policy, 8 October 1969," *FRUS, 1969–1976, Vol. XXIII: Arab-Israeli Dispute, 1969–1972* (Washington, DC: GPO, 2015), https://history.state.gov/historicaldocuments/frus1969-76v23/d55.

[124] "Memorandum of Conversation Between Assistant to the President for National Security Affairs Henry Kissinger and Israeli Ambassador Yitzhak Rabin, 23 February 1970, Top Secret/Sensitive," *DNSA collection: Kissinger Conversations: Supplement I, 1969–1977* (Ann Arbor, MI: ProQuest, 2016), p. 2, http://search.proquest.com.ezproxy.library.tufts.edu/docview/1679087713?accountid=14434.

[125] Avner Cohen, *The Worst-Kept Secret: Israel's Bargain with the Bomb* (New York: Columbia University Press, 2010), pp. 23–28.

consequences, namely accelerated Soviet arms transfers to Egypt and Syria and undermining the NPT.[126]

Nixon, Kissinger, and other administration officials appear to have been less concerned about reactive proliferation by the Arab states than were their predecessors. Indeed, in April 1968, Rusk told Eban that US intelligence did not foresee "any Arab nuclear capability in the foreseeable future."[127] At this point, nuclear domino theory (or at least the hypothesis set out in chapter 2) essentially drops out as a plausible alternative explanation for Nixon administration's policies. According to a July 1969 State Department assessment, the main negative consequences of overt Israeli nuclear weapons possession were a heightened risk of US-Soviet military confrontation in the Middle East, a sharp reduction in the chance for an Arab-Israeli peace settlement, accusations of US complicity in the Israeli nuclear effort, and the collapse of the NPT.[128]

Kissinger and Laird agreed that avoiding a superpower confrontation in the Middle East was the top priority. Kissinger observed the Israeli nuclear problem "could draw USSR even more into the Mid-East with some form of guarantee for the Arabs."[129] Richardson opined, "Our main diplomatic effort . . . has been predicated on concern over the risk of an US-USSR confrontation in the Middle East." The Arab states' discovery of an Israeli nuclear weapons capability, he warned, "would seem to increase the likelihood of a local confrontation—increasing [the] possibility of [the] eventual involvement of the US and USSR." Wheeler concurred, warning "the Arabs might even go to war to prevent Israel from achieving full nuclear capability, while the Soviets 'rattled their own rockets in the background.'"[130] By late summer 1969, however, Nixon and Kissinger

---

[126] Or Rabinowitz and Nicholas L. Miller, "Keeping the Bombs in the Basement: U.S. Nonproliferation Policy Toward Israel, South Africa, and Pakistan," *International Security*, Vol. 40, No. 1 (2015), pp. 47–86.

[127] "155. Telegram from the Department of State to the Embassy in Israel, Re: Letter from Secretary of State Rusk to Israeli Foreign Minister Eban, 28 April 1968," *FRUS, 1964–1968, Vol. XX: Arab-Israeli Dispute, 1967–1968* (Washington, DC: GPO, 2001), https://history.state.gov/historicaldocuments/frus1964-68v20/d155.

[128] "Summary of Intelligence Information Gained Concerning Israel's Nuclear Capability, and Its Impact upon U.S.-Israeli Relations, Top Secret, Department of State, 19 July 1969," *US Declassified Documents Online* (Farmington Hills, MI: Gale, 2007), http://tinyurl.galegroup.com/tinyurl/3bptP6.

[129] "5. Minutes of a National Security Council Meeting, 4 February 1969, 10 A.M.," *FRUS, 1969–1976, Vol. XXIII: Arab-Israeli Dispute, 1969–1972* (Washington, DC: GPO, 2015), https://history.state.gov/historicaldocuments/frus1969-76v23/d5.

[130] "35. Memorandum for the Record, Re: NSC Ad Hoc Review Group Meeting on NSSM 40—Israeli Nuclear Program, 20 June 1969," *FRUS, 1969–1976, Vol. XXIII: Arab-Israeli Conflict, 1969–1972* (Washington, DC: GPO, 2015), https://history.state.gov/historicaldocuments/frus1969-76v23/d35.

became willing to accept Israel as a nuclear-armed state, as long as Israel's nuclear weapons capability remained opaque.[131]

It was worth remembering that while US newspapers periodically reported on AEC scientists' visits to Dimona and the rumors of Israeli nuclear and missile programs since 1959, much of the US-Israel nonproliferation dispute occurred behind closed doors. The "no introduction of nuclear weapons" pledge in the March 1965 MOU for the A-4 Skyhawks, as well as the reaffirmation of that pledge in the November 1968 MOU for the F-4s, were not public information at the time. The CIA apparently did not share intelligence on Israel's nuclear program with Congress until July 1970. Comments by Senator Stuart Symington (D-MO), a member of the Foreign Relations Committee, about a "somber appraisal" of the Israeli nuclear program given by Helms prompted the New York Times to run a front page story.[132] Threatening to withhold the F-4s to coerce Israeli compliance on the nuclear issue risked the Meir government making its dispute public, thus upending the goal of keeping Israel's nuclear capability from becoming "an internationally established fact." Kissinger believed that if the administration held up the deliveries of the F-4s, "The Jewish community in the United States would run amok and make a public confrontation."[133]

On 6 November 1969, Kissinger initiated National Security Study Memoranda (NSSM) 81 and 82. NSSM 81 directed an NSC Ad-hoc Group to "examine the balance of Arab/Israeli military capabilities given alternative levels of US and Soviet armaments over the next five years" and to "analyze Israel's force requirements to meet a variety of alternative defense objections," including the maintenance of general deterrence, and the preemption of an attack by its neighbors.[134] NSSM 82 directed a study of economic policy toward Israel including "the availability of foreign exchange ... to finance Israel's defense requirements" and "the alternative means of financing US economic assistance to Israel."[135]

---

[131] For a discussion of the strategy of nuclear opacity, see Avner Cohen and Benjamin Frankel, "Opaque Nuclear Proliferation," Journal of Strategic Studies, Vol. 13, No. 3 (1990), pp. 14–44.

[132] Hendrick Smith, "U.S. Assumes the Israelis Have A-Bomb or Its Parts," New York Times, 18 July 1970, 1.

[133] "35. Memorandum for the Record, Re: NSC Ad Hoc Review Group Meeting on NSSM 40—Israeli Nuclear Program, 20 June 1969," FRUS, 1969–1976, Vol. XXIII: Arab-Israeli Conflict, 1969–1972 (Washington, DC: GPO, 2015), https://history.state.gov/historicaldocuments/frus1969-76v23/d35.

[134] "National Security Study Memorandum No. 81, Re: US Arms Transfer Policy Toward Israel, 6 November 1969, Secret/Sensitive," US Declassified Documents Online (Farmington Hills, MI: Gale, 2009), http://tinyurl.galegroup.com/tinyurl/3k7Jv9.

[135] "National Security Study Memorandum No. 82, Re: US Economic Assistance Policy Toward Israel, 6 November 1969, Secret/Sensitive," US Declassified Documents Online (Farmington Hills, MI: Gale, 2009), http://tinyurl.galegroup.com/tinyurl/3k7Jw7.

Egypt's War of Attrition against Israel had been ongoing for several months by the time of Nixon and Meir's first meeting. Preoccupied with the Vietnam War and other issues, Nixon initially delegated responsibility for managing the Arab-Israeli conflict to Rogers and the State Department. Skirmishes between Israeli and Egyptian forces in the Suez Canal Zone continued, despite the parallel efforts by Rogers and the UN special representative for the Middle East, Gunnar Jarring, to broker Arab-Israeli peace negotiations along the line of UN Security Council Resolution 242.[136] Helms wrote to Nixon in September 1969 that "The re-equipment of the Egyptian military has been accomplished more rapidly than the Israelis had expected. By 1970 the number of aircraft and tanks in the Egyptian armed forces will be double that of June 1967." He added, "The only reason why renewed full-scale war has not erupted since 1967 is because the Arabs and the Soviets have concluded their chances of waging a successful battle are in doubt."[137] According to an INR assessment, "Were the Arabs and the Soviets to conclude that Israel's capacity for long-term defense planning is now to be subjected to the limitations of a restrictive aircraft supply, the prospects of all-out war will automatically increase."[138]

The Israeli request to purchase an additional 25 F-4s and 100 A-4s created yet another dilemma. Officials in Washington sought to strike a balance between selling Israel enough arms to defend the ceasefire line, but not enough to enable Israel to escalate to full-scale hostilities with Egypt.[139] "The sale of sophisticated equipment carries the implied obligation to continue supply regardless of the Israeli use of the equipment," Kissinger wrote to Nixon on 28 August.[140]

---

[136] For the documentary history of Jarring missions (1969–1970) and the Rogers Middle East Peace Plan (1969), see *FRUS, 1969–1976, Vol. XXIII: Arab-Israeli Dispute, 1969–1972* (Washington, DC: GPO, 2013). Also see William B. Quandt, *Peace Process: American Diplomacy and the Arab-Israeli Conflict Since 1967* (Washington, DC: Brookings Institution Press, 2005), chapter 3. See "UNSC Resolution 242 of 22 November 1967," https://documents-dds-ny.un.org/doc/RESOLUTION/GEN/NR0/240/94/PDF/NR024094.pdf (accessed 2 May 2017).

[137] "Memorandum from Richard Helms for President Nixon, 24 September 1969," folder "Israel Vol. II: June 1, 1969 to Sep 20, 1969," box 605, NSC Files, Country Files (Yorba Linda, CA: RMNL, 1969), p. 5.

[138] "The Situation in the Middle East—Summary, 24 September 1969," folder "Israel Vol. II: 1 June 1969 to 20 Sept. 1969," box 605, NSC Files, Country Files (Yorba Linda, CA: RMNL 1969).

[139] "U.S. Military Assistance Policy Toward Israel [Attribution to National Security Council Based on Format], Top Secret, 9 December 1969," *DNSA Collection: Presidential Directives on National Security. Part I. From Truman to Clinton* (Ann Arbor, MI: ProQuest, 2015), p. 33, http://search.proquest.com.docview/1679053044.

[140] "47. Memorandum from the President's Assistant for National Security Affairs (Kissinger) to President Nixon, 10 September 1969," *FRUS, 1969–1976, Vol. XXIII: Arab-Israeli Dispute, 1969–1972* (Washington, DC: GPO, 2015).

Conceivably, a militarily strong Israel might help the United States frustrate the Soviet Union's designs in the Middle East. "Assume for the sake of discussion that there is no domestic political pressure and that there is no moral question of continuing support, would the US foreign policy interests be served by dumping Israel?" During a 10 December 1969 NSC meeting, Nixon stated, "Looking at this from the Soviet viewpoint, if we save [Egypt's] bacon, the Soviets would gain by our act. In my view, Soviet-US relations are the overriding concern," according to the president.[141] Yet, there was still the risk the sale of more sophisticated combat aircraft and additional weapons might embolden a nuclear-armed Israel into launching a full-scale retaliation against Egypt, which would heighten Soviet involvement in the region.

Nixon decided to postpone a decision on the Israeli request for the additional F-4s in March 1970, concluding, "our detailed analysis has identified no military need for the additional aircraft Israel has requested for the time being. If as a result of actions by others, in particular the Soviet Union or France, or as a result of unusual losses, Israel's clear-cut air superiority is threatened, we would be in a position to move quickly to maintain Israel's margin of safety."[142] The Meir government argued the balance of power was rapidly shifting against Israel. The Soviets accelerated arms shipments to Egypt, culminating in the deployment of the SA-3 anti-aircraft missile batteries and Soviet military personnel to operate them. According to report from the Israeli Embassy in Washington, "With the presence of missiles, Israel has no choice but to face the prospect of increased air losses at the very time when its request for more aircraft is being held up." The report's authors warned, "This is a new situation ... represents a material shift in the balance of power."[143]

Despite Israeli claims, some Nixon administration officials concluded the balance of power would favor Israel for the next few years. Laird wrote to Kissinger in April 1970 that he "cannot realistically conceive of a situation in which both we and Israel would not have substantial warning—probably several weeks or months—of any developments sufficiently adverse as either to require the necessity of additional aircraft, or to necessitate emergency resupply." He added

---

[141] "74. Minutes of a National Security Council Meeting, 10 December 1969, 10 A.M.," *FRUS, 1969–1976, Vol. XXIII: Arab-Israeli Dispute, 1969–1972* (Washington, DC: GPO, 2015), pp. 239–257, at p. 254.

[142] "Department of State Telegram 29464, 21 March 1970," folder "Israel Vol. IV: 01 Mar 70 to 21 May 70," box 606, Country Files, NSC Files (Yorba Linda, CA: RMNL, 1970).

[143] "'The US Response to Israel's Aircraft Needs—an Assessment,' Embassy of Israel, Washington, DC, 26 March 1970," folder "Israel Vol. IV: 01 Mar 70 to 21 May 70," box 606, Country Files, NSC Files (Yorba Linda, CA: RMNL, 1970).

that by transferring additional F-4s, the United States would essentially give the IAF a "ready reserve" and thus encourage "Israeli high-risk attack policies."[144]

Fears that providing additional combat aircraft might embolden the Israelis into launching air strikes deeper into Egyptian territory, which would result in even more Soviet arms sales to Egypt and/or the outbreak of another Arab-Israeli war, were recurrent themes in memoranda sent by various senior and mid-level officials. In the words of one State Department analyst, "The USSR senses that, with the US boxed in by commitments to Israel, long-term trends are strongly in its favor throughout the Arab world."[145]

Officials also worried that providing Israel with a stronger security guarantee would undermine their efforts to negotiate a political settlement. While noting that the presence of Soviet forces in Egypt was a "geo-political fact of the greatest consequence," Kissinger also argued that "a defense treaty with Israel would call on us to pay too high a political price in the Arab countries."[146] An earlier interagency study concluded that it would not be in Washington's interests "to offer a firm, formal guarantee of Israel's security. We should avoid any open-ended and uncontrollable commitment because it would subordinate the United States to Israeli concepts of defense and security, and because it would polarize the area between us and the USSR."[147]

By summer 1970, the deployment of SA-2 and SA-3 anti-aircraft missiles to the Suez Canal Zone, the growing number of Soviet military advisers, and Soviet MIG jets providing cover for Egyptian ground forces, prompted Nixon administration officials to reconsider.[148] Rogers wrote to Nixon in June that "Your decision in March to hold in abeyance Israel's request for additional aircraft was based on the judgment that Israel's qualitative superiority compensated amply for its numerical inferiority in planes." Since March, he noted, "the Soviet presence has

---

[144] "Memorandum for the Assistant to the President for National Security Affairs from Secretary of Defense Melvin Laird, Re: Military Assistance to Israel, 6 April 1970," folder "Israel Vol. IV: 01 Mar 70 to 21 May 70," box 606, Country Files, NSC Files, (Yorba Linda, CA: RMNL, 1970).

[145] See "Memorandum by David E. Mark (INR), Undated," folder "Israel Vol. IV: 01 Mar 70 to 21 May 70," box 606 (Yorba Linda, CA: RMNL, 1970). Also see "Memorandum to Henry A. Kissinger from Ambassador Charles W. Yost, 18 May 1970," folder "Israel Vol. IV: 01 Mar 70 to 21 May 70," box 606, Country Files, NSC Files (Yorba Linda, CA: RMNL, 1970).

[146] "119. Memorandum for the Record, Re: Meeting of the NSC Special Review Group on the Middle East, 28 May 1970," *FRUS, 1969–1976, Vol. XXIII: Arab-Israeli Dispute, 1969–1972* (Washington, DC: GPO, 2015), pp. 394–399.

[147] "8. Paper Prepared by the Interdepartmental Group for Near East and South Asia, NSCIG/NEA 69–2a (Revised), 'Further Studies on Middle East Policy,' 20 February 1969," *FRUS, 1969–1976, Vol. XXIII: Arab-Israeli Dispute, 1969–1972* (Washington, DC: GPO, 2015) pp. 30–39.

[148] "Cable from Dick Kennedy to Winston Lord, Enclosing Memorandum for the Secretary of Defense, Re: Israeli Requests for ECM against SA-2 and SA-3 Missiles, 4 July 1970," folder "Israel Vol. V [1 of 3]: 22 May 70–Jul 70," Country Files, NSC Files (Yorba Linda, CA: RMNL, 1970).

reduced the Israeli qualitative superiority" and "the Arab-Israeli military balance now depends on Soviet actions and decisions which have already created a situation in which Israel's air superiority could be rapidly neutralized."[149]

The Meir government requested electronic jamming equipment to counter the SA-2 and SA-3 missiles, but Laird opined, "to provide this capability would, of course, give the Israelis the ability to mount deep raids against Soviet manned targets in Egypt." He sought written guarantees that the Israelis would only use the jamming equipment along the canal.[150] In a meeting with Laird and other Defense Department officials, Rabin offered assurances that Israeli jets would not attack Soviet positions in the Egyptian heartland. He reiterated Israel's interest in purchasing additional F-4s and A-4s on an accelerated delivery schedule, as well as cluster bombs (CBUs), AGM-45 Shrike anti-radiation surface-to-air missiles, unmanned aerial vehicles, and RF-4Cs, which were F-4s modified for surveillance missions.[151] While Laird and Packard remained wary of the Israeli request, Kissinger argued, "The provision of more security to Israel to enable her to cope with Egyptians would be the factor most likely to deter Israeli thoughts of attack."[152]

After a second meeting with Meir in September 1970, Nixon directed Rogers and Laird to develop "a suitable further package of military equipment to offset the military advantages gained by the [Egyptians] in violations of the military standstill" and to make recommendations for Israel's longer-term equipment needs in 1971 and 1972.[153] Nasser's death in September 1970 and the ascension of Anwar al-Sadat to the Egyptian presidency appeared to provide an opening to break the Egyptian-Israeli stalemate. While Sadat did make some early overtures to Washington, including an extension of the August 1970 ceasefire and offers to draw down Egyptian forces in the canal zone, the Israelis refused to negotiate.[154]

---

[149] "123. Memorandum from Secretary of State Rogers to President Nixon, Re: Next Steps in the Middle East, 9 June 1970," *FRUS, 1969–1976, Vol. XXIII: Arab-Israeli Dispute, 1969–1972* (Washington, DC: GPO, 2015), pp. 415–418.

[150] "Cable from Dick Kennedy to Winston Lord, Enclosing Memorandum for the Secretary of Defense, Re: Israeli Requests for ECM against SA-2 and SA-3 Missiles, 4 July 1970," folder "Israel Vol. V [1 of 3]: 22 May 70–Jul 70," Country Files, NSC Files (Yorba Linda, CA: RMNL, 1970).

[151] "Memorandum of Conversation, Re: Discussion with Ambassador Yitzhak Rabin About Israeli Military and Financial Requirements, 29 July 1970," folder "Israel Vol. V [1 of 3]: 22 May 70–Jul 70," box 607, Country Files, NSC Files (Yorba Linda, CA: RMNL, 1970).

[152] "Memorandum for the President from Henry Kissinger, re: Israel Intentions to Resume Bombing Raids, 29 September 1970," folder "Israel August 1, 1970–September 30, 1970," box 607, Country Files, NSC Files (Yorba Linda, CA: RMNL, 1970).

[153] "163. Memorandum from President Nixon to Secretary of State Rogers and Secretary of Defense Laird, re: Follow up Actions with Israel, 23 September 1970," *FRUS, 1969–1976, Vol. XXIII: Arab-Israeli Dispute, 1969–1972* (Washington, DC: GPO, 2015).

[154] "195. Minutes of a Senior Review Group Meeting, 11 January 1971, 10:55–11:45 A.M," *FRUS, 1969–1976, Vol. XXIII: Arab-Israeli Dispute, 1969–1972* (Washington, DC: GPO, 2015).

Kissinger wrote to Nixon in December 1970 about the "progress the Soviet Union has recently made in establishing hegemony in the Near East," noting that "the Soviets have . . . substantially increased their military presence in the region" in the past year.[155] He recommended a military assistance package for Israel designed to achieve three objectives: (1) to alleviate Israeli security concerns and thus enable the United States to pressure Israel to make territorial concessions; (2) to make the Arab states realize that any peace settlement would depend on cooperation with Washington, not Moscow; and (3) to make the Kremlin realize that its Middle East strategies threatened vital US interests and therefore risked superpower confrontation.[156] Nixon stated during an NSC meeting in late February 1971, "We will go all the way with Israel in maintaining the military balance in its favor." He added, however, "If Israel starts a conflict where it has been responsible for the breakdown in the peace talks, it cannot count on US support."[157] Accordingly, Nixon withheld the shipment of the additional F-4s and A-4s to Israel throughout 1971, despite repeated pleas from the Israeli government and contrary to Kissinger's recommendations.[158]

Rogers held talks with Sadat about an interim settlement in the Suez Canal Zone and the removal of the Soviet military personnel from Egypt.[159] In late May 1971, Nixon wrote to Rogers that "Under no circumstances would I take a position on aid to Israel which I felt would be in conflict with the national security interests of the United States." Furthermore, on the question of an interim settlement in the Suez, the president felt Meir and other Israeli leaders "diddled us along through the 1970 election and now are planning to follow the same tactics through the 1972 elections." Nixon said he came "Hard on the side of

---

[155] "Memorandum for the President from Kissinger, Re: The Middle East, December 1970," folder "Israel December 1–January 30, 1970," box 608, Country Files, NSC Files (Yorba Linda, CA: RMNL, 1970).

[156] "Memorandum for the President from Kissinger, Re: The Middle East, December 1970," folder "Israel December 1–January 30, 1970," box 608, Country Files, NSC Files (Yorba Linda, CA: RMNL, 1970).

[157] "209. Memorandum of Conversation of a National Security Council Meeting, 26 February 1971, 11:45 A.M," *FRUS, 1969–1976, Vol. XXIII: Arab-Israeli Dispute, 1969–1972* (Washington, DC: GPO, 2015), pp. 757–762.

[158] "243. Memorandum for the Record, Subject: NSC Meeting on the Middle East and South Asia, San Clemente, 16 July 1971," *FRUS, 1969–1976, Vol. XXXIII: Arab-Israeli Dispute, 1969–1972* (Washington, DC: GPO, 2015), https://history.state.gov/historicaldocuments/frus1969-76v23/d243; "244. Telegram from the Department of State to the Embassy in Israel, 21 July 1971, 0105z," https://history.state.gov/historicaldocuments/frus1969-76v23/d244; and "249. Memorandum from the President's Assistant for National Security Affairs (Kissinger) to President Nixon, Re: Letter from Mrs. Meir, 23 September 1971," Ibid., https://history.state.gov/historicaldocuments/frus1969-76v23/d249.

[159] Craig A. Daigle, "The Russians Are Going: Sadat, Nixon, and the Soviet Presence in Egypt, 1970–1971," *MERIA: Middle East Review of International Affairs*, Vol. 8, No. 1 (2004), pp. 1–15.

Israel in maintaining the balancing of power in the area when Soviet influence in Egypt and other countries surrounding Israel has been particularly strong." Nonetheless, he argued, "It is essential that no more aid programs for Israel be approved until they agree to some kind of interim action on the Suez and other issues."[160]

In November 1971, the INR, in collaboration with the CIA and the DIA, produced a major reassessment of the Arab-Israeli military balance. "Israel's military superiority has been reduced because of Egypt's much improved air defense system that would make impossible a preemptive air strike such as that in 1967," the report concluded. It went on to note that "The Israelis received 119 new jet aircraft from the US in the 1970 and 1971 while Egypt received 125 [from the USSR]."[161] Kissinger wrote to Nixon on 27 November, "The shift in the balance has taken place a result of the Soviet-installed defense capability mainly affective Israel's pre-emptive strike capability.... The other important element in the picture is the continuing buildup of the USSR's own position in Egypt."[162] He added, "Everyone here admits that Israel will need more planes over a 1–3 year span to continue normal modernization and upgrading of its air force. The main question is when those planes will be provided and in what political context."[163]

Nixon approved the transfer of 69 F-4 Phantoms, at a rate of three per month from February 1972 through December 1973, and an additional 82 A-4s Skyhawks during the same period, intended to maintain Israeli air superiority for years to come.[164] The steady growth of US military assistance to Israel continued over the next two years, notwithstanding Sadat's expulsion of 15,000 Soviet military advisers and the opening of a backchannel between his national security adviser, Hafiz Ismail, and Kissinger in July 1972.[165] The CIA

---

[160] "233. Memorandum from President Nixon to Secretary of State Rogers, 26 May 1971," *FRUS, 1969–1976, Vol. XXXIII: Arab-Israeli Dispute, 1969–1972* (Washington, DC: GPO, 2015).

[161] "266. Memorandum from the President's Assistant for National Security Affairs (Kissinger) to President Nixon, 27 November 1971," *FRUS, 1969–1976, Vol. XXIII: Arab-Israeli Dispute, 1969–1972* (Washington, DC: GPO, 2015), pp. 948–951.

[162] Ibid.

[163] Ibid.

[164] "271. Memorandum of Conversation Between Assistant Secretary of State for Near East Affairs Joseph Sisco and Israeli Ambassador Yitzhak Rabin, 29 December 1971," *FRUS, 1969–1976, Vol. XXIII: Arab-Israeli Dispute, 1969–1972* (Washington, DC: GPO, 2015), pp. 962–967; and "272. Memorandum from the Assistant Secretary of Defense for International Security Affairs (Nutter) to Secretary of Defense Laird, Re: President's Decision on Aircraft for Israel, 30 December 1971," *FRUS, 1969–1976, Vol. XXXIII: Arab-Israeli Dispute, 1969–1972* (Washington, DC: GPO, 2015), pp. 967–969.

[165] "296. Memorandum of Conversation Between Ashraf Ghorbal, head of UAR Interest Section, and Henry A. Kissinger, 27 June 1972, 12:15–12:45 P.M.," *FRUS, 1969–1976, Vol. XXIII: Arab-Israeli Dispute, 1969–1972* (Washington, DC: GPO, 2015), pp. 1015–1019.

reported, "Moscow's pursuit of détente with the US and Cairo's expulsion of Soviet military advisers from Egypt have added to the mutual distrust that has permeated Soviet-Egyptian relations for several years."[166] Officials in Jerusalem and Washington reacted to Sadat's February 1973 peace overtures with skepticism. Kissinger characterized Sadat's overtures as "far reaching, but one sided."[167] Nixon decided to assist Israel in the production of at least 100 Super Mirage aircraft and guaranteed the supply pipeline for the A-4s and the F-4s would continue through fiscal years (FY) 1974 and 1975, although the exact number would be determined in negotiations.[168]

In the period between September 1969 and October 1973, the Nixon administration concluded that the United States confronted a favorable power distribution in the Middle East, but short time horizons for emerging threats. The deployment of SA-2 and SA-3 anti-aircraft missiles, the large numbers of Soviet military advisers to the Suez Canal Zone, and the deployment of Soviet MIG jets to provide air cover for Egyptian ground forces raised the prospect of a direct engagement between Israeli and Soviet forces that, in turn, might draw in the United States. Officials agreed that Israel currently enjoyed a favorable military balance vis-à-vis Egypt. They disagreed among themselves, and with the Meir government, however, about the time frame in which Soviet arms transfers would shift the balance.

As noted in chapter 2, where the United States faces a favorable regional power distribution and short time horizons for emerging threats, policymakers will prefer to pursue a hybrid strategy. The September 1969 to October 1973 period illustrates this. On the whole, senior officials in Washington were inclined to pursue accommodative strategies in the form of a large military assistance package to Israel. The main disagreements within the Nixon administration revolved around the transfer of specific weapons systems, such as electronic jamming equipment, and over the delivery schedule for additional F-4 and A-4

---

[166] "66. Intelligence Memorandum Prepared in the Central Intelligence Agency, No. 1652/73: The Status of Soviet Relations with Egypt and the Palestinians, June 1973," *FRUS, 1969–1976, Vol. XXV: Arab-Israeli Crisis and War, 1973* (Washington, DC: GPO, 2011) pp. 195–198.

[167] Quoted in Uri Bar-Joseph, "Last Chance to Avoid War: Sadat's Peace Initiative of February 1973 and Its Failure," *Journal of Contemporary History*, Vol. 41, No. 3 (2006), p. 549. Also see "28. Memorandum from the President's Assistant for National Security Affairs (Kissinger) to President Nixon, Re: My Talks with Hafiz Ismail, 24–25 February 1973," *FRUS, 1969–1976, Vol. XXV: Arab-Israeli Crisis and War, 1973* (Washington, DC: GPO, 2011), pp. 80–84.

[168] "37. Memorandum from the President's Assistant for National Security Affairs (Kissinger) to Secretary of State Rogers and Secretary of Defense Richardson, 2 March 1973," *FRUS, 1969–1976, Vol. XXV: Arab-Israeli Crisis and War, 1973* (Washington, DC: GPO, 2011), pp. 116–117. See also "35. Memorandum of Conversation Between President Nixon and Israeli Prime Minister Golda Meir, 1 March 1973, 11:03–12:25 A.M.," Ibid., pp. 105–113.

aircrafts. The coercive element lay in the implicit threat that the Nixon administration might not transfer electronic jamming equipment at all or delay delivery of the F-4s and A-4s, unless the Meir government made territorial concessions.

The Nixon administration encountered low mobilization hurdles during this period. It was able to sell major weapons to Israel and to calibrate both the types of weapons and the delivery schedule with little effective interference from Congress. On the contrary, arms transfers to Israel had strong support in Congress. Although Nixon deferred a decision on the Israeli request for additional F-4s and A-4s from March 1970 to December 1971, he ultimately authorized two major military assistance packages to maintain Israeli air superiority until the mid-1970s.

The Nixon-Meir Understanding Tested: The October 1973 War Ceasefire

The October 1973 Arab-Israeli (or Yom Kippur) War was a "test" of the Nixon-Meir understanding of September 1969, although not for the reasons often cited. Other scholars argue one or more of the following episodes tested that understanding: (1) Secretary of State Henry Kissinger's warning against Israel launching a preemptive attack to forestall the coordinated Syrian and Egyptian offensives on 5 October; (2) Prime Minister Golda Meir's rejection of a proposal on 9 October from her defense minister, Moshe Dayan, to detonate a nuclear device as a demonstration; and (3) Israel's readying of nuclear-capable Jericho missiles on 17 and 18 October in an attempt to blackmail the Nixon administration into resupplying the combat aircraft, tanks, and missiles to replace those that had been lost or destroyed since 6 October.[169] Instead, the real test of the Nixon-Meir understanding occurred between 24 October and 11 November, after the tide of battle on both fronts turned in Israel's favor and after the superpowers agreed to support a ceasefire resolution in the UN Security Council.

On 6 October 1973, columns of Soviet-equipped Egyptian and Syrian armor and infantry, backed by heavy artillery, launched an offensive into the Suez Canal Zone and the Golan Heights, overwhelming the Israeli defensive lines. The offensives were a strategic and operational surprise. The IDF incurred heavy losses of weapons, equipment, and soldiers during the first days of the fighting. Neither offensive, however, breached Israel's pre-June 1967 borders. The war

---

[169] The US Senate confirmed Nixon's nomination of Kissinger to be secretary of state on 21 September 1973. Kissinger concurrently served as secretary of state and assistant to the president for national security affairs until 3 November 1975.

aims of Sadat and President Hafez al-Assad of Syria appear to have been confined to recapturing the territories lost in June 1967.[170]

Israeli intelligence provided a few hours of warning about the coordinated Egyptian and Syrian attacks and the Meir government conveyed that intelligence to Washington.[171] Kissinger urgently warned Israel not to launch a preemptive strike.[172] Meir assured US ambassador Kenneth Keating on 5 October, "We will not strike first," mindful of Kissinger's warning.[173] Nixon, Kissinger, Secretary of Defense James D. Schlesinger, and other senior officials in Washington expected the IDF to quickly defeat the Egyptians and the Syrians on both fronts. As Kissinger admitted to Israeli ambassador Simcha Dinitz on the morning of 9 October, "Our strategy was to give you until Wednesday evening, by which time, I thought the whole Egyptian army would be wrecked."[174] Consequently, during the first week of hostilities the administration "deflected" the Meir government's urgent appeals for military hardware, such as additional F-4s and Sidewinder missiles, and only grudgingly agreed to send "consumables" such as ammunition.[175]

---

[170] For analysis of how Israel's nuclear opacity may have influenced the calculations of the Egyptian and Syrian leaders and military strategists in October 1973, see Paul C. Avey, "Who's Afraid of the Bomb? The Role of Nuclear Non-Use Norms in Confrontations Between Nuclear and Non-Nuclear Opponents," *Security Studies*, Vol. 24, No. 4 (2015), pp. 563–596; and Shlomo Aronson, "The Nuclear Dimension of the Arab-Israeli Conflict: The Case of the Yom Kippur War," *Jerusalem Journal of International Relations*, Vol. 7, No. 1–2 (1984), pp. 107–142. For a dissenting view, see Yair Evron, "The Relevance and Irrelevance of Nuclear Options in Conventional Wars: The 1973 October War," *Jerusalem Journal of International Relations*, Vol. 7, No. 1–2 (1984), pp. 143–176.

[171] "Deputy Assistant to the President for National Security Brent Scowcroft to Kissinger, 5 October 1973, Enclosing Message from Israeli Prime Minister Golda Meir (Passed through Israeli Chargé Shalev)," in William Burr, ed., *NSA Electronic Briefing Book no. 98* (Washington, DC: National Security Archive, 2003), http://nsarchive.gwu.edu/NSAEBB/NSAEBB98/octwar-07.pdf.

[172] "Message from Secretary Kissinger, New York, to White House Situation Room, for Delivery to President Nixon at 9:00 A.M., 6 October 1973," in William Burr, ed., *NSA Electronic Briefing Book no. 98* (Washington, DC: National Security Archive, 2003), http://nsarchive.gwu.edu/NSAEBB/NSAEBB98/octwar-10.pdf; and U.S. Embassy Israel, Cable 7766 to Department of State, 6 October 1973, "GOI Concern About Possible Syrian and Egyptian Attack Today," in William Burr, ed., *NSA Electronic Briefing Book no. 98* (Washington, DC: National Security Archive, 2003), http://nsarchive.gwu.edu/NSAEBB/NSAEBB98/octwar-09.pdf.

[173] "Memcon Between Dinitz and Kissinger, 7 October 1973, 8:20 P.M.," in William Burr, ed., *NSA Electronic Briefing Book no. 98* (Washington, DC: National Security Archive, 2003), http://nsarchive.gwu.edu/NSAEBB/NSAEBB98/octwar-18.pdf.

[174] "Memcon Between Dinitz and Kissinger, 9 October 1973, 8:20–8:40 A.M," in William Burr, ed., *NSA Electronic Briefing Book no. 98* (Washington, DC: National Security Archive, 2003), http://nsarchive.gwu.edu/NSAEBB/NSAEBB98/octwar-21a.pdf.

[175] David Rodman, "The Impact of American Arms Transfers to Israel During the 1973 Yom Kippur War," *Israel Journal of Foreign Affairs*, Vol. 7, No. 3 (2013), p. 108. On Nixon's pledge to send Israel consumables, such as ammunition, see "Memcon Between Dinitz and Kissinger, 9 October 1973, 6:10–6:35 P.M.," in William Burr, ed., *NSA Electronic Briefing Book no. 98* (Washington,

Kissinger candidly told Ambassador Huang Zhen, the head of the People's Republic of China (PRC) Liaison Office in Washington, on the evening of 6 October, "Our strategic objective is to prevent the Soviet Union from getting the dominant position in the Middle East. That is our basic objective. Israel is a secondary emotional problem having to do with domestic politics here." He added, "Our objective, as always, when the Soviet Union appears, to demonstrate whoever gets help from the Soviet Union cannot achieve his objective, whatever it is."[176]

Nixon administration officials actually *wanted* Israel to decisively defeat the Syrian and Egyptian offensives. They did not, however, want the Israelis to launch a counteroffensive beyond the June 1967 ceasefire lines or to take any action that might prompt the Kremlin to intervene militarily on behalf its Arab clients. "We could not tolerate an Israeli defeat," Kissinger told his senior staff at the State Department on 23 October, but added, "we could not make our policy hostage to the Israelis, because our interests, while parallel in respect to that I have outlined, are not identical in overall terms."[177]

Nixon and Kissinger abandoned restraint in resupplying Israel due a combination of the following: the massive Soviet airlift and sealift of military hardware to Syria and Egypt, which began on 8 October; the refusal of the Egyptian government to accept an immediate ceasefire; and intense lobbying by Senators Frank Church (D-IA), Hubert Humphrey (D-MN), and others on Israel's behalf.[178] Nixon authorized a massive airlift, later supplemented by a sealift, of 16 F-4 Phantoms, 30 A-4 Skyhawks, 200 Sidewinder missiles, and other weapons

DC: National Security Archive, 2003), http://nsarchive.gwu.edu/NSAEBB/NSAEBB98/octwar-21b.pdf.

[176] "Memcon Between Kissinger and Ambassador Huang Zhen, PRC Liaison Office, 6 October 1973, 9:10–9:30 P.M.," in William Burr, ed., *NSA Electronic Briefing Book no. 98* (Washington, DC: National Security Archive, 2003), http://nsarchive.gwu.edu/NSAEBB/NSAEBB98/octwar-17.pdf.

[177] "250. Minutes of the Secretary of State's Staff Meeting, 23 October 1973," *FRUS, 1969–1976, Vol. XXV: Arab-Israeli Crisis and War, 1973* (Washington, DC: GPO, 2011), pp. 689–700.

[178] On reports about the Soviet resupply of Egypt and Syria, see "144. Transcript of Telephone Conversation Between Secretary of Defense Schlesinger and the Chairman of the Joint Chiefs of Staff (Moorer), 10:02 A.M., 10 October 1973," and 145. Diary Entry by the Chairman of the Joint Chiefs of Staff (Moorer), 10 October 1973, *FRUS, 1969–1976, Vol. XXV: Arab-Israeli Crisis and War, 1973* (Washington, DC: GPO, 2011), pp. 4224–4425. Also see "169. Memorandum from William B. Quandt of the National Security Council Staff to Secretary of State Kissinger, 13 October 1973," Ibid., pp. 473–475. On senators' demands that the Nixon administration immediately send replacement tanks and combat aircraft to Israel, see "Memorandum of Telephone Conversation Between Senator Frank Church and Secretary of State Henry Kissinger, 11:48 A.M., 9 October 1973," and "Memorandum of Telephone Conversation Between Senator Hubert Humphrey and Secretary of State Henry Kissinger, 2:30 P.M., 12 October 1973," *DNSA Collection: Kissinger Telephone Conversations, 1969–1977* (Ann Arbor, MI: ProQuest, 2004).

systems and equipment to Israel.[179] He took this step despite threats from the foreign ministers of Saudi Arabia, Kuwait, and Oman and later from King Faisal bin Abdul Aziz of Saudi Arabia to cut oil production by 5 percent per month unless the United States suspended arms shipments to Israel and the IDF withdrew to the pre-June 1967 borders in accordance with UN Security Council Resolution 242.[180] Between 14 October, when the first Galaxy C-5 transport planes of the Military Assistance Command (MAC) landed, until the end of the operation on 14 November, the United States transported 12,000 tons of materials.[181] Nixon requested Congress to approve a $2.2 billion emergency assistance package for Israel on 19 October.[182]

Other scholars identify at least two instances during the October 1973 War when Israeli leaders contemplated "nuclear steps."[183] According to Cohen, following a war cabinet meeting on 9 October, Dayan raised the possibility of staging a demonstration of Israel's nuclear weapons capability. Deputy Prime Minister Yigal Allon and Minister-Without-Portfolio Israel Galili told Meir such a move was premature and unnecessary, and she agreed.[184] The second nuclear

---

[179] "Seymour Weiss, Director, Bureau of Politico-Military Affairs, Department of State, to Kissinger, 'Armed Shipments to Israel,' 15 October 1973," in William Burr, ed., *NSA Electronic Briefing Book no. 98* (Washington, DC: National Security Archive, 2003), http://nsarchive.gwu.edu/NSAEBB/NSAEBB98/octwar-31.pdf.

[180] See Memorandum of Conversation Among President Richard M. Nixon, Secretary of State Henry A. Kissinger, Minister of State for Foreign Affairs of Saudi Arabia Omar Shaqqaf, and Others, 11:10 A.M., 17 October 1973, *FRUS, 1969–1976, Vol. XXV: Arab-Israeli Crisis and War, 1973* (Washington, DC: GPO, 2011), pp. 565–571. Also see "U.S. Embassy Kuwait Cable 3801 Cable to State Department, 'Atiqi Comment on OPEC Meeting,' 18 October 1973," in William Burr, ed., *NSA Electronic Briefing Book no. 89* (Washington, DC: National Security Archive, 2003), http://nsarchive.gwu.edu/NSAEBB/NSAEBB98/octwar-38.pdf; "Assistant Secretary for Near Eastern Affairs Joseph Sisco to Kissinger, 'Proposed Presidential Message to King Faisal,' 12 October 1973, with State Department Cable Routing Message Attached," Ibid., http://nsarchive.gwu.edu/NSAEBB/NSAEBB98/octwar-28.pdf; and State Department Cable 203672 to U.S. Embassy, Saudi Arabia, "Message to the King from the Secretary, 14 October 1973," Ibid., http://nsarchive.gwu.edu/NSAEBB/NSAEBB98/octwar-29a.pdf.

[181] The figure comes from Zach Levey, "Anatomy of an Airlift: United States Military Assistance to Israel During the 1973 War," *Cold War History*, Vol. 8, No. 4 (2008), pp. 481–501, at p. 481.

[182] Richard Nixon: "Special Message to the Congress Requesting Emergency Security Assistance Funding for Israel and Cambodia," 19 October 1973. Online by Gerhard Peters and John T. Woolley, The American Presidency Project, http://www.presidency.ucsb.edu/ws/?pid=4012.

[183] Or Rabinowitz, *Bargaining on Nuclear Tests: Washington and Its Cold War Deals* (Oxford: Oxford University Press, 2014), p. 90.

[184] Cohen, *Worst Kept Secret*, p. 80; and Avner Cohen, "When Israel Stepped Back from the Brink," *New York Times*, 3 October 2003. In 2008, Cohen interviewed Arnan Azaryahu, a close aide to Galili who was present during the 7 October meeting in Meir's office in which Dayan allegedly suggested a nuclear demonstration. See "Interview with Arnan 'Sini' Azaryahu by Avner Cohen," *History and Public Policy Program Digital Archive, Personal Collection of Avner Cohen* (Washington, DC: Woodrow

step allegedly occurred on 17 or 18 October, in response to a state of alert of Soviet-made SCUD missiles in Egypt. According to this account, the Meir government initiated a strategic alert, which involved readying the nuclear-capable Jericho missiles for launch.[185]

Whether the Jericho missiles were actually armed with nuclear warheads is disputable. Likewise, it is debatable whether the alert was an attempt at nuclear signaling or an attempt to blackmail the Nixon administration into resupplying Israel with conventional weapons to replace those lost during the first week of the war.[186] For example, Vipin Narang argues, "The goal of the operational checks was to compel the Nixon administration to resupply Israel with the necessary conventional material to thwart the combined Arab assails and enable counteroffensives" and that Kissinger "was effectively pursuing a strategy of allowing Israel to get its nose bloodied before the United States would intervene."[187]

Declassified US documents and interviews with the surviving US and Israeli participants, however, suggest that while Israel likely did take steps associated with readying its missiles during the opening days of the war, such steps were largely precautionary. The Meir government and the IDF staff apparently did not intend them to be signals to Washington or Cairo. More important, while the CIA and other US intelligence agencies did observe these Israeli activities and disseminated reports to senior policymakers, those reports did not have a major impact on Nixon's decision to resupply Israel with conventional weapons and equipment on 12 October.[188]

Wilson International Center for Scholars, 2008), http://digitalarchive.wilsoncenter.org/document/117848.

[185] Avner Cohen, "Nuclear Arms in Crisis Under Secrecy: Israel and the Lessons of the 1967 and 1973 Wars," in Peter Lavoy, Scott D. Sagan, and James J. Wirtz, eds., *Planning the Unthinkable: How New Powers Will Use Nuclear, Biological, and Chemical Weapons* (Ithaca, NY: Cornell University Press, 2000), pp. 118–119. On this second alleged Israeli nuclear alert Cohen cites Yuval Ne'eeman, "The USA-Israel Connection in the Yom Kippur War (6–24 October)," in Michael Wheeler and Kemper V. Gay, eds., *Nuclear Weapons and the 1973 Middle East War*, Center for National Security Negotiations, Occasional Paper, Nuclear Lessons and Legacies Project Monograph, no. 3 (1996).

[186] See Seymour M. Hersh, *The Samson Option: Israel's Nuclear Arsenal and American Foreign Policy* (New York: Random House, 1991), pp. 225–231. For a dissenting view see David Tal, "A Tested Alliance: The American Airlift to Israel in the 1973 Yom Kippur War," *Israel Studies*, Vol. 19, No. 3 (2014), pp. 29–54.

[187] Vipin Narang, *Nuclear Strategy in the Modern Era: Regional Powers and International Conflict* (Princeton, NJ: Princeton University Press, 2014), p. 189. Narang's account draws heavily on Hersh, *The Samson Option*, pp. 225–231 and Avner Cohen, "Nuclear Arms in Crisis Under Secrecy: Israel and the Lessons of the 1967 and 1973 Wars," in Peter Lavoy, Scott D. Sagan, and James J. Wirtz, eds., *Planning the Unthinkable: How New Powers Will Use Nuclear, Biological, and Chemical Weapons* (Ithaca, NY: Cornell University Press, 2000) pp. 104–124.

[188] This is one of the main conclusions in Elbridge A. Colby, Avner Cohen, William F. McCants, Bradley Morris, and William G. Rosenau, *The Israeli "Nuclear Alert" of 1973: Deterrence and Signaling*

The more significant episodes occurred during the last week of October 1973, after the superpowers tentatively agreed to support a UN Security Council resolution for an immediate ceasefire.[189] Kissinger went to Moscow on 20–21 October to confer with CPSU general-secretary Leonid I. Brezhnev and Foreign Minister Andrei A. Gromyko on the draft ceasefire resolution.[190] During a 22 October stopover in Tel Aviv, en route back to Washington, Kissinger told Meir, "You won't get violent protests in Washington if something happens during the night, while I'm flying. Nothing can happen in Washington until noon tomorrow."[191] The Soviets planned to introduce the resolution in the Security Council the following day, which called for Israeli and Egyptian forces to hold their battle lines as of 22 October.[192]

Brezhnev, acting on behest of Sadat, used the US-Soviet hotline on 24 October to protest Israeli violations of Resolutions 338 and 339. He proposed the deployment of a joint US-Soviet military continent to the Suez Canal Zone to enforce the ceasefire.[193] Brezhnev's hotline message read in part: "Israel's continuing noncompliance with the Security Council's decisions . . . suggests the idea that the measures undertaken on the part of the United States to influence Israel to immediately fulfill the Security Council's resolutions are not only ineffective and inadequate, but, as evident enable Israel to continue its . . . actions."[194]

---

in Crisis (Washington, DC: Center for Naval Analysis, 2013). Also see Rabinowitz, *Bargaining on Nuclear Tests*, p. 50.

[189] "U.S. Embassy Soviet Union Cable 13148 to Department of State, 21 October 1973," in William Burr, ed., *NSA Electronic Briefing Book no. 98* (Washington, DC: National Security Archive, 2003), http://nsarchive.gwu.edu/NSAEBB/NSAEBB98/octwar-51.pdf.

[190] "Memcon Between Brezhnev and Kissinger, 20 October 1973, 9:15–11:30 P.M.," in William Burr, ed., *NSA Electronic Briefing Book no. 98* (Washington, DC: National Security Archive, 2003), http://nsarchive.gwu.edu/NSAEBB/NSAEBB98/octwar-46.pdf; "Memcon Between Brezhnev and Kissinger, 21 October 1973, 12:00 Noon–4:00 P.M.," Ibid., http://nsarchive.gwu.edu/NSAEBB/NSAEBB98/octwar-49.pdf; and "Memcon of Luncheon for Kissinger's Party, 22 October, 2:30–4:30 P.M.," Ibid., http://nsarchive.gwu.edu/NSAEBB/NSAEBB98/octwar-55.pdf.

[191] "Memcon Between Meir and Kissinger, 22 October 1973, 1:35–2:15 P.M.," in William Burr, ed., *NSA Electronic Briefing Book no. 98* (Washington, DC: National Security Archive, 2003) http://nsarchive.gwu.edu/NSAEBB/NSAEBB98/octwar-54.pdf

[192] "Memcon Between Gromyko and Kissinger, 22 October 1973, 8:45–9:45 A.M.," in William Burr, ed., *NSA Electronic Briefing Book no. 98* (Washington, DC: National Security Archive, 2003), http://nsarchive.gwu.edu/NSAEBB/NSAEBB98/octwar-53.pdf.

[193] "UNSC Resolution 338 (1973) of 22 October 1973," http://www.un.org/en/ga/search/view_doc.asp?symbol=S/RES/338(1973) (accessed 30 April 2017); and "UNSC Resolution 339 (1973) of 23 October 1973," http://www.un.org/en/ga/search/view_doc.asp?symbol=S/RES/339(1973) (accessed 30 April 2017).

[194] "Hotline Message from Brezhnev to Nixon, 26 October 1973, Complete Translation Received 29 October 1973," in William Burr, ed., *NSA Electronic Briefing Book no. 98* (Washington, DC: National Security Archive, 2003), http://nsarchive.gwu.edu/NSAEBB/NSAEBB98/octwar-83.pdf.

Kissinger and other members of the Washington Special Actions Group (WSAG), acting on Nixon's behalf, responded by raising the alert status of US conventional and nuclear forces worldwide to DEFCOM III.[195] Kissinger demanded Israel observe the 22 October ceasefire terms. "I have to say again your course is suicidal," he warned Dinitz on the night of 26 October, "you will not be permitted to destroy this army." He added, "It is inconceivable that the Soviets will permit the destruction of the Egyptian army and that the Egyptians will withdraw their army. It will bring down Sadat."[196]

Meir arrived in Washington for an official visit on 1 November. Kissinger accused the Israeli prime minister and her war cabinet of "blindsiding" him. He told Meir, "In ignorance of what your strategic plans were ... we made a ceasefire agreement, with direct negotiations which was always your position. ... Then you took the Third Army after the ceasefire, which was not expected."[197] Later, during a meeting in the Oval Office, Nixon also told Meir that Israel had no alternative but to accept the 22 October ceasefire, at least in principle. The president reaffirmed that Kissinger's Moscow trip was intended to buy forty-eight hours for the IDF to consolidate its position on the Suez front before the Security Council voted on a ceasefire resolution. "We did not press for an early ceasefire because your ambassador at the time said you were at a disadvantage."[198]

Kissinger reminded Meir, "We have kept the Security Council off your back by saying that we're talking to the Egyptians, and we told the Egyptians that any proposal that comes to us through the Russians is dead."[199] Essentially, Kissinger

---

[195] See "269. Memorandum for the Record, Re: NSC/JCS Meeting, Wednesday/Thursday, 24/25 October 1973, 2230-0330 (U)," *FRUS, 1969–1976, Vol. XXV: Arab-Israeli Crisis and War, 1973* (Washington, DC: GPO, 2011) pp. 738–742. Chaired by Kissinger, the WSAG was the crisis management group within the NSC system during the Nixon administration. The participants in the rump WSAG that met on the night of 24–25 October were Kissinger; Schlesinger; Lt. Gen. Alexander M. Haig, the White House chief of staff; Admiral Thomas Moorer, the chairman of the JCS; Lt. Gen. Brent Scowcroft, the deputy assistant to the president for national security affairs; and DCI William Colby.

[196] "289. Transcript of Telephone Conversation Between Secretary of State Kissinger and the Israeli Ambassador (Dinitz), 10:58 P.M., 26 October 1973," *FRUS, 1969–1976, Vol. XXV: Arab-Israeli Crisis and War, 1973* (Washington, DC: GPO, 2011), pp. 771–784. For the argument that Soviet threats were designed to get the United States to pressure Israel to comply with the 22 October ceasefire, see Benjamin Miller, *When Opponents Cooperate: Great Power Conflict and Collaboration in World Politics* (Ann Arbor: University of Michigan Press, 1995), pp. 164–165.

[197] "Memcon Between Kissinger, Meir, Dinitz, and General Yariv. 1 November 1973, 8:10 A.M.–10:25 A.M.," in William Burr, ed., *NSA Electronic Briefing Book no. 98* (Washington, DC: National Security Archive, 2003), http://nsarchive.gwu.edu/NSAEBB/NSAEBB98/octwar-91a.pdf.

[198] Ibid.

[199] "Memcon Between Kissinger, Meir, and Party, 2 November 1973, 10:00 P.M.–12:45 A.M.," in William Burr, ed., *NSA Electronic Briefing Book no. 98* (Washington, DC: National Security Archive, 2003), http://nsarchive.gwu.edu/NSAEBB/NSAEBB98/octwar-93a.pdf.

threatened to abandon Israel in the Security Council. The Meir government agreed to allow non-military supplies to reach the Third Army on 28 October, while Israeli and Egyptian military representatives met at Kilometer 101 in the Suez Canal Zone to discuss the ceasefire implementation. After meetings with Sadat in Cairo, Kissinger announced the terms of the first disengagement agreement on 9 November, which Israeli and Egyptian representatives signed on 11 November.[200]

The US-Israeli confrontation over the ceasefire is significant because it illustrated the limits of the United States' security commitment to Israel. The IDF's encirclement of the Egyptian Third Army, after the ceasefire was supposed to go into effect, precipitated a crisis between the two superpowers when Brezhnev threatened to unilaterally deploy Soviet peacekeepers to the Canal Zone. The Nixon administration quickly switched from an accommodative strategy toward Israel to a strategy that bended accommodation and coercion (a hybrid strategy): the continuation of the air and sealift of US weapons and equipment, coupled with private threats of abandonment in the UN Security Council.

Neoclassical realist theory would expect policymakers in Washington to subordinate their nonproliferation objectives to the immediate need to shore up the United States' overall position in a geographic region, if the regional power distribution were unfavorable and there were short time horizons for emerging threats to US interests in the region. However, in this period (24 October to 11 November 1973), Israeli nuclear proliferation was not really an issue. Nuclear weapons possession may have actually emboldened the Meir cabinet and the IDF staff to seek operational gains at Egypt's expense. Nonetheless, Israel was highly dependent on US conventional weapons and equipment to replace its earlier losses in the war.

Nixon and Kissinger did not encounter any domestic mobilization hurdles. The airlift of advanced weapons and military equipment, which Nixon ordered on 13 October, enjoyed broad support in Congress. Also, there was not much disagreement between the administration and the congressional leadership about the desirability of an early ceasefire in the October War.[201] Lastly, Nixon

---

[200] For a recent analysis of Egyptian-Israeli ceasefire negotiations, see Yinon Shlomo, "The Israeli-Egyptian Talks at Kilometer 101," *British Journal of Middle Eastern Studies*, Vol. 43, No. 1 (2016), pp. 1–17.

[201] On 8 October, Senator Mike Mansfield (D-MT), the majority leader, and Senator Hugh Scott (R-PA), the minority leader, co-sponsored a resolution calling for an immediate ceasefire and a return of Israeli and Egyptian forces to the lines they held as of 6 October 1973. See Deploring the Outbreak of Hostilities in the Middle East, S. Res. 179, 93rd Cong. (1973) and 119 Cong. Rec. S33180-33181 (daily ed. 8 October 1973) (Statement of Senator Mansfield) https://congressional-proquest.com/congressional/docview/t19.d20.cr-1973-1008? The resolution in referenced in "127. Transcript of Telephone Conversation Between President Nixon and Secretary of State Kissinger, 2:35 P.M., 8 October 1973," *FRUS, 1969–1976, Vol. XXV: Arab-Israeli Crisis and War, 1973* (Washington, DC: GPO, 2011), pp. 373–374, fn. 4.

and Kissinger privately communicated their threats and made no attempt to link Israeli compliance with the ceasefire to a continuation of US military and economic assistance.

Conclusions: Prioritizing Containment over Nonproliferation in the Middle East

The twelve-year confrontation between the United States and Israel over the latter's clandestine nuclear weapons program generally supports neoclassical realist theory. Averting containment failure in the Middle East was the overriding strategic objective of the Kennedy, Johnson, and Nixon administrations from 1961 to 1973. Thwarting the Israeli nuclear weapons program was a secondary objective.

During the early 1960s, faced with a favorable power distribution in the Middle East, along with long time horizons for emerging threats to US interests in the region, the Kennedy administration opted for a coercive strategy to halt Israel's nuclear program. Specifically, Kennedy and his national security team pressured Ben-Gurion into inviting AEC scientists to "visit" the Dimona reactor complex, hinting that non-compliance would result in a serious rupture in US-Israeli relations; declining the Israeli prime minister's request for a mutual defense treaty; and only grudgingly approving Israeli requests to purchase anti-aircraft missile batteries. The Kennedy administration was able to pursue such a strategy because the domestic mobilization hurdles it faced were low.

When the pursuit of the nuclear nonproliferation and containment objectives in the Middle East came into conflict with each other, as they began to do in the mid-1960s when the Soviet Union's arms transfers to Egypt and Syria increased, the Johnson administration prioritized containment. Johnson and his advisers jettisoned Kennedy's coercive strategy of demanding twice-yearly "visits" by AEC scientists to the Dimona complex. Instead, they embarked an accommodative strategy of selling the Eshkol government conventional weapons (the M48 tanks and the A-4 Skyhawks) in exchange for pledges that Israel would not be the first state to "introduce nuclear weapons" into the Middle East. However, by opening the door on sales of advanced weapons to Israel in 1964 and 1965, the Johnson administration inadvertently raised the domestic mobilization hurdle it and its successors would have to overcome in order to pursue a coercive nonproliferation strategy. These hurdles made it difficult for the Johnson administration and later the Nixon administration to link the transfer of the more sophisticated F-12 aircraft to Israeli concessions on the nuclear issue. By autumn 1969, Nixon and Kissinger were not only prepared to "live with" a nuclear-armed Israel, they were also prepared to let the United States become Israel's main supplier of advanced weapons, in order to contain Soviet Union's influence in the Middle East.

The nuclear domino theory hypothesis finds, at best, limited empirical support during the early years of the US-Israeli proliferation dispute. Kennedy and Rusk did tell Ben-Gurion and Eban that suspicions about the Dimona complex might prompt Egypt to undertake a nuclear weapons program. Nonetheless, the possibility of reactive nuclear proliferation by Egypt appears not to have been the main driver for Kennedy's insistence that AEC scientists "visit" Dimona. Instead, Kennedy and his advisers were more concerned that Israeli nuclear activities might prompt the Soviets to increase conventional arms transfers to Syria and Egypt.

The October 1973 Arab-Israeli War was a watershed for the Washington's engagement in the Middle East. Israel emerged from the war as an unambiguous ally of the United States, albeit one without a formal defense treaty. Kissinger brokered the second Egyptian-Israeli disengagement agreement (Sinai II) in 1975 and President Jimmy Carter brokered the Camp David Accords in 1978 that led to a peace treaty between Israel and Egypt.[202] The alliance has endured despite periodic intra-alliance disputes and subsequent attempts by US presidential administrations (of both parties) to restrain their Israeli counterparts from pursuing strategies they deemed harmful to broader US interests in the Middle East. A partial list of intra-alliance disputes include the 1982 Israeli invasion of Lebanon (Operation Peace for Galilee), possible Israeli retaliation against Iraqi Scud missile strikes during the 1991 Persian Gulf War, and possible Israeli preventive military strikes on Iran's nuclear facilities in the mid-2000s.[203] Yet none of these disputes resulted in a lasting rupture between Israel and the United States.

The Nixon-Meir special understanding of September 1969 paved the way for a de facto alliance between the United States and Israel. While that

---

[202] For a recent analysis of the Ford administration's role in brokering Sinai II, see Galen Jackson, "The Showdown That Wasn't: U.S.-Israeli Relations and American Domestic Politics, 1973–75," *International Security*, Vol. 39, No. 4 (2015), pp. 130–169. For a recent analysis of Carter's role in brokering the Camp David Peace Accords and the 1979 Israeli-Egyptian Peace Treaty, see Norrin M. Ripsman, *Peacemaking from Above, Peace from Below: Ending Conflict Between Regional Rivals* (Ithaca, NY: Cornell University Press, 2016), pp. 74–80.

[203] For analyses of efforts by the Reagan, George H. W. Bush, and George W. Bush administrations to restrain Israel see Pressman, *Warring Friends*, pp. 78–120. For an analysis of the Obama administration's efforts see Daniel Sobelman, "Restraining an Ally: Israel, the United States, and Iran's Nuclear Program, 2010–2012," *Texas National Security Review*, Vol. 1, No. 4 (2018), at https://tnsr.org/2018/08/restraining-an-ally-israel-the-united-states-and-irans-nuclear-program-2011-2012/

understanding resolved the US-Israeli proliferation dispute, it did not resolve the underlying issue of how policymakers in Washington might respond to the nuclear aspirations of allies in other volatile geographic regions. Over the next several years, the United States would have nonproliferation disputes with other allies in South Asia and East Asia.

4

The United States and Pakistan's Nuclear Weapons Program, 1975–1990

Pakistan initiated a secret nuclear weapons program in the aftermath of its catastrophic defeat in the 1971 war with India. The Pakistani president and later prime minister, Zulfikar Ali Bhutto, had long advocated developing nuclear weapons. As early as 1965, Bhutto, then-foreign minister in the government of President Field Marshal Mohammad Ayub Khan, said in an interview with the *Manchester Guardian*: "If India makes an atom bomb, then even if we have to feed on grass and leaves—even if we have to starve—we shall also produce an atom bomb as we would be left with no other alternative."[1] On 20 January 1972, Bhutto, who succeeded General Muhammad Yahya Khan as Pakistan's president the previous month, was quoted as telling a meeting of some 400 scientists and engineers in Multan: "We are fighting a thousand year war with India, and we will make an atomic bomb even if we have to eat grass."[2] In May 1973, Bhutto's government signed a secret contract with a French nuclear engineering firm, Saint Gobian Technique Nouvelle, to build a uranium reprocessing plant at Chashma. Once completed, the plant would be able to extract weapons-grade plutonium

---

[1] Quoted in Feroz Hassan Khan, *Eating Grass: The Making of the Pakistani Bomb* (Stanford, CA: Stanford University Press, 2012), p. 7. Field Marshal Mohammad Ayub Khan, the commander-in-chief of the Pakistani Army, seized power in a coup against the president of Pakistan, Iskandar Ali Mirza, on 27 October 1958. Ayub Khan served as president of Pakistan until his resignation on 24 March 1969. General Agha Muhammad Yahya Khan (no relation) succeeded him as president and chief martial law administrator.

[2] Quoted in Khan, *Eating Grass*, p. 87. For a discussion of the origins of the Pakistan Atomic Energy Commission (PAEC), the debates between the nuclear weapons enthusiasts and skeptics during Ayub Khan's tenure, and Ayub Kahn's non-decision regarding a nuclear weapon capability in 1967, see Khan, *Eating Grass*, pp. 59–68.

from the spent fuel of the Canadian-supplied uranium reactor Pakistan acquired in 1972.[3]

Unlike Israel in the late 1950s, however, in the early 1970s Pakistan was formally an ally of the United States when it started its nuclear weapons program. Most notably, it was a founding member of the Central Treaty Organization (CENTO), a multilateral alliance to contain the Soviet Union's influence in the Middle East and South Asia. For much of the Cold War, the United States' overriding strategic objective in South Asia was to contain the Soviet Union, and secondarily the People's Republic of China (at least until the Sino-Soviet split in the mid-1960s). From the partition of British India in 1947 onward, Pakistan's overriding strategic objective was defense against its more powerful neighbor, India.[4] The United States, however, had no treaty obligation to come to Pakistan's defense in the event of war with India.[5] Consequently, US security guarantees to Pakistan were always limited and highly conditional.[6]

The United States denied Pakistani requests for military assistance through CENTO during the 1965 India-Pakistan War, the second war the South Asian rivals fought over the disputed region of Kashmir.[7] President Lyndon B. Johnson imposed an arms embargo on India and Pakistan that remained in place for a decade.[8] The United States officially remained neutral during the early months of 1971 South Asia crisis, which began when President Yahya Khan authorized the army's brutal suppression of a Bengali campaign to win greater autonomy for

---

[3] Jeffrey Richelson, *Spying on the Bomb: American Nuclear Intelligence from Nazi Germany to Iran and North Korea* (New York: Norton, 2006), p. 328; and Dennis Kux, *The United States and Pakistan, 1947–2000: Disenchanted Allies* (Baltimore: Johns Hopkins University Press, 2001), p. 212.

[4] For an analysis of the interplay of geopolitics and ideational factors in driving Pakistan's rivalry with India, see T. V. Paul, *The Warrior State: Pakistan in the Contemporary World* (New York: Oxford University Press, 2014), pp. 94–126.

[5] Office of the Legal Adviser Treaty Affairs Staff, US Department of State, ed., *Treaties in Force: A List of Treaties and Other Agreements of the United States in Force as of 1 January 2016* (Washington, DC: GPO, 2016), https://www.state.gov/documents/organization/264509.pdf.

[6] See Evan Braden Montgomery, *In the Hegemon's Shadow: Leading States and the Rise of Regional Powers* (Ithaca, NY: Cornell University Press, 2016), pp. 104–109.

[7] For analyses of the Kennedy and the Johnson administrations' attempt to deter India and Pakistan from going to war over Kashmir, see Timothy W. Crawford, *Pivotal Deterrence: Third-Party Statecraft and the Pursuit of Peace* (Ithaca, NY: Cornell University Press, 2003), pp. 135–168; and Montgomery, *In the Hegemon's Shadow*, pp. 109–116.

[8] See "185. Telegram from the Department of State to the Embassy in Pakistan, Washington, 5 September 1965, 3:57 P.M.," *FRUS, 1964–1968, Vol. XXV: South Asia* (Washington, DC: GPO, 2000), pp. 358–359; "190. Memorandum from Robert Komer of the National Security Council Staff to President Johnson, 7 September 1965, 7:30 P.M.," Ibid., pp. 367–368; and "194. Telegram from the Department of State to the Embassy in India, Washington, 8 September 1965, 7:12 P.M.," Ibid., p. 372.

East Pakistan.[9] Henry Kissinger, then President Richard Nixon's national security adviser, disingenuously told the Indian minister of external affairs, Swaran Singh, on the eve of his first secret trip to the People's Republic of China in July 1971,[10] "Unlike other major powers from outside the region, the US has an essentially disinterested concern in developments in South Asia."[11] Despite Kissinger's assurances to Singh, he and Nixon were extremely wary of India, which had been a major Soviet arms purchaser. Indian prime minister Indira Gandhi's tilt toward the Soviet Union exacerbated their suspicion.[12]

As the South Asia crisis escalated in autumn 1971, Nixon and Kissinger feared that another India-Pakistan war—resulting in the certain dismemberment of Pakistan—would not only undermine their nascent rapprochement with China, but also lead allies and adversaries alike to question the United States' resolve. On 3 December 1971, the Indian army launched a full-scale offensive into East Pakistan, routing the Pakistani army units deployed there in a few days. Nixon sent the aircraft carrier USS *Enterprise* to the Bay of Bengal in a show of American resolve.[13] Kissinger observed, "We have a country [India], supported

---

[9] For an overview of the events leading to the outbreak of the 1971 South Asia Crisis, see Srinath Raghavan, *1971: A Global History of the Creation of Bangladesh* (Cambridge, MA: Harvard University Press, 2013), pp. 14–33. For analyses of the Pakistani army's suppression of the Bengali secessionist movement and its escalation to genocide (Operation Searchlight), see Raghavan, *1971*, pp. 34–53; and Ashan I. Butt, *Secession and Security: Explaining State Strategies Against Separatists* (Ithaca, NY: Cornell University Press, 2017), pp. 49–63. For an indictment of the Nixon administration's failure to respond to the slaughter of the Bengalis, see Gary Jonathan Bass, *The Blood Telegram: Nixon, Kissinger, and a Forgotten Genocide* (New York: Vintage Books, 2014).

[10] Yahya provided the main backchannel between Nixon and Kissinger and PRC premier Zhou Enlai between autumn 1970 and summer 1971. See "Memcon, Meeting Between the President and Pakistan President Yahya, 25 October 1970, Top Secret/Sensitive," in William Burr, ed., *NSA Electronic Briefing Book no. 66* (Washington, DC: National Security Archive, 2002), http://nsarchive2.gwu.edu/NSAEBB/NSAEBB66/ch-03.pdf; "Kissinger to Nixon, 'Chinese Communist Initiative,' c. 10 December 1970, Enclosing Draft Note Verbal and Message from Zhou Enlai, as Conveyed by Hilaly, with Comments by Yahya, Top Secret/Sensitive," Ibid., http://nsarchive2.gwu.edu/NSAEBB/NSAEBB66/ch-06.pdf; "Memo by Hilaly, Record of a Discussion with Mr. Henry Kissinger on [Sic] the White House on 16th December 1970," Ibid. http://nsarchive2.gwu.edu/NSAEBB/NSAEBB66/ch-07.pdf; "Memo of Record by Col. Richard T. Kennedy, 16 December 1970, Enclosing Response to PRC Via Hilaly and Yahya, Top Secret/Sensitive, Delivered in Beijing on 5 January 1971," Ibid., http://nsarchive2.gwu.edu/NSAEBB/NSAEBB66/ch-08.pdf; "Message from Zhou to Nixon, 29 May 1971, with Commentary, Conveyed by Hilaly to White House," Ibid., http://nsarchive2.gwu.edu/NSAEBB/NSAEBB66/ch-26.pdf.

[11] "92. Memorandum of Conversation, 7 July 1971," *FRUS, 1969–1976, Vol. XI: South Asia Crisis, 1971* (Washington, DC: GPO, 2005), pp. 227–231.

[12] See George Perkovich, *India's Nuclear Bomb: The Impact on Global Proliferation* (Berkeley: University of California Press, 1999), pp. 162–163. Also see Vojtech Mastny, "The Soviet Union's Partnership with India," *Journal of Cold War Studies*, Vol. 12, No. 3 (2010), pp. 50–90.

[13] For an analysis of Nixon and Kissinger's "tilt" toward Pakistan in the last months of the 1971 South Asia Crisis, see Raghavan, *1971*, pp. 235–263. Also see Kux, *United States and Pakistan,*

and equipped by the Soviet Union, turning one-half of another country [East Pakistan] into a satellite state and the other half [West Pakistan] into an impotent vassal."[14]

The scale of Pakistan's defeat in December 1971, resulting in the loss of one-third of its territory to the new state of Bangladesh, was the main impetus for Bhutto to initiate a nuclear weapons program.[15] India's underground test of a nuclear device on 8 May 1974, which Gandhi termed a peaceful nuclear explosion (PNE), was an additional impetus.[16]

An interagency working group convened by Secretary of State Kissinger immediately after the Indian PNE concluded, "Pakistan is seeking security assistance from the US and other major powers, a relaxation of US arms restrictions, and possibly in time, its own nuclear test program." Since "limiting the number of nuclear weapons states" and "attaining a peaceful and stable South Asia" remained major US interests, it was crucial to dissuade Pakistan from following India's example.[17] SNIE 4-1-74, released in August 1974, acknowledged that without substantial foreign assistance, Pakistan was unlikely to have a nuclear weapon before 1980. Nonetheless the Pakistanis would continue their nuclear weapons program.[18] Over the coming months, concerns about Pakistani nuclear intentions and reports about a contract to purchase a French-designed uranium

---

1947–2000, pp. 178–214; Montgomery, *In the Hegemon's Shadow*, pp. 120–124; and Robert J. McMahon, "The Dangers of Geopolitical Fantasies: Nixon, Kissinger, and the South Asia Crisis of 1971," in Fredrik Logevall and Andrew Preston, eds., *Nixon in the World: American Foreign Relations, 1969–1977* (Oxford: Oxford University Press, 2008), pp. 249–268. On the alleged deployment of the USS *Enterprise* to the Bay of Bengal, see Raghavendra Mishra, "Revisiting the 1971 'USS *Enterprise* Incident': Rhetoric, Reality, and Pointers for the Contemporary Era," *Journal of Defence Studies*, Vol. 9, No. 2 (2015), pp. 49–80.

[14] "Minutes of Washington Special Actions Group Meeting, 8 December 1971," *FRUS, 1969–1976, Vol. XI: South Asia Crisis, 1971* (Washington, DC: GPO, 2005), pp. 690–699.

[15] Zulkufar Ali Bhutto succeeded Yahya Khan as the president of Pakistan on 20 December 1971 and served in that post until 13 August 1973. Bhutto then served as prime minister from 14 August 1973 until his ouster in a coup on 5 July 1977.

[16] "Central Intelligence Bulletin—India, 20 May 1974, Top Secret," *DNSA Collection: Weapons of Mass Destruction* (Ann Arbor, MI: ProQuest, 2016), p. 3, http://search.proquest.com/docview/1679128688.

[17] "Memo from Sidney Sober to Henry A. Kissinger, re: Indian Nuclear Development—NSSM 156 [Includes Revised Report; Annex Not Included], 31 May 1974," *DNSA Collection: Presidential Directives, Part II* (Ann Arbor, MI: ProQuest, 2016), p. 67, http://search.proquest.com/docview/1679070697.

[18] "Special National Intelligence Estimate 4-1-74, 'Prospects for Further Proliferation of Nuclear Weapons,' 23 August 1974, Top Secret, Excised Copy," in William Burr and Jeffrey Richelson, eds., *NSA Electronic Briefing Book no. 240* (Washington, DC: National Security Archive, 2008), http://nsarchive.gwu.edu/NSAEBB/NSAEBB240/snie.pdf.

reprocessing plant sparked a confrontation between the United States and Pakistan that lasted until the end of the Cold War.

How did three successive US administrations—those of Gerald R. Ford, Jimmy Carter, and Ronald Reagan—attempt to balance competing nonproliferation and containment objectives in South Asia in the 1970s and 1980s? What might explain the oscillations of US strategies toward Pakistan from coercion to accommodation, and then back to coercion, over the span of approximately fifteen years? This chapter examines the confrontation between the United States and Pakistan over the latter's clandestine nuclear weapons program between 1975 and 1990.

I have chosen to restrict the analysis to this period for three reasons. First, given the moving twenty-five-year wall for declassification, many documents from the administrations of Presidents George H. W. Bush, William J. Clinton, and George W. Bush remain classified. Second, this period marked the height of the nonproliferation confrontation. Pakistan reached the threshold for testing a nuclear device in the late 1980s, but it did not conduct full-yield tests until May 1998, in part because Reagan and Pakistan's military dictator, General Muhammad Zia-ul-Haq, reached a non-testing understanding in 1982, somewhat comparable to the 1969 Nixon-Meir understanding.[19] Third, Bush's decision not to certify Pakistan's non-possession of a nuclear weapon in October 1990 resulted in the termination of $600 million in annual US foreign military and economic assistance, including the transfer of thirty F-16 aircrafts. This move was tantamount to the end of the US-Pakistan alliance.[20]

Averting containment failure in South Asia was the overriding aim of the Ford, Carter, and Reagan administrations from the mid-1970s to the late 1980s. Slowing or halting the Pakistani race to the bomb was always a subordinate aim. The United States' policies toward Pakistan were driven primarily by policymakers' assessments of the current power distribution in South Asia and the time horizons of emerging threats to US interests in that region. That power distribution became decidedly unfavorable and the time horizons for emerging threats grew dramatically shorter when the Soviet Union invaded Afghanistan in December 1979. From that point onward, officials in the Carter and Reagan administrations generally favored accommodative strategies toward

---

[19] Or Rabinowitz, *Bargaining on Nuclear Tests: Washington and Its Cold War Deals* (Oxford: Oxford University Press, 2014), p. 137.

[20] On Pakistani views of the George H. W. Bush administration's termination of military and economic assistance in October 1990 as tantamount to abandonment and the termination of US-Pakistan alliance, see Kux, *United States and Pakistan, 1947–2000*, pp. 309–311; and Ḥusain Ḥaqqānī, *Magnificent Delusions: Pakistan, the United States, and an Epic History of Misunderstanding* (New York: Public Affairs, 2013), pp. 283–284.

Pakistan's clandestine nuclear program. Both administrations sought to bolster Pakistan as a frontline ally against Soviet-occupied Afghanistan and as a conduit for covert military assistance to the Afghan insurgency. The Reagan administration extracted pledges from Zia that the nuclear program would not cross certain "red lines." In exchange for adhering to those red lines, Pakistan would receive billions of dollars of US arms and economic assistance. The various nonproliferation laws enacted by Congress in the late 1970s and 1980s, however, constituted the domestic mobilization hurdles for the two administrations' preferred South Asia policies.

In this chapter, I juxtapose the hypotheses from neoclassical realist theory against those from nuclear domino theory and credible sanctions theory. Nuclear domino theory would attribute any variation in the nonproliferation strategies that the Ford, Carter, and Reagan administrations pursued toward Pakistan to changed estimates in the likelihood of reactive proliferation in South Asia. During the period examined, India was already a nuclear latent state. Therefore, nuclear domino theory would expect US policymakers to pursue coercive nonproliferation strategies toward Pakistan to the extent they saw an increased likelihood that India might weaponize its nuclear capability. Conversely, when US policymakers perceived a lower risk of reactive proliferation (or weaponization) by India, they should be less inclined to pursue coercive nonproliferation strategies toward Pakistan.

As noted in chapter 2, the US-Pakistan nonproliferation dispute straddled the passage of the Symington Amendment. Credible sanctions theory suggests that following the passage of stringent and universal nonproliferation legislation, the Carter and Reagan administrations would consistently pursue coercive nonproliferation strategies toward other states, including allies like Pakistan. Yet, after the Soviet invasion of Afghanistan, the Carter and Reagan administrations repeatedly undermined the credibility of nonproliferation sanction in order to bolster Pakistan's military capability as a frontline ally.

The remainder of the chapter proceeds chronologically, beginning with the Ford administration's discovery of Pakistan's contract to acquire a French reprocessing plant in 1975 and ending with the Bush administration's termination of military and economic assistance to Pakistan in 1990.

The Ford Administration and the Pakistani Reprocessing Plant Contract (1975–1977)

Three months after the Indian PNE, Nixon resigned due to the Watergate scandal and Vice President Gerald R. Ford succeeded to the presidency. The

Ford administration adopted a two-pronged strategy to forestall Pakistan's nuclear weapons development: (1) the application of diplomatic pressure on allies to cancel contracts to sell nuclear technology to Pakistan; and (2) the resumption of US arms sales to Pakistan, in exchange for observance of International Atomic Energy Agency (IAEA) safeguards. On 5 February 1975, Ford and Kissinger met with Bhutto and other senior Pakistani officials. Kissinger asked the Pakistani prime minister to pledge that his government would "observe [IAEA] safeguards and ... not undertake any experiments outside the scope of the safeguards" as a precondition for US arms sales. Bhutto readily agreed. The Pakistani foreign minister, Aziz Ahmed, asked whether Pakistan could develop "peaceful nuclear explosives." Kissinger responded, "Absolutely not. Our position on safeguards is clear."[21]

A few weeks later, Kissinger assured Senator John Sparkman (D-AL), the chairman of the Foreign Relations Committee, "Pakistan has given us assurances not to go into nuclear explosives."[22] On 24 March 1975, Ford lifted the arms embargo that Johnson imposed on Pakistan during the 1965 war, but with the conditions that future arms sales would be on a cash-only basis and should not "restore the pre-1965 situation where the US was a major regional arms supplier."[23] The Ford administration approved Pakistan's request to purchase 20 TOW launchers and 450 missiles in late September 1975, but Kissinger informed Ahmed that more time was needed to evaluate the request for 110 A-7 jet fighters.[24]

In December 1975, US intelligence confirmed the secret Pakistani contract to purchase a French reprocessing plant, in addition to the contact to obtain a heavy water production facility from the Federal Republic of Germany.[25] Undersecretary of State for Political Affairs Joseph J. Sisto informed the Pakistani

---

[21] "189. Memorandum of Conversation, Washington, 5 February 1975, 2:30–3:30 P.M.," *FRUS, 1969–1976, Vol. E-8: Documents on South Asia, 1973–1976* (Washington, DC: GPO, 2007), https://history.state.gov/historicaldocuments/frus1969-76ve08/d189.

[22] "Memo of Telephone Conversation Between Secretary Kissinger and Senator John Sparkman, 20 February 1975, 6:45 P.M.," *DNSA Collection: Kissinger Telephone Conversations* (Ann Arbor, MI: ProQuest, 2016), p. 1, http://search.proquest.com/docview/1679103165.

[23] "193. National Security Decision Memorandum 289, Washington, 24 March 1975," *FRUS, 1969–1976, Vol. E-8: Documents on South Asia, 1973–1976* (Washington, DC: GPO, 2007), https://history.state.gov/historicaldocuments/frus1969-76ve08/d193.

[24] "210. Memorandum of Conversation, New York, 30 September 1975, 11:30 A.M.–12:30 P.M.," *FRUS, 1969–1976, Vol. E-8: Documents on South Asia, 1973–1976* (Washington, DC: GPO, 2007), https://history.state.gov/historicaldocuments/frus1969-76ve08/d210.

[25] "Memorandum to Holders, Special National Intelligence Estimate, 'Prospects for Further Proliferation of Nuclear Weapons,' SNIE 4-1-74, 18 December 1975," in William Burr, ed., *NSA Electronic Briefing Book no. 333* (Washington, DC: National Security Archive, 2010), http://www.gwu.edu/~nsarchiv/nukevault/ebb333/doc01.pdf.

ambassador, Sahabzada Yaqub Khan, about growing concern within the administration, Congress, and the American public about Pakistan's nuclear activities. Sisco warned, "Pakistan's apparent effort to acquire complete, indigenous nuclear fuel cycle is open to misinterpretation and question" and urged the Pakistani government to cancel the contracts with France and West Germany.[26] President Ford delivered a similar warning in a March 1976 letter to Bhutto warning that "The establishment of sensitive nuclear facilities under national control inevitably gives rise to perceptions in many quarters that ... non-peaceful uses may be contemplated."[27]

The Ford administration offered to sell Pakistan 100 A-7 attack aircraft in exchange for canceling the reprocessing plant contract.[28] In September 1976, Kissinger told Yaqub Khan that Pakistan's nuclear program had become an issue in the US presidential election campaign.[29] He warned: "If the Democrats win, you will face an assault and they will attack you. Credit and arms sales will be much more difficult, even impossible."[30] The following month, Kissinger warned Ahmed that if Pakistan did not cancel the contract, the Democrats in Congress would call to impose sanctions, as stipulated by the Symington Amendment. He added, however, if Bhutto cut a deal with Ford before the US election, those sanctions might be averted: "After November 2, if we are elected, Congress will act. If [Jimmy] Carter is elected, Congress and the President will act against you."[31]

---

[26] "224. Telegram 40475 from the Department of State to the Embassy in Pakistan, 19 February 1976, 2317z.," *FRUS, 1969–1976, Vol. E-8: Documents on South Asia, 1973–1976* (Washington, DC: GPO, 2007), https://history.state.gov/historicaldocuments/frus1969-76ve08/d224.

[27] "225. Letter from President Ford to Pakistani Prime Minister Bhutto, Washington, 19 March 1976," *FRUS, 1969–1976, Vol. E-8: Documents on South Asia, 1973–1976* (Washington, DC: GPO, 2007), https://history.state.gov/historicaldocuments/frus1969-76ve08/d225.

[28] "Memo of Conversation in Brent Scowcroft's Office, re: Progress on Proposal to Sell 110 A-7s to Pakistan and Problem Concerning Nuclear Sale by France to Pakistan, 20 September 1976," *US Declassified Documents Online* (Farmington Hills, MI: Gale, 1996), http://tinyurl.galegroup.com/tinyurl/3cbYd1.

[29] See Kathleen Teltsch, "Carter Proposes a Nuclear Limit," *New York Times*, 14 May 1976, pp. 1, 13.
Arms control and nuclear proliferation also came up during presidential debates. See Transcript of the Second Ford-Carter Presidential Debate at the Palace of Fine Arts Theater, San Francisco, CA, 6 October 1976, Commission on Presidential Debates, http://www.debates.org/index.php?page=october-6-1976-debate-transcript, accessed 9 July 2017.

[30] "235. Memorandum of Conversation, Washington, 11 September 1976, 3:07 P.M.," *FRUS, 1969–1976, Vol. E-8: Documents on South Asia, 1973–1976* (Washington, DC: GPO, 2007), https://history.state.gov/historicaldocuments/frus1969-76ve08/d235.

[31] "236. Memorandum of Conversation, New York, 6 October 1976, 10:30–11:28 A.M.," *FRUS, 1969–1976, Vol. E-8: Documents on South Asia, 1973–1976* (Washington, DC: GPO, 2007), https://history.state.gov/historicaldocuments/frus1969-76ve08/d236.

Following Carter's election, Kissinger made a final effort to persuade the Pakistanis. In December 1976, he met with Yaqub Khan to offer the A7s and even US financing for a French-built nuclear reactor, in exchange for Bhutto quietly terminating the contract. Kissinger warned, "Early in January and it will be a new administration which was elected on a plank of non-proliferation. And I think I can assure you that it won't avail itself of escape clauses, or Symington amendments."[32]

The United States faced a stable, although not necessarily favorable, distribution of power in South Asia in the early to mid-1970s. India and the Soviet Union renewed their treaty of alliance and friendship in 1970. India continued to purchase Soviet-made arms throughout the decade. New Delhi's relations with Washington during the premierships of Indira Gandhi and Rajiv Desai remained cool.[33] At the same time, there was little indication that the Soviet Union planned to expand its influence into South Asia in the mid-1970s. The Ford administration began the process of normalizing diplomatic relations with China, India's adversary and Pakistan's erstwhile ally. From the perspective of officials in Washington, therefore, the threat of containment failure in South Asia appeared remote. Likewise, in 1974–1976, Ford administration officials operated from long time horizons: the short-term likelihood of additional Soviet penetration in South Asia appeared to be low.

Neoclassical realist theory would expect senior officials in the Ford administration to prefer a coercive strategy to halt Pakistan's nuclear weapons program in the period from March 1975 to December 1976. Instead, officials pursued accommodative strategies toward Pakistan: Ford lifted the 1965 arms embargo with the proviso that any future US arms sales would be on a cash basis. Ford and Kissinger subsequently offered to sell 100 A-7 aircraft to Pakistan in exchange for Bhutto's pledge to terminate the reprocessing plant contract. In December 1976, Kissinger made a last-ditch offer to Yaqub Khan: the outgoing administration would provide additional A-7s and even US-financing for the construction of a French nuclear reactor in exchange for Bhutto's commitment to cancel the reprocessing plant contract. This behavior is an anomaly for the neoclassical realist hypothesis.

What might explain the Ford administration's accommodative strategies toward Pakistan's nuclear weapons program, despite the United States' confronting

---

[32] "239. Memorandum of Conversation, Washington, 17 December 1976, 3:20–4 P.M.," *FRUS, 1969–1976, Vol. E-8: Documents on South Asia, 1973–1976* (Washington, DC: GPO, 2007), https://history.state.gov/historicaldocuments/frus1969-76ve08/d239.

[33] Gandhi, the leader of the Indian National Congress, served as prime minister from 15 March 1971 to 24 March 1977. Desai, the leader of Janata Party, served as prime minister from 24 March 1977 to 28 July 1977.

a favorable power distribution in South Asia and long time horizons for threats to its interests there in 1975 and 1976? The failure of US intelligence agencies to anticipate the Indian PNE in May 1974 and the muted response by the Nixon administration to it prompted the Congress to take an increasingly assertive role in trying to shape US nonproliferation policy.[34] In June 1976, Congress passed the Symington Amendment to the 1961 Foreign Assistance Act (FAA), which prohibited economic and military assistance, as well as export credits, to countries that acquire, receive, or transfer nuclear enrichment technologies not in compliance with IAEA regulations. That amendment went into effect in August 1977.

Two considerations appear to have driven the Ford administration's strategies toward Pakistan's nascent nuclear weapons program. The first was a desire to restore limited alliance ties with Pakistan as a potential hedge against the more powerful and Soviet-leaning India. The second was a desire to head off a confrontation with Bhutto over the reprocessing plant contract, which would play into the hands of the Carter presidential campaign and the Democratic majority in Congress.

The Carter Administration and Symington Amendment Sanctions (1977–1981)

As Kissinger warned, the incoming Carter administration was more even determined to thwart Pakistan's nuclear ambitions than the Ford administration had been. In April 1977, Deputy Secretary of State Warren Christopher sent a memorandum to President Jimmy Carter outlining various options for negotiations over Pakistan's uranium reprocessing efforts. Christopher recommended that Carter offer several incentives for Bhutto to cancel the French reprocessing contract. These included the cash sale of F-5Es, and if necessary, A-4s, as well as the possible sale of C-130 transport planes, general utility helicopters, self-propelled howitzers, helicopters armed with TOW anti-aircraft missiles, and two surplus destroyers. Christopher also suggested the president consider economic and energy-related inducements such as a $100–$125 million increase in development assistance over the next two year or three years, an increase in Title I PL-480 food assistance, and perhaps some agreement on US holding of Pakistani rupees, if Congress did not object. Finally, he suggested renewing Kissinger's offer to help Pakistan finance the purchase of a French nuclear reactor and

---

[34] See George Perkovich, *India's Nuclear Bomb: The Impact on Global Proliferation* (Berkeley: University of California Press, 1999), p. 184; and Mitchell Reiss, *Without the Bomb: The Politics of Nuclear Nonproliferation* (New York: Columbia University Press, 1988), p. 232.

low-grade uranium (LEU) reprocessing facility, in lieu of a uranium enrichment facility. Carter rejected selling A-4s, increasing development assistance, or renewing Kissinger's offer to finance purchase a nuclear reactor and LEU reprocessing facility.[35]

Alfred Atherton, the assistant secretary of state for Near Eastern Affairs, and Douglas Bennet, the assistant secretary of state for legislative affairs, warned in June 1977 that articles in the *Washington Post* and the trade publication *Nucleonics Week* regarding Saint Gobian's transfer of reprocessing technology to Pakistan might spark additional press and congressional inquiries about the Carter administration's hesitation in invoking the Symington Amendment. "Obviously invocation of the Symington Amendment, especially at this point in US-Pakistan relations, would be highly damaging," Atherton and Bennet observed. As an alternative, they recommended that Secretary of State Cyrus Vance, Christopher, and other senior officials reach out to key members of Congress, demonstrating the administration's willingness to achieve the law's objective, without having to invoke it and cut off assistance to Pakistan. The new administration asked France to cancel, or at least postpone, the reprocessing plant contract. Atherton and Bennet acknowledged that "The chances of the French accepting our position in isolation from other nuclear questions of interest to France are slight in view of the political implications in France of this question."[36]

General Muhammad Zia-ul-Haq, the chief of the Pakistani Army Staff, overthrew Bhutto on 5 July 1977 after mass riots prompted by allegations of vote-rigging by the prime minister's Pakistan People's Party (PPP). Zia declared himself chief martial law administrator and president of Pakistan.[37] In September 1977, the Carter administration suspended development aid to Pakistan over concerns about its pursuit of French reprocessing technology. The State Department did not make a formal announcement to minimize

---

[35] "Acting Secretary of State Warren Christopher to the President, 'Reprocessing Negotiations with Pakistan: A Negotiating Strategy,' 2 April 1977, Secret," in William Burr, ed., *NSA Electronic Briefing Book no. 333* (Washington, DC: National Security Archive, 2010), http://www.gwu.edu/~nsarchiv/nukevault/ebb333/doc02.pdf.

[36] Assistant Secretaries Alfred L. Atherton and Douglas J. Bennet, Jr., Through Mr. Habib to the Acting Secretary, "Pakistan's Purchase of a Nuclear Fuel Reprocessing Plant: The Symington Amendment and Consultations with Congress, 23 June 1977, Confidential, with Cover Note from Christopher to 'Roy' Atherton," in William Burr, ed., *NSA Electronic Briefing Book no. 333* (Washington, DC: National Security Archive, 2010), http://nsarchive.gwu.edu/nukevault/ebb333/doc03.pdf.

[37] "Army Coup Is Reported in Pakistan," *Washington Post*, 5 July 1977, p. 2; "Pakistani Military, Now Ruling Nation, Promises Elections," *New York Times*, 6 July 1977, p. 53; "Army Coup Is Reported in Pakistan," *Washington Post*, 5 July 1977, p. 2; Harry Kramer, "Military Ousts Bhutto in Bloodless Coup, Hoping to End Pakistani Political Unrest," *Wall Street Journal*, 6 July 1977, p. 2; and Associated Press, "Pakistani Military, Now Ruling Nation, Promises Elections," *New York Times*, 6 July 1977, p. 1.

diplomatic fallout. A month later, however, Hummel proposed resuming development aid for two reasons: first, Pakistan had technically not violated the 1977 Glenn Amendment (which banned the provision of US military and economic assistance, as well as export credits, to countries that acquire or transfer nuclear reprocessing technology or explode or transfer a nuclear device); and second, the French government was desperately trying to find a justification for canceling the reprocessing plant contract. Hummel argued, "It now appears we have virtually achieved our objective," adding "to continue the current suspension of new economic assistance places us in a punitive posture, when it is no longer appropriate," would do further damage to US-Pakistan relations.[38]

Arthur Hartman, the US ambassador to France, took the opposite view, arguing the US needed assurances that the reprocessing contract was in fact dead. "To resume economic assistance," Hartman argued, "would suggest to the French we may not be as serious as we say about the non-proliferation issue and that we are squandering potential leverage without any visible return." Vance, Christopher, and other State Department officials agreed with Hartman, concluding it was better to defer a decision on economic aid and to see how the French-Pakistani negotiations developed, rather than to face "very tough questions" from members of Congress and the "choice of providing unconvincing justifications or risking embarrassment."[39]

In late May 1978, President Valéry Giscard d'Estaing of France informed Carter of his intention to cancel the reprocessing plant contract. Giscard said, however, he wanted to delay officially informing the Pakistani government.[40] In order to guard against an "intemperate" response once the French decision became public, as well as to dissuade the Pakistanis from seeking enrichment technology from other suppliers, Vance told Hummel that the administration planned to offer General Zia "a package of tangible inducements and some political support."[41] On the political side, this would entail sending Undersecretary of State for Political Affairs David Newsom to Islamabad to meet with Zia and Foreign Minister Agha Shahi, sending a US aircraft carrier to make a port call in

---

[38] "Alfred L. Atherton and George S. Vest Thru: Mr. Christopher, Mr. Habib, Mrs. Benson to the Secretary, 'the Nuclear Reprocessing Issue with Pakistan and France: Whether to Resume Aid to Pakistan,' 18 October 1977, with Draft Instructions and Telegrams from Embassies in Paris and Islamabad Attached, Secret," in William Burr, ed., *NSA Electronic Briefing Book no. 333* (Washington, DC: National Security Archive, 2010), http://www.gwu.edu/~nsarchiv/nukevault/ebb333/doc04.pdf.

[39] Quoted in Ibid.

[40] "State Department Cable 136685 to Embassy Islamabad, 'Reprocessing Issue,' 30 May 1978, Secret," in William Burr, ed., *NSA Electronic Briefing Book no. 333* (Washington, DC: National Security Archive, 2010), http://nsarchive.gwu.edu/nukevault/ebb333/doc06.pdf.

[41] Ibid.

Karachi, and enhancing US-Pakistan intelligence liaison regarding Soviet activities in Afghanistan.[42]

Vance instructed Hummel to tell Shahi that the Carter administration shared Pakistani concerns about instability in Afghanistan, where Nur Muhammad Taraki and the People's Democratic Party of Afghanistan (PDPA) staged a coup against President Mohammed Daoud Khan.[43] Vance also instructed Hummel to warn Shahi that "Neither the Congress, nor the administration, could support any aid program or military sales if Pakistan seeks to develop reprocessing capability on its own or takes any further steps toward the development of nuclear explosives."[44]

Newsom told Yaqub Khan in August 1978 that if Pakistan decided not to go forward with the French reprocessing plant, the United States would not require written assurance or a public statement that Pakistan would refrain from "indigenous construction" of a uranium enrichment facility. He added, however, that members of Congress were mindful of the "intent" of the Glenn Amendment and that, if asked, administration officials would provide "estimates of Pakistan's future intentions on reprocessing."[45]

A meeting between Newsom and Senator John Glenn (D-OH), a member of the Senate Foreign Relations Committee, and Rep. Clement Zablocki (D-WI), the chairman of the House Foreign Affairs Committee, on 12 August 1978, illustrates the depth of congressional concern about Pakistan's nuclear program. Zablocki told Newsom that while the Glenn Amendment did provide for a presidential waiver on the cutoff of US military and economic assistance, such a waiver would not be popular with members of Congress unless concerns about Pakistani reprocessing were addressed. Glenn warned Newsom that if doubts remained about Pakistani nuclear intentions, there were members of Congress who would propose specific prohibitions on US aid to Pakistan.[46]

---

[42] Ibid.

[43] For an analysis of the PDPA coup against Daoud in April 1978 and the ensuing Saur Revolution, see David B. Edwards, *Before Taliban: Genealogies of the Afghan Jihad* (Berkeley: University of California Press, 2002), pp. 22–56.

[44] "State Department Cable 136685 to Embassy Islamabad, 'Reprocessing Issue,' 30 May 1978, Secret," in William Burr, ed., *NSA Electronic Briefing Book no. 333* (Washington, DC: National Security Archive, 2010), http://nsarchive.gwu.edu/nukevault/ebb333/doc06.pdf.

[45] "State Department Cable 191467 to Embassy Islamabad, 'Pak Ambassador's Call on Undersecretary Newsom,' 1 August 1978, Secret," in William Burr, ed., *NSA Electronic Briefing Book no. 333* (Washington, DC: National Security Archive, 2010), http://nsarchive.gwu.edu/nukevault/ebb333/doc08.pdf.

[46] "State Department Cable 204785 to Embassy Islamabad, 'Pakistan Reprocessing,' 12 August 1978, Secret," in William Burr, ed., *NSA Electronic Briefing Book No. 352* (Washington, DC: National Security Archive, 2010), http://nsarchive.gwu.edu/nukevault/ebb333/doc12.pdf.

Newsom met with Shahi the following day and informed him that the administration was aware of the ongoing French-Pakistani negotiations regarding the reprocessing plant. He also wanted to share the results of his consultations with Glenn and Zablocki. Newsom stated, "our ability to gain congressional concurrence would be facilitated by some kind of Pakistani assurance on their future intentions." Shahi indicated "it would be impossible for the GOP [government of Pakistan] to provide public or private assurances on [its] future intentions on reprocessing," adding that "Pakistan has the unfettered right to do what it wishes and will retain all its options."[47]

Giscard sent a letter to Zia on 21 August 1978, formally notifying him of the cancellation of the reprocessing plant contract.[48] The Pakistani government publicly announced the cancellation on 23 August.[49] Vance met with Shahi at the UN General Assembly in October and informed him the Carter administration was prepared to resume development aid to Pakistan and might even consider military aid as well. Shahi asked Vance for clarification on the administration's policy on the possible sale of A-7s to Pakistan, especially in light of India's plan to purchase 200 deep-penetration strike aircraft from the Soviet Union. Vance replied that he warned the Indian external affairs minister that the planned purchase would set off a regional arms race. Vance said that if India proceeded with the purchase of the Soviet strike aircraft, then the Carter administration would review its policy on the sale of the A-7s to Pakistan.[50]

In November 1978, Harold Saunders, the assistant secretary of state for Near Eastern Affairs, and Anthony Lake, the director of policy planning, argued that a more supportive US-Pakistan relationship, especially in the areas of military supply and development aid, "may reduce Pakistan's paranoia and give us some influence over their nuclear program, but not decisive leverage." In a fourteen-page memorandum to Vance, Saunders and Lake wrote they supported linking

---

[47] "State Department Cable 205550 to Embassy Islamabad, 'Discussion Between Undersecretary Newsom and Pakistan's Minister of State for Foreign Affairs Agha Shahi on the Reprocessing Issue,' 14 August 1978, Secret," in William Burr, ed., *NSA Electronic Briefing Book no. 333* (Washington, DC: National Security Archive, 2010), http://nsarchive.gwu.edu/nukevault/ebb333/doc13.pdf.

[48] "U.S. Embassy Islamabad to Cable 8167 to State Department, 'Reprocessing Plant,' 21 August 1978, Secret," in William Burr, ed., *NSA Electronic Briefing Book no. 333* (Washington, DC: National Security Archive, 2010), http://nsarchive.gwu.edu/nukevault/ebb333/doc14.pdf.

[49] "US Embassy Paris Cable 28414 to State Department, 'French Views on Pakistan Reprocessing Plant,' 25 August 1978, Confidential," in William Burr, ed., *NSA Electronic Briefing Book no. 333* (Washington, DC: National Security Archive, 2010), http://nsarchive.gwu.edu/nukevault/ebb333/doc17.pdf.

[50] "Memo to Chris [Warren Christopher] from Steve [Oxman], 4 October 1978, Enclosing Edits to Draft Cable to Islamabad and 'Evening Reading' Reports to President Carter on Pakistan, Secret, Excerpts," in William Burr, ed., *NSA Electronic Briefing Book no. 333* (Washington, DC: National Security Archive, 2010), http://www.gwu.edu/~nsarchiv/nukevault/ebb333/doc18.pdf.

assistance to the nuclear issue, but there was also a need to rebuild bilateral ties to a point where Zia and his advisers might actually perceive the severance of US ties to be "disadvantageous to their national interests."[51]

Just as the Carter administration prepared to resume economic aid, intelligence analysts became increasingly concerned that Pakistan would pursue other options to acquire weapons-grade nuclear fuel, including development of an indigenous centrifuge enrichment capacity.[52] CIA analysts warned in December 1978, "Pakistani efforts to acquire foreign equipment . . . have been more extensive and sophisticated than previously indicated" and that they "may succeed in acquiring the main missing components for a strategically significant gas centrifuge enrichment capability."[53] In January 1979, the CIA warned Pakistan "may already have succeeded in acquiring the main missing components for a gas centrifuge plant and ancillary facilities" and might be able to produce "highly enriched uranium for weapons, perhaps even by 1982."[54]

Saunders and Thomas Pickering, the assistant secretary of state for oceanic, environmental, and scientific affairs, proposed "buying off" Pakistan. They envisioned a three-stage process: (1) consideration of a military and economic assistance package to Pakistan, including the sale of conventional weapons like the F-16s and Cobra helicopters with TOW missiles as well as $290 million in economic aid for FY 1980; (2) revisiting the idea of a nuclear non-development/non-use agreement between India and Pakistan; and (3) consideration of waiving the March 1980 nuclear fuel cutoff date for India, if New Delhi adhered to a "no nuclear weapons" pact and the Comprehensive Test Ban Treaty (CTBT), as well

---

[51] "Harold Saunders and Anthony Lake Through Mr. Newsom and Mrs. Benson to the Secretary, 'PRC Meeting, November 30, 1978–Pakistan,' 29 November 1978, Secret," in William Burr, ed., *NSA Electronic Briefing Book no. 333* (Washington, DC: National Security Archive, 2010), http://nsarchive.gwu.edu/nukevault/ebb333/doc20.pdf.

[52] "Memorandum of Conversation, Prepared by Assistant Secretary of State Joseph Nye, 'Consultations on Pakistan: Details on Indigenous Nuclear Capabilities (Supplement to Memcon Prepared by Ambassador Hummel),' 6 October 1978, Secret," in William Burr, ed., *NSA Electronic Briefing Book no. 333* (Washington, DC: National Security Archive, 2010), http://www.gwu.edu/~nsarchiv/nukevault/ebb333/doc19.pdf.

[53] "John Despres, National Intelligence Officer for Nuclear Proliferation via Deputy Director for National Foreign Assessment [and] National Intelligence Officer for Warning to Director of Central Intelligence, 'Monthly Warning Report—Nuclear Proliferation,' 'Warning Report' Attached, 5 December 1978, Secret," in William Burr, ed., *NSA Electronic Briefing Book no. 333* (Washington, DC: National Security Archive, 2010), http://www.gwu.edu/~nsarchiv/nukevault/ebb333/doc21.pdf.

[54] "John Despres, NIO for Nuclear Proliferation, to Interagency Intelligence Working Group on Nuclear Proliferation, 'Monthly Warning Report,' 18 January 1979, Top Secret," in William Burr, ed., *NSA Electronic Briefing Book no. 333* (Washington, DC: National Security Archive, 2010), http://nsarchive.gwu.edu/nukevault/ebb333/doc22.pdf.

as maintained an open dialogue with Islamabad.[55] The Saunders-Pickering proposal never went anywhere. Other State Department officials and NSC staffers deemed the proposal had not been sufficiently analyzed and the Carter administration would have great difficulty selling such a deal to a skeptical Congress.[56]

The Policy Review Committee (PRC) of the National Security Council (NSC), chaired by Deputy National Security Adviser David Aaron, met on 22 January 1979. Based upon the latest intelligence, they concluded Pakistan was developing a nuclear explosive capacity and that key components were likely in place before August 1977, when the Symington Amendment went into effect. Hummel and Robert Goheen, the US ambassador to India, would be asked to approach Desai about the possibility of a joint Indian-Pakistani agreement not to develop nuclear weapons. On the diplomatic front, officials endorsed discussions with Chinese vice premier Deng Xiaoping and "selected European" leaders about cutting off the flow of nuclear technology to Pakistan. They considered asking Congress to amend the Symington Amendment to provide a presidential waiver "to permit continued cooperation with Pakistan while seeking to dissuade them from the nuclear option," but only after consulting key senators and representatives. In the meantime, Hummel would raise the nuclear program issue with Zia and "point out to him the implications for US-Pakistan relations."[57]

In early March 1979, Christopher traveled to Islamabad and delivered a *démarche* to Zia: unsafeguarded uranium enrichment activities would trigger the imposition of sanctions on Pakistan, under the terms of Symington Amendment. According to the handwritten notes taken by NSC staff member Thomas Thornton, Christopher spoke in "tough terms" about the nuclear issue and Shahi characterized his words as an "ultimatum." Christopher also said that the enrichment program was fundamentally different from the abortive French reprocessing plant deal because the Pakistanis were undertaking the

---

[55] "Steve [Oxman] to Chris [Warren Christopher], 5 March 1979, Enclosing Memorandum from Harold Saunders and Thomas Pickering Through Mr. Newsom and Mrs. Benson to the Secretary, 'a Strategy for Pakistan,' 5 March 1979, Secret," in William Burr, ed., *NSA Electronic Briefing Book no. 333* (Washington, DC: National Security Archive, 2010), https://www2.gwu.edu/~nsarchiv/nukevault/ebb333/doc28.pdf.

[56] "Marshall Shulman, Paul Kreisberg, and Robert Barry to Mr. Newsom, 'the "Mini-PRC" Meeting on Pakistani Nuclear Intentions,' 22 January 1979, Secret," in William Burr, ed., *NSA Electronic Briefing Book no. 333* (Washington, DC: National Security Archive, 2010), http://nsarchive.gwu.edu/nukevault/ebb333/doc23b.pdf.

[57] "Presidential Review Committee Meeting, January 22, 1979, 'Summary of Conclusions: Mini-PRC on Pakistani Nuclear Matters,' 23 January 1979, Secret, Excised Copy," in William Burr, ed., *NSA Electronic Briefing Book no. 333* (Washington, DC: National Security Archive, 2010), http://nsarchive.gwu.edu/nukevault/ebb333/doc23c.pdf.

former in a clandestine manner.[58] Zia and Shahi did not deny that Pakistan was building reprocessing and enrichment facilities. Nor did they agree to refrain from enriching uranium to weapons grade.[59] Instead, Shahi told Christopher that the Zia regime might support a South Asia nuclear weapons–free zone, if India and Pakistan agreed to reciprocal inspections of their nuclear facilities.[60] Shahi declared Pakistan "is not capable of pursuing a nuclear option" and that Pakistanis scientists and engineers were "not using our reprocessing capability to make nuclear weapons."[61]

In the aftermath of Christopher's trip, Hummel was quite pessimistic. "We lack the leverage to force Pakistan out of the nuclear business," he wrote in a cable to Washington, suggesting "only by a bold initiative of US policy—with its own attendant risks— . . . can we hope to prevent nuclear proliferation." Hummel laid out three options: (1) a reciprocal agreement between India and Pakistan for an inspections regime or signing the NPT (which as ideal, but also highly unlikely), (2) "pinching off" the Pakistani nuclear option by getting supplier countries to tighten export controls (which was unworkable as a long-term solution, but it would buy time), or (3) multilateral guarantees against an Indian nuclear attack, with additional support for Pakistani conventional defense capabilities (which would risk US-India relations and might face congressional opposition).[62]

The PRC met on 9 March 1979 to discuss three items: (1) the imposition of the Symington Amendment sanctions; (2) additional measures to stop Pakistan from acquiring a nuclear explosive capability, including more-stringent export restrictions; and (3) options to maintain the "best possible relations

---

[58] "Handwritten Notes, Warren Christopher Meetings with General Zia and Foreign Minister Shahi, 1 and 2 March 1979," in William Burr, ed., *NSA Electronic Briefing Book no. 333* (Washington, DC: National Security Archive, 2010), http://nsarchive.gwu.edu/nukevault/ebb333/doc26b.pdf.

[59] "U.S. Embassy Islamabad Cable 2769 to State Department, 'Nuclear Aspects of DEPSEC Visit Discussed with UK and French Ambassadors,' 7 March 1979," in William Burr, ed., *NSA Electronic Briefing Book no. 333* (Washington, DC: National Security Archives, 2010), http://nsarchive.gwu.edu/nukevault/ebb333/doc26a.pdf.

[60] "U.S. Embassy Islamabad to Cable 2413 to State Department, 'Pakistan Nuclear Program: Technical Team Visit,' 27 February 1979, Secret," in William Burr, ed., *NSA Electronic Briefing Book no. 333* (Washington, DC: National Security Archive, 2010), http://nsarchive.gwu.edu/nukevault/ebb333/doc25.pdf.

[61] "Handwritten Notes, Warren Christopher Meetings with General Zia and Foreign Minister Shahi, 1 and 2 March 1979," in William Burr, ed., NSA Electronic Briefing Book no. 333 (Washington, DC: National Security Archive, 2010), http://nsarchive.gwu.edu/nukevault/ebb333/doc26b.pdf.

[62] "U.S. Embassy Islamabad to Cable 2655 to State Department, 'Pakistan's Nuclear Program: Hard Choices,' 5 March 1979, Secret," in William Burr, ed., *NSA Electronic Briefing Book no. 333* (Washington, DC: National Security Archive, 2010), http://nsarchive.gwu.edu/nukevault/ebb333/doc27.pdf.

with Pakistan under the circumstances."[63] The administration announced the suspension of US economic and military aid to Pakistan on 6 April 1979. In identical letters to Giscard, British prime minister James Callaghan, Canadian prime minister Pierre Trudeau, and West German chancellor Helmut Schmidt, Carter wrote that US law obligated him to suspend aid to Pakistan. He found this especially regrettable "at a time when there is a possibility of increasing Soviet involvement in Afghanistan and when political instability persists in Iran." Nonetheless, Carter warned that if left unchecked, Pakistani efforts to acquire a nuclear weapons capability would "disturb the stability of the sub-continent and the region."[64]

Following the invocation of the Symington Amendment, the Carter administration continued trying to broker an India-Pakistan agreement against the development or testing of nuclear weapons. Desai reacted coolly to the proposal. The Indian prime minister ominously told Goheen that if he learned Pakistan was ready to test a bomb or if it actually tested one, he "would act at once to smash it."[65] Averting a possible Pakistani nuclear test became the administration's objective in summer 1979. Peter Constable, then deputy chief of mission in Islamabad, however, questioned whether Pakistan would emulate India by conducting a nuclear test. In a 6 June cable, Constable suggested the Pakistanis might be content to master the nuclear fuel cycle without actually testing a device. Therefore, instead of trying to dismantle the Pakistani nuclear program entirely, he suggested the Carter administration seek a "special understanding" with General Zia patterned on the Nixon-Meir agreement in September 1969.[66]

Ambassador Gerald C. Smith, the special envoy on nonproliferation issues, argued the United States was already vulnerable to charges of hypocrisy because of the disconnect between its commitment to nuclear nonproliferation, on the one hand, and its "special understanding" about Israel's undeclared nuclear arsenal, on the other hand. "A second exception would drain the consistency [from]

---

[63] "Presidential Review Committee [Sic] Meeting, March 9, 1979, 'Pakistan,' n.d., Secret, Excised Copy," in William Burr, ed., *NSA Electronic Briefing Book no. 333* (Washington, DC: National Security Archive, 2010), http://nsarchive.gwu.edu/nukevault/ebb333/doc29.pdf.

[64] "Paul H. Kreisberg to Mr. Newsom, 'Presidential Letter on Pakistan Nuclear Program to Western Leaders,' 30 March 1979, Secret," in William Burr, ed., *NSA Electronic Briefing Book no. 333* (Washington: National Security Archive, 2010), http://nsarchive.gwu.edu/nukevault/ebb333/doc33.pdf.

[65] "U.S. Embassy New Delhi Cable 9979, 'India and the Pakistan Nuclear Problem,' 7 June 1979, Secret," in William Burr, ed., *NSA Electronic Briefing Book no. 333* (Washington, DC: National Security Archive, 2010), http://nsarchive.gwu.edu/nukevault/ebb333/doc35b.pdf.

[66] "US Department of State Cable 145139 to US Embassy India [Repeating Cable Sent to Embassy Pakistan], 'Non-Proliferation in South [Asia],' 6 June 1979, Secret," in William Burr, ed., *NSA Electronic Briefing Book no. 377* (Washington, DC: National Security Archive, 2012), https://www.documentcloud.org/documents/347012-doc-1-6-6-79.html.

your nonproliferation policy," he added. Apparently, Carter agreed with Smith's assessment, since he penciled the word "true" in the margins of the memo.[67]

Noting that the United States' relations with India and Pakistan were at an impasse and that "Our nonproliferation goals [were] in great jeopardy," on 19 June, National Security Adviser Zbigniew Brzezinski asked Vance to convene an interagency working group, chaired by Smith, to review the administration's policy options in South Asia.[68] In July, CIA analysts warned that, in response to the rapid advances in Pakistan's nuclear program, India would likely move toward nuclear weapons production, although that would take "at least two years." India would try to improve its range of "unilateral military options," should diplomacy fail to slow Pakistani production of weapons-usable materials. Although analysts thought it unlikely the Zia government would transfer any nuclear explosives abroad, Pakistan might already be sharing sensitive technologies with states such as Saudi Asia, Libya, and Iraq.[69]

Shahi traveled to Washington in October 1979 for talks with Vance and other US officials. He hoped that a series of adverse developments in the Middle East and South Asia in recent months would make the Carter administration more flexible on the Pakistani nuclear program. These adverse developments included: the ouster the shah of Iran, Mohammad Reza Pahlavi, in late 1978 and the Islamic Revolution earlier in the year; the growing Afghan insurgency against the PDPA; the ouster and the subsequent execution of Taraki by his deputy Hazifullah Amin in October 1978; and the growing tensions between the Soviet Union and the Amin regime in Kabul.[70] Instead, Vance asked Shahi for commitments that Pakistan: (1) would not transfer nuclear technology to other states; (2) would open its nuclear facilities to international inspections, and (3) would not test a nuclear device. Shahi agreed to only the first condition. On the second, he replied that Pakistan would not permit international

---

[67] "Gerard C. Smith, Special Representative of the President for Non-Proliferation Matters, to the President, 'Nonproliferation in South Asia,' 8 June 1979, Secret," in William Burr, ed., *NSA Electronic Briefing Book no. 333* (Washington, DC: National Security Archive, 2010), http://nsarchive.gwu.edu/nukevault/ebb333/doc36.pdf.

[68] "Brzezinski to the Secretary of State, 'the South Asian Nuclear Problem,' 19 June 1979, Secret," in William Burr, ed., *NSA Electronic Briefing Book no. 333* (Washington, DC: National Security Archive, 2010), http://nsarchive.gwu.edu/nukevault/ebb333/doc37.pdf.

[69] "John Despres, NIO for Nuclear Proliferation via Deputy Director for National Foreign Assessment [and] National Intelligence Officer for Warning to Director of Central Intelligence, 'Monthly Warning Report—Nuclear Proliferation,' 24 July 1979, Secret, Excised Copy," in William Burr, ed., *NSA Electronic Briefing Book no. 333* (Washington, DC: National Security Archive, 2010), http://nsarchive.gwu.edu/nukevault/ebb333/doc41.PDF.

[70] "Department of State to Multiple Embassies, Re: U.S.-Pak. Talks: Regional Issues, Confidential, 24 October 1979," *DNSA Collection: Nuclear Nonproliferation* (Ann Arbor, MI: ProQuest, 2016), p. 8, http://search.proquest.com/docview/1679138908.

inspection of Kahuta and other nuclear facilities unless India did likewise. On the third item, Shahi said that "Pakistan had not yet reached that stage." The Pakistani foreign minister said his government would review the pros and cons of conducting a nuclear test once it had the capacity to do so.[71]

In mid-November 1979, Saunders, Pickering, and Lake proposed multilateral collaboration with Pakistan on a power generation program that might give Zia and his advisers "a political 'out' for discontinuing their sensitive nuclear facilities." Additionally, they proposed continued consultations with European allies to increase pressure on Pakistan regarding its nuclear activities and an offer to sell Pakistan two Gearing-class destroyers "to keep the nuclear dialogue going."[72] However, before Vance could raise this proposal at the PRC meeting scheduled for 16 November, Smith reported disappointing results from his recent talks in European capitals. The British, French, Dutch, and West German foreign ministers told him they doubted "any combination of available disincentives or incentives will influence Pakistan's nuclear course." Smith felt his case was not made easier by the fact that Chinese premier Hua Goufeng recently urged the British, French, and West German governments to "bolster Pakistan as a barrier to Soviet adventurism in the region."[73]

The Carter administration confronted a stable, if not exactly favorable, power distribution in South Asia and long time horizons for threats to US interests there when it took office in January 1977. Those interests always entailed denying the Soviet Union access to South Asia, and by extension to the Persian Gulf. Until late summer 1979, the risk of increased Soviet military penetration in the region was relatively low. Instead, the more pressing threat to US interests appeared to be Pakistan's pursuit of a nuclear weapons option—first through the acquisition of reprocessing facilities from France, and later through the construction of an indigenous uranium enrichment plant.

From April to December 1979, the power distribution in South Asia became decidedly less favorable from the United States' standpoint. Further, the time horizons for emerging threats to US interests grew shorter. The situation in Afghanistan became highly volatile, due to the mounting insurgency against the PDPA regime and the growing rivalry between Amin and Taraki. The Soviet

---

[71] Quoted in Kux, *United States and Pakistan, 1947–2000*, pp. 240–241.

[72] "Assistant Secretaries Harold Saunders, Thomas Pickering, and Anthony Lake Through Mr. Christopher, Mr. Newsom, and Mrs. Benson to the Secretary, 'November 14 PRC Meeting on South Asian Nuclear Issues,' 10 November 1979, Secret," in William Burr, ed., *NSA Electronic Briefing Book no. 333* (Washington, DC: National Security Archive, 2010), http://www.gwu.edu/~nsarchiv/nukevault/ebb333/doc44.pdf.

[73] "Gerard C. Smith to the Secretary, 'Consultations in Europe on Pakistan,' 15 November 1979, Secret," in William Burr, ed., *NSA Electronic Briefing Books no. 333* (Washington, DC: National Security Archive, 2010), http://nsarchive.gwu.edu/nukevault/ebb333/doc45.pdf.

Army deployed a combat brigade to the Bagram Air Base outside of Kabul in July. The Soviet Foreign Ministry dispatched a high-ranking delegation to Kabul to mediate between Taraki and Amin in August.[74]

The US Embassy in Kabul warned about a growing Soviet military presence in Afghanistan and the acceleration of arms shipments to the PDPA regime.[75] "One of the major difficulties that Soviet decision makers have faced this year," the CIA reported on 21 September, "has been to determine whether the regime, which has increasingly been at odds with the rest of the country, is salvageable."[76] Five days later, the CIA reported that while it had "not seen indications that the Soviets are at the moment preparing for a large-scale military intervention in Afghanistan," such a large scale-military intervention was a distinct possibility in the coming months.[77]

On 10 September, Director of Central Intelligence (DCI) Admiral Stansfield Turner told the NSC that "Soviet leaders may be on the threshold of a decision to commit their own forces to prevent the collapse of the Taraki regime and protect their own sizable stake in Afghanistan." Turner added that "The Soviets may now be more inclined to gamble on a substantial intervention in Afghanistan because of their perception of the downturn in relations with the US and the uncertain prospects of the SALT [II] treaty in the Senate."[78] Noting that a steady buildup of Soviet air and ground forces near the Afghan border had been underway since

---

[74] "US Embassy Soviet Union to the State Department, re: Soviet Views About Afghanistan, Confidential Cable, 16 August 1979," *DNSA Collection: Afghanistan* (Ann Arbor, MI: ProQuest, 2015), p. 1, http://search.proquest.com/docview/1679077774; and "White House Situation Room to US Embassy, Beijing, Re: USSR-Afghanistan: Continued Soviet Support, Intelligence Support Cable, Top Secret, 26 August 1979," *DNSA Collection: Afghanistan* (Ann Arbor, MI: ProQuest, 2015), p. 4, http://search.proquest.com/docview/1679095556.

[75] "Cable, 'An Assessment of Soviet Influence and Involvement in Afghanistan,' [J. Bruce] Amstutz to Secretary of State, 6 September 1979," in Svetlana Savranskaya and Malcolm Byrne, eds., *Carter-Brezhnev Project* (Washington, DC: National Security Archive, 2016), http://nsarchive.gwu.edu/carterbrezhnev/docs_intervention_in_afghanistan_and_the_fall_of_detente/doc53.pdf; "Cable, 'Soviet Combat Troops in Afghanistan,' Amstutz to the Secretary, 3 October 1979," in Svetlana Savranskaya and Malcolm Byrne, eds., *Carter-Brezhnev Project* (Washington, DC: National Security Archive, 2016), http://nsarchive.gwu.edu/carterbrezhnev/docs_intervention_in_afghanistan_and_the_fall_of_detente/doc56.pdf.

[76] "CIA, National Intelligence Daily: USSR-Afghanistan: Soviet Involvement and Options [Includes Map], 21 September 1979," *DNSA Collection: CIA Covert Operations: From Carter to Obama, 1977–2010* (Ann Arbor, MI: ProQuest, 2015), p. 4, http://search.proquest.com/1679096635.

[77] "Interagency Intelligence Memorandum, CIA, 'Soviet Options in Afghanistan,' 27 September 1979," in Svetlana Savranskaya and Malcolm Byrne, eds., *NSA Electronic Briefing Book no. 396* (Washington, DC: National Security Archive, 2012), http://nsarchive.gwu.edu/NSAEBB/NSAEBB396/docs/1979-09-27%20Soviet%20Options%20in%20Afghanistan.pdf.

[78] "Memorandum from the Director of Central Intelligence to the National Security Council, re: Alert Memorandum on USSR-Afghanistan [Includes Attachment; Differently Excised Versions Appended], Top Secret, 10 September 1979," *DNSA Collection: CIA Covert Operations: From Carter*

July, Turner told the PRC on 17 December that there were approximately 5,300 Soviet troops already in Afghanistan, in addition to approximately 3,000 Soviet civilians.[79]

The Carter administration confronted high domestic mobilization hurdles in the pursuit of its preferred nonproliferation strategies toward Pakistan. This was evident in the deliberations following the discovery of Pakistani uranium enrichment facilities in winter 1979. The Symington Amendment prohibited economic and military assistance, as well as export credits, to states that acquire, receive, or transfer nuclear enrichment technologies not in compliance with IAEA safeguards. At that time, the law had no provisions for the president to waive imposing sanctions.

Senior officials recognized that the sudden termination of US economic and military aid was unlikely to coerce Zia into ceasing uranium enrichment and allowing international inspections of nuclear sites. Nonetheless, they felt compelled to invoke the Symington Amendment. Then, having imposed sanctions, they struggled to find incentives for Pakistan to refrain from continuing with unsafeguarded enrichment, the export of nuclear technologies, and possibly conducting a nuclear test. Between January 1977 and December 1979, therefore, the administration's strategies toward Pakistan oscillated from outright coercion to offers of limited economic inducements and intelligence cooperation, especially with respect to collection and limited covert operations against the PDPA regime in Afghanistan.[80]

The Soviet Union invaded Afghanistan on 24 December 1979. The CIA reported that as many as 215 Soviet transports, including AN-22s, AN-12s, and IL-76s, crossed the Soviet-Afghan border the following day.[81] On 27 December, Soviet special forces killed Amin in his palace on the outskirts of Kabul and installed Babrak Kamal as the new chairman of the Revolutionary Council and

---

to Obama, 1977–2010 (Ann Arbor, MI: ProQuest, 2015), p. 10, http://search.proquest.com/docview/1679096321.

[79] "Summary of Conclusions, 'Iran,' Special Coordination Committee Meeting, [Excerpt on Afghanistan], 17 December 1979," in Svetlana Savranskaya and Malcolm Byrne, eds., *Carter-Brezhnev Project* (Washington, DC: National Security Archive, 2016), http://nsarchive.gwu.edu/carterbrezhnev/docs_intervention_in_afghanistan_and_the_fall_of_detente/doc60.pdf.

[80] Carter authorized limited covert assistance to Afghan insurgents fighting Taraki's government in July 1979. See Bruce Riedel, *What We Won: America's Secret War in Afghanistan, 1979–1989* (Washington, DC: Brookings Institution Press, 2014), p. 99; Ḥusain Ḥaqqānī, *Magnificent Delusions*, p. 242; and Robert M. Gates, *From the Shadows: The Ultimate Insider's Story of Five Presidents and How They Won the Cold War* (New York: Simon and Schuster, 1996), p. 143.

[81] "245. Summary of Conclusions of a Special Coordinating Committee Meeting, 9:30–10:30 A.M., 26 December 1979," *FRUS, 1977–1980, Vol. VII: Soviet Union* (Washington, DC: GPO, 2013).

PDPA general-secretary.[82] In Washington, Carter and his national security team determined that strengthening Pakistan would be a major component of the administration's response to the Soviet invasion.[83] Secretary of Defense Harold Brown raised the option of decoupling military aid to Pakistan from the nuclear nonproliferation issue, suggesting that the administration draw a distinction between the Pakistani nuclear program and actual testing of a nuclear device. Vance replied that he had tried to do this earlier, noting that Shahi told him in October that Zia agreed not to test a nuclear device for at least six months.[84]

The Symington Amendment prohibited foreign military sales (FMS) credit to countries that did not comply with IAEA safeguards. Nonetheless, Vance observed Congress was unlikely to object to selling US weapons to Pakistan on a cash basis, if the administration claimed doing so would stabilize the region. "Isn't the point one of generating more confidence in Pakistan so that they do not feel they are alone in a deteriorating situation?" Brzezinski asked. He added, "This means moving ahead on the non-proliferation issue. We should supply them arms. It doesn't matter all that much what the arms are."[85] The PRC recommended putting together an emergency military aid package for Pakistan, exploring whether Saudi Arabia might finance Pakistan's purchase of US military hardware, increased funding for Afghan refugees, and negotiating with Congress about a presidential waiver to the Symington Amendment.[86]

At an NSC meeting on 27 December, Carter approved the four initiatives the PRC recommended. In addition, he decided to send a high-level delegation to Islamabad, headed by Christopher and Brzezinski, to confer with Zia as soon as possible. Finally, he approved Vance's recommendation to ask Zia to reaffirm that Pakistan would not build nuclear weapons, transfer sensitive technology to other countries, or conduct a nuclear test during Zia's tenure in office. Over the next several days, Carter publicly reaffirmed the 1959 Bilateral Agreement. Privately, the administration put together a $400 million assistance package composed of $100 million in economic support in FY 1980 and FY 1981, and a similar amount of FMS credit over the same period. By early January, the CIA

[82] Rodric Braithwaite, *Afgantsy: The Russians in Afghanistan, 1979–89* (New York: Oxford University Press, 2011), pp. 99–103.

[83] "245. Summary of Conclusions of a Special Coordinating Committee Meeting, 9:30–10:30 A.M., 26 December 1979," *FRUS, 1977–1980, Vol. VII: Soviet Union* (Washington, DC: GPO, 2013).

[84] "NSC PRC Minutes [Includes Attachment Dated 27 December 1979], Secret, Action Memorandum, 4 January 1980," *DNSA Collection: CIA Covert Operations: From Carter to Obama, 1977–2010* (Ann Arbor, MI: ProQuest, 2016), p. 16 http://search.proquest.com/docview/1679096200.

[85] Ibid.
[86] Ibid.

estimated that were at least 40,000 Soviet troops in Afghanistan.[87] Carter signed a presidential finding on 20 January, authorizing the CIA to begin a covert action to supply small arms to the Afghan insurgents.[88] Congress appropriated $50 million annually for this program.[89]

News of the proposed $400 million package for Pakistan leaked to the media before the State Department could formally present it. Zia rejected the package as far too small to meet Pakistan's economic and defense meets. A *New York Times* article on 18 January 1980 quoted Zia as dismissing the aid offer as "peanuts."[90] Zia argued that the $400 million aid package would provoke the Soviet Union without contributing enough to Pakistan's security to justify that risk. In a private meeting with an American journalist, Selig Harrison, in early March, Zia explained that the Carter administration's effort to have Congress affirm the 1959 Bilateral Agreement and approve a $400 million aid package would be viewed by Pakistan as inadequate.[91]

Zia urged the Carter administration not to submit the aid package to Congress, despite warnings from Brzezinski and Christopher that the budget window was closing. In a speech to some 400 provincial and local officials a few days later, Shahi stated it would be unwise for Pakistan to depend on the United States to guarantee its security. Noting the ambiguities of the 1959 Agreement, "US assistance by way of armed force is conditional on the consent of the Congress of the US, which may or may not be forthcoming," Shahi argued.[92] The Pakistani foreign ministry informed the State Department that it would forgo US military assistance altogether, rather than accept the amount offered in January 1980. Nonetheless, Zia was still interested in economic aid, and said the rescheduling of Pakistan's debt payments were his immediate priority.[93]

---

[87] "251. Summary of Conclusions of a Special Coordination Committee Meeting, re: Soviet Forces in Afghanistan, 9:30–10:30 A.M., 2 January 1980," *FRUS, 1977–1980, Vol. VI: Soviet Union* (Washington, DC: GPO, 2013), pp. 725–726.

[88] Carter's 29 January 1980 authorization for the CIA to provide lethal weapons to the Afghan mujahidin is cited in Kux, *Disenchanted Allies*, p. 252; and Ridel, *What We Won*, p. 103.

[89] Riedel, *What We Won*, p. 103.

[90] William Borders, "Pakistani Dismisses $400 Million in Aid Offered by U.S. as 'Peanuts'," *New York Times*, 18 January 1980, p. 2.

[91] "Hummel to Department to State, re: U.S.-Pakistan Relations: Zia Expounds to American Scholar, Confidential Cable, 9 March 1980," *DNSA Collection: U.S. Nuclear Non-Proliferation Policy, 1945–1991* (Ann Arbor, MI: ProQuest, 2016). p. 3 http://search.proquest.com/docview/1679128521.

[92] "Hummel to Department of State, re: Agha Shahi Publicly Rejects Proposed U.S. Assistance Package, Unclassified Cable, 6 March 1980," *DNSA Collection: U.S. Nuclear Non-Proliferation Policy, 1945–1991* (Ann Arbor, MI: ProQuest, 2016), p. 5 http://search.proquest.com.ezproxy/docview/1679139986.

[93] "Hummel to Department of State, re: U.S.-Pakistan Relations: Zia Expounds to American Scholar, Confidential Cable, 9 March 1980," *DNSA Collection: U.S. Nuclear Non-Proliferation*

In May 1980, Constable, who had returned to Washington as the deputy assistant secretary of state for Near Eastern Affairs, warned Secretary of State Edmund Muskie about the perceived gap between the administration's rhetorical support for Pakistan and its performance. "This problem of credibility will become acute," Constable wrote, "when it becomes apparent that we plan no assistance to Pakistan, other than food [aid], for another 18 months."[94] CIA and Defense Intelligence Agency (DIA) estimates in July 1980 reported on Soviet forces' steps to deter Pakistani assistance to the Afghan insurgents and various factors limiting the escalation of Soviet military pressure on Pakistan.[95]

At a 17 July PRC meeting, Turner reported that Soviet forces would likely to concentrate on stabilizing the Afghan side of the border, although they may launch limited probes against insurgent safe havens inside Pakistan. Aaron again raised the prospect of asking Congress for a sanction waiver. He asked, "Congress was after all prepared to act earlier.... Perhaps we could provide some continuing role for Congress if we were to take further steps on waiving the Symington Amendment?" Muskie and Christopher, however, raised the practical difficulties of securing congressional support for a waiver, given the decreased likelihood of a Soviet move into Pakistan, fears that the any increased US involvement in South Asia might be a slippery slope, and the nonproliferation question.[96] During that meeting, Muskie, Turner, Brzezinski, and General David C. Jones, the chairman of the Joint Chiefs of Staff (JCS), debated Pakistan's requirements for US military assistance and whether those requirements could be met without congressional approval.[97]

Pakistan quickly became the major conduit for providing US weapons and equipment to Afghan *mujahidin* fighting against the Soviet Red Army and the Afghan National Army. There was, however, no major US military or economic

Policy, 1945–1991 (Ann Arbor, MI: ProQuest, 2016), p. 3 http://search.proquest.com/docview/1679128521.

[94] "Memo from Peter D. Constable to Secretary of State Edmund Muskie, re: Assistance for Pakistan, Secret, Briefing Memorandum, 22 May 1980," *DNSA Collection: U.S. Nuclear Non-Proliferation Policy, 1945–1991* (Ann Arbor, MI: ProQuest, 2016), p. 3, http://search.proquest.com/docview/1679127443.

[95] "Pakistan: Military Buildup Opposite Afghanistan, [Classification Excised], Report, Defense Intelligence Agency, 9 July 1980," *DNSA Collection: Afghanistan* (Ann Arbor, MI: ProQuest, 2016), p. 3, http://search.proquest.com/docview/1679077708; and "Soviet Intentions Vis-à-Vis Pakistan, Top Secret, Intelligence Report, 14 July 1980, Central Intelligence Agency," *DNSA Collection: CIA Covert Operations: From Carter to Obama, 1977–2010* (Ann Arbor, MI: ProQuest, 2016), p. 4, http://search.proquest.com/docview/1679108682.

[96] "Minutes, NSC Policy Review Committee Meeting on Pakistan, Top Secret, Sensitive, 17 July 1980," *DNSA Collection: CIA Covert Operations: From Carter to Obama, 1977–2010* (Ann Arbor, MI: ProQuest, 2016), p. 11, http://search.proquest.com/docview/1679109671.

[97] Ibid.

assistance package for Pakistan during the Carter administration's remaining months in office. Carter met with Zia in the Oval Office on 3 October 1980. Carter characterized the media coverage and the public statements by US and Pakistani officials regarding the abortive $400 million aid package as "mutually embarrassing." He raised the prospect of allowing Pakistan to purchase F-16s (on a cash basis), but Zia demurred and said that debt relief was his government's immediate priority.[98]

From 27 December 1979, until it left office on 20 January 1981, the Carter administration confronted an unfavorable power distribution in South Asia and short time horizons for emerging threats to US interests in that region. The near-term likelihood of containment failure in South Asia dramatically increased, as Soviet airborne forces and light infantry quickly seized control of Kabul in late December 1979. While the prospect that Soviet forces might launch a full-scale offensive across the Afghan-Pakistani border diminished in January 1980, the outflow of Afghan refugees threatened to overwhelm Pakistan. Officials in the Carter administration concluded that CPSU general-secretary Leonid Brezhnev and other members of the Politburo were willing to pay a high price to shore up the tottering PDPA government in Kabul.

As neoclassical realist hypothesis would expect, the unfavorable power distribution in South Asia and the short time horizons for threats to US interests in the region after late December 1979 led senior officials in the Carter administration to favor pursuing an accommodative strategy toward the Pakistani nuclear program. Their priority was to provide an emergency package of military and economic assistance to Islamabad, even if that meant downplaying US nonproliferation concerns, at least in the short term. The administration, however, had to overcome high domestic mobilization hurdles in the form of the Symington Amendment sanctions it had imposed on Pakistan in April 1979 and congressional reluctance to approve a presidential waiver. Ultimately, the Carter administration was unable to put together a military and economic assistance package that would meet Pakistan's immediate security requirements.

Nuclear domino theory would attribute the Carter administration's imposition of Symington Amendment sanctions on Pakistan to policymakers' assessment of heightened risk of reactive proliferation and nuclear arms racing in South Asia. In April 1979, Carter told Giscard, Schmidt, and Callaghan that revelations about Pakistan's unsafeguarded uranium enrichment facilities would have a destabilizing effect on the region, which implied a risk of an India-Pakistan nuclear arms race. Yet there are few references to the risk of reactive

---

[98] "Meeting with Pakistani President Zia, Memorandum of Conversation, Secret, 3 October 1980," *DNSA Collection: CIA Covert Operations: From Carter to Obama, 1977–2010* (Ann Arbor, MI: ProQuest, 2016), p. 4, http://search.proquest.com/docview/1679108058.

proliferation or India's possible weaponization of its latent nuclear capacity in the records of PRC meetings and State Department cables to the US Embassy in Islamabad in late 1978 and early 1979. Administration officials only made a concerted effort to broker an Indian-Pakistani pact against nuclear weapons development and testing in summer 1979, that is, after the imposition of sanctions on Pakistan.

The Carter administration's scramble to put together an emergency military and economic assistance package for Pakistan and to ask Congress to approve a presidential waiver of Symington Amendment sanctions appear anomalous for the credible sanctions theory hypothesis. In April 1979, Carter carried out the threat conveyed to Pakistani officials over the previous year: unsafeguarded uranium enrichment activities would trigger Symington Amendment sanctions. After the Soviet invasion of Afghanistan, however, Carter and his national security team began to look for ways to provide Pakistan with an emergency aid package and persuade Congress to allow the president to waive Symington sanctions. Although the administration was unsuccessful on both counts, these moves were a harbinger of what would become a pattern over the next eight years: in order to bolster Pakistan as a frontline ally, the Carter and Reagan administrations would repeatedly undermine the credibility of nonproliferation sanctions.[99]

The Reagan Administration: Four Red Lines for Pakistan's Nuclear Program (1981–1988)

The Reagan administration found itself balancing long-term nonproliferation objectives in South Asia against immediate containment objectives in that region. Yet, to a far greater extent than Carter, President Ronald Reagan and his national security team were willing to pursue accommodative strategies toward Pakistan's nuclear weapons program in order to halt the expansion of Soviet influence in South Asia. That accommodation took the form of billions of dollars of US arms sales and economic aid over the next seven years, in exchange for Zia's pledge that the Pakistani nuclear program would not cross certain "red lines." Yet when confronted with flagrant violations of those "red lines," Reagan administration officials circumvented US nonproliferation laws to continue the flow of conventional weapons and economic assistance to Pakistan, as well as to the Afghan insurgents.

---

[99] Nicholas L. Miller, *Stopping the Bomb: The Sources and Effectiveness of US Nonproliferation Policy* (Ithaca, NY: Cornell University Press, 2018), pp. 202–203.

Soon after taking office, Reagan and William Casey, the director of central intelligence, expand the covert operation of providing military hardware and funding to the Afghan *mujahidin*.[100] Since Pakistan was the only viable conduit for any US assistance to reach the insurgents, however, the Reagan administration first needed to persuade Congress to pass a waiver to the Symington Amendment, thus allowing for a resumption of US military and economic assistance to Islamabad. At the same time, the administration needed an agreement with Zia on the nuclear program, so as not to jeopardize the restored US-Pakistan alliance and the flow of covert military assistance to the Afghan insurgents.

The Reagan administration requested that Congress provide $50 million in economic assistance to Pakistan in FY 1982 under the PL-480 (Food for Security) program in late January 1981.[101] The following month, the State Department recommended a $750 million package of economic and military assistance to Islamabad in FY 1983, in addition to an immediate package of $100 million of economic and military assistance in FY 1982.[102] An interagency working group chaired by Nicholas Veliotes, the assistant secretary of state for Near Eastern Affairs, recommended a minimum five-year security assistance program "which will give Pakistan confidence in our commitment to its security and provide us reciprocal benefits in terms of our regional interests," and noting, "we seek to use a new security relationship to influence Pakistani nuclear decision making."[103]

Secretary of State Alexander M. Haig met with the Pakistani foreign minister, Agha Shahi, Lt. Gen. Khalid Mahmud Arif, Zia's chief of staff, and Sahabzada Yaqub Khan, the former Pakistani ambassador to Washington, on 20 and 21 April at the State Department. Haig underscored the administration's determination to stop Soviet expansion in Southwest Asia and its desire for "strong bilateral relations with friendly states" in the region. Haig and Shahi agreed that addressing Pakistan's economic and security requirements would require a multiyear effort. Haig, however, also warned that "The explosion of a nuclear device would make it very difficult for us to maintain our support," and that

---

[100] Riedel, *What We Won*, pp. 110–127.

[101] "Secretary of State to US Embassy in Pakistan, re: FY 82 Assistance for Pakistan, Confidential Cable, 12 January 1981," *DNSA Collection: Nuclear Nonproliferation* (Ann Arbor, MI: ProQuest, 2016), p. 1, http://search.proquest.com/docview/1679128548.

[102] "Security Assistance for Pakistan, Secret, Action Memorandum, 16 February 1981," *DNSA Collection: US Nuclear Non-Proliferation Policy, 1945–1991* (Ann Arbor, MI: ProQuest, 2016), p. 6, http://search.proquest.com/docview/1679139930.

[103] "Assistant Secretary of State for Near East and South Asia Affairs (Designate) Nicholas A. Veliotes to Deputy Secretary of State William B. Clark, re: Interagency Working Group Meeting on Pakistan, Security Assistance and Its Relationship to the Nuclear Issue, Secret, Action Memorandum, 7 March 1981," *DNSA Collection: US Nuclear Non-Proliferation Policy, 1945–1991* (Ann Arbor, MI: ProQuest, 2016), p. 2, http://search.proquest.com/docview/1679112294.

resumption of US assistance depended on congressional approval of changes to the Symington Amendment.[104]

Undersecretary of State for Security Assistance James Buckley traveled to Islamabad in June 1981 for meetings with Zia, Shahi, and other Pakistani officials. Buckley offered a six-year package of economic and security assistance that would include the following: cash military sales for the remainder of FY 1981, a five-year program of economic supporting funds, development assistance, and FMS loans totaling approximately $3 billion, subject to annual congressional approval. The summit communiqué also stated that the United States would sell Pakistan F-16 attack aircraft to improve Pakistani air defenses against Soviet and Afghan incursions, although the number of aircraft, funding, and timing of delivery would be determined later.[105]

On 14 July, Richard V. Allen, Reagan's national security adviser, received a memorandum from his deputy John Nance stating, "Buckley may well have conveyed an implicit commitment to early delivery in his discussions with Zia. If we back away from this implicit commitment, we risk a cooling of relations and loss of faith in Southwest Asia." Whereas Buckley thought Saudi Arabia might finance Pakistan's purchase of the F-16s, Nance warned, "experience shows the gap between Saudi promises and actual Saudi funding can be measured in light years."[106]

By midsummer 1981, the Reagan administration embarked upon a concerted effort to persuade Congress to approve a presidential waiver for the Symington Amendment, while assuring them that arms sales would provide an incentive for Zia to refrain from nuclear testing.[107] In September 1981, Reagan sent the proposal for a five-year $3.2 billion package of economic and military assistance to Congress, along with a request for a presidential waiver of the Symington Amendment sanctions. A month later, he notified Congress of his intent to sell Pakistan 40 F-16 aircraft. "As praiseworthy as the intentions of the Symington

---

[104] "Secretary of State to Multiple Embassies, re: Visit of Pakistan Foreign Minister, Secret, Cable, 25 April 1981," *DNSA Collection: Afghanistan* (Ann Arbor, MI: ProQuest, 2016), p. 4, http://search.proquest.com/docview/1679078657.

[105] "Joint U.S.-Pakistan Statement [Relating to Undersecretary of State for Security Assistance James Buckley's Talks with Pakistan on Mutual Security], Unclassified, Press Release, Department of State, 15 June 1981," *DNSA Collection: Afghanistan* (Ann Arbor, MI: ProQuest, 2016), p. 2, http://search.proquest.com/docview/1679078386.

[106] "Memo from James W. Nance to Richard V. Allen, re: National Security Planning Group (NSPG) Meeting—Tuesday, 14 July 1981, 1:45–2:30 P.M.—Situation Room," *DNSA Collection: CIA Covert Operations: From Carter to Obama, 1977–2010* (Ann Arbor, MI: ProQuest, 2016), p. 5, http://search.proquest.com/docview/1679109442.

[107] "Department of State to Multiple Embassies, re: U.S. Policy Towards Pakistan, Confidential Cable, 1 April 1981," *DNSA Collection: Nuclear Nonproliferation* (Ann Arbor, MI: ProQuest, 2016), p. 4, http://search.proquest.com/docview/1679139181.

Amendment may have been, it is clear that it has failed to stop Pakistan from pursuing unsafeguarded portions of its nuclear program," Buckley told the Senate Foreign Relations Committee in November 1981.[108]

In response to a question from Senator Mark Hatfield (R-OH) about how the Reagan administration would react to a Pakistani nuclear test, Haig wrote, "In all probability, we would choose to cut off our assistance and major sales programs," adding that the Pakistani government "is fully aware of this probability."[109] Congress approved the $3.2 billion aid package and a five-year presidential waiver of the Symington Amendment in November 1982. The legislation, however, also stipulated that military and economic assistance would stop if Pakistan carried out a nuclear test.[110]

The debate over the $3.2 billion aid package and the F-16 sale unfolded against a backdrop of US intelligence about rapid developments in the Pakistani nuclear weapons program. In March 1981, INR warned that policymakers should have no illusions that Pakistan would give up its nuclear ambitions in exchange for US aid, because the nuclear weapons program was too closely associated with Pakistani nationalism and status competition with India.[111] A month later, CIA analysts reported Pakistan was "probably capable of producing a workable device at this time," but would not "have sufficient fissile material to test a device until late 1982 or early 1983." Noting that domestic and regional factors might affect a decision on testing, analysts added, "the martial law rulers of Pakistan at the very least apparently want to give the impression that Pakistan is moving toward an explosives capacity."[112] SNIE 31-32/81, released in September 1981,

---

[108] "U.S. Cooperation with Pakistan [Statements by James L. Buckley, Undersecretary of State for Security Assistance, Science and Technology, and M. Peter McPherson, Administrator of the Agency for International Development, Before the Senate Foreign Relations Committee, 12 November 1981]," DNSA Collection: Afghanistan (Ann Arbor, MI: ProQuest, 2016), p. 6, http://search.proquest.com/docview/1679055279.

[109] "Secretary of State Alexander Haig to Senator Mark Hatfield (R-OR), 21 November 1981, Confidential," in William Burr, ed., NSA Electronic Briefing Book no. 377 (Washington, DC: National Security Archive, 2012), https://assets.documentcloud.org/documents/347023/doc-10-11-22-81.pdf.

[110] "Memo from Assistant Secretary of State for Legislative Affairs Richard Fairbanks to Secretary of State Alexander Haig, re: Daily Legislative Report [Restrictions on Aid Package to Pakistan], 14 December 1981," DNSA Collection: Afghanistan (Ann Arbor, MI: ProQuest, 2016), p. 1, http://search.proquest.com/docview/1679128387.

[111] "Bureau of Intelligence and Research, U.S. Department of State, 'Pakistan and the US: Seeking Ways to Improve Relations,' Report 97-Pa, 23 March 1981, Secret," in William Burr, ed., NSA Electronic Briefing Book no. 377 (Washington, DC: National Security Archive, 2012), https://www.documentcloud.org/documents/347017-doc-4-3-23-81-inr-report.html.

[112] "Special Assistant for Nuclear Proliferation Intelligence, National Foreign Assessment Center, Central Intelligence Agency, to Resource Management Staff, Office of Program Assessment et al., 'Request for Review of Draft Paper on the Security Dimension of Non-Proliferation,' 9 April 1981,

warned, "If Pakistan persists toward nuclear weapons production, or if Pakistan moves to acquire a strategic stockpile of nuclear material, then New Delhi will face a choice of accepting the high probability of a nuclear arms race or destroying Pakistan's nuclear facilities."[113]

In July 1982, Reagan sent a special envoy, Lt. Gen. Vernon Walters (ret.), a former deputy director of central intelligence, to Rawalpindi to meet with Zia, Arif, Foreign Minister Yaqub Khan, and Munir Khan, the chairman of the Pakistan Atomic Energy Commission (PEAC). Walters told Zia that Washington had "incontrovertible intelligence" that Pakistani representatives had transferred designs and specifications for nuclear weapons components to purchasing agents in several countries and that, under law, the Reagan administration would have to inform Congress. Zia denied the existence of a weapons program and repeated assurances that he had given to Buckley that he had no intention of developing or exploding a nuclear device. In a cable to the State Department reporting on the meeting, Walters commented that "Either [Zia] really does not know or he is the most superb and patriotic liar I have ever met."[114]

During a second meeting with Walters, Zia said, "The President must be right, your information must be right—I accept its authenticity." He asked Walters, "Tell us, who in Munir's outfit" is responsible for seeking nuclear components in other countries. According to Walters, upon hearing incontrovertible information about Pakistani nuclear acquisition efforts, Zia "describe[d] such information as [a] total fabrication, given assurances that Pakistan neither poses nor has transmitted any designs or specifications of nuclear weapons to anyone else."[115]

Walters returned to Islamabad in late October 1982 to warn Zia that continued US military assistance was in great jeopardy. He showed Zia drawings of

---

Secret, Excised Copy," in William Burr, ed., *NSA Electronic Briefing Book no. 377* (Washington, DC: National Security Archive, 2012), https://www.documentcloud.org/documents/347018-doc-5-4-9-81-state-dept-draft-paper.html.

[113] "John N. McMahon, Deputy Director for National Foreign Assessment, to Ambassador Richard T. Kennedy, Undersecretary of State for Management, 'Special National Intelligence Estimate on Indian Reactions to Nuclear Developments in Pakistan,' 21 September 1981, Enclosing SNIE 31-32/81, Secret, Excised Copy," in William Burr, ed., *NSA Electronic Briefing Book no. 377* (Washington, DC: National Security Archive, 2012), https://assets.documentcloud.org/documents/347022/doc-9-9-21-81.pdf.

[114] "U.S. Embassy Pakistan Cable 10239 to State Department, 'My First Meeting with President Zia,' 5 July 1982, Secret," in William Burr, ed., *NSA Electronic Briefing Book no. 377* (Washington, DC: National Security Archive, 2012), https://assets.documentcloud.org/documents/347027/doc-13-a-7-5-82.pdf.

[115] "U.S. Embassy Pakistan Cable 10276 to State Department, 'My Final Meeting with President Zia,' 6 July 1982, Secret," in William Burr, ed., *NSA Electronic Briefing Book no. 377* (Washington, DC: National Security Archive, 2012), https://assets.documentcloud.org/documents/347028/doc-13-b-7-6-82.pdf.

Chinese-influenced nuclear weapons designs obtained by US intelligence. Zia told Walters that after their July meeting, he ordered an investigation into the alleged illicit procurement of nuclear components abroad, but that the investigation turned up nothing. He added, "Nothing could be hidden from US intelligence. The CIA is capable of penetrating anywhere, and it would be foolish to act on any other assumption." According to Walters, Zia also gave Reagan his "word of honor" that Pakistan would not develop nuclear weapons.[116]

Pakistan's request that F-16s come equipped with the ALR-69 radar warning system became a major source of contention. Secretary of Defense Caspar Weinberger and other Defense Department officials were reluctant to transfer the ALR-69, but Zia was adamant that Pakistan would not take possession of the F-16s unless they came equipped with this radar system.[117] In early November, Deputy Director of Central Intelligence John N. McMahon wrote to Deputy Secretary of Defense Frank Carlucci that "The sale of the AN/ALR-69 Radar Warning Receiver to Pakistan entails a significant risk of the equipment being exploited by China.... For the near term, however, we believe Pakistan probably will safeguard the new US arms it receives to protect its arms supply relationship with the US."[118] McMahon attached the key judgments of an undated NIE to his memo. "Islamabad sees nuclear weapons as critical to its survival and continues to develop a nuclear explosive capacity," but Zia was unlikely to authorize a nuclear detonation so long as the $3.2 billion aid package remained on track. The NIE also concluded, "The Pakistanis continue to doubt the reliability of US commitments and US steadfastness in times of crisis. These doubts—based on

---

[116] "US Embassy Pakistan Cable 15696 to State Department, 'Pakistan Nuclear Issue: Meeting with General Zia,' 17 October 1982, Secret; State Department Cable 299499 to US Embassy Islamabad, 'Pakistan Nuclear Issue: Meeting with General Zia,' 25 October 1982, Secret," in William Burr, ed., *NSA Electronic Briefing Book no. 377* (Washington, DC: National Security Archive, 2012), https://www.documentcloud.org/documents/347029-doc-14-a-10-17-82.html.

[117] "Undersecretary of Defense for Policy Fred Ikle to Undersecretary of State for Political Affairs Lawrence Eagleburger, 29 September 1982," *US Declassified Documents Online* (Farmington Hills, MI: Gale, 2000), http://tinyurl.galegroup.com/tinyurl/3ev98X; and "US Embassy Pakistan to Secretary of State, re: Summary of Meeting between Rep. Charles Wilson (D-Texas) and Pakistani Air Chief Marshal M. Anwar Shamin, Confidential, 5 November 1982," *US Declassified Documents Online* (Farmington Hills, MI: Gale, 2000), http://tinyurl.galegroup.com/tinyurl/3p4j59.

[118] "Excerpt from Intelligence Report, 'Pakistan-US: Démarche on F-16 Equipment,' 8 November 1982, Enclosed with Memorandum from Deputy Director of Central Intelligence John N. McMahon to Deputy Secretary of Defense Frank Carlucci, 'Risk Assessment of the Sale of an/ALR-69 Radar Warning Receiver to Pakistan,' 8 November 1982, with Excerpt from National Intelligence Estimate on Pakistan Attached, n.d., Secret," in William Burr, ed., *NSA Electronic Briefing Book no. 377* (Washington, DC: National Security Archives, 2012), https://assets.documentcloud.org/documents/347031/doc-15-a-11-8-82.pdf.

earlier disappointments—color current Pakistani concerns about the funding of the US arms package and the precise equipment to be supplied."[119]

Zia was scheduled to arrive in Washington on 5 December 1982 for a state visit. "There is overwhelming evidence that Zia has been breaking his assurances to us," Secretary of State George P. Shultz wrote in a 26 November memorandum to Reagan. Shultz continued, "The intelligence community on balance believes that if forced to choose between US aid and nuclear weapons capability, Zia will opt for the latter." He advised Reagan to raise the nuclear program with Zia and laid out a number of options ranging from an overt threat to cut off US military assistance to a more subtle warning that the pursuit of certain nuclear activities would "seriously jeopardize our security relationship, including the ability of the US to provide military and economic assistance to Pakistan."[120]

Reagan met privately with Zia in the Oval Office on 6 December 1982. Although no record of that meeting is currently available, Kenneth Adelman, the director of the Arms Control and Disarmament Agency (ACADA), wrote in a June 1986 memorandum that Reagan established four "red lines" for the Pakistani nuclear program: (1) no reprocessing of spent uranium fuel into plutonium; (2) no assembly of a nuclear explosive device; (3) no testing of a nuclear explosive device; and (4) no transfer of sensitive nuclear technologies to or from other countries. According to Adelman's memorandum, Zia assured Reagan that Pakistan would not cross those four red lines.[121] In late December 1982, Reagan, acting upon the State Department's recommendation, signed a determination that he had received reliable assurances that Pakistan "would not transfer sensitive US equipment, materials or technology in violation of agreements entered into under the Arms Export Control Act," thereby allowing the sale of 40 F-16 aircraft equipped with advanced radar.[122]

Despite Zia's assurances, intelligence about clandestine Pakistani uranium enrichment and nuclear procurement continued. On 21 May 1984,

---

[119] Ibid.

[120] "Secretary of State George Shultz to President Reagan, 'How Do We Make Use of the Zia Visit to Protect Our Strategic Interests in the Face of Pakistan's Nuclear Weapons Activities,' 26 November 1982, Secret," in William Burr, ed., *NSA Electronic Briefing Book no. 377* (Washington, DC: National Security Archive, 2012), https://www.documentcloud.org/documents/347090-doc-16-11-26-82.html.

[121] "Kenneth Adelman, Director, Arms Control and Disarmament Agency, to Assistant to the President for National Security Affairs, 'Pakistan's Nuclear Weapons Programs and U.S. Security Assistance,' 16 June 1986, Top Secret," in William Burr, ed., *NSA Electronic Briefing Book no. 377* (Washington, DC: National Security Archive, 2012), https://www.documentcloud.org/documents/347039-doc-20-6-16-86.html.

[122] "Memo from Acting Secretary of State Kenneth Dam to the President, re: Determination for Pakistan, 24 December 1982," *US Declassified Documents Online* (Farmington Hills, MI: Gale, 2000), http://tinyurl.galegroup.com/tinyurl/3f7L70.

Ambassador-at-Large Richard Kennedy delivered a "non-paper" to Yaqub Khan reiterating the "red lines" that Reagan established in December 1982. Kennedy warned "that the US would be obligated to terminate security assistance if Pakistan assembles or tests a nuclear device, transfers technology for such a device, violates international safeguards or undertakes unsafeguarded reprocessing."[123] Ambassador Deane Hinton met with Zia on 21 July 1984 to convey the administration's continuing concern about uranium enrichment. Zia repeated earlier assurances and said there would be no uranium enrichment above the 5 percent level. He declined, however, to open the uranium enrichment facility to US observers or IAEA inspectors.[124]

During a National Security Planning Group (NSPG) meeting on 31 August 1984, Shultz told Reagan, "Zia needs to understand that he must commit to limits on enrichment and this must be done quickly if we are to save our security assistance program for Pakistan from congressional assaults." Weinberger added, "our focus with Zia should be on the difficult time we are going to have in Congress and with US public opinion unless there is a foundation that allays fears about Pakistan's intentions in the nuclear field." He recommended offering Zia inducements for agreeing to the 5 percent level limit, such as accelerated delivery of M48 A5 tanks, and a commitment to sell up to 30 AIM-9L (Sidewinder) missiles within two weeks.[125]

Reagan wrote to Zia on 12 September 1984 that "enrichment of uranium above 5% would be of the same significance as those nuclear activities, such as unsafeguarded reprocessing, which I personally discussed with you in December 1982 and would have the same implications for our security program and relationship." This was effectively a fifth red line. Reagan noted the growing congressional concern about the Pakistan's nuclear program and warned India might use that program as a pretext for "untoward military action."[126] Hinton received instructions to inform Zia the administration not only planned to expedite the

---

[123] "Arnold Kanter, Acting Assistant Secretary of State for Politico-Military Affairs and Richard Murphy, Assistant Secretary of State for Near East and South Asian Affairs, to Under Secretary of State for Political Affairs Michael Armacost, 'Memo on Pakistan Nuclear Issue for the NSC,' 24 August 1984, with Enclosure, 'Responding to Pakistan's Continuing Efforts to Acquire Nuclear Explosives,' Secret," in William Burr, ed., *NSA Electronic Briefing Book no. 351* (Washington, DC: National Security Archive, 2015), http://nsarchive.gwu.edu/nukevault/ebb531-U.S.-Pakistan-Nuclear-Relations,-1984-1985/documentsdoc%204%208-24-84%20interagency%20memo.pdf.

[124] Ibid.

[125] "Minutes of National Security Planning Group (NSPG) Meeting, re: Pakistan and NSDD-99 Work Program, 11:00 A.M. to 12:15 P.M., 7 September 1984, Top Secret," *DNSA Collection: CIA Covert Operations: From Carter to Obama, 1977–2010* (Ann Arbor, MI: ProQuest, 2016), p. 14, http://search.proquest.com.docview/1679096416.

[126] "President Reagan to General Zia, 12 September 1984," in William Burr, ed., *NSA Electronic Briefing Book no. 351* (Washington, DC: National Security Archive, 2015), http://nsarchive.gwu.edu/

delivery of 35 of the 100 M48A5 tanks and 500 I-TOW missiles, but was also prepared to discuss near-term enhancements of Pakistani air defenses, including "an evaluation of E-2c aircraft in Pakistan's operational environment." Finally, Hinton received instructions to say that the Reagan administration was prepared to approach Congress about the possible sale of AIM-9L missiles to Pakistan in January 1987.[127]

Zia replied to Reagan's letter on 7 November, the day after Reagan won reelection to a second term. He wrote Pakistan's enrichment facility produced HEU only for research purposes. Zia added that his government "will do nothing to embarrass your administration," but he did not explicitly address Reagan's demand to refrain from enriching uranium above the 5 percent level.[128]

In late November 1984, Senators Glenn and Sam Nunn (D-GA), accompanied by staff member Leonard Weiss, went to Islamabad, where they met with the PAEC chairman Munir Khan and the Pakistani foreign secretary, Naiz Naik.[129] Munir repeated claims that Pakistan did not seek nuclear weapons. Glenn responded that Zia's predecessor, Bhutto, "clearly sought a weapons capability" and that the arrest of a Pakistani citizen, Nazir Ahmed Vaid, on suspicion of smuggling fifty krypton switches (used in nuclear weapons triggers) in Houston, Texas, in June 1984 raised serious concerns. Glenn "thought Pakistan, like Israel, might be planning to develop weapons, but stop short of testing." Weiss observed that Pakistani attempts to export sensitive nuclear technologies, such as trigger mechanisms and high explosive lenses from the United States, seemed rather odd since Zia repeatedly disavowed wanting to develop a nuclear weapon. He also noted that every time US assistance programs to Pakistan came before Congress, "A rabbit is pulled from a hat."[130]

---

nukevault/ebb531-U.S.-Pakistan-Nuclear-Relations,-1984-1985/documents/Doc%207A%209-12-84%20reagan%20letter.pdf.

[127] "'Talking Points for Use in Delivering Letter to General Zia,' n.d., Secret," in William Burr, ed., *NSA Electronic Briefing Book no. 351* (Washington, DC: National Security Archive, 2015), http://nsarchive.gwu.edu/nukevault/ebb531-U.S.-Pakistan-Nuclear-Relations,-1984-1985/documents/Doc%207B%20%209-84%20talking%20points%20for%20delivering%20letter.pdf.

[128] "Letter, General Zia to President Reagan, 7 November 1984, Confidential," in William Burr, ed., *NSA Electronic Briefing Book no. 351* (Washington, DC: National Security Archive, 2015), http://nsarchive.gwu.edu/nukevault/ebb531-U.S.-Pakistan-Nuclear-Relations,-1984-1985/documents/Doc%209%20%2011-7-1984%20Zia%20letter.pdf.

[129] As foreign secretary, Naik was the bureaucratic head of the Pakistani Ministry of Foreign Affairs in Islamabad. He was subordinate to the foreign minister, Yaqub Khan.

[130] "U.S. Embassy Pakistan Telegram 24145 to State Department, 'Nuclear Non-Proliferation,' 29 November 1984, Secret," in William Burr, ed., *NSA Electronic Briefing Book no. 351* (Washington, DC: National Security Archive, 2015), http://nsarchive.gwu.edu/nukevault/ebb531-U.S.-Pakistan-Nuclear-Relations,-1984-1985/documents/Doc%2011%2011-27-84%20glenn-nunn-munir.pdf.

Vaid accepted a plea deal and was deported in October 1984. The case prompted Rep. Stephen A. Solarz (D-NY) and Senator Larry Pressler (R-SD) to introduce more-stringent nonproliferation bills. The Solarz Amendment to Section 670(a)(1) of the FAA (the Glenn Amendment) that Congress passed in August 1985 required terminating US economic and military assistance to any country that: "exports illegally or attempts to export illegally any material, equipment, or technology which could significantly contribute to the ability of such country to manufacture a nuclear explosive device, if the president determines."[131] The amendment, did however, include a waiver to prevent an aid cutoff, if the president determined such action would threaten US national security.[132] The Pressler Amendment to Section 620E(e) of the FAA, which also passed in August 1985, required terminating military and economic assistance to Pakistan unless the president annually certified that Pakistan did not possess a nuclear weapon or components of a weapon.[133]

By summer 1985, the Reagan administration found its containment and its nonproliferation objectives in South Asia were becoming mutually exclusive. Officials wanted to continue the covert flow of US arms to the Afghan insurgents. The Solarz and the Pressler amendments posed hurdles to the administration's strategy in South Asia, since cutting off military and economic assistance to Pakistan would also mean cutting off the flow of arms to the Afghan *mujahidin*. Therefore, for the next three years, administration officials attempted to circumvent these laws, while continually warning Pakistani officials that clandestine nuclear procurement and enrichment above 5 percent would jeopardize US military and economic assistance.

The first "test" of the Solarz and the Pressler amendments came in September 1985, when the State Department learned that a Pakistani trading firm based in Lahore, Multinational, Inc., contacted two West German firms about the purchase of aluminum tubes. Officials suspected these tubes were intended for the

---

[131] "Department of State, Classified Congressional Briefing on Pakistani Clandestine Nuclear-Related Procurement, 'Circa 26 July 1987, Secret,'" in William Burr, ed., *NSA Electronic Briefing Book no. 446* (Washington, DC: National Security Archive, 2013), http://nsarchive.gwu.edu/nukevault/ebb446/docs/12.pdf.

[132] "Department of State, Memorandum from Ted Borek to Mr. Peck [et al.], 'Solarz Amendment: Legal Memorandum for Mr. Armacost,' 20 July 1987, Limited Official Use," in William Burr, ed., *NSA Electronic Briefing Book no. 446* (Washington, DC: National Security Archive, 2013), http://nsarchive.gwu.edu/nukevault/ebb446/docs/7.pdf.

[133] For the full text of the Pressler Amendment see *International Security and Development Cooperation Act of 1985*. Public Law 99-83, 99 Stat. 190, 268. 99th Congress, 1st Sess., 8 August 1985. Rabinowitz, *Bargaining on Nuclear Tests*, p. 152. According to an interview Rabinowitz conducted with Ambassador Teresita Schaffer, former deputy assistant secretary of state for South Asia in 1984–1985, Zia's government actively supported the passage of the Pressler Amendment as a means to ensure an uninterrupted flow of US military assistance. Ibid., p. 152, n. 100.

manufacture of gas centrifuges to produce highly enriched uranium (HEU). Furthermore, Multinational was a known procurement agent for the A. Q. Khan Research Laboratory, the organization chiefly responsible for Pakistani uranium enrichment.[134]

In late May 1986, Solarz went on a fact-finding trip to Islamabad. He warned senior Pakistani officials that the nuclear issue had the potential to derail congressional approval for a new five-year aid package. Solarz confronted Zia and Prime Minister Muhammad Khan Junejo, who denied that Pakistan had enriched or would enrich uranium over 5 percent. Zia argued that his "word" would have to be accepted if "there was to be any basis for the relationship" between Islamabad and Washington.[135]

The second and more serious "test" for the Solarz Amendment began with the arrest of another Pakistani citizen, Arshed Pervez, on 10 July 1987, on suspicion of trying to illegally procure 25 tons of maraging steel. The grand jury for the US District Court in the Eastern District of Pennsylvania indicted Pervez, the president of A. P. Enterprises in Willowdale, Ontario, Canada, and his codefendant, Lt. Gen. Inam-ul-Haq (retd.), the managing director of Multinational, on eight counts including conspiracy, providing false statements, and export violations. The key charges revolved around the effort to illegally export 350-maraging steel for use "in a uranium enrichment plant to manufacture nuclear weapons" and beryllium for use as a neutron trigger for a nuclear weapon.[136]

The Pervez case threatened to derail the Reagan administration's South Asia policies. By 1987, the Afghanistan war had indeed become a quagmire for the Soviet Union, thanks in large part to the covert US military assistance to the Afghan insurgents funneled through Pakistan.[137] The five-year waiver on the

---

[134] "Department of State Telegram 287763 to Embassy Bonn, 'Export of Uranium Enrichment Equipment to Pakistan,' 19 September 1985, Secret," in William Burr, ed., *NSA Electronic Briefing Book no. 446* (Washington, DC: National Security Archive, 2013), http://nsarchive.gwu.edu/nukevault/ebb446/docs/1A.pdf; and "Embassy Bonn Telegram 35237 to Department of State, 'Export of Uranium Enrichment to Pakistan,' 22 November 1985, Secret," in William Burr, ed., *NSA Electronic Briefing Book no. 446* (Washington, DC: National Security Archive, 2013), http://nsarchive.gwu.edu/nukevault/ebb446/docs/1B.pdf.

[135] "Embassy Islamabad Cable 11791 to Department of State, 'Nuclear: Solarz Conversation with GOP,' 29 May 1986," in William Burr, ed., *NSA Electronic Briefing Book no. 446* (Washington, DC: National Security Archive, 2013), http://nsarchive.gwu.edu/nukevault/ebb446/docs/2.pdf.

[136] "US District Court, 'Indictment: United States of America vs. Arshad Pervez and Inam Ul-Haq,' 28 July 1987," in William Burr, ed., *NSA Electronic Briefing Book no. 446* (Washington, DC: National Security Archive, 2013), http://nsarchive.gwu.edu/nukevault/ebb446/docs/11.pdf.

[137] "CIA, Directorate of Intelligence, Office of Soviet Analysis, the Costs of Soviet Involvement in Afghanistan, February 1987," *DNSA Collection: CIA Covert Operations: From Carter to Obama, 1977–2010* (Ann Arbor, MI: ProQuest, 2000), p. 25, http://search.proquest.com/docview/1679135434; and "CIA, Directorate of Intelligence, Office of Soviet Analysis, Moscow's Afghan Quagmire: No End in Sight After Eight Years, 20 September 1987," *DNSA Collection: CIA Covert Operations: From*

Symington Amendment sanctions, however, was due to expire on 30 September. As the first installment of a new five-year $4.2 billion aid package to Pakistan (FY 1988–1993), Reagan requested that Congress approve an installment of $290 million in military assistance and $290 million in economic assistance in FY 1988. Pakistan could not receive that aid unless Congress extended the Symington Amendment waiver.[138]

The Pervez case also exposed divisions within the administration. On 14 July, Adelman expressed irritation with the "business-as-usual" tone in the State Department's talking points about the case. "We have warned Pakistan repeatedly to halt nuclear procurement activities in the United States and they have assured us that appropriate orders have been given to halt such activities," he wrote to Undersecretary of State for Political Affairs Michael Armacost. Adelman added, "Now, when the administration is struggling to maintain congressional support for the Pakistan program, we are confronted with the most blatant nuclear procurement case since the Vaid krytron case."[139]

During a 24 July hearing, the House Foreign Affairs Committee questioned Assistant Secretary of State for Near Eastern Affairs Robert Murphy and other officials about Pakistani complicity in the Pervez operation and whether the evidence was sufficient to trigger the Solarz Amendment. In his opening statement, Solarz said that the criminal charges against Pervez "assuming they are true, represent a flagrant and provocative challenge to US nonproliferation objectives."[140] During the hearing, however, Rep. Jim Leach (D-IA) observed, "the problem with the Solarz Amendment, and particularly with its early exercise, is that it puts the administration so much on the spot that a national security waiver is virtually inevitable."[141] Two days before the hearing, Rep. Dante B. Fascell (D-FL), the chairman of the Foreign Affairs Committee, and Rep. Don Bonker (D-WA), the chairman of the International Economic Policy Subcommittee,

---

Carter to Obama, 1977–2010 (Ann Arbor, MI: ProQuest, 2007), p. 10, http://search.proquest.com/docview/1679145215.

[138] "Aid for Pakistan," *CQ Almanac 1987* (Washington, DC: Congressional Quarterly, 1988), http://library.cqpress.com.

[139] "Arms Control and Disarmament Agency, Memorandum from Kenneth Adelman to Under Secretary of State for Political Affairs, 'Your Meeting with Ambassador Merker,' 14 July 1987, Secret," in William Burr, ed., *NSA Electronic Briefing Book no. 446* (Washington, DC: National Security Archive, 2013), http://nsarchive.gwu.edu/nukevault/ebb446/docs/4.pdf.

[140] "Arms Control and Disarmament Agency, Briefing Memorandum from Anthony Salvia to the Director, 'HFAC Asia Subcommittee Hearing on Pakistan,' 24 July 1987, Unclassified, with Bonker-Fascell Letter to Reagan Attached," in William Burr, ed., *NSA Electronic Briefing Book no. 446* (Washington, DC: National Security Archive, 2013), http://nsarchive.gwu.edu/nukevault/ebb446/docs/10.pdf.

[141] Ibid.

sent a letter to Reagan, urging him to suspend all assistance and "to review with Pakistani leaders the future direction of our relations and of our mutual security interests in South Asia."[142]

In early August 1987, Armacost went to Islamabad to meet with Zia, Junejo, and Yaqub Khan on a range of topics including nuclear procurement and uranium enrichment, the Pervez case, growing congressional suspicion of Islamabad's nuclear intentions, and the Afghanistan war. In a cable to Shultz, Armacost said he stressed the need for the Pakistani government "to demonstrate to an aroused Congress and a skeptical administration that no further illegal procurement actives would take place" and to provide "verifiable assurances there would be no further enrichment of weapons-grade uranium."[143]

In a series of tense meetings on 5 and 6 August, Zia rejected Armacost's proposals for intrusive verifications of Pakistani nuclear facilities, denied any connection between the Pakistani government and Pervez, and claimed the criminal case appeared to be an "effort to hang one Pakistani in order to hang the entire government" at a time when the United States and Pakistan "were supposed to be cooperating."[144] At one point, Armacost said some believed Pakistani officials calculated they could illegally export nuclear components with impunity because the US-Pakistan "security relationship was so important and our shared interests in Afghanistan so significant that the [US government] would 'wink' at such violations." Zia replied, "No, because we were [in Afghanistan] before you were. I tried to convince your Democratic president for 18 months. Afghanistan is our commitment—you were the latecomers."[145] Zia also repeated a claim made by the Pakistani foreign ministry two weeks earlier: the Pervez case was a conspiracy to divide Washington and Islamabad.[146]

---

[142] Ibid.

[143] "Embassy Islamabad Telegram 16294 to Department of State, 'First Day in Islamabad—August 2,' 3 August 1987, Secret," in William Burr, ed., *NSA Electronic Briefing Book no. 446* (Washington, DC: National Security Archive, 2013), http://nsarchive.gwu.edu/nukevault/ebb446/docs/14A.pdf.

[144] "Embassy Islamabad Telegram 16556 to Department of State, 'Undersecretary Armacost Meeting with Zia,' 5 August 1987, Secret," in William Burr, ed., *NSA Electronic Briefing Book no. 446* (Washington, DC: National Security Archive, 2013), http://nsarchive.gwu.edu/nukevault/ebb446/docs/14B.pdf.

[145] "Department of State Telegram 244270 to the Embassy in Islamabad, 'Undersecretary Armacost Meeting with Zia,' 7 August 1987, Secret," in William Burr, ed., *NSA Electronic Briefing Book no. 446* (Washington, DC: National Security Archive, 2013), http://nsarchive.gwu.edu/nukevault/ebb446/docs/14C.pdf.

[146] Ibid. On the statement by the Pakistani foreign secretary see "Embassy Islamabad Telegram 16052 to Department of State, 'Pervez Nuclear Arrest Case—July 23 Statement by MFA Spokesman Gives Greater Emphasis to Conspiracy,' 30 July 1987, Confidential," in William Burr, ed., *NSA Electronic Briefing Book no. 446* (Washington, DC: National Security Archive, 2013), http://nsarchive.gwu.edu/nukevault/ebb446/docs/14D.pdf.

Before the August recess, the House and the Senate passed a non-binding resolution calling on the president to warn that "Pakistan's verifiable compliance with these past commitments is vital to any further United States military assistance."[147] This suggested the possibility of tougher nonproliferation legislation targeting Pakistan. As the trial date in the Pervez case drew near, the State Department asked the Canadian government and the Justice Department for permission to review documents seized from Pervez's office to make a recommendation to Reagan "concerning a decision on the applicability of the Solarz Amendment."[148]

In early November 1987, Adelman wrote to Armacost again calling for a hardline strategy toward Pakistan, observing that, under the most likely congressional scenario, the president would not have renewed authority to waive Symington Amendment sanctions before 15 January 1988. Adelman recommended invoking the Solarz Amendment immediately and postponing any decision about a sanction waiver until January. "Dribbling these actions out between now and a Symington waiver," he warned, "would not only expose the president to two additional opportunities for criticism but would incrementally remove any pressure on Pakistan to curtail its nuclear programs."[149]

Shultz recommended that Reagan immediately certify that Pakistan did not possess a nuclear explosive device. Adelman sent a memorandum to Reagan on 21 November, urging him to delay certification, noting that no significant deliveries of military equipment could arrive before December, and that any new assistance would be prohibited until Congress granted new waiver authority. He wrote, "Our failure to invoke the Solarz Amendment—when the facts clearly support such a finding—can only strengthen the 'business-as-usual' perception both here and in Pakistan."[150]

---

[147] "Arms Control and Disarmament Agency, Memorandum from Norman Wulf to the Director, 'Recent Activities Related to the Pakistani Procurement Case,' 10 August 1987, Secret," in William Burr, ed., *NSA Electronic Briefing Book no. 446* (Washington, DC: National Security Archive, 2013), http://nsarchive.gwu.edu/nukevault/ebb446/docs/15.pdf.

[148] "State Department Telegram 278631 to U.S. Embassy Ottawa, 'Access to Canadian Documents in Pervez Case,' 5 September 1987, Secret," in William Burr, ed., *NSA Electronic Briefing Book no. 446* (Washington, DC: National Security Archive, 2013), http://nsarchive.gwu.edu/nukevault/ebb446/docs/19C.pdf.

[149] "Arms Control and Disarmament Agency, Memorandum from Kenneth Adelman to Under Secretary of State for Political Affairs, 'a Strategy on Pakistan,' 4 November 1987, Secret," in William Burr, ed., *NSA Electronic Briefing Book no. 446* (Washington, DC: National Security Archive, 2013), http://nsarchive.gwu.edu/nukevault/ebb446/docs/20.pdf.

[150] "Arms Control and Disarmament Agency, Memorandum from Kenneth Adelman for the President, 'Certification on Pakistan,' 21 November 1987, Secret," in William Burr, ed., *NSA Electronic Briefing Book no. 446* (Washington, DC: National Security Archive, 2013), http://nsarchive.gwu.edu/nukevault/ebb446/docs/22.pdf.

Despite Adelman's admonition, Reagan accepted Shultz's recommendation. The president sent a letter on 17 December to the speaker of the House of Representatives, Thomas P. O'Neill (D-MA), about his determination that Pakistan did not possess a nuclear weapon. Reagan wrote, "I am convinced that our security relationship and assistance program are the most effective means available to us for dissuading Pakistan from acquiring nuclear explosive devices."[151] That same day, a federal jury convicted Pervez and Inam (in absentia) on five of the eight counts, including conspiracy, attempted export of beryllium without an export license, and submitting false end-use statements for the export of maraging steel.[152] The foreign aid bill Congress passed on 20 December 1987 gave the president authority to exempt Pakistan from the Symington Amendment for eighteen months (that is, until 1 April 1990). The legislation, however, reduced the FY 1988 military and economic aid installment to $480 million for FY 1988.[153]

On 15 January 1988, Reagan invoked the Solarz Amendment and then promptly waived the sanctions, thus allowing for continued US military assistance to Pakistan.[154] The White House statement read in part, "The Government of Pakistan is aware of our continuing concern over certain aspects of its nuclear program. Despite these problem areas, there are crucial nonproliferation criteria which Pakistan continues to honor."[155]

Between 1982 and 1988, the Pakistani nuclear program did not cross Reagan's second and third "red lines." The Pakistanis, however, flagrantly crossed Reagan's fourth and fifth lines: no transfers of sensitive nuclear technologies and no uranium enrichment above the 5 percent level.[156] The Reagan administration

---

[151] "President Reagan to Speaker of the House, 17 December 1987, Enclosing Presidential Determination," in William Burr, ed., *NSA Electronic Briefing Book no. 446* (Washington, DC: National Security Archive, 2013), http://nsarchive.gwu.edu/nukevault/ebb446/docs/24%20Reagan%2017%20Dec%2087.pdf.

[152] "Department of State Telegram to U.S. Embassy Islamabad, 'Pervez Case Verdict,' 17 December 1987, Unclassified," in William Burr, ed., *NSA Electronic Briefing Book no. 446* (Washington, DC: National Security Archive, 2013), http://nsarchive.gwu.edu/nukevault/ebb446/docs/23B.pdf.

[153] "Unpopular Foreign Aid Escapes Severe Cuts," *CQ Almanac 1987* (Washington, DC: Congressional Quarterly, 1988), http://library.cqpress.com.

[154] "Presidential Determination No. 88-5 of 15 January 1988, *Federal Register*, Vol. 83, No. 24, 5 February 1988," in William Burr, ed., *NSA Electronic Briefing Book no. 446* (Washington, DC: National Security Archive, 2013), http://nsarchive.gwu.edu/nukevault/ebb446/docs/27A%20Statement%20on%20Reagan%20determinaton%201-15-88.pdf.

[155] "White House Statement on Continuation of Military Aid to Pakistan, 15 January 1988," in William Burr, ed., *NSA Electronic Briefing Book no. 446* (Washington, DC: National Security Archive, 2013), http://nsarchive.gwu.edu/nukevault/ebb446/docs/27A%20Statement%20on%20Reagan%20determinaton%201-15-88.pdf.

[156] "U.S. Arms Control and Disarmament Agency, Memorandum from Kenneth Adelman for the Undersecretary of State for Political Affairs, 'The Pakistani Procurement Cases,' 23 July 1987, Secret,"

confronted an unfavorable power distribution in South Asia and short time horizons for threats to US interests there. Containment failure would occur if Soviet forces succeed in defeating the Afghan insurgency and stabilizing the regimes of Kamal and later Mohammad Najibullah in Kabul. The threat of a large-scale Soviet incursion into Pakistan diminished by the time Reagan took office on 20 January 1981. Nonetheless, the Soviet campaign to crush the Afghan insurgency and refugee flows into Pakistan threatened to destabilize South Asia.

Since the only viable way to supply US weapons to the Afghan *mujahidin* was overland through Pakistani territory, the Reagan administration was prepared to sell advanced weapon systems, including F-16s equipped with advanced radar, M48 A5 tanks, and Sidewinder missiles, while also providing economic assistance to Zia's government, in exchange for restrictions on the Pakistani nuclear weapons program. Reagan, Shultz, Weinberger, Armacost, Adelman, and other administration officials were aware of Pakistani nuclear program crossing the fourth and the fifth red lines, as well as Zia's mendacity. They disagreed, however, over how explicit threats for Pakistani noncompliance with the red lines ought to be. When intelligence revealed continued uranium enrichment over the 5 percent level and the efforts by Pakistani agents to secretly purchase nuclear materials in the United States were exposed, officials quickly moved to thwart congressional efforts to cut off military and economic assistance to Islamabad.

Epilogue: The Bush Administration and the "Abandonment" of Pakistan (1989–1990)

The waning of the Cold War changed the geopolitics of South Asia and the dynamics of the US-Pakistani nonproliferation dispute. The depth of the Soviet Union's decline prompted General-Secretary Mikhail Gorbachev and his advisers to begin liquidating costly security commitments.[157] Following the signing of the UN-sponsored Geneva Accords between the Najibullah government and the coalition of Afghan insurgents, Gorbachev announced Soviet troop withdrawals would begin in May 1988 and be complete by February 1989.[158] On 16 February 1989, Lt. Gen. Boris Gromov, the commander of the

---

in William Burr, ed., *NSA Electronic Briefing Book no. 446* (Washington, DC: National Security Archive, 2013), http://nsarchive.gwu.edu/nukevault/ebb446/docs/8.pdf.

[157] M. Kalinovsky Artemy, *A Long Goodbye, the Soviet Withdrawal from Afghanistan* (Cambridge, MA: Harvard University Press, 2011), pp. 74–92.

[158] "Soviet Union Embassy in the United States, News and Views from the USSR: Soviet Government Statement on Geneva Accords, 27 April 1988," *DNSA Collection: Afghanistan* (Ann Arbor, MI: ProQuest, 2015), http://search.proquest.com.docview/1679075254. Also see "United Nations, the Geneva Accords: Agreements on the Settlement of the Situation Relating to

Soviet Fortieth Army, led a column of tanks and personnel carriers across the "Friendship Bridge" over the Amu Dar'ya River, marking the Soviet-Afghan border.[159] A few weeks later, the coalition of Peshawar-based *mujahidin* (the self-styled Afghan Interim Government or AIG), supported by Pakistan's Inter-Service Intelligence (ISI), renewed their campaign to oust Najibullah regime.[160]

The end of the Soviet war in Afghanistan coincided with leadership transitions in Washington and Islamabad. On 18 August 1988, Zia, along with US ambassador Arnold Raphel, died when his Pakistani air force plane mysteriously exploded in midair and crashed after taking off from Bahawalpur, some 60 miles west of the Indian border.[161] Ghulam Ishaq Khan, the president of the Pakistani Senate, succeeded Zia and called new parliamentary elections for November 1988. Benazir Bhutto, the daughter of the executed Zulfikar Ali Bhutto and leader of the PPP, was elected prime minister by the National Assembly on 2 December 1988. Meanwhile in the United States, Vice President George H. W. Bush defeated the Democratic candidate, Massachusetts governor Michael Dukakis, in the November 1988 election. Bush took office on 20 January 1989.

The CIA, DIA, the National Security Agency (NSA), and other intelligence agencies assembled a comprehensive picture of the Pakistani nuclear weapons program from the following: satellite images of the Pakistan Institute of Nuclear Science and Technology (PINSTECH) near Rawalpindi, the Kahuta enrichment plant, and the ongoing construction at Chashma and other facilities; communications intercepts of Pakistani scientists and military officers; and human sources in Pakistan and China.[162] Additionally, Pakistani scientists and engineers gave magazine interviews about their ability to "produce five or six nuclear bombs with around 70 to 80 kgs. of enrichment uranium."[163] In May 1989, Director of Central Intelligence William Webster testified to the Senate

---

Afghanistan, July 1988," *DNSA Collection: Afghanistan* (Ann Arbor, MI: ProQuest, 2015), http://search.proquest.com/docview/1679076527.

[159] Bill Keller, "Afghanistan: Last Man Out," *New York Times*, 16 February 1989, p. 1.

[160] Kux, *The United States and Pakistan, 1947–2000*, pp. 297–299.

[161] Elaine Sciolino, "Zia of Pakistan Killed as Blast Downs Plane: US Envoy, 28 Others Die," *New York Times*, 18 August 1988. Also see Ronald Reagan: "Statement on the Deaths of President Mohammed Zia-ul-Haq of Pakistan and United States Ambassador Arnold Raphel," 17 August 1988. Online by Gerhard Peters and John T. Woolley, *The American Presidency Project*, https://www.presidency.ucsb.edu/node/255380.

[162] Richelson, *Spying on the Bomb*, p. 344.

[163] "United States Embassy, Pakistan, Press Article on Pak Nuclear Enrichment Program, Unclassified, Cable, 16 May 1989," *DNSA Collection: Weapons of Mass Destruction* (Ann Arbor, MI: ProQuest, 2015), http://search.proquest.com/docview/1679139738.

Governmental Operations Committee that "Clearly Pakistan is engaged in developing a nuclear [weapon] capability."[164]

On 24 February 1989, Bush and Bhutto met in Tokyo, while both were attending the state funeral of the Shōwa emperor (Hirohito). Bhutto said her government intended to "follow the message of President Reagan's [1982] letter," but she warned that non-certification of Pakistan would have dire consequences, including a nuclear arms race in South Asia. She hoped that the current level of US military and economic assistance to Pakistan—worth approximately $600 million per year— could be sustained. Bush noted the goodwill Bhutto enjoyed in the United States but added that she needed to understand the Pakistani nuclear program was a serious issue and "one over which the president of the United States cannot exert total control." He warned that Congress "is serious and independent, and it needs assurances."[165]

"Speaking for Pakistan," Bhutto told a joint meeting of Congress on 7 June, "I can declare that we do not possess, nor do we intend to make a nuclear device. That is policy."[166] She made similar statements during her meeting with Bush at the White House.[167] Despite her assurances, Bhutto appears to have played only a marginal role in Pakistani nuclear decision-making. President Khan and General Mirza Aslam Beg, the new chief of Army Staff, retained de facto control over the nuclear program. They also facilitated A. Q. Khan's network to supply nuclear technology to other states on the black market.[168]

Throughout 1988 and 1989, the US Embassy in Bonn reported on continued Pakistani smuggling of nuclear components from West Germany.[169] In October 1989, the CIA concluded that "A relative decline in the deterrent value of

---

[164] "Nuclear and Missile Proliferation," Senate Committee on Governmental Operations, *101st Cong., 1st sess.* (Washington, DC: GPO, 1989), pp. 23; Stephen Engelberg, "US Sees Pakistan Seeking an A-Bomb," *New York Times*, 11 June 1989, p. 5.

[165] "Memorandum of Conversation, re: President's Meeting with Prime Minister Benazir Bhutto of Pakistan, American Ambassador's Residence, Tokyo, Japan, 24 February 1989," Bush Presidential Records (College Station, TX: George Bush Presidential Library, 1989), https://bush41library.tamu.edu/files/memcons-telcons/1989-02-24--Bhutto.pdf.

[166] Quoted in Kux, *United States and Pakistan, 1947–2000*, p. 302. Also see Benazir Bhutto, "Address by Her Excellency, Mohtrama Benazir Bhutto, Prime Minister of the Islamic Republic of Pakistan, 7 June 1989," *135 Cong Rec H 2352*, Vol. 135, No. 73 (1989), p. H2354.

[167] George H. W. Bush, "Remarks Following Discussions with Prime Minister Benazir Bhutto of Pakistan, 6 June 1989," *The Public Papers of the President of the United States: George Bush, 1989* (Washington, DC: GPO, 1989), https://bush41library.tamu.edu/archives/public-papers/506.

[168] Khan, *Eating Grass*, pp. 253–254; and Kux, *United States and Pakistan, 1947–2000*, p. 299.

[169] "United States Embassy, Germany, Statement of the Hanau Prosecutor on the Allegedly Illegal Exports of Nuclear Assembly Parts, 28 December 1988," *DNSA Collection: Weapons of Mass Destruction* (Ann Arbor, MI: ProQuest, 2015), http://search.proquest.com/docview/1679127939; "United States Consulate General Frankfurt am Main, Nuclear Proliferation Expert Harald Mueller on Illegal FRG Exports of Nuclear Technology, Limited Official Use, Cable, 18 January

Pakistan's conventional forces is leading Islamabad to seek ballistic missiles and the rapidly deployable nuclear weapons capability."[170] Nonetheless, that same month Bush certified that Pakistan did not possess a nuclear explosive device.[171]

In May 1990, renewed tensions over Kashmir brought India and Pakistan to the brink of war.[172] US intelligence analysts concluded that the Pakistanis had taken the last step toward assembling a nuclear explosive device by matching HEU with bomb cores.[173] During a visit to Islamabad in June, Deputy National Security Adviser Robert Gates raised the issue with Khan and Beg, both of whom claimed Pakistan's nuclear status had not changed. Gates warned that the nuclear program had come dangerously close to crossing Reagan's second "red line" and that unless the bomb cores were melted down, Bush would be unable to certify Pakistan's status in October.[174] On 6 August 1990, Khan dismissed Bhutto as prime minister, charging her with corruption and nepotism, and called a new parliamentary election for October 1990. Meanwhile, CIA, DIA, and other intelligence agencies informed the White House that Pakistan likely possessed a nuclear explosive device.[175]

On 19 September, US ambassador Robert Oakley delivered a letter from Bush to Khan. Bush wrote, "We have obtained information giving us reason to believe that the status of your nuclear program has changed.... [Under] present circumstances, it not possible for me to certify Pakistan's compliance with the law." Noting the upcoming Pakistani election, the president expressed a willingness to ask the Congress for authority to delay terminating US assistance "but only if I can offer them some realistic prospect that Pakistan will do its part to warrant its flexibility."[176]

1989," *DNSA Collection: Weapons of Mass Destruction* (Ann Arbor, MI: ProQuest, 2015), http://search.proquest.com/docview/1679111511.

[170] "Directorate of Intelligence, Central Intelligence Agency, Science and Weapons Review [Pakistan—Progress Toward Advanced Weapons; Heavily Excised], Top Secret, Periodical, 13 October 1989," *DNSA Collection: Weapons of Mass Destruction* (Ann Arbor, MI: ProQuest, 2015), http://search.proquest.com/docview/1679115154.

[171] George Bush: "Memorandum on Determination Pursuant to Section 620E(e) of the Foreign Assistance Act of 1961, as Amended," 5 October 1989. Online by Gerhard Peters and John T. Woolley, *The American Presidency Project*, https://www.presidency.ucsb.edu/node/255380.

[172] For analyses of the 1990 Kashmir Crisis, see Sumit Ganguly and Devin T. Hagerty, *Fearful Symmetry: India-Pakistan Crises in the Shadow of Nuclear Weapons* (Seattle: University of Washington Press, 2005), pp. 82–114; and Devin T. Hagerty, *The Consequences of Nuclear Proliferation: Lessons from South Asia* (Cambridge, MA: MIT Press, 1998), pp. 133–171.

[173] Kux, *United States and Pakistan, 1947–2000*, pp. 306–307.

[174] Ibid., pp. 306–307; and Richardson, *Spying on the Bomb*, p. 345.

[175] Richardson, *Spying on the Bomb*, p. 346; Kux, *United States and Pakistan, 1947–2000*, p. 308.

[176] "Email to Richard N. Haass from White House Situation Room (WHSR), re: Cable from Secretary of State to US Embassy, Pakistan, re: Presidential Letter on Certification, 19 September 1990, 10:54 EST," George H. W. Bush Presidential Records, Richard N. Haass Files, National Security

By declining to certify Pakistan did not possess a nuclear device, Bush terminated $600 million in annual military and economic development assistance and froze the transfer of thirty F-16 jets that the Pakistani government had already purchased. Pakistani officials, military officers, and politicians saw the sudden termination of US assistance as a betrayal and abandonment.[177] Nawaz Sharif became prime minister on 1 November 1990, after his Pakistan Muslim League-N and its conservative coalition partners defeated Bhutto's PPP in the election. Sharif tried to persuade the Bush administration to restore the aid package and to accept Pakistan as a latent nuclear power. The administration, however, was unable to persuade Congress to approve a waiver of the Pressler Amendment, absent credible guarantees that the Pakistanis would melt down the bomb cores.[178] In February 1992, Pakistani foreign secretary Shahyar Khan confirmed in an interview with the *Washington Post* that his country had the "elements, which if put together, would become a [nuclear] device," including HEU weapons cores.[179] For all intents and purposes, the US-Pakistan alliance had collapsed.

After the Soviet withdrawal from Afghanistan in February 1989, the United States again confronted a favorable power distribution in South Asia and the time horizons for emerging threats to US interests in that region grew longer. The Reagan administration had been willing to circumvent the Solarz and the Pressler amendments in order to continue the flow of military and economic assistance to Zia's government as a hedge against Soviet expansion in South Asia. The Bush administration, however, faced different international circumstances in the region. After the Soviet withdrawal, the strategic rationale for US military and economic aid to Pakistan vanished. Absent the threat of containment failure in South Asia, it was more difficult for the administration to justify military and economic assistance to an ally determined to acquire nuclear weapons in defiance of US nonproliferation laws. The mobilization hurdles for pursuing such a strategy were too high.

Council, Working Files—India/Pakistan, 1989–1992, CFO1304 (College Station, TX: George Bush Presidential Library, 1990), 3 pages.

[177] See Steve Coll, "Rifts Appear in U.S.-Pakistani Alliance; Islamabad's Nuclear and Electoral Initiatives Raise Concerns," *Washington Post*, 22 October 1990, p. A13; and Barbara Crossette, "U.S. Aid Judgment Upsets Pakistanis," *New York Times*, 16 October 1990, p. 5. Also see Kux, *United States and Pakistan, 1947–2000*, p. 310.

[178] See Michael R. Gordon, "End to Pakistan Aid Is Sought over Nuclear Issue," *New York Times*, 25 September 1990, p. 8; Neal A. Lewis, "Key Congressman Urges Halt in Pakistan Aid," *New York Times*, 3 October 1990, p. 7; and R. Jeffrey Smith, "Administration Unable to Win Hill Support for Continued Aid to Pakistan," *Washington Post*, 10 October 1990, p. A14.

[179] Quoted in R. Jeffrey Smith, "Pakistan Official Affirms Capacity for Nuclear Device; Foreign Minister Vows to Contain Technology," *Washington Post*, 7 February 1992, p. A18.

This chapter juxtaposed hypotheses from neoclassical realist theory, nuclear domino theory, and credibility sanctions theory to explain variation in the types of nonproliferation strategies the United States pursued toward Pakistan between 1975 and 1990. Overall, neoclassical realist theory explains the variation in the strategies undertaken by the Carter, Reagan, and Bush administrations. Averting containment failure in South Asia was the overriding strategic objective of the Ford, Carter, and Reagan administrations, while thwarting Pakistani nuclear ambitions was a secondary objective. When the pursuit of the two objectives came into conflict with each other, as they did after the Soviet invasion of Afghanistan in late December 1979, the Carter and Reagan administrations prioritized containment.

As neoclassical realist theory would expect, when confronted with an unfavorable regional power distribution and short time horizons for emerging threats to US interests post December 1979, policymakers in Washington pursued accommodative strategies toward Pakistan's nuclear activities. When confronted with a stable (if not favorable) regional power distribution in South Asia and long time horizons for threats to US interests in the region, however, policymakers pursued coercive nonproliferation strategies. The strategies pursued by the Carter administration prior to December 1979 and by the George H. W. Bush administration after April 1989 are consistent with this hypothesis.

Neoclassical realist theory, however, confronts an anomaly in the Ford administration's pursuit of an accommodative strategy toward Pakistan in 1975 and 1976. During that time, the United States confronted a stable, if not exactly favorable, power distribution in South Asia and long time horizons for threats to its interest. Yet Ford lifted the decade-old arms embargo and Kissinger offered Bhutto various inducements—100 A-7 aircraft, US financing for a LEU nuclear reactor, and even F-7s—in exchange for canceling the French reprocessing plant contract. Ford and Kissinger's willingness to offer Bhutto inducement for nuclear restraint was a function of US domestic political calculations, specifically a desire to deny the Democratic presidential nominee, Jimmy Carter, another opportunity to criticize the administration on the nuclear nonproliferation issue.

The two alternative theories, nuclear domino and credible sanctions, fare less well against the empirical record. There are occasional references in US intelligence assessments about how Pakistani nuclear activities might prompt India to weaponize its nuclear capabilities. Those references came in early summer 1979, after the Carter administration had invoked the Symington Amendment, not before. Still there is little evidence that senior officials pursued coercive nonproliferation strategies toward Pakistan due to the likelihood of Indian nuclear weaponization.

The US-Pakistan nonproliferation straddles the passage of the Symington, Glenn, Solarz, and Pressler amendments. The Carter administration's invocation of Symington Amendment sanctions in April 1979 is consistent with this theory, as was the Bush administration's refusal to certify Pakistan did not possess a nuclear weapon in October 1990. Yet the continual efforts by the Reagan administration to obtain congressional approval for sanctions waivers, and later efforts to circumvent the Glenn, Solarz, and Pressler amendments, are difficult to square with the credible sanctions theory hypothesis.

President George H. W. Bush's decision not to certify Pakistani nonpossession of a nuclear weapon in October 1990 effectively ended the US-Pakistan alliance, at least in its Cold War incarnation. In the days following the 9/11 terrorist attacks, President George W. Bush's administration "revived" the alliance, by threatening to take military action against Pakistan unless the regime of General Pervez Musharraf fully cooperated with the "global war on terrorism." The second Bush administration demanded and received from Musharraf forward basing and overflight rights, as well as intelligence cooperation, in support of military operations against Al-Qaeda and the Taliban in neighboring Afghanistan and later tribal regions in Pakistan. Over the ensuing sixteen years, the revived US-Pakistan alliance has proven to be just as fractious and dysfunctional as its prior incarnation had been in the 1970s and the 1980s.

5

The United States and South Korea's Nuclear Weapons Program, 1970–1981

The nuclear proliferation dispute between the United States and the Republic of Korea (ROK or South Korea) was the unintended consequence of the Nixon administration's pursuit of three broad objectives in East Asia and Southeast Asia in the early 1970s. The first objective was to extricate the United States from the Vietnam War. The second objective was to reduce US troop deployments throughout Southeast Asia and East Asia. The third objective was to seek a rapprochement with the People's Republic of China (PRC) and enlist it as an ally of convenience against the Soviet Union.[1]

The pursuit of these three objectives had adverse implications for the credibility of US extended deterrence on the Korean peninsula.[2] It was in this context that South Korea's president, Park Chung-hee, authorized a clandestine program to develop nuclear weapons and long-range missiles.[3] Like Israel in late 1950s and early 1960s and Pakistan in the 1970s, South Korea in the early 1970s faced an existential threat from a neighboring state, in its case the Democratic People's

---

[1] On the concept of allies of convenience see Evan N. Resnick, "Strange Bedfellows: U.S. Bargaining Behavior with Allies of Convenience," *International Security*, Vol. 35, No. 3 (2010), pp. 144–184.

[2] See Terence Roehrig, "The US Nuclear Umbrella over South Korea: Nuclear Weapons and Extended Deterrence," *Political Science Quarterly*, Vol. 132, No. 4 (2017), pp. 651–684; and Se Young Jang, "The Evolution of US Extended Deterrence and South Korea's Nuclear Ambitions," *Journal of Strategic Studies*, Vol. 39, No. 4 (2016), pp. 502–520.

[3] See, for example, Sung Gul Hong, "The Search for Deterrence: Park's Nuclear Option," in Byung-Kook Kim and Ezra F. Vogel, eds., *The Park Chung Hee Era: The Transformation of South Korea* (Cambridge, MA: Harvard University Press, 2011), pp. 483–510; and Seung-Young Kim, "Security, Nationalism, and the Pursuit of Nuclear Weapons and Missiles: The South Korean Case, 1970–82," *Diplomacy & Statecraft*, Vol. 12, No. 4 (2001), pp. 53–80.

Republic of Korea (DPRK or North Korea). Unlike Israel and Pakistan, South Korea had a bilateral alliance treaty with the United States.[4]

Several books and articles purport to explain Park's pursuit of a nuclear weapons option, the efficacy of US threats and inducements on shuttering much of the nuclear weapons program in the mid-1970s, and South Korea's nuclear forbearance since its transition to democratic rule in the late 1980s.[5] Yet several questions about the United States' policies toward South Korea before, during, and after the proliferation dispute remain unanswered, or at least inadequately answered, by the extant literature.

Given the ROK's vulnerability, what prompted the Nixon administration to unilaterally withdraw 20,000 US combat troops in 1971? Why did the Ford administration employ a mixture of coercive and accommodative strategies to get the Park government to cancel a contract for a French reprocessing plant in 1975 and 1976? Why, despite residual concerns about South Korean nuclear intentions, did the Carter administration propose the phased withdrawal of the remaining 40,000 US troops and tactical nuclear weapons in 1977? What prompted the Reagan administration to reaffirm the US security commitment to South Korea and provide a generous military aid package and legitimacy for Park's successor, Chun Doo-hwan, in early 1981?

The shifts in the strategies the United States pursued toward South Korea between 1970 and 1981 were products of US policymakers' assessments of power distributions and the time horizons for emerging threats in East Asia. Domestic mobilization hurdles, specifically the degree of congressional support or opposition to the proposed initiatives of the Nixon, Ford, Carter, and Reagan administrations, however, sometimes skewed the types of strategies they ultimately pursued.

---

[4] Mutual Treaty of Defense between the United States and the Republic of Korea, http://avalon.law.yale.edu/20th_century/kor001.asp (accessed 11 April 2018).

[5] See, for example, T. V. Paul, *Power Versus Prudence: Why Nations Forgo Nuclear Weapons* (Montreal: McGill–Queen's University Press, 2000), pp. 120–124; Jonathan D. Pollack and Mitchell B. Reiss, "South Korea: The Tyranny of Geography and the Vexations of History," in Kurt M. Campbell, Robert J. Einhorn, and Mitchell B. Reiss, eds., *The Nuclear Tipping Point: Why States Reconsider Their Nuclear Choices* (Washington, DC: Brookings Institution Press, 2004), pp. 254–292; Etel Solingen, *Nuclear Logics: Contrasting Paths in East Asia and the Middle East* (Princeton: Princeton University Press, 2007), pp. 82–94; Eugene B. Kogan, "Coercing Allies: Why Friends Abandon Nuclear Plans" (PhD diss., Brandeis University, 2013), pp. 93–131; Alexandre Debs and Nuno P. Monteiro, *Nuclear Politics: The Strategic Causes of Proliferation* (New York: Cambridge University Press, 2016), pp. 377–394; Nicholas L. Miller, *Stopping the Bomb: The Sources and Effectiveness of US Nonproliferation Policy* (Ithaca, NY: Cornell University Press, 2018), pp. 137–139; and Alexander Lanoszka, *Atomic Assurance: The Alliance Politics of Nuclear Proliferation* (Ithaca, NY: Cornell University Press, 2018), pp. 110–131.

The Nixon administration reduced the US troop presence because the military balance on the Korean peninsula would still favor the ROK and the near-term likelihood of a North Korean attack appeared low. Nixon and his advisers confronted low domestic mobilization hurdles to the troop reductions. As the Vietnam War continued, Congress actually supported decreasing US troop deployments elsewhere in East Asia and Southeast Asia.

The "critical phase" of the proliferation dispute occurred between March 1974 and January 1976. Like their predecessors, Ford and his advisers perceived a stable power distribution in East Asia and temporally distant threats to US interests in that region. Officials sought to thwart South Korea's acquisition of a French reprocessing plant because they feared it might complicate their efforts to normalize US-China diplomatic ties. At the same time, the administration faced high domestic mobilization hurdles. Prominent senators and representatives, however, were concerned about the Park regime's authoritarianism, as well as global nuclear proliferation. The Ford administration pursued a hybrid strategy toward Park's regime. Officials threatened to withhold an Export-Import Bank loan for a nuclear power reactor and suspend civil nuclear cooperation. But they also promised a moratorium on US troop reductions and the sale of advanced combat aircraft. Park canceled the reprocessing plant contract in January 1976.

Carter's 1976 campaign pledge to withdraw the remaining 40,000 US troops was also predicated on a favorable East Asian power distribution and long time horizons for threats to US interests there. Carter and his advisers sought to normalize US-China diplomatic relations. However, the troop withdrawal plan and Carter's subsequent pledge of $800 million in "compensatory" equipment transfers to the ROK succumbed to both high mobilization hurdles and changing strategic circumstances on the Korean peninsula. From the outset, members of Congress opposed a complete troop withdrawal, as did the uniformed military, intelligence analysts, and even senior political appointees in Carter's administration. In spring 1978, updated intelligence estimates of North Korean military capabilities indicated the power distribution in East Asia had shifted in an unfavorable direction and that threats to US interests were not temporally distant.

Finally, unfavorable power distributions in East Asia and shorter time horizons for emerging threats in 1980 led the incoming Reagan administration to seek a "reset" in the US-ROK alliance. Reagan abandoned Carter's criticism of South Korean human rights abuses. He also offered Chun a generous military assistance package, including the sale of advanced aircraft. In exchange, Chun downsized the missile development program and agreed to abide by US nonproliferation policies.

The "acute" phase of the proliferation dispute meets the scope conditions for all three of the alternative theories outlined in chapter 2. The remainder of the chapter is organized chronologically, beginning with Park's abandonment fears in the late 1960s and early 1970s and ending with Reagan and Chun's effort to "reset" the alliance in early 1981.

Park's Abandonment Fears, the Nixon Doctrine, and Project 890, 1968–1973

From the late 1950s until the end of the Cold War, the credibility of the United States' extended deterrence on the Korean peninsula rested upon three pillars: (1) the forward deployment of US combat troops and conventional weapons systems; (2) the forward deployment of tactical nuclear weapons; and (3) conventional arms transfers to South Korea, initially through grant military assistance and then, after 1974, through the provision of foreign military sales (FMS) credits for purchases of US weapons systems.

The US-ROK alliance was always highly asymmetric in terms of both the two allies' relative power and their strategic interests. For South Korean officials, the alliance was primarily a vehicle to deter an attack from North Korea. Therefore, South Korean leaders sought maximum "reassurance" from Washington in the form of large US troop deployments, military grants-in-aid (and later FMS), and conventional arms transfers. According to a July 1975 Department of Defense (DoD) policy paper: "The Koreans are somewhat paranoid, but not without reason. . . . South Korea's only reliable ally, the US, is 10,000 miles away and increasing Korean doubts about our constancy are reinforced by the continuing debates within the US over our foreign policy and Korean policy."[6]

For Washington policymakers, the alliance with South Korea was part of a network of bilateral security treaties designed to facilitate the US hegemonic role in East Asia. Preventing the Soviet Union from increasing its military, diplomatic, and economic penetration was their overriding objective. Until 1969–1970, a secondary objective was to prevent "Communist China" from expanding its influence in East Asia.

North Korea had a larger industrial base, as well as a numerical advantage in ground forces. Pyongyang also received substantial assistance from the Soviet Union, China, and other Communist bloc states in postwar reconstruction and industrialization.[7] In 1961, Kim Il-sung, the North Korean premier and

---

[6] "274. Study Prepared by the Office of International Security Affairs in the Department of Defense, Washington, Updated," *FRUS, 1969–1976, Vol. E-12: Documents on East and Southeast Asia, 1973–1976* (Washington, DC: GPO, 2011).

[7] See Charles K. Armstrong, "'Fraternal Socialism': The International Reconstruction of North Korea, 1953–62," *Cold War History*, Vol. 5, No. 2 (2005), pp. 161–187.

chairman (later general secretary) of the Korea Workers' Party, signed treaties of alliance and friendship with China and the Soviet Union.[8]

The strength of the United States Forces in Korea (USFK), which had reached 325,000 troops at the height of the Korean War, declined to 85,000 by 1955. By 1970, there were approximately 63,000 US combat troops deployed in South Korea and the Demilitarized Zone (DMZ), giving the combined USFK and ROK ground forces a two-to-one advantage over the Korean People's Army (KPA).[9] The Eisenhower administration first deployed tactical nuclear weapons to South Korea in January 1958.[10] At the peak in 1967, the United States had eight weapons systems totaling 950 tactical nuclear warheads in the country.[11]

Between 1950 and 1982, 99 percent of the ROK armed forces' weapons systems and equipment were US imports.[12] Additionally, all nuclear and conventional military forces in South Korea were under US command.[13] As Andrew

---

[8] See Treaty of Friendship, Cooperation, and Mutual Assistance Between the Union of Soviet Socialist Republics and the Democratic People's Republic of Korea, signed at Moscow on 6 July 1961, https://www.documentcloud.org/documents/3005971-1961-Treaty-of-Friendship-Cooperation-and-Mutual.html (accessed 19 April 2018); and Treaty of Friendship, Co-operation, and Mutual Assistance Between the People's Republic of China and the Democratic People's Republic of Korea, signed at Peking, 11 July 1961, https://www.marxists.org/subject/china/documents/china_dprk.htm (accessed 19 April 2018). Also see "Journal of Soviet Ambassador in the DPRK A. M. Puzanov for 10 February 1960," February 10, 1960, History and Public Policy Program Digital Archive, AVPRF fond 0102, opis 16, delo 6, p.28–61. Translated for NKIDP by Gary Goldberg, http://digitalarchive.wilsoncenter.org/document/116279.

[9] "55. Draft Minutes of a National Security Council Meeting, 4 March 1970," *FRUS, 1969–1976, Vol. XIX, Part 1: Korea, 1969–1972* (Washington, DC: GPO, 2010), pp. 142–147.

[10] For an indication of the North Korean reaction to the US deployment of tactical nuclear weapons in South Korea, see "Journal of Soviet Ambassador in the DPRK A. M. Puzanov for 22 March 1960," March 22, 1960, History and Public Policy Program Digital Archive, AVPRF fond 0102, opis 16, delo 6, p.72–122. Translated for NKIDP by Gary Goldberg, http://digitalarchive.wilsoncenter.org/document/116170.

[11] See Hans M. Kristensen and Robert S. Norris, "A History of US Nuclear Weapons in South Korea," *Bulletin of the Atomic Scientists*, Vol. 73, No. 6 (2017), pp. 349–357. South Korea remains under the US nuclear umbrella as of 2018, although President George H. W. Bush withdrew tactical nuclear weapons from the peninsula in 1991. See George H. W. Bush, "Address to the Nation on Reducing United States and Soviet Nuclear Weapons, 27 September 1991," *Public Papers of the Presidents of the United States: George H. W. Bush, 1991* (Washington, DC: GPO, 1991), https://bush41library.tamu.edu/archives/public-papers/3438 (accessed 14 April 2018).

[12] Stockholm International Peace Research Institute (SIPRI), "Arms Transfer Database," http://www.sipri.org/databases/armstransfers (accessed 11 April 2018).

[13] ROK president Syngman Rhee transferred command and operational responsibility over the ROK armed forces to General Douglas MacArthur, the commander of the United Nations Command and commander of US Forces in the Far East during the opening weeks of the Korean War. See UN Security Council Resolution 84, Complaint of Aggression upon the Republic of Korea, S/Res/84 (1950), 14 July 1950, http://www.un.org/en/ga/search/view_doc.asp?symbol=S/RES/84(1950) (accessed 12 April 2018). Also see "The Chargé (Drumright) in Korea to the Secretary of State, 14 July 1950," *FRUS, 1950, Vol. VI: Korea* (Washington, DC: GPO, 1976), p. 388.

O'Neil observes, there were no mechanisms for allied consultation "regarding the modalities for command and control of the nuclear forces stationed on South Korean sovereign territory."[14] According to one estimate, in 1958, US military assistance totaled $358 million, which was 2.5 times the ROK's official defense budget of $143 million.[15]

Major General Park Chung-hee and his allies orchestrated a coup against the civilian government of Prime Minister Chang Myon on 16 May 1961.[16] Park won election as president in October 1963 and then set about consolidating a military dictatorship under the guise of civilian rule.[17] Park and other ROK leaders had a deep-seated fear that the United States might "abandon" South Korea, just as it had in the interval between the departure of US occupation troops in June 1949 and the outbreak of the Korean War on 25 June 1950. Specifically, Park worried that President Lyndon B. Johnson might redeploy US combat troops and weapons from South Korea to the Republic of Vietnam (RVN or South Vietnam).[18]

To forestall this possibility, Park undertook two initiatives. First, he negotiated a treaty to normalize diplomatic relations with Japan, Korea's former colonial master and the other US treaty ally in the region.[19] Second, he responded to Johnson's request for troop contributions to the Vietnam War.[20] Park dispatched

---

[14] Andrew Neil, *Asia, the US, and Extended Nuclear Deterrence: Atomic Umbrellas in the Twenty-First Century* (London; New York: Routledge, Taylor & Francis Group, 2013), p. 61.

[15] Chung-in Moon and Sangkeun Lee, "Military Spending and the Arms Race on the Korean Peninsula," *Asian Perspective*, Vol. 33, No. 4 (2009), pp. 69–99.

[16] For analysis of the causes of the 16 May 1961 coup see Yong-Sup Han, "The May Sixteenth Military Coup," in Kim Byung-Kook and Ezra F. Vogel, eds., *The Park Chung Hee Era: The Modernization of South Korea* (Cambridge, MA: Harvard University Press, 2011), pp. 35–57.

[17] Taehyun Kim and Chang Jae Baik, "Taming and Tamed by the United States," in Byung-Kook Kim and Ezra F. Vogel, eds., *The Park Chung Hee Era: The Transformation of South Korea* (Cambridge, MA: Harvard University Press, 2011), pp. 58–84.

[18] See Min Yong Lee, "The Vietnam War: South Korea's Search for National Security," in Byung-Kook Kim and Ezra F. Vogel, eds., *The Park Chung Hee Era: The Transformation of South Korea* (Cambridge, MA: Harvard University, 2011), pp. 409–411. Also see Glenn Baek, "Park Chung-Hee's Vietnam Odyssey: A Study in Management of the US-ROK Alliance," *The Korean Journal of Defense Analysis*, Vol. 25, No. 2 (2013), pp. 147–170, esp. pp. 151–154.

[19] For analyses of Park's efforts to seek a rapprochement between South Korea and Japan, see Jung-Hoon Lee, "Normalization of Relations with Japan: Toward a New Partnership," in Kim Byung-Kook and Ezra F. Vogel, eds., *The Park Chung Hee Era: The Transformation of South Korea* (Cambridge, MA: Harvard University Press, 2011), pp. 430–456. For documentation, see "US Efforts to Encourage Normalization of Relations Between the Republic of Korea and Japan," *FRUS 1964–1968, Vol XIX, Part 1: Korea* (Washington, DC: GPO, 2000), documents 332 to 369.

[20] "48. Memorandum of Conversation Between President Lyndon B. Johnson and President Park Chung Hee of Korea, 28 May 1965," *FRUS, 1964–1968, Vol. XIX, Part 1: Korea* (Washington, DC: GPO, 2000).

the two best-trained ROK army divisions (approximately 55,000 troops) to the war in 1965 and 1966. Moreover, he did this even though South Korea had no treaty obligation to South Vietnam.[21] As Ming Young Lee observes, "For the first time in the volatile and fragile alliance relationship, South Korea was to have leverage over US security policy by joining the United States' war in a distant place."[22] Annual US foreign military aid increased from $163 million in the 1961–1964 period to $336 million in the 1965–1970 period.[23]

Events in the late 1960s exacerbated Park's "abandonment" fears. On 21 January 1968, North Korean special operations forces (Unit124) infiltrated the DMZ and launched an assault on the Blue House, the ROK presidential residence in Seoul.[24] Forty-eight hours after the Blue House raid, North Korean patrol ships intercepted the naval intelligence ship USS *Pueblo* (AGER-2) in international waters. Johnson and his advisers concluded that Kim Il-sung likely wanted to harass US and ROK forces, rather than initiate full-scale hostilities.[25] The North Korean dictator would not risk a full-scale war unless he had explicit Chinese or Soviet backing and such backing was not likely.[26] When Park pressed US ambassador William J. Porter on how Johnson would respond, he replied, "The US would not retaliate" and that "any South Korean attempts at retribution

---

[21] The United States' military intervention in defense of South Vietnam was ostensibly undertaken as part of its obligations as a member of the Southeast Asia Treaty Organization (SEATO). South Korea was never a member of SEATO.

[22] Lee, "The Vietnam War," pp. 405–406.

[23] Ibid., p. 420. For an analysis of the other economic benefits South Korea received as a direct and indirect consequence of troop deployments to South Vietnam, see Se Jin Kim, "South Korea's Involvement in Vietnam and Its Economic Impact," *Asian Survey*, Vol. 10, No. 6 (1970), pp. 519–532.

[24] This operation was part of Kim Il-sung's ongoing militant strategy, intended to undermine domestic support for Park's government, spark a Communist insurgency, and test the resolve of the US-ROK. See Balazs Szalontai, "In the Shadow of Vietnam: A New Look at North Korea's Militant Strategy 1962–1970," *Journal of Cold War Studies*, Vol. 14, No. 4 (2012), pp. 122–166. For a chronology of North Korean incidents between 1965 and 1969, see "11. Briefing for Director of Central Intelligence Helms for a National Security Council Meeting, 16 April 1969," *FRUS, 1969–1976, Vol. XIX, Part 1: Korea, 1969–1972* (Washington, DC: GPO, 2010), pp. 23–26.

[25] See "215. Memorandum from Director of Central Intelligence Helms to Secretary Defense McNamara, Re: North Korean Intentions, 23 January 1968"; "217. Summary Minutes of Meeting, 10:30–11:45 A.M., 24 January 1968," *FRUS, 1964–1968, Vol. XXIX, Part 1: Korea* (Washington, DC: GPO, 2000), pp. 464–465 and pp. 469–474. Also see "Central Intelligence Agency, Special National Intelligence Estimate 14.2-68, 'The Likelihood of Major Hostilities in Korea,' 16 May 1968, Secret," in John Prados and Jack Cheevers, eds., *NSA Electronic Briefing Book No. 453* (Washington, DC: National Security Archive, 2014), https://nsarchive2.gwu.edu/NSAEBB/NSAEBB453/docs/doc18.pdf.

[26] See "State Department, Embassy Moscow Cable 2853, 'Kosygin on Korea,' 20 February 1968, Confidential," in John Prados and Jack Cheevers, eds., *NSA Electronic Briefing Book No. 453* (Washington, DC: National Security Archive, 2014), https://nsarchive2.gwu.edu/NSAEBB/NSAEBB453/docs/doc11.pdf.

would meet strong US opposition."[27] In a cable to the State Department, Porter wrote that Park said Johnson appeared more "worried about reprisals from the ROK government than with getting satisfaction from the North Koreans."[28]

Johnson sent a special envoy, the former deputy secretary of defense Cyrus Vance, to Seoul in February 1968 to ensure that the "ROKG [Republic of Korea Government] will take no independent military actions against North Korea." Vance wrote to Johnson that Park "doubted both the resolve of the United States and her commitment in Korea, partially because of US involvement in SEA [Southeast Asia] and partially because of alleged delays in providing military equipment to ROK military forces and in modernizing those forces."[29]

On 15 April 1969, a North Korean MIG-21 jet shot down a US EC-121 reconnaissance plane over the Sea of Japan, killing all thirty-one crew members. The National Security Council (NSC) met the following day to consider options, including retaliatory airstrikes.[30] According to Director of Central Intelligence (DCI) Richard Helms, Kim viewed downing the EC-121 as a "relatively low-risk opportunity to reopen the propaganda campaign against 'US aggressive designs.'"[31]

Nixon decided against a military retaliation, although he authorized the resumption of reconnaissance flights within a week.[32] During a 16 April NSC meeting, Undersecretary of State Elliot Richardson asked about the South Korean reaction to the EC-121 downing. General Earle Wheeler, the chairman

---

[27] Quoted in Victor D. Cha, *Alignment Despite Antagonism: The United States-Korea-Japan Security Triangle* (Stanford, CA: Stanford University Press, 1999), p. 63.

[28] "145. Telegram from the Embassy in Korea to the Department of State, 24 January 1968," *FRUS, 1964–1968, Vol. XXIX, Part I: Korea* (Washington, DC: GPO, 2000), pp. 311–312.

[29] "181. Memorandum from Cyrus R. Vance to President Johnson, 20 February 1968," *FRUS, 1964–1968, Vol. XXIX, Part 1: Korea* (Washington, DC: GPO, 2000), pp. 384–385. Vance served as deputy secretary of defense from 28 January 1964 to 30 June 1967.

[30] "12. Memorandum from the President's Military Adviser (Haig) to the President's Assistant for National Security Affairs (Kissinger), 16 April 1969," *FRUS, 1969–1976, Vol. XIX, Part 1: Korea, 1969–1972* (Washington, DC: GPO, 2010), pp. 26–27; and "13. Minutes of a National Security Council Meeting, 16 April 1969," Ibid., pp. 28–31.

[31] "11. Briefing for Director of Central Intelligence Helms for a National Security Council Meeting, 16 April 1969," *FRUS, 1969–1976, Vol. XIX, Part 1: Korea, 1969–1972* (Washington, DC: GPO, 2010), pp. 23–26. Also, SNIE 14.2-69 stated: "We conclude that, under present circumstances, Pyongyang does not intend to invade South Korea; nor do we believe that Pyongyang is deliberately trying to provoke the Republic of Korea (ROK) (and/or the US) into a resumption of major hostilities." See "1. Special National Intelligence Estimate, SNIE 14.2-69, 30 January 1969," Ibid, pp. 1–2.

[32] "19. Record of a Telephone Conversation Between President Nixon and the President's Assistant for National Security Affairs (Kissinger), 18 April 1969"; and "20. Memorandum by the President's Assistant for National Security Affairs (Kissinger), 29 April 1969," *FRUS, 1969–1976, Vol. XIX, Part I: Korea, 1969–1972* (Washington, DC: GPO, 2010), pp. 44–46.

of the Joint Chiefs of Staff (JCS), replied, "They are apprehensive we won't do anything." Nixon added, "They are very jittery."[33]

Two weeks before the EC-121 incident, ROK prime minister Chung Il-kwon met with Nixon to request that the US military assistance remain at $160 million per year. He also asked Nixon to maintain two army divisions in South Korea once the Vietnam War ended.[34] Unbeknownst to Chung and Park, Nixon had ordered an interagency review of the US troop deployments in South Korea, as well as various military contingencies, in February 1969.[35] The EC-121 downing led him to postpone any discussion of US troop reductions.[36]

While visiting Guam on 25 July 1969, Nixon responded to a reporter's question about future military commitments in East Asia and Southeast Asia. The president said he would honor alliance treaty commitments but added, "That as far as the problems of military defense, except for the threat of a major power involving nuclear weapons, that the United States is going to encourage and has a right to expect that this problem will be handled by, and responsibility for it taken by, the Asian nations themselves."[37]

Nixon met Park in San Francisco on 21 August 1969. "I believe that your government's efforts toward military and economic self-reliance are the correct road to take," Nixon told him. Park responded that the US troop presence in South Korea was critical in deterring a North Korean attack. He added, "I believe we can meet the North Korean threat without increasing the present level of US forces in South Korea, if [military] equipment is strengthened."[38]

---

[33] "13. Minutes of a National Security Council Meeting, 16 April 1969," *FRUS, 1969–1976, Vol. XIX, Part 1: Korea, 1969–1972* (Washington, DC: GPO, 2010), p. 31.

[34] "5. Memorandum of Conversation Between President Nixon and Prime Minister Chung Il Kwon of Korea, 1 April 1969," *FRUS, 1969–1976, Vol. XIX, Part 1: Korea, 1969–1972* (Washington, DC: GPO, 2010), pp. 8–10

[35] National Security Study Memorandum 27, 22 February 1969, *FRUS, 1969–1976, Vol. XIX, Part 1: Korea, 1969–1972* (Washington, DC: GPO, 2010), p. 8.

[36] Kissinger later admitted as much. See "46. Memorandum from the President's Assistant for National Security Affairs (Kissinger) to President Nixon, 25 November 1969," *FRUS, 1969–1976, Vol. XIX, Part 1: Korea, 1969–1972* (Washington, DC: GPO, 2010), pp. 117–118.

[37] See "Informal Remarks with Newsmen, 25 July 1969," *Public Papers of the Presidents of the United States: Richard Nixon, 1969* (Washington, DC: GPO, 1969), pp. 544–556, at p. 555. Nixon later elaborated on the Guam (or Nixon) Doctrine in a televised address on the Vietnam War. See Richard M. Nixon, "Address to the Nation on the Vietnam War, 3 November 1969," in Gerhard Peters and John T. Woolley, eds., *The American Presidency Project*, UCSB, http://www.presidency.ucsb.edu/ws/?pid=2303 (accessed 11 July 2018).

[38] "35. Memorandum of Conversation Between President Nixon and President Pak, 21 August 1969," *FRUS, 1969–1976, Vol. XIX, Part 1: Korea, 1969–1972* (Washington, DC: GPO, 2010), pp. 96–105. For a comprehensive analysis of the Nixon Doctrine's impact on South Korea, see Joo-Hong Nam, *America's Commitment to South Korea: The First Decade of the Nixon Doctrine* (Cambridge: Cambridge University Press, 1986).

Nixon wrote to his national security adviser, Henry Kissinger, on 29 November 1969, that the time had come to reduce US troop levels in South Korea. While the United States ought to maintain its sea and air presence at "whatever level is necessary for the retaliatory strike we planned," Nixon wrote, the troop level should be cut over the next year.[39] Kissinger warned, "The implementation of your decision to reduce the US presence in Korea will require a sound approach to consultations with the ROK so that we can minimize the likelihood of a confrontation with President Park or a pullout of ROK troops from Vietnam."[40]

On 20 January 1970, Secretary of Defense Melvin Laird informed the ROK ambassador, Kim Dong-jo, of growing political pressure to reduce the US troop numbers.[41] Laird told Kim the president would ask Congress to approve a $164 million military assistance package (MAP) for South Korea in FY 1971. The defense secretary also said no US troops would depart until the modernization of the ROK armed forces got underway.[42]

"We have had 64,000 troops in Korea since 1953 and someone should have looked at this long before now," Nixon observed during a 4 March 1970 NSC meeting. He added that "What we are looking for is not a way to get out of Korea, but a way to be able to stay in by means of a long-range viable posture."[43] Kissinger issued National Security Decision Memorandum 48 (NSDM-48) on 20 March 1970, ordering the withdrawal of the Seventh Infantry Division by the end of FY 1971.[44]

Porter later testified to a congressional committee that he first informed Park about possible troop reductions in December 1969. Likewise, Laird and U. Alexis Johnson, the undersecretary of state for political affairs, also told Kim Dong-jo about an imminent troop reduction announcement.[45] Nonetheless,

---

[39] "45. Memorandum from President Nixon to the President's Assistant for National Security Affairs (Kissinger), 24 November 1969," *FRUS, 1969–1976, Vol. XIX, Part 1: Korea, 1969–1972* (Washington, DC: GPO, 2010), p. 117.

[40] "47. Memorandum from the President's Assistant for National Security Affairs (Kissinger) to President Nixon, 12 December 1969," *FRUS, 1969–1976, Vol. XIX, Part 1: Korea, 1969–1972* (Washington, DC: GPO, 2010), pp. 118–119.

[41] See "34. Minutes of a National Security Council Meeting, 14 August 1969," *FRUS, 1969–1976, Vol. XIX, Part 1: Korea, 1969–1972* (Washington, DC: GPO, 2010), pp. 89–95, esp. fn. 13 on p. 92.

[42] "49. Telegram from the Department of State to the Embassy in Korea, re: Map and US Force Levels, 29 January 1970," *FRUS, 1969–1976, Vol. XIX, Part 1: Korea, 1969–1972* (Washington, DC: GPO, 2010), pp. 121–122.

[43] "55. Draft Minutes of a National Security Council Meeting, 4 March 1970," *FRUS, 1969–1976, Vol. XIX, Part 1: Korea, 1969–1972* (Washington, DC: GPO, 2010), pp. 142–147.

[44] "56. National Security Decision Memorandum 48, 20 March 1970," *FRUS, 1969–1976, Vol. XIX, Part 1: Korea, 1969–1972* (Washington, DC: GPO, 2010), pp. 148–150.

[45] US House of Representatives Subcommittee on International Organizations of the Committee on International Relations, *Investigation of Korean-American Relations* (Washington, DC: GPO, 1978), p. 63.

Park claimed Nixon's decision was a "profound shock" and that US troop reductions prior to the modernization of the ROK armed forces "would have profound effects on Korea."[46] In a 15 June 1970 letter to Nixon, Park argued that if US troop numbers decreased, other measures would be necessary "to relieve the apprehensions of the Korean people ... and to prevent the danger of irrevocable calamities, which might be caused by miscalculations on the part of ... the North Koreans and the Chinese Communists."[47] Nixon replied that the residual US troop presence and military assistance would show "friend and enemy our commitment to Korea's defense and security."[48]

Park tried unsuccessfully to obtain a guarantee there would be "no further reduction of the level of remaining US forces until such time as the modernization program has been implemented and ROK defenses increased."[49] Secretary of State William P. Rogers told Nixon that "President Park was probably motivated by the need—for both domestic and diplomatic reasons—to show satisfactory results in his negotiations with us."[50]

Recognizing that Nixon's decision was irrevocable, Park and his ministers decided to bargain for increased foreign military assistance. In July 1970, they suggested that $200 million per year for five years "would be required to bring their forces to a state at which genuine modernization could begin." Furthermore, they requested US assistance in establishing ROK defense industries. Deputy Secretary of Defense David Packard's offer to leave behind the military equipment of the departing US troops (e.g., 286 M-48 tanks), plus the regular MAP appropriation of $140 million per year, was "met with silence" by ROK officials. Minister of National Defense Jung Nae-hiuk said that Packard's offer "would not be of any help because that equipment was already in Korea and therefore leaving it there would not increase Korea's defense capability."[51] Park told Porter

---

[46] "57. Telegram from the Department of State to the Embassy in Korea, 23 April 1970," *FRUS, 1969–1976, Vol. XIX, Part 1: Korea, 1969–1972* (Washington, DC: GPO, 2010), pp. 150–152.

[47] "61. Telegram from the Embassy in Korea to the Department of State, 15 June 1970," *FRUS, 1969–1976, Vol. XIX, Part 1: Korea, 1969–1972* (Washington, DC: GPO, 2010), pp. 59–61.

[48] "64. Letter from President Nixon to Korean President Park, 7 July 1970," *FRUS, 1969–1976, Vol. XIX, Part 1: Korea, 1969–1972* (Washington, DC: GPO, 2010), pp. 164–165.

[49] "71. Backchannel Telegram from the Ambassador to Korea (Porter) to the President's Assistant for National Security Affairs (Kissinger), 25 August 1970," *FRUS, 1969–1976, Vol. XIX, Part 1, Korea, 1969–1972* (Washington, DC: GPO, 2010), pp. 183–184. Also see "68. Telegram from the Embassy in Korea to the Department of State, 4 August 1970," *FRUS, 1969–1976, Vol. XIX, Part 1: Korea, 1969–1972* (Washington, DC: GPO, 2010), pp. 174–179.

[50] "78. Memorandum from Secretary of State Rogers to President Nixon, 10 November 1970," *FRUS, 1969–1976, Vol. XIX, Part 1: Korea, 1969–1972* (Washington, DC: GPO, 2010), pp. 197–198.

[51] "67. Telegram from the Commander in Chief, Pacific (McCain) to the Department of State, 23 July 1970," *FRUS, 1969–1976, Vol. XIX, Part 1: Korea, 1969–1972* (Washington, DC: GPO, 2010), pp. 170–173.

in August 1970, "If the United States proceeds to reduce [its troop levels] he will not object, but he will not cooperate."⁵²

Nixon sent Vice President Spiro Agnew to Seoul in September 1970 with the task of securing Park's acquiescence to the troop reduction in exchange for a larger five-year MAP. After a six-hour meeting with Agnew, Park agreed to a statement (which Porter drafted) that he had "no objection to US force reduction of 20,000, provided ROK forces equipment is modernized, and national defense capability is increased," and provided there would be no further US troop withdrawals until the "modernization program has been implemented and ROK force strength increased."⁵³ Agnew exacerbated Park's anxiety when he stated during a press conference that Nixon intended to withdraw all US troops within five years.⁵⁴ In December 1970, Prime Minister Kim Jong-pil told Kissinger that everyone in South Korea understood the US troop reduction "to mean a detachment of the US commitment to support Korea and the establishment of an Asian defense system."⁵⁵

In February 1971, the Nixon administration and the Park government announced an agreement on the conditions for US troop reductions and ROK force modernization, as well as an agreement for annual high-level security consultations.⁵⁶ The US Second Infantry Division left South Korea in June 1971. The following month, Laird traveled to Seoul for the first annual US-ROK Security Consultative Meeting. Park told Laird he had "no intent of asking US troops to stay in the Republic of Korea indefinitely," but that he hoped the United States "would retain its capacity in South Korea until the ROK did attain self-sufficiency."⁵⁷ In September 1971, the Nixon administration proposed a MAP for South Korea totaling $1.5 billion between FY 1971 and 1975, composed of grant military assistance programs, the sale of excess defense articles, and no-cost transfers of equipment to the ROK armed forces.⁵⁸

---

⁵² "68. Telegram from the Embassy in Korea to the Department of State, 4 August 1970," *FRUS, 1969–1976, Vol. XIX, Part 1: Korea, 1969–1972* (Washington, DC: GPO, 2010), pp. 174–179.

⁵³ "71. Backchannel Telegram from the Ambassador to Korea (Porter) to the President's Assistant for National Security Affairs (Kissinger), 25 August 1970," *FRUS, 1969–1976, Vol. XIX, Part 1, Korea, 1969–1972* (Washington, DC: GPO, 2010), pp. 183–184.

⁵⁴ *Investigation of Korean-American Relations*, p. 67.

⁵⁵ "81. Memorandum of Conversation, re: Kim Chong Pil's Remarks on US-Korea Relations, 2 December 1970," *FRUS, 1969–1976, Vol. XIX, Part I: Korea, 1969–1972* (Washington, DC: GPO, 2010), pp. 213–216.

⁵⁶ See "79. Memorandum from John H. Holdridge of the National Security Council Staff to the President's Assistant for National Security Affairs (Kissinger), 16 November 1970," *FRUS, 1969–1972, Vol. XIX, Part 1: Korea, 1969–1972* (Washington, DC: GPO, 2010), pp. 198–199.

⁵⁷ "101. Memorandum from Secretary of Defense Laird to President Nixon, 19 July 1971," *FRUS, 1969–1976, Vol. XIX, Part 1: Korea, 1969–1972* (Washington, DC: GPO, 2010), pp. 254–263.

⁵⁸ "107. National Security Decision Memorandum 129, 2 September 1971," *FRUS, 1969–1976, Vol. XIX, Part 1: Korea, 1969–1972* (Washington, DC: GPO, 2010), pp. 277–278.

Nixon ordered the troop reduction because he and his advisers perceived the United States as confronting a favorable power distribution in East Asia and long time horizons for emerging threats. This assessment might seem odd, since at the time, the United States was still mired in the Vietnam War. However, US policymakers made a distinction between East Asia, or more properly Northeast Asia (e.g., China, Korea, Japan, and Taiwan), and Southeast Asia (e.g., Vietnam, Cambodia, Laos, Thailand, Burma, Malaysia, Singapore, Indonesia, and the Philippines).

National Intelligence Estimate (NIE) 42-70-2 concluded that South Korea's economy and military capabilities had dramatically improved over the past several years, so much so that the ROK army "poses a substantial deterrent to any North Korean invasion." Withdrawing one US army division would not adversely impact the military balance. That NIE warned, however, that Park's increasing authoritarianism would make the ROK political system less stable, thus rendering South Korea more susceptible to North Korean propaganda and subversion.[59]

Neither the Soviet Union nor China was likely to support a North Korean attack in the foreseeable future. The Sino-Soviet rivalry nearly escalated to war when an armed clash between Chinese and Soviet border troops erupted on the disputed Zhenbao (or Damanskii) Island on the Ussuri River on 2 March 1969.[60] Border clashes on that island and elsewhere continued into summer 1969. At one point, some analysts at the Central Intelligence Agency (CIA) and the State Department's Bureau of Intelligence and Research (INR) and policymakers in the Nixon administration feared that the Soviets might launch a preventive air strike on Chinese nuclear facilities.[61]

The Nixon administration encountered low domestic mobilization hurdles to pursuing its preferred strategy in South Korea. There was actually congressional support for the US troop reductions in Southeast Asia and East Asia. During an NSC meeting at Nixon's San Clemente retreat on 14 August 1969, Laird observed that congressional support for a five-year MAP for South Korea was contingent on US troop reductions. Nixon added, "With regard to our 60,000

---

[59] "80. National Intelligence Estimate, the Changing Scene in South Korea, NIE 42-70, 2 December 1970," *FRUS, 1969–1976, Vol. XIX, Part 1: Korea, 1969–1972* (Washington, DC: GPO, 2010), pp. 200–212.

[60] See Viktor M. Gobarev, "Soviet Policy Toward China: Developing Nuclear Weapons 1949–1969," *Journal of Slavic Military Studies*, Vol. 12, No. 4 (1999), pp. 1–53; Yang Kuisong, "The Sino-Soviet Border Clash of 1969: From Zhenbao Island to Sino-American Rapprochement," *Cold War History*, Vol. 1, No. 1 (2000), pp. 21–52; William Burr, "Sino-American Relations, 1969: The Sino-Soviet Border War and Steps Towards Rapprochement," *Cold War History*, Vol. 1, No. 3 (2001), pp. 73–112.

[61] On this see Burr, "Sino-America Relations, 1969," pp. 86–95.

troops in Korea, Congress would love to see a reduction."⁶² In November 1970, Nixon reported to Congress that his administration had withdrawn 6,000 troops from the Philippines, 6,000 from Thailand, and 165,000 from South Vietnam, in addition to 20,000 from South Korea.⁶³

The third catalyst for Park's decision to pursue a nuclear weapon option was the rapprochement between the United States and China. In 1967, Nixon published an article in *Foreign Affairs* on the desirability of US-China rapprochement.⁶⁴ In autumn 1970, he and Kissinger began to pursue this initiative in earnest. Nixon's brief televised announcement on 15 July 1971 about Kissinger's secret talks with PRC premier Zhou En-lai and his own planned visit to Beijing in February 1972 stunned the world.⁶⁵ None of the three US treaty allies in East Asia—South Korea, Japan, or Taiwan—was consulted beforehand.

Park wrote to Nixon in September 1971 to say that while he welcomed the US president's upcoming trip to Beijing and hoped that it would ease tensions on the Korean peninsula, he was nonetheless concerned by speculation that Zhou might raise the US-ROK Mutual Security Treaty and the US troop presence in South Korea.⁶⁶ Foreign Minister Kim Yong-sik and Hahn Pyong-cho, Park's assistant for political affairs, conveyed similar concerns during their

---

⁶² "34. Minutes of a National Security Council Meeting, 14 August 1969," *FRUS, 1969–1976, Vol. XIX, Part 1: Korea, 1969–1972* (Washington, DC: GPO, 2010), pp. 89–95, especially note 13 at p. 94. Following Vance's mission to Seoul in February 1968, Johnson directed Undersecretary of State Nicholas deB. Katzenbach to initiate a comprehensive review of US policy toward South Korea. A draft State Department report recommended reducing the US troop presence. "201. Paper Prepared by the Policy Planning Council of the Department of State, 15 June 1968," *FRUS, 1964–1968, Vol. XXIX, Part 1: Korea, 1969–1972* (Washington, DC: GPO, 2000), p. 433. A Senior Interdepartmental Group was established in September 1968 to prepare options for consideration by the NSC, but it did not finish its work before Johnson left office on 20 January 1969. See "211. Memorandum from the Under Secretary of State (Katzenbach) to President Johnson, 23 December 1968," *FRUS, 1964–1968, Vol. XXIX, Part 1: Korea* (Washington, DC: GPO, 2000), pp. 455–458. The NSSM 27 process that Kissinger initiated on 22 February 1969 essentially picked up where Johnson's NSC staff had left off.

⁶³ Richard M. Nixon, "Special Message to the Congress Proposing Supplemental Foreign Assistance Appropriations, 18 November 1970," in Gerhard Peters and John T. Woolley, eds., *The American Presidency Project*, UCSB, http://www.presidency.ucsb.edu/ws/?pid=2822 (accessed 11 July 2018).

⁶⁴ Richard M. Nixon, "Asia After Viet-Nam," *Foreign Affairs*, Vol. 46, No. 1 (1967): 113–125.

⁶⁵ "Remarks to the Nation Announcing Acceptance of an Invitation to Visit the People's Republic of China," 15 July 1971, *Public Papers of the Presidents of the United States: Richard Nixon, 1971* (Washington, DC: GPO, 1972), pp. 819–820.

⁶⁶ "109. Telegram from the Department of State to the Embassy in Korea, re: Kim Yong-Sik in Washington, 23 September 1971," *FRUS, 1969–1976, Vol. XIX, Vol. 1: Korea, 1969–1972* (Washington, DC: GPO, 2010) pp. 279–280.

respective meetings with Rogers, Kissinger, and Brig. Gen. Alexander M. Haig, then deputy national security adviser, in Washington in September.[67]

Ambassador Philip C. Habib, who succeeded Porter in October 1971, warned in May 1972 that "We are seeing a rising trend of Korean concern that the US takes them for granted and that we also are less than prepared to share in advance those discussions of strategy and actions which we are pursuing in regard to matters directly affecting Korea's forces and Korea's future."[68] In December 1972, Defense Minister Yu Chae-hung informed Habib that the withdrawal of ROK troops from Vietnam would start in January 1973 and finish by June 1973, regardless of the outcome of the Paris negotiations between the United States and North Vietnam.[69]

According to a 1978 CIA estimate, Park authorized a clandestine nuclear weapons program in late 1974, but he had not yet made a decision as to whether to actually seek to develop a nuclear weapon.[70] Other sources suggest Park made the decision much earlier. Kim Jong-pil recalled that Park discussed a nuclear weapons option with him as early as 1970, as did Park Geun-hye, Park's daughter.[71] Kim further recalled that Park said, "We do not know when the United States will leave, so let us research [on] nuclear weapons," adding "Even if we cannot develop those weapons because of the US interference with our project, it would be still beneficial for us to have sufficient technology to make

---

[67] "106. Memorandum of Conversation Between Pyong-Choon Hahn, Special Assistant to the President of Korea for Political Affairs, and Brigadier General Alexander M. Haig, Deputy Assistant to the President for National Security Affairs, 1 September 1971," FRUS, 1969–1976, Vol. XIX, Part 1: Korea, 1969–1972 (Washington, DC: GPO, 2010), pp. 272–277; "109. Telegram from the Department of State to the Embassy in Korea, 23 September 1971," Ibid., pp. 279–280; and "110. Memorandum of Conversation between Kim Yong-Sink, Foreign Minister of the Republic of Korea, Kim Dong-Jo, Korean Ambassador to the US, and Henry A. Kissinger, Assistant to the President for National Security Affairs, 29 September 1971," Ibid., pp. 281–285.

[68] "141. Telegram from the Embassy in Korea to the Department of State, re: Vietnam and Korea, 19 May 1972," FRUS, 1969–1976, Vol. XIX, Part 1: Korea, 1969–1972 (Washington, DC: GPO, 2010), pp. 350–351.

[69] "171. Telegram from the Embassy in Korea to the Department of State, re: ROK Forces in Viet-Nam, 16 December 1972," FRUS, 1969–1976, Vol. XIX, Part 1: Korea, 1969–1972 (Washington, DC: GPO, 2010), pp. 446–447.

[70] National Foreign Assessment Center (NFAC), "South Korea: Nuclear Developments and Strategic Decision Making," US Central Intelligence Agency, June 1978, DOC-0001254259. nautilus.org/wp-content/.../CIA_ROK_Nuclear_DecisionMaking.pdf.

[71] See Jang, "The Evolution of US Extended Deterrence," p. 514; and Hong, "Search for Deterrence," p. 488. Jang and Hong both cite an interview with Park Geun-hye in Weekly Chosen, 12 January 2010. Park Geun-hye was elected ROK president in February 2013 and served until her impeachment by the National Assembly on corruption charges in December 2016. The ROK Constitutional Court upheld the impeachment and formally removed the younger Park from office in March 2017.

the weapons when necessary."[72] Similarly, Oh Won-chul, the senior secretary for economic affairs in the Blue House, remembered that Park raised the nuclear weapon option during negotiations over the Seventh Infantry Division's withdrawal.[73] Oh also recalled meeting in November 1971 with Minister of Science and Technology Choe Hyong and Yoon Young-ku, president of the Korea Atomic Energy Institute (KAERI), to discuss plans for a clandestine nuclear weapons program.[74]

South Korea was a beneficiary of Eisenhower's Atoms for Peace Program. South Korean scientists began peaceful nuclear research in 1956. The ROK joined the International Atomic Energy Agency (IAEA) the following year. KAERI began operations in 1959 and later became affiliated with the Ministry of Science and Technology (MOST). With US assistance, KAERI oversaw the construction of a General Dynamics–designed Triga Mark-II (250 KW) research reactor. In the late 1960s, KAERI decided to master the nuclear fuel cycle. It built a 500 MW nuclear power reactor (the Kori-I), which began operations in 1970, and planned to start nuclear fuel and reprocessing by 1976.[75] In 1968, South Korea signed the Nuclear Nonproliferation Treaty (NPT), although the Park government did not submit it to the National Assembly for ratification because North Korea had not yet signed.[76]

In August 1970, Park established two new entities: the Agency for Defense Development (ADD), an autonomous agency within the Ministry of National Defense (MND); and the Weapons Exploration Committee (WEC), a Blue House coordinating body. The ADD and WEC would support the three legs of Park's strategy to make South Korea "self-sufficient" in national defense. The first was a five-year Force Improvement Plan (FIP) to augment the capabilities of ROK ground forces to repel a North Korean invasion with only US air and logistical support. The second was a major expansion of ROK defense industries.[77]

---

[72] See Jang, "Evolution of US Extended Deterrence," p. 514. This statement allegedly made by Park appears in "Interview with Kim Jong-pil," *JoongAng Ilbo*, 10 July 2015 http://news.joins.com/article/18210193 (accessed 4 May 2018). I am quoting See Jang's English translation of Kim Jong-pil's recollection of Park's statement. The published interview with Kim is in Korean.

[73] See Jang, "The Evolution of US Extended Deterrence," p. 514; and Sung Gul Hong, "Search for Deterrence," p. 488.

[74] Ibid., p. 488. Hong later writes, "The Ministry of National Defense was excluded from the entire project not only because of its lack of expertise but also because of its wholesale institutional integration with the U.S. military establishment, which made the clandestine development of nuclear weapons impossible." Ibid., p. 490

[75] Jungmin Kang and H. A. Feiveson, "South Korea's Shifting and Controversial Interest in Spent Fuel Reprocessing," *Nonproliferation Review*, Vol. 8, No. 1 (2001), pp. 70–78.

[76] Hong, "The Search for Deterrence," pp. 486–487. North Korea did not sign the NPT until 1985.

[77] National Foreign Assessment Center, "South Korea: Nuclear Developments and Strategic Decision Making," p. 5

The third leg was Project 890, a clandestine program to develop the capacity for nuclear weapons and delivery systems.

The ADD oversaw Project 890, which had three compartmentalized teams: a nuclear warhead design team, a chemical warhead design team, and a missile design team.[78] The ADD started with 169 researchers but soon embarked on a campaign to recruit Korean nuclear scientists and engineers who had trained in North American and Western European universities, with the lure of high salaries and generous benefits. In less than five years, the ADD grew from 169 researchers to over 2,000 employees.[79]

KAERI received instructions to purchase uranium reprocessing facilities and fuel fabrication technologies from foreign suppliers. This was ostensibly to help the fledgling nuclear power industry master the fuel cycle and start large-scale electricity generation.[80] In reality, this technology would be used to provide fissile material for a nuclear weapon. As Sung Gul Hong notes, "Because KAERI and the ADD could pursue their respective technological missions [independently] of each other, the division of labor helped Park's effort to hide the nuclear weapons program from the United States as long as possible."[81]

Two other developments impacted the proliferation dispute and the broader US-ROK alliance. First, Park's government became increasingly authoritarian. In April 1971, Park defeated Kim Dae-jung, the leader of the New Democratic Party of Korea, to win a third presidential term. In December, the National Assembly granted Park emergency powers. The following year, he unveiled a new constitution that strengthened the powers of the presidency and allowed him to serve as president for life. A rigged plebiscite approved the so-called *Yushin* ("revitalizing reform") constitution in December 1972.[82]

Park's moves provoked unrest at home and criticism from abroad, including from members of the US Congress. One episode that sparked international outrage was the abduction of Kim Dae-jong from a Tokyo hotel in August 1973 by KCIA operatives, who apparently intended to kill him. Diplomatic intervention by Habib and an international outcry led to Kim's release.[83] In December 1974,

---

[78] Ibid., pp. 5–8.

[79] Quoted from National Foreign Assessment Center, Central Intelligence Agency, "Korea: The Agency for Defense Development," 12 May 1978, Remote Archives Capture (RAC) NLC 4-39-1-9-5, Jimmy Carter Presidential Library (JCPL). Obtained by Alexander Lanoszka.

[80] See Hong, *The Search for Deterrence*, p. 489; and Lyong Choi, "The First Nuclear Crisis in the Korean Peninsula, 1975–76," *Cold War History*, Vol. 14, No. 1 (2014), p. 72.

[81] Hong, "The Search for Deterrence," p. 491.

[82] See Hyug Baeg Im, "The Origins of the Yushin Regime Machiavelli Unveiled," in Byung-Kook Kim and Ezra F. Vogel, eds., *The Park Chung Hee Era: The Transformation of South Korea* (Cambridge, MA: Harvard University Press, 2011) pp. 233–262.

[83] See Yong-Jick Kim, "The Security, Political, and Human Rights Conundrum, 1974–1979," in Byung-Kook Kim and Ezra F. Vogel, eds., *The Park Chung Hee Era: The Modernization of South Korea*

Congress voted to reduce the Ford administration's request for a $238 million MAP to South Korea in FY 1975 to $145 million, but with the proviso the amount could increase to $165 million if the president certified there had been a "significant improvement" in the Park government's compliance with international human rights standards. Ford declined to make that certification.[84]

Second, in September 1970, Park and his advisers authorized South Korean lobbyists in Washington, led by business executive Park Tong-sun, to intensity efforts to secure more military assistance and improve the ROK's image in Washington. Over the next seven years, Park Tong-sun and his fellow lobbyists, many of whom were also KCIA agents, would provide cash, gifts, and illegal campaign donations to members of Congress, congressional staff, and other US officials.[85]

The Ford Administration and South Korean Reprocessing Acquisition, 1974–1976

The CIA station in the US Embassy in Seoul first learned about KAERI's interest in purchasing uranium reprocessing facilities and nuclear reactors (without IAEA safeguards) from Canadian, French, and Belgian firms in summer 1974.[86] In December, the embassy reported the evidence it had received in the past few months "justifies [a] strong presumption that the Korean [government] had decided to proceed with the initial phases of a nuclear weapons development program."[87]

In June 1974, Habib warned about a "Visceral feeling . . . based only on growing independence of Korean attitude toward defense matters and increasing

(Cambridge, MA: Harvard University Press, 2011), pp. 457–482; and Don Oberdorfer and Robert Carlin, *The Two Koreas: A Contemporary History* (New York: Basic Books, 2014), pp. 30–38.

[84] *Investigation of Korean-American Relations*, pp. 46–47.

[85] For details of the illegal lobbying of members of Congress by Park Tung-sun and other South Korean nationals, see *Investigation of Korean-American Relations*, pp. 89–112.

[86] "US Embassy in Republic of Korea Telegram 7328 to Department of State, 'Canadian Nuclear Reactor Program in Korea,' 4 November 1974, Secret," in William Burr, ed., *NSA EBB no. 582* (Washington, DC: National Security Archive, 2017), http://nsarchive.gwu.edu/dc.html?doc=3513492-Document-03-U-S-Embassy-in-Republic-of-Korea.

[87] "US Embassy Seoul Telegram 8023 to Department of State, 'ROK Plans to Develop Nuclear Weapons and Missiles,' 2 December 1974, Secret, Excised Copy Attached to W. R. Smyser and David Elliott to Secretary Kissinger, 'Development of U.S. Policy Toward South Korean Development of Nuclear Weapons,' 28 February 1975, Secret," in William Burr, ed., *NSA EBB no. 582* (Washington, DC: National Security Archive, 2017), http://nsarchive.gwu.edu/dc.html?doc=3513496-Document-06-U-S-Embassy-Seoul-telegram-8023-to.

doubts about the durability of US commitments."[88] The US Mission to the IAEA in Vienna reported that "[The] Koreans have made at least preliminary survey of nuclear fuel reprocessing technology in Europe with view to considering construction of plant in Korea."[89] In November 1974, Ambassador Richard Sneider, who had replaced Habib in Seoul two months earlier, reported that his Canadian counterpart, J. A. Stiles, informed him about KAERI's negotiations to purchase two nuclear power reactors.[90]

A November 1974 INR and Policy Planning Staff report to Secretary of State Henry Kissinger warned, "President Park privately told Korean newsmen last August that he had ordered Korean scientists to develop 'atom bombs' by 1977." The report further warned that a South Korean effort to develop a nuclear weapon capability "could have a deeply unsettling effect on regional stability and our non-proliferation strategy, as it became known to other powers."[91] Intelligence about KAERI's efforts to acquire reprocessing facilities and fuel fabrication technology continued to reach US policymakers in winter 1974–1975.[92]

In April 1975, KAERI signed an interim contract to purchase a uranium fuel reprocessing plant from the French nuclear engineering firm Saint-Gobain Techniques Nouvelles. It signed a second contract to purchase nuclear fuel fabrication facilities from the Belgian firm Belgonucléaire.[93] KAERI also entered

---

[88] "US Embassy in Republic of Korea Telegram 4957 to Department of State, 'Korean Accession to NPT,' 30 July 1974, Confidential," in William Burr, ed., *NSA EBB No. 582* (Washington, DC: National Security Archive, 2017), http://nsarchive.gwu.edu/dc.html?doc=3513489-Document-01-U-S-Embassy-in-Republic-of-Korea.

[89] "U.S. Mission to IAEA, Vienna, Telegram 7090 to Department of State, 'Korean Accession to the NPT,' 13 August 1974, Confidential," in William Burr, ed., *NSA EBB no. 582* (Washington, DC: National Security Archive, 2017), http://nsarchive.gwu.edu/dc.html?doc=3513491-Document-02-U-S-Mission-to-IAEA-Vienna-telegram.

[90] "US Embassy in Republic of Korea Telegram 7328 to Department of State, 'Canadian Nuclear Reactor Program in Korea,' 4 November 1974, Secret," in William Burr, ed., *NSA EBB no. 582* (Washington, DC: National Security Archive, 2017), http://nsarchive.gwu.edu/dc.html?doc=3513492-Document-03-U-S-Embassy-in-Republic-of-Korea.

[91] "Winston Lord, Director, Policy Planning Staff, and Martin Packman, Deputy Director, Office of Intelligence and Research, 'Second Alert Report,' 20 November 1974, Secret," in William Burr, ed., *NSA EEB no. 582* (Washington, DC: National Security Archive, 2017), http://nsarchive.gwu.edu/dc.html?doc=3513493-Document-04-Winston-Lord-director-Policy.

[92] See "US Embassy Seoul Telegram 1089 to State Department, ROK Nuclear Program, 20 February 1975, Secret," in William Burr, ed., *NSA EBB no. 584* (Washington, DC: National Security Archives, 2017), https://nsarchive2.gwu.edu/dc.html?doc=3535258-Document-02A-U-S-Embassy-Seoul-Telegram-1089-to; and "Draft Telegram to State Department Intelligence and Research [RCI], 3 March 1975, Secret," in William Burr, ed., *NSA EBB no. 584* (Washington, DC: National Security Archives, 2017), https://nsarchive2.gwu.edu/dc.html?doc=3535259-Document-02B-Draft-Telegram-to-State-Department.

[93] Hong, "Search for Deterrence," p. 491.

into negotiations to acquire two CANDU (Canada Deuterium Uranium) heavy-water reactors, which would provide spent nuclear fuel, and a National Research Experimental (NRX) heavy-water reactor.[94] The NRX was the same type of reactor that India had used to obtain plutonium.[95]

The Ford administration embarked upon a four-fold strategy to thwart the fledgling nuclear weapons program. First, officials would try to persuade France and Canada to restrict nuclear technology exports to South Korea. Second, they would threaten to suspend the 1972 US-ROK civil nuclear cooperation agreement and withhold a $252 million Export-Import Bank loan for the construction of a Westinghouse-supplied Kori-II power reactor. Third, they would pressure the Park government to ship spent nuclear reactor fuel to an as-yet-unbuilt regional reprocessing facility. Fourth, they would pledge to maintain current US troop levels and to transfer F-4, F-5, and A-37 aircraft.[96] The second and third parts would be overtly coercive: noncompliance by the Park government would trigger the imposition of "sanctions." The fourth part of the strategy, however, would be accommodative. By pledging to stabilize US troop levels, transfer F-4, F-5, and A-37s, and enhance civil nuclear cooperation, the administration would seek to diminish Park's demand for a nuclear weapon option. Hence, the overall strategy was a hybrid of coercion and accommodation.

Canadian prime minister Pierre Trudeau's government moved to impose conditions on nuclear technology sales to South Korea even before the Ford administration acted.[97] In January 1975, Secretary of State for External Affairs Allan MacEachen sent a letter to Foreign Minister Kim Dong-ju stating that Canada would not export the CANDU and NRX reactors unless South Korea ratified the NPT.[98] When Sneider raised the NPT issue with Lho Shing-yong,

---

[94] Ibid.; CIA NFAC, "South Korea: Nuclear Developments and Strategic Decision Making."

[95] "US National Security Council Memorandum, Sale of Canadian Nuclear Reactor to South Korea," November 14, 1974, History and Public Policy Program Digital Archive, Gerald R. Ford Presidential Library, Office of the Asst. to the President for National Security Affairs, Henry Kissinger and Brent Scowcroft Files (1972), 1974–1977, Temporary Parallel File, A1, Korea 10-74-1-75. Obtained by Charles Kraus, http://digitalarchive.wilsoncenter.org/document/114631.

[96] See "John Marcum to Brent Scowcroft, 24 July 1975, Enclosing Jan M. Lodal and David Elliott Memorandum to Secretary Kissinger, 'Approach to South Korea on Reprocessing,' 24 July 1975, Secret, Excised Copy," in William Burr, ed., *NSA EBB no. 582* (Washington, DC: National Security Archive, 2017), http://nsarchive.gwu.edu/dc.html?doc=3513507-Document-16-John-Marcum-to-Brent-Scowcroft-24.

[97] Se Young Jang, "Bringing Seoul into the Nonproliferation Regime: The Effect of ROK-Canada Reactor Deals on South Korea's Ratification of the NPT," *Nuclear Proliferation International History Program Working Paper* no. 10 (Washington, DC: Woodrow Wilson International Center for Scholars 2017), pp. 20–23.

[98] Cited in Lyong Choi, "The First Nuclear Crisis in the Korean Peninsula, 1975–76," Cold War History, Vol. 14, No. 1 (2014), pp. 71–90, at p. 75.

the vice foreign minister, on 25 February, Lho replied that Park government had already submitted the NPT to the National Assembly for ratification.[99]

During talks in London to establish the NSG in June 1975, George Vest, assistant secretary of state for politico-military affairs, informed French officials that the Ford administration would try to discourage South Korea's acquisition of a reprocessing capacity. In reply, Bertrand Goldschmidt, the French representative to the IAEA Board of Governors, said that "There wasn't much money in reprocessing sales and that France would not object to Korean cancellation of the deal if Saint Gobain was reimbursed for termination costs."[100]

In April 1975, Park told Sneider about plans to develop missile production capabilities to provide the means for attacking North Korean air bases and urban centers. While Park said that his government had no plans to develop nuclear weapons, he was determined to build up the ROK's self-reliance and defense production, especially its missile capabilities. Sneider told the State Department, "It should be feasible to develop a US policy which gives [the] ROK [a] reasonable sense of security in [the] effective defense of Korea even in contingency of [a] US withdrawal."[101]

Meanwhile, the Ford administration debated the Lockheed Propulsion Company's contract to sell advanced missile technology to South Korea. Deputy Secretary of Defense William Clements recommended approval, while officials in the State Department and the Arms Control and Disarmament Agency (ACDA) opposed it. A State Department memorandum to Lt. Gen. Brent Scowcroft, then deputy national security adviser, argued, "We believe that SSMs, even without nuclear warheads, could be destabilizing in the hands of the present ROK leadership," adding that the South Korea's strategic location in East

---

[99] "US Embassy Seoul Telegram 1239 to Department of State, 'Non-Proliferation Treaty,' 26 February 1975, Confidential," in William Burr, ed., *NSA EBB no. 582* (Washington, DC: National Security Archive, 2017), http://nsarchive.gwu.edu/dc.html?doc=3513498-Document-08-U-S-Embassy-Seoul-telegram-1239-to. The ROK National Assembly ratified the NPT on 25 April 1975. See "Republic of Korea: Ratification of Treaty on the Non-Proliferation of Nuclear Weapons (NPT)," 23 April 1975, United Nations Office of Disarmament Affairs, http://disarmament.un.org/treaties/a/npt/republicofkorea/rat/washington (accessed 19 June 2018).

[100] "US Embassy London Telegram 09295 to State Department, 'Nuclear Export Policy: Bilateral with France,' 18 June 1975, Secret," in William Burr, ed., *NSA EBB no. 582* (Washington, DC: National Security Archive, 2017), http://nsarchive.gwu.edu/dc.html?doc=3513504-Document-13-U-S-Embassy-London-telegram-09295-to.

[101] "US Embassy Seoul Telegram 3090 to State Department, Meeting with President Park: Missile Strategy, 1 May 1975, Secret," in William Burr, ed., *NSA EBB no. 584* (Washington, DC: National Security Archives, 2017), https://nsarchive2.gwu.edu/dc.html?doc=3535261-Document-04-U-S-Embassy-Seoul-Telegram-3090-to.

Asia made the linkage between nuclear weapon and long-range missile development all the more serious.[102]

The engineers in the Project 890 missile development team focused on modifying command-guidance systems of the US-made Nike Hercules. Without modifications, and when launched from behind the DMZ, the Hercules could target Pyongyang, as well as the ports of Nampo and Wonsan. Engineers modified the missile to strike targets within an arc of 240 kilometers and to carry heavier payloads.[103] Due to the Ford administration's opposition to exports of propellant, as well as to the Lockheed contract, the ADD agreed to limit the missile range to 180 kilometers and the warhead weight to 440 kilograms.[104]

Sneider reported on a March 1975 meeting between MacEachen and Park on the terms for the CANDU and NRX reactor transfers. Park unequivocally stated his government had no plans to develop nuclear weapons. Yet, in an earlier meeting with the Canadian trade minister, Alistair Gillespie, Park made a link between the possible withdrawal of the US nuclear umbrella from South Korea and the need to develop a nuclear weapon.[105]

A cable from the US Embassy in Seoul sent ahead of a meeting between Vice President Nelson Rockefeller and Kim Chong-pil in April 1975 observed: "[South Korean] security rests heavily on [the] deterrent effect US force presence and military assistance provide.... Decline of military assistance below levels earlier agreed and criticism in US of [South Korea] have already created concerns over US intentions toward its commitments."[106] NSC staff members Jan M. Lodal and David Elliott warned Kissinger that South Korea's "exercise of a nuclear option would depend on the continuation of US security guarantees."[107] A DoD policy review noted that while the intra-Korean military

---

[102] "US Department of State Memorandum, Sale of Rocket Propulsion Technology to South Korea," February 04, 1975, History and Public Policy Program Digital Archive, Gerald R. Ford Presidential Library, National Security Adviser Presidential Country Files for East Asia and the Pacific, Box 9, Korea (3). Obtained by Charles Kraus, http://digitalarchive.wilsoncenter.org/document/114634.

[103] Hong, "Search for Deterrence," pp. 495–496.

[104] National Foreign Assessment Center, *South Korea: Nuclear Developments*, p. 9.

[105] "US Embassy Seoul Telegram 4902 to Department of State, 'Canadian/ROK Talks on Nuclear Energy,' 3 July 1975, Confidential," in William Burr, ed., *NSA EBB no. 582* (Washington, DC: National Security Archive, 2017), http://nsarchive.gwu.edu/dc.html?doc=3513505-Document-14-U-S-Embassy-Seoul-telegram-4902-to.

[106] Department of State Telegram, "Vice President's Meeting with ROK Prime Minister Kim Chong-Phil," April 1975, folder: "Korea—State Department Telegrams: From SECSTATE to NODIS (3)," box 11, National Security Adviser, Presidential Country Files for East Asia and the Pacific, GRFL, obtained by Alexander Lanoszka.

[107] "John Marcum to Brent Scowcroft, 24 July 1975, Enclosing Jan M. Lodal and David Elliott Memorandum to Secretary Kissinger, 'Approach to South Korea on Reprocessing,' 24 July 1975, Secret, Excised Copy," in William Burr, ed., *NSA EBB*

balance appeared stable, "President Park's fears of isolation and the possible withdrawal of US forces have led him to embark on a secret program to develop nuclear weapons and long-range surface-to-surface missiles to deliver the weapons."[108]

Kissinger and Habib, then assistant secretary of state for East Asian and Pacific Affairs, instructed Sneider to inform ROK officials that a reprocessing facility "could be perceived as destabilizing and thus impair our ability to sustain US-Korean peaceful nuclear cooperation." Sneider also received instructions to convey that "cognizant committees of Congress have indicated that they would be unlikely to approve" an Export-Import Bank loan for the construction of the Kori-II reactor "unless they can be assured that the ROK has terminated its plans to acquire a pilot reprocessing plant."[109]

Sneider told Choe that, in the interest of future civil nuclear cooperation, the Ford administration asked the Park government to cancel the French contract and to instead explore possibilities for multilateral reprocessing. Choe expressed surprise at the extent of US concern and said the French plant would be used only as a learning tool, not for the production of weapons-grade plutonium.[110]

Sneider met with Yoon, who claimed that the French-designed facility would train Korean scientists and engineers in fuel element fabrication, reprocessing, and waste management. Yoon claimed that only a minimal amount of plutonium would result. Sneider informed the State Department that "Koreans are not willing to accept anything less than a laboratory in Korea of [the] kind purchased from [the] French," and that KAERI officials questioned "whether the US can impose a policy on Korea which forbids Korea entry into a legitimate business aspect of nuclear power; an aspect in which, for example, Japan is very heavily involved."[111] "Unequivocally negative" was Sneider's assessment of the

---

no. 582 (Washington, DC: National Security Archive, 2017), http://nsarchive.gwu.edu/dc.html?doc=3513507-Document-16-John-Marcum-to-Brent-Scowcroft-24.

[108] "274. Study Prepared by the Office of International Security Affairs in the Department of Defense, Washington, Updated," *FRUS, 1969–1976, Vol. E-12: Documents on East and Southeast Asia, 1973–1976* (Washington, DC: GPO, 2011), https://history.state.gov/historicaldocuments/frus1969-76ve12/d274.

[109] "State Department Telegram 195214 to US Embassy Seoul, 'ROK Nuclear Fuel Reprocessing Plans,' 16 August 1975, Secret, Excised Copy," in William Burr, ed., *NSA EBB no. 582* (Washington, DC: National Security Archive, 2017), http://nsarchive.gwu.edu/dc.html?doc=3513547-Document-18-State-Department-telegram-195214-to.

[110] "US Embassy Seoul Telegram 6495 to Department of State, 'ROK Nuclear Fuel Reprocessing Plans,' 23 August 1975, Secret," *NSA EBB no. 582* (Washington, DC: National Security Archive, 2017), http://nsarchive2.gwu.edu/dc.html?doc=3513548-Document-19-U-S-Embassy-Seoul-telegram-6495-to.

[111] "US Embassy Seoul Telegram 6608 to Department of State, 'ROK Nuclear Fuel Reprocessing Plans,' 26 August 1975, Secret," in William Burr, ed., *NSA EBB no. 582*

reactions of Yoon, Choe, and Deputy Prime Minister Nam Duk-woom to the regional reprocessing facility.[112]

On 9 October 1975, Deputy Secretary of State Robert Ingersoll summoned Ambassador Hahm Pyong-choon to reiterate the "seriousness [that the United States] attach[es] to the reprocessing issue." Hahn responded that the plant would have no plutonium production capacity and that South Korea would "obtain all necessary assurances by direct application of supplementary safeguard measures." Ingersoll replied that the "physical existence of reprocessing capability in Korea" was problematic and that, "in perception of others, the implications of this could not be overcome by any control arrangements."[113] He also told Hahm that the administration would be unable to convince members of Congress, even with significant safeguards, of South Korea's peaceful intentions with the plant.[114]

The Ford administration's various efforts to thwart the reprocessing plant transfer occurred alongside renewed efforts to reassure Park about the United States' security commitment. During a visit to Seoul in November 1974, Ford told Park there were no plans for further US troop withdrawals and that his administration would continue to support ROK force modernization.[115] In January 1975, Ford authorized the sale of an F-4D squadron, as well as the rehabilitation of two F-5A squadrons under the Enhance Plus Agreement, and the gradual shift from military grant assistance to FMS credits for future ROK arms purchases.[116]

In late August 1975, Secretary of Defense James D. Schlesinger traveled to Seoul for meetings with Park and other ROK officials. Schlesinger told Park that he foresaw no basic changes in US force levels in South Korea over the next five years, especially since congressional pressures to reduce overseas troop

(Washington, DC: National Security Archive, 2017), http://nsarchive2.gwu.edu/dc.html?doc=3513550-Document-20-U-S-Embassy-Seoul-telegram-6608-to.

[112] "US Embassy Seoul Telegram 74642 to Department of State, 'ROK Nuclear Fuel Reprocessing Plant,' 30 September 1975, Secret," in William Burr, ed., *NSA EBB no. 582* (Washington, DC: National Security Archive, 2017), http://nsarchive.gwu.edu/dc.html?doc=3513552-Document-22-U-S-Embassy-Seoul-telegram-74642-to.

[113] "State Department Telegram 240692 to US Embassy Seoul, 'Deputy Secretary Ingersoll's Meeting with Ambassador Hahm of Korea,' 9 October 1975, Secret," in William Burr, ed., *NSA EBB no. 582* (Washington, DC: National Security Archive, 2017), http://nsarchive.gwu.edu/dc.html?doc=3513554-Document-24-State-Department-telegram-240692-to.

[114] Ibid.

[115] See "259. Memorandum of Conversation, Seoul, November 1974," *FRUS, 1969–1976, Vol. E-12: Documents on East and Southeast Asia, 1973–1976* (Washington, DC: GPO, 2011), https://static.history.state.gov/frus/frus1969-76ve12/pdf/d259.pdf.

[116] "National Security Decision Memorandum 282: Korean Force Modernization," 9 January 1975, National Security Adviser's Files, Box 1, NSDM File, 1974–1977, GRFL, https://www.fordlibrarymuseum.gov/library/document/0310/nsdm282.pdf.

deployments had diminished. He indicated that the administration would assist in the development of ROK defense industries.[117] Schlesinger also warned Park: "We can deter Soviet nuclear threats while the ROK could not and a ROK effort to develop its own nuclear weapons would end up providing the Soviets with justification for threatening the ROK with nuclear weapons."[118]

Schlesinger assured Defense Minister Suh Jyong-chul that neither China nor the Soviet Union appeared overly concerned about US troops in South Korea or showed any signs of backing North Korean provocations. He announced that the Ford administration would proceed with the transfer of F-4 and F-5s, which the Park government had requested, and offered 18 A-37s on an "as-is basis" at a low cost. When Suh inquired if the transfer of 21 F-5Es would be part of the assistance package, Schlesinger replied they would not.[119]

Lho told Sneider on 24 October that it would be "impossible to cancel the French contract at this stage." Sneider warned, "adverse US congressional reaction may very well not be limited to rejection [of] Kori-II [reactor] loan and supply of fuel elements but could apply in many areas [the] ROKS need US support." He also rejected Lho's comparison of Korean and Japanese reprocessing, noting that Japan "was not on [the] DMZ," and saying that "Korea is [a] critical area where [North Korean] and Sino/Soviet reaction needed to be considered."[120]

Kissinger instructed Sneider and Habib to seek meetings with Kim Chong-pil, and if necessary, with Park. Failure to cancel the reprocessing plant would lead the Ford administration to withdraw support for the Export-Import Bank loan and forbid the reprocessing of any US-derived nuclear fuel. In addition, any future South Korean action to separate and stockpile plutonium "would seriously affect our security and political relationship" and have an "unsettling" impact in the region.[121]

---

[117] "Memoranda of Conversations between James R. Schlesinger and Park Chung Hee and Suh Jyong-chul," 26 August 1975, History and Public Policy Program Digital Archive, Gerald R. Ford Presidential Library, National Security Adviser Presidential Country Files for East Asia and the Pacific, Box 9, Korea (11), obtained by Charles Kraus, http://digitalarchive.wilsoncenter.org/document/114633.

[118] "272. Memorandum of Conversation, Seoul, 27 August 1975," *FRUS 1969–1973, Vol. E-12: Documents on East and Southeast Asia, 1973–1976* (Washington, DC: GPO, 2011).

[119] Ibid.

[120] "US Embassy Seoul Telegram 8278 to Department of State, 'ROKG Rejects Our Representations on Nuclear Reprocessing,' 24 October 1975, Secret," in William Burr, ed., *NSA EBB no. 582* (Washington, DC: National Security Archive, 2017), http://nsarchive.gwu.edu/dc.html?doc=3513555-Document-25-U-S-Embassy-Seoul-telegram-8278-to.

[121] "State Department Telegram 230171 to US Embassy Seoul, ROK Nuclear Reprocessing, 4 December 1975, Secret," in William Burr, ed., NSA EBB no. 584 (Washington, DC: National Security Archives, 2017), https://nsarchive2.gwu.edu/dc.html?doc=3535264-Document-07-State-Department-telegram-230171-to.

Ford's December 1975 meeting with Vice Premier Deng Xiaoping in Beijing is significant. At the time, the distribution of power in East Asia appeared favorable to the United States. Sino-Soviet tensions had markedly diminished since 1969, but the two Communist powers still viewed each other warily. "Throughout this century, Peking's foreign policy will probably continue to be shaped in part by hatred and fear of the USSR," according to a CIA assessment. "China will attempt to use US influence to deter the USSR from attacking China and to offset Soviet efforts to encircle or contain China."[122]

From March 1975 to December 1976, Ford administration officials perceived a stable power distribution and long time horizons for threats in East Asia. Again, this assessment stands in sharp contrast to Southeast Asia, where the US strategic position faced imminent collapse in spring 1975. The Khmer Rouge captured the Cambodian capital, Phnom Penh, on 17 April. South Vietnam's capital, Saigon, fell to the People's Army of Vietnam and the Viet Cong on 25 April. Meanwhile, Pathet Lao insurgents continued to seize territory in neighboring Laos.[123]

In East Asia, by comparison, the power distribution among the major states appeared stable. There were few indications of near- or medium-term expansion by the Soviet Union or its allies in that region. Indeed, North Korea was the USSR's only ally in East Asia in 1975 and 1976. "The structure of the Major Power balance in the Far East appears unchanged in its essentials, despite some new uncertainties," Policy Planning Staff director Winston Lord wrote to Kissinger in October 1975, adding, "The Soviets are looking for political openings, but they've probably lost as much ground (versus China) in Northeast Asia (Korea, Japan) as they have gained in Southeast Asia (Hanoi)."[124] Intelligence analysts concluded the conventional military balance between the two Koreas was near parity. The near-term likelihood of renewed instability in East Asia appeared low. As a March 1974 INR assessment put it: "Given Pyongyang's desire neither to strengthen Park against his critics nor to displease the Chinese and Soviets

---

[122] "84. Paper Prepared in the Central Intelligence Agency, July 1974," *FRUS, 1969–1976, Vol. XVIII: China, 1973–1976* (Washington, DC: GPO, 2006). Also see "147. Editorial Note," *FRUS, 1969–1976, Vol. XVIII: China, 1973–1976* (Washington, DC: GPO, 2006).

[123] See "65. Minutes of the Secretary of State's Staff Meeting, Washington, 30 April 1975, 8 A.M."; and "67. Memorandum for Secretary Kissinger, Washington, 2 May 1975," *FRUS, 1969–1976, Vol. E-12: Documents on East and Southeast Asia, 1973–1976* (Washington, DC: GPO, 2011).

[124] "21. Memorandum from the Director of the Policy Planning Staff (Lord) to Secretary of State Kissinger, Washington, 16 October 1975," *FRUS, 1969–1976, Vol. E-12: Documents on East and Southeast Asia, 1973–1976* (Washington, DC: GPO, 2011).

unnecessarily, Northern moves which might seriously destabilize the situation in the peninsula are unlikely."[125]

Nixon's summit with Zhou and CCP chairman Mao Zedong in February 1972 started the rapprochement between the United States and China. However, it fell to the Ford administration to begin the process of normalizing US-China diplomatic ties. This, in turn, required finessing a number of complex political and security issues in East Asia, one of which was the divided Korean peninsula. North Korea was China's buffer against the US military presence in South Korea and Japan. Officially, Deng and other Chinese leaders supported the North Korean position that all foreign troops should withdraw from the Korean peninsula.[126] Privately, however, they did not object to the US troop presence in South Korea and actually saw it as necessary for regional stability, as Schlesinger told Park in August 1975.[127]

Ford, Kissinger, Habib, and Scowcroft sought Chinese leaders' assurances to restrain Kim Il-sung in order to reassure Park. Deng told Ford, "We are not worried like you are about a military attack against the South," but he also expressed a "hope that the American side would keep an eye on Park Chung Hee."[128] Habib briefed Park on the Ford-Deng meeting. When Park asked whether Deng sought to maintain the status quo in Korea, Habib responded "that [the] PRC apparently accepts [the] present status quo since it wishes no problems either with [the] US or [the] USSR."[129]

The domestic mobilization hurdles the Ford administration had to overcome were congressional wariness about the Park government's authoritarianism, as well as growing congressional concern about worldwide nuclear proliferation.

---

[125] Bureau of Intelligence and Research, "North Korean Military Forces: Gradual Growth," 29 March 1974, Gerald R. Ford Presidential Library, National Security Adviser, NSC East Asian and Pacific Affairs Staff: Files, (1969) 1973–1976, Box 5, Folder: Korea (4), obtained by Charles Krause.

[126] See, for example, "109. Memorandum of Conversation Between Ambassador Huang Chen, Chief of the PRC Liaison Office in Washington, and Secretary of State Henry A. Kissinger, 9 May 1975," *FRUS, 1969–1976, Vol. XVIII: China, 1973–1976* (Washington, DC: GPO, 2006) pp. 665–671.

[127] "Memoranda of Conversations Between James R. Schlesinger and Park Chung Hee and Suh Jyong-chul," 26 August 1975, History and Public Policy Program Digital Archive, Gerald R. Ford Presidential Library, National Security Adviser Presidential Country Files for East Asia and the Pacific, Box 9, Korea (11), obtained by Charles Kraus, http://digitalarchive.wilsoncenter.org/document/114633.

[128] "137. Memorandum of Conversation, Beijing, 4 December 1975," *FRUS 1969–1976, Vol. XVIII: China, 1972–1976* (Washington, DC: GPO, 2006), pp. 892–907.

[129] "US Embassy Seoul Telegram 9439 to State Department, Assistant Secretary Habib's Meeting with President Park, 9 December 1975, Secret," in William Burr, ed., *NSA EBB no. 584* (Washington, DC: National Security Archives, 2017), https://nsarchive2.gwu.edu/dc.html?doc=3535268-Document-11A-U-S-Embassy-Seoul-telegram-9439-to.

Kissinger wrote to Ford: "Distaste in Congress for Park's handling of his domestic political situation did not in the end reduce our military assistance to South Korea by as much as earlier seemed likely," noting that Congress had recently authorized a $145 million MAP for FY 1975, plus an additional $20 million, if the president certified the Park government made "substantial progress" on human rights.[130]

As the Park government became more repressive, however, some members of Congress became more vocal in their criticism of US policy toward South Korea. According to one DoD study, "We have witnessed Congressional efforts... to pressure Park to liberalize his administration by denying aid and threatening a US withdrawal."[131] Indeed, in February 1976, Representative Donald M. Fraser (D-MN), the chairman of the Subcommittee on International Organizations, submitted a report on the illegal activities of the KCIA in the United States. Three months later, Fraser and 118 House members sent a letter to Ford asking him to suspend military aid to the ROK because of the Park government's human rights abuses.[132]

The French reprocessing plant dispute occurred against the backdrop of increased attention to nuclear nonproliferation in Congress. In March 1975, Senator Stuart Symington (D-MO) called for "linking certain [US assistance] programs and trade privileges to membership in the Nuclear Nonproliferation Treaty and subscription to International Atomic Energy Agency 'safeguards.'"[133] In June, Senator Charles Percy (R-IL) introduced legislation to grant the new Nuclear Regulatory Commission the power to approve or deny nuclear technology exports, as well as imposing more-stringent criteria for such exports.[134]

---

[130] "260. Memorandum from the President's Assistant for National Security Affairs (Kissinger) to President Ford, 3 January 1975," *FRUS, 1969–1976, Vol. E-12: Documents on East and Southeast Asia* (Washington, DC: GPO, 2011).

[131] "274. Study Prepared by the Office of International Security Affairs in the Department of Defense, Washington, circa 16 January 1976," *FRUS, 1969–1976, Vol. E-12: Documents on East and Southeast Asia, 1973–1976* (Washington, DC: GPO, 2011), https://history.state.gov/historicaldocuments/frus1969-76ve12/d274.

[132] See *Investigation of Korean-American Relations* (Washington, DC: GPO, 1978), pp. 89–110; and "275. Information Memorandum from the Acting Assistant Secretary for International Security Affairs in the Department of Defense (Bergholt) to Secretary of Defense Rumsfeld, Washington, 16 March 1976," *FRUS, 1969–1976, Vol. E-12: Documents on East and Southeast Asia, 1973–1976* (Washington, DC: GPO, 2011). Also see Chronology of Events in Christian F. Ostermann, James Person, and Charles Kraus, eds., *The Carter Chill: US-ROK-DPRK Trilateral Relations, 1976–1979: A Critical Oral History Conference* (Washington, DC: Woodrow Wilson International Center for Scholars, 2013), p. iii.

[133] Stuart Symington, "Controlling the Cancer of Nuclear Proliferation, 13 March 1975," in United States Senate Committee on Government Operations, *Peaceful Nuclear Exports and Weapons Proliferation: A Compendium* (Washington, DC: GPO, 1975) p. 528.

[134] David Burnham, "Nuclear Equipment Sales Spark Debate," *New York Times*, 15 June 1975, p. 1. The Nuclear Regulatory Commission is the successor agency to the Atomic Energy Commission.

In October 1975, Senators Alan Cranston (D-CA), Charles Mathias (R-MD), and Bill Brock (R-TN) sponsored a resolution calling on the Ford administration to take further steps to control nuclear proliferation, including tighter export controls. On 12 December, the Senate passed a resolution calling upon the president to impose strict conditions on nuclear technology transfers, including enrichment and reprocessing facilities.[135]

On 6 December 1975, Ingersoll met sequentially with French ambassador Jacques Kosciusko-Morizet and Canadian ambassador Jack Warren at the State Department. He told both envoys that the Ford administration "concluded that a secret program to develop a future nuclear weapon capability is now underway in the ROK" and that KAERI's planned acquisition of reprocessing facilities and heavy-water reactors were integral to that program.[136] Ingersoll said that he wanted to keep Paris "fully informed" about the ROK nuclear program and told Kosciusko-Morizet that the Park government had rejected US requests to cancel the reprocessing plant deal. Kosciusko-Morizet replied that President Valéry Giscard d'Estaing was "personally interested" in the matter.[137] Ingersoll then asked Warren to persuade the Trudeau government to delay the CANDU and NRX reactor sales and support the US position on the reprocessing plant.[138]

Four days later, Warren informed Ingersoll and Vest that the Trudeau government had decided to postpone finalizing CANDU reactor sale, telling ROK officials that ministerial schedules prevented any action before January 1976.[139] Stiles informed Sneider that the Trudeau government wished to know "what

[135] S. Res. 221 reprinted in Joint Committee on Atomic Energy, "S. 1439 Export Reorganization Act of 1976: Hearing Before the Joint Committee on Atomic Energy, Congress of the United States, 94th Congress, Second Session, 22 June 1976," *Joint Committee on Atomic Energy Digital Archive* (Stanford, CA: Stanford University Press, 1976), pp. 198–201.

[136] "Policy Planning Staff Director Winston Lord and Acting Assistant Secretary of State for East Asian and Pacific Affairs Robert H. Miller to Deputy Secretary of State, Your Meetings with the French and Canadian Ambassadors on Korean Reprocessing, 4 December 1975, Secret," in William Burr, ed., *NSA EBB no. 584* (Washington, DC: National Security Archives, 2017), https://nsarchive2.gwu.edu/dc.html?doc=3535265-Document-08-Policy-Planning-Staff-director.

[137] "State Department Telegram 288551 to US Delegation, ROK Nuclear Reprocessing Plant Negotiation, 6 December 1975, Secret," in William Burr, ed., *NSA EBB No. 584* (Washington, DC: National Security Archives, 2017), https://nsarchive2.gwu.edu/nukevault/ebb584-The-U.S.-and-the-South-Korean-Nuclear-Program,-1974-1976,-Part-2/.

[138] "State Department Telegram 288550 to US Delegation, ROK Nuclear Reprocessing Plant Negotiation, 6 December 1975, Secret," in William Burr, ed., *NSA EBB no. 584* (Washington, DC: National Security Archives, 2017), https://nsarchive2.gwu.edu/dc.html?doc=3535267-Document-10-State-Department-telegram-288550-to.

[139] "State Department Telegram 291712 to US Embassy Seoul, ROK Nuclear Reprocessing Plant, 10 December 1975, Secret," in William Burr, ed., *NSA EBB no. 584* (Washington, DC: National Security Archives, 2017), https://nsarchive2.gwu.edu/dc.html?doc=3535272-Document-14-State-Department-telegram-291712-to.

nuclear material will be available for reprocessing in [the] French plant."[140] MacEachen told Kissinger, "The impending conclusion of our agreement with Korea has been postponed because of the information you have given us. You have knowledge that Korea is gearing up for a nuclear capability."[141]

Meanwhile, Ingersoll informed Hahm that the Ford administration rejected KAERI's economic and technical arguments. The deputy secretary emphasized the dangers of the reprocessing plant for US-ROK "mutual interests." Hahm responded by offering American "participation and control" of the facility and raised the prospect of Washington offering a "concrete fuel fabrication proposal which would allow [the] ROKG to cancel [the] reprocessing deal."[142] Vice Minister of Science and Technology Yi Chong-sok met with Sneider and inquired what nuclear assistance the United States was prepared to offer if South Korea canceled the French reprocessing plant. "It is quite possible ROKG officials are seeking [a] rationale in terms of positive gains for pulling out of suspending of [the] French project," Sneider cabled.[143] Sneider met with Kim Chom-yom, the presidential secretary-general in the Blue House, who assured him that "Any final action on the further final action on [the] purchase of [the] French plant will be held off until our reply is received." Kim added, "President Park [was] fully aware of the high political stakes involved."[144]

In late December 1975, Sneider warned, "Reversal of [the] decision on [the] French reprocessing [plant] involves [the] personal prestige of President Park," and advised that a "reversal on ostensibly technical grounds, rather than

---

[140] "State Department Telegram 295 to US Embassy Tokyo et al., Forwarding US Embassy Seoul Telegram 9661, ROK Nuclear Reprocessing Plant: Canadian Approach, 16 December 1975, Secret," in William Burr, ed., *NSA EBB no. 584* (Washington, DC: National Security Archives, 2017), https://nsarchive2.gwu.edu/dc.html?doc=3535275-Document-17-State-Department-telegram-295-to-U-S.

[141] "Memorandum of Conversation, 17 December 1975, 10:45 A.M., Hotel Raphael, Paris, Secret," in William Burr, ed., *NSA EBB no. 584* (Washington, DC: National Security Archives, 2017), https://nsarchive2.gwu.edu/dc.html?doc=3535276-Document-18-Memorandum-of-conversation-17.

[142] "State Department Telegram 293834 to US Embassy Seoul, Acting Secretary Discusses Nuclear Reprocessing with Korean Ambassador, 12 December 1975, Secret," in William Burr, ed., *NSA EBB no. 584* (Washington, DC: National Security Archives, 2017), https://nsarchive2.gwu.edu/dc.html?doc=3535273-Document-15-State-Department-telegram-293834-to.

[143] "State Department Telegram 295 to US Embassy Tokyo et al., Forwarding US Embassy Seoul Telegram 9661, ROK Nuclear Reprocessing Plant: Canadian Approach, 16 December 1975, Secret," in William Burr, ed., *NSA EBB no. 584* (Washington, DC: National Security Archives, 2017), https://nsarchive2.gwu.edu/dc.html?doc=3535275-Document-17-State-Department-telegram-295-to-U-S.

[144] "State Department telegram 295 to US Embassy Tokyo et al., Forwarding US Embassy Seoul telegram 9661, 'ROK Nuclear Reprocessing Plant: Canadian Approach,' 16 December 1975, Secret" in William Burr, *NSA EBB, no. 584* (Washington, DC: National Security Archive, 2017), https://nsarchive2.gwu.edu//dc.html?doc=3535275-Document-17-State-Department-telegram-295-to-U-S.

response to US *force majeure* may prove easier to swallow."[145] Kissinger instructed Sneider to discuss the "positive aspects" of bilateral nuclear cooperation in "non-sensitive areas" should Park cancel the deal with the French.[146] In other words, in addition to the assurances about US troop levels, military aircraft transfers (the F-4s, the F-5s, and A-37s), and support for ROK force modernization, Kissinger was now prepared to offer additional inducements in civil nuclear cooperation.

Unable to secure a meeting with Park, Sneider instead met with Kim Chong-yom on 26 December 1975. Kim suggested a compromise: the ROKG would postpone any action on reprocessing for six months, while it held talks with the Ford administration about nuclear cooperation. As part of this reconsideration, South Korea would be "prepared" to cancel the French contract if its nuclear research and development requirements could be met.[147] Sneider received instructions to warn ROK officials that an "extended delay in reaching a final decision on our request may adversely affect public and congressional attitudes towards bilateral nuclear cooperation with the ROK."[148]

The State Department dispatched a team of proliferation and nuclear energy experts to Seoul in order to give ROK officials an "an early occasion to cancel" the French deal.[149] Led by Myron Kratzer, acting assistant secretary of state for Oceans, International Environment, and Scientific Affairs (OES), the team arrived in Seoul on 22 January. During the talks, Choe "affirmed that [the] ROKG had no intention whatsoever [to] develop nuclear weapons, since it could not afford such development and it relied completely on [the] US nuclear umbrella." However, South Korean and US officials disagreed over the linkage between the

---

[145] "US Embassy Seoul Telegram 9813 to Department of State, ROK Nuclear Reprocessing, 22 December 1975, Secret," in William Burr, ed., *NSA EBB no. 584* (Washington, DC: National Security Archives, 2017), https://nsarchive2.gwu.edu/dc.html?doc=3535278-Document-20-U-S-Embassy-Seoul-telegram-9813-to.

[146] "State Department Telegram 302043 to US Embassy Seoul, ROK Nuclear Reprocessing, 24 December 1975, Secret," in William Burr, ed., *NSA EBB no. 584* (Washington, DC: National Security Archives, 2017), https://nsarchive2.gwu.edu/dc.html?doc=3535280-Document-22-State-Department-telegram-302043-to.

[147] "US Embassy Seoul Telegram 9928 to Department of State, ROK Nuclear Reprocessing, 26 December 1975, Secret," in William Burr, ed., *NSA EBB no. 584* (Washington, DC: National Security Archives, 2017), https://nsarchive2.gwu.edu/dc.html?doc=3535281-Document-23-U-S-Embassy-Seoul-telegram-9928-to.

[148] "State Department Telegram 305630 to US Embassy Seoul, ROK Nuclear Reprocessing, 31 December 1975, Secret," in William Burr, ed., *NSA EBB no. 584* (Washington, DC: National Security Archives, 2017), https://nsarchive2.gwu.edu/dc.html?doc=3535283-Document-25-State-Department-telegram-305630-to.

[149] "State Department Telegram 008531 to US Embassy Seoul, ROK Nuclear Reprocessing, 13 January 1976, Secret," in William Burr, ed., *NSA EBB no. 584* (Washington, DC: National Security Archives, 2017), https://nsarchive2.gwu.edu/dc.html?doc=3535286-Document-28-State-Department-telegram-008531-to.

French reprocessing plant and future nuclear cooperation. While Choe avoided making any direct link between the two, Kratzer insisted the French plant cancellation was a prerequisite for civil nuclear cooperation.[150]

On the sidelines of the NATO foreign ministers' meeting in Brussels on 23 January, MacEachen informed Kissinger that the CANDU transfer would be contingent on the cancellation of the French reprocessing plant contract. MacEachen said, "We are working with the ROK to soften them up, but I don't know if we can deliver a knockout blow." Kissinger said he was confident that the Canadian action was indeed the "knockout blow," and that, as far as he was concerned, "there will be no reprocessing plant."[151]

On 25 January 1976, the Park government signed an agreement with Canada stating South Korea "is not pursuing acquisition of the reprocessing facility" and "the projected reprocessing facility has been shelved indefinitely ... at least until after the [ROK's] negotiations with the United States on further nuclear co-operation are resolved."[152] The following day, Park notified the French government of the cancellation of the Saint-Gobain contract.[153] The ROK government canceled the contract with Belgonucléaire for the purchase a plutonium reprocessing facility in November 1977.[154]

Park terminated Project 890 and assigned oversight of all nuclear programs to Oh Won-chul in December 1976. The nuclear fuel reprocessing program, which had been under KAERI, became the Chemical Fuel Replacement Plan under the auspices of the new Korea Nuclear Fuel Development Institute (KNFDI).[155] KNFDI had the dual mission of developing indigenous capabilities for nuclear fuel fabrication and obtaining plutonium by reprocessing the spent fuel from

---

[150] "US Embassy Seoul Telegram 0516 to Department of State, ROK Nuclear Reprocessing, 22 January 1976, Secret," in William Burr, ed., *NSA EBB no. 584* (Washington, DC: 2017), https://nsarchive2.gwu.edu/dc.html?doc=3535288-Document-30-U-S-Embassy-Seoul-telegram-0516-to.

[151] "Memorandum of Conversation, Middle East; ROK Nuclear Reactor, 24 January 1976, Secret," in William Burr, ed., *NSA EBB no. 584* (Washington, DC: National Security Archives, 2017), https://nsarchive2.gwu.edu/dc.html?doc=3535291-Document-33-Memorandum-of-conversation-Middle.

[152] "US Embassy Seoul Telegram 0552 to Department of State, ROK Nuclear Reprocessing; Canadian Reactor Sale, 25 January 1976, Secret," in William Burr, ed., *NSA EBB no. 584* (Washington, DC: National Security Archives, 2017), https://nsarchive2.gwu.edu/dc.html?doc=3535292-Document-34-U-S-Embassy-Seoul-telegram-0552-to.

[153] See Hong, "Search for Deterrence," p. 508; and Kim, "Security, Nationalism, and the Pursuit of Nuclear Weapons," p. 66. Also see "French A-Plant Purchase Cancelled," *Facts on File World News Digest*, 7 February 1976, Lexis-Nexis, web.lexis.nexis.com.

[154] Kim, "Security, Nationalism, and the Pursuit of Nuclear Weapons," p. 66; and Jungmin Kang and H. A. Feiveson, "South Korea's Shifting and Controversial Interest in Spent Fuel Reprocessing," *Nonproliferation Review*, Vol. 8, No. 1 (2001), p. 72.

[155] See Korea Atomic Energy Research Development Institute, "Brief History," https://www.kaeri.re.kr/english/sub/sub01_03.jsp (accessed 19 June 2018).

existing light uranium (LEU) reactors.[156] The technology and expertise developed could potentially be translated into military applications. Also, the long-range missile development team continued within the ADD. Therefore, Park left open the possibility of a nuclear weapon option at some point in the future.[157]

Neoclassical realist theory would expect the Ford administration to have pursued a hybrid strategy—a mixture of coercion and accommodation—to thwart the Park government's acquisition of nuclear reprocessing technology. Recall the theory would expect policymakers to pursue a hybrid nonproliferation strategy toward an ally under three circumstances: (1) when they perceive a favorable power distribution and short time horizons for emerging threats in the region, but also face high domestic hurdles; (2) when they perceive an unfavorable power distribution and long time horizons for emerging threats in the region, but also face high domestic mobilization hurdles; and (3) when they perceive a favorable power distribution and long time horizons for emerging threats in the region, but also face high domestic mobilization hurdles. The Ford administration found itself in the third circumstance in the 1974–1976 period.

Credible commitment theory would expect that Ford administration to have pursued accommodative strategies to forestall South Korea's reprocessing plant acquisition. Specifically, it would expect officials to pledge to maintain current US troop levels in South Korea indefinitely as a means of assuaging Park's fear. The pledges by Ford and Schlesinger are consistent with this hypothesis. The credible commitment hypothesis, however, does not account for the coercive aspect of the Ford administration's strategy, namely the threats to withhold the Export-Import Bank loan for the Kori-II reactor and to suspend civil nuclear cooperation.

Did the perceived likelihood of reactive proliferation lead the Ford administration to adopt a coercive strategy to forestall South Korea's acquisition of reprocessing facilities, as nuclear domino theory would expect? Although some memoranda and diplomatic cables from 1974 and 1975 speculated that South Korean nuclear activities might prompt reactive proliferation, there are few declassified intelligence estimates on North Korean proliferation from that period.[158] North Korea only became a serious proliferation concern for the

---

[156] See CIA National Foreign Assessment Center, "South Korea: Nuclear Development and Strategic Decisionmaking," p. 12; and Hong, "Search for Deterrence," p. 509.

[157] Hong, "Search for Deterrence," p. 509.

[158] North Korea's first nuclear reactor, which it purchased from the Soviet Union, began operations in 1967. Soviet intelligence became concerned that Kim Il-sung might seek to develop a nuclear weapon in the early 1970s. The Soviets pressured North Korea to join the International Atomic Energy Agency (IAEA) in 1975, but it did not sign the Nuclear Nonproliferation Treaty (NPT) until 1985. Kim likely authorized a nuclear weapons program at Yongbyon in the late 1970s. See Georgy Bulychev and Alexnander Vorontsov, "North Korea: An Experiment in Nuclear Proliferation,"

US Intelligence Community in 1986, a decade after Park terminated Project 890.[159]

Likewise, there is little evidence to suggest that the Ford administration saw increased likelihood of Japanese nuclear proliferation as a direct result of South Korean nuclear behavior. Japan had operational reprocessing plants by 1968 and the requisite number of centrifuges to produce enough highly enriched uranium (HEU) to fuel a nuclear weapon by 1970.[160] Some scholars argue that Prime Minister Satō Eisaku deliberately embarked upon a strategy of nuclear hedging—a strategy of maintaining, or appearing to maintain, an indigenous capacity to rapidly develop a nuclear weapon.[161] Other scholars contend that Japan did not, in fact, develop a latent nuclear weapon capability largely because of disagreements among various political actors.[162] There is little evidence that the Ford administration perceived an increased likelihood of Japanese proliferation and therefore pursued a coercive nonproliferation strategy toward South Korea.

Did congressional concern about nuclear proliferation in 1975 and 1976 push the Ford administration to adopt a coercive strategy to thwart South Korea's

---

in Alexei Arbatov, ed. *At the Nuclear Threshold: The Lessons of North Korea and Iran for the Nuclear Non-Proliferation Regime* (Moscow: Carnegie Moscow Center, 2007), p. 14; and Alexandre Y. Mansourov, "The Origins, Evolution, and Current Politics of the North Korean Nuclear Program," *The Nonproliferation Review*, Vol. 2, No. 3 (1995), pp. 25–38.

[159] See CIA Directorate of Intelligence, "North Korea: Potential for Nuclear Weapon Development," September 1986, declassification date unknown, publicly available at http://www.foia.cia.gov/sites/default/files/document_conversions/89801/DOC_0000835124.pdf.

[160] Matthew Fuhrmann and Benjamin Tkach, "Almost Nuclear: Introducing the Nuclear Latency Dataset," *Conflict Management and Peace Science*, Vol. 32, No. 4 (2015), pp. 443–461.

[161] See Ariel E. Levite, "Never Say Never Again: Nuclear Reversal Revisited," *International Security*, Vol. 27, No. 3 (2002), pp. 59–88, at p. 71. For various arguments that Japan has pursued a strategy of nuclear hedging (or nuclear latency) since Satō's tenure as prime minister (1964–1972), see Lanoszka, *Atomic Assurances*, pp. 83–93; Paul, *Power Versus Prudence*, pp. 37–61; Solingen, *Nuclear Logics*, pp. 57–81; Solingen, "The Perils of Prediction: Japan's Once and Future Nuclear Status," in William C. Potter and Gaukhar Mukhatzhanova, eds., *Forecasting Nuclear Proliferation in the 21st Century: A Comparative Perspective* (Stanford, CA: Stanford University Press, 2010), pp. 131–157; Kurt M. Campbell and Tsuyoshi Sunohara, "Japan: Thinking the Unthinkable," in Kurt M. Campbell, Robert J. Einhorn, and Mitchell Reiss, eds., *The Nuclear Tipping Point: Why States Reconsider Their Nuclear Choices* (Washington, DC: Brookings Institution Press, 2004), pp. 218–253; and Toshi Yoshihara and James Holmes, "Thinking About the Unthinkable: Tokyo's Nuclear Option," in Toshi Yoshihara and James R. Holmes, eds., *Strategy in the Second Nuclear Age: Power, Ambition, and the Ultimate Weapon* (Washington, DC: Georgetown University Press, 2012), pp. 99–113.

[162] See, for example, Llewelyn Hughes, "Why Japan Will Not Go Nuclear (Yet): International and Domestic Constraints on the Nuclearization of Japan," *International Security*, Vol. 31, No. 4 (2007), pp. 67–96; Jacques E. C. Hymans, "Veto Players, Nuclear Energy, and Nonproliferation: Domestic Institutional Barriers to a Japanese Bomb," *International Security*, Vol. 36, No. 2 (2011), pp. 154–189; and Akira Kurosaki, "Nuclear Energy and Nuclear-Weapon Potential: A Historical Analysis of Japan in the 1960s," *The Nonproliferation Review*, Vol. 24, No. 1–2 (2017), pp. 47–65.

acquisition of reprocessing technology, as credible sanctions theory would expect? The evidence is, at best, mixed. India's PNE in May 1974 unquestionably had a catalyzing effect on how Ford administration officials and members of Congress thought about the risks of nuclear proliferation and the necessity of tighter export controls on nuclear technology.[163]

Yet it is difficult to draw a causal link between nonproliferation legislation and the strategies the Ford administration pursued. First, there is the problem of timing. Congress passed the Symington Amendment in June 1976. Furthermore, the amendment did not go into effect until April 1977. Second, although US officials occasionally warned about congressional proliferation concerns, they never threatened to suspend foreign military or economic assistance to South Korea. They did, however, threaten to suspend civil nuclear cooperation, including the Export-Import Bank loan for the Kori-II reactor, and warned of unspecified negative repercussions for the bilateral relationship.

By late January 1976, the Ford administration and the Park government reached a set of tacit agreements to resolve the proliferation dispute. However, Ford's defeat in the November 1976 presidential election by the Democratic nominee, former Georgia governor Jimmy Carter, threatened to unravel these agreements.

The Carter Chill, 1976–1979: Troop Withdrawals and US-ROK Alliance in Crisis

Three calculations appear to have prompted President Carter's bid to withdraw all US combat troops and tactical nuclear weapons from South Korea. The first was his desire to reduce US troop deployments in East Asia, and by doing so, prevent future involvement in another "Vietnam" quagmire. The second was his moral opposition to authoritarian governance and widespread human rights abuses, especially by allies of the United States.[164] The third was Carter's calculation about a favorable power distribution in East Asia and long time horizons for threats to US interests there.

---

[163] On this point, I agree with Miller, *Stopping the Bomb*, pp. 74–75. See National Security Decision Memorandum 225: Security and Other Aspects of the Growth and Dissemination of Nuclear Power Industries, 3 June 1974, National Security Council Institutional Files, Box H-208, RMNL, https://www.nixonlibrary.gov/virtuallibrary/documents/nsdm/nsdm_255.pdf.

[164] For an overview of Carter's human rights agenda and its implementation with respect to US allies in Central America, East Asia, Southeast Asia, and the Middle East, see Tony Smith, *America's Mission: The United States and the Worldwide Struggle for Democracy* (Princeton: Princeton University Press, 2012), pp. 239–265.

By the mid-1970s, South Korea had an increasingly prosperous economy. The ROK army appeared to have a numerical and firepower advantage over the KPA. Since the Soviet Union and China shared the United States' interest in preserving stability on the Korean peninsula, they would restrain North Korea.[165] Carter concluded he had leeway to withdraw US troops and tactical nuclear weapons, while simultaneously pressuring Park to curtail human rights abuses and increase defense spending.[166] What Carter did not appreciate were the complex linkages among the US troop presence in the South Korea; Park's willingness to forgo a nuclear weapons option entirely; the credibility of the US extended deterrence in East Asia; and the near-term prospects for normalizing US-China diplomatic relations.

There is little documentary evidence to suggest that Carter or his advisers intended the troop withdrawal as a strategy to coerce Park into closing ADD's long-range missile team or KNFDI's nuclear fuel fabrication program. Nevertheless, the episode was significant. South Korean interest in pursuing a nuclear weapons option did not end with Project 890 in December 1976.[167] The proposed withdrawal of the US Second Infantry Division and tactical nuclear weapons provided an incentive to keep the long-range missile and nuclear fuel fabrication programs operational should South Korea ever need to resume a drive to develop a nuclear weapon in the future.

Carter's withdrawal plan and his promise of compensatory military assistance to South Korea are consistent with the neoclassical realist hypothesis: When policymakers perceive a favorable power distribution and long time horizons for emerging threats in the region, but confront high domestic mobilization hurdles, they will likely pursue a hybrid strategy toward a nuclear-proliferating ally. The coercive element was the phased withdrawal of US ground forces over a period of four or five years. Carter hoped to use the US troop withdrawal as leverage to get Park to increase the ROK defense budget. The accommodative element was the promise of compensatory military assistance—in the form of no-cost equipment transfers—to make up for the near-term gap in the ROK army's capabilities.

---

[165] Larry A. Niksch, "U.S. Troop Withdrawal from South Korea: Past Shortcomings and Future Prospects," *Asian Survey*, Vol. 21, No. 3 (1981), pp. 325–341.

[166] Carter did make personal appeals to Park on both issues during their quarrelsome summit meeting in Seoul on 30 June 1979. See "Memoranda of Conversation, President Jimmy Carter, South Korean President Park Chung Hee, et al., 30 June 1979, Secret," in Robert A. Wampler, ed., *NSA EBB no. 595* (Washington, DC: National Security Archives, 2017), at https://nsarchive2.gwu.edu//dc.html?doc=3696535-Document-08-Memoranda-of-Conversation-President.

[167] See Paul Kerr, "IAEA: Seoul's Nuclear Sins in Past," *Arms Control Today*, Vol. 34 (December 2004), at https://www.armscontrol.org/print/1714 (accessed 29 June 2018).

Credible commitment theory would expect the Carter administration to have pursued an accommodative strategy of maintaining current US troop levels as a means to avoid South Korean backsliding on nuclear proliferation. Instead, the administration attempted to do the exact opposite. By proposing the phased withdrawal of the remaining 40,000 US ground troops, as well as tactical nuclear weapons, over a four-to-five-year period, Carter reignited Park's abandonment fears and gave the South Korean president an incentive to keep the long-range missile and nuclear fuel fabrication programs operational.[168]

The empirical evidence does not support the nuclear domino hypothesis. Carter and senior officials in his administration received no intelligence on the heightened likelihood of North Korean or Japanese proliferation in the 1977 to 1979 period. Likewise, credible sanctions theory is not applicable because the Carter administration never contemplated, let alone threatened, to invoke Symington Amendment sanctions on South Korea.

In March 1976, then presidential candidate Carter said in a *Washington Post* interview that, if elected, he would consider removing the 700 US tactical nuclear weapons from South Korea.[169] On 23 June, Carter announced, "I believe that it will be possible to withdraw our ground forces from South Korea on a phased basis over a time span to be determined after consultation with both South Korea and Japan."[170] While reaffirming support for South Korea, the July 1976 Democratic Party Platform stated, "We can redeploy, and gradually phase out, the US ground forces, and can withdraw the nuclear weapons now stationed in Korea without endangering that support."[171]

Two weeks before the November 1976 election, the *Washington Post* reported the Justice Department and the Federal Bureau of Investigation (FBI) had informed the White House about an extensive South Korean bribery scheme. Park Tung-sin and his associates, acting on the direct instructions from the Blue House, had dispensed between $500,000 and $1 million annually in cash, gifts, and illegal campaign donations to ninety members of Congress and their staff members over the previous several years.[172] Dubbed "Koreagate" because of the

---

[168] See Lanoszka, *Atomic Assurances*, pp. 126–127.

[169] Jules Witcover, "Jimmy Carter: The Candidate on the Issues: An Interview," *Washington Post*, 21 March 1976, p. 2.

[170] Quoted in Committee on Administration, US Congress, House of Representatives, *The Presidential Campaign, 1976* (Washington, DC: GPO, 1978), Vol. 1, Part 1, p. 278. Also quoted in Lyong Choi, "Human Rights, Popular Protest, and Jimmy Carter's Plan to Withdraw U.S. Troops from South Korea," *Diplomatic History*, Vol. 41, No. 5 (2017), p. 935.

[171] Democratic Party Platforms: "1976 Democratic Party Platform," 12 July 1976, in Gerhard Peters and John T. Woolley, eds., *The American Presidency Project*, UCSB, http://www.presidency.ucsb.edu/ws/?pid=29606 (accessed 13 June 2018).

[172] Maxine Cheshire and Scott Armstrong, "Seoul Gave Millions to U.S. Officials," *Washington Post*, 24 October 1976, pp. 1 and 10.

parallels with the Watergate scandal, this scandal led to two years of congressional investigations that cast a pall over the US-ROK alliance.[173]

On 26 January 1977, Carter directed the NSC to oversee a broad review of policies on Korean peninsula, including the phased withdrawal of all US ground forces and tactical nuclear weapons from South Korea.[174] An Interagency Group for East Asia, chaired by Richard C. Holbrooke, the assistant secretary of state for East Asian and Pacific Affairs, convened shortly thereafter. William H. Gleysteen, Holbrooke's deputy and later the US ambassador to Seoul (from July 1978), recalls that the White House told Secretary of State Cyrus Vance that the group should not consider the political and strategic consequences of a complete US troop withdrawal, but only the timetable for implementation.[175]

Carter wrote to Park on 15 February to reiterate his decision for a phrased troop withdrawal, as well as his criticisms of Park's authoritarianism and human rights record. But he also promised to send Congress a FY 1978 request for $275 million in FMS guaranteed loans for South Korea.[176] Park asked for a delay, citing North Korea's aggressive designs and the need to complete the FIP.[177] Kim Chong-yom told Sneider that Park's moves against the opposition were both legal under the 1972 ROK Constitution and similar to actions taken by the governments of Ethiopia, Uganda, and Chile. Kim added, "If the American people and Congress knew the real situation in Korea, they would have no misgivings."[178]

In March 1977, Carter wrote to Vance and Zbigniew Brzezinski, the national security adviser, that not only would US ground troops be withdrawn, but also that "US-Korean relations as determined by Congress and American people

---

[173] For a summary of the eighteen-month congressional investigations into Koreagate, see "Congress Ends 'Koreagate' Lobbying Probe," *CQ Almanac*, Vol. 34 (1978), pp. 803–812, at http://library.cqpress.com/ezproxy.library.tufts.edu/cqakmanac/cqal78-1237310 (accessed 3 July 2018).

[174] Presidential Review Memorandum/NSC 13, 26 January 1977, folder: "Presidential Review Memoranda (1135)," Box 105, Vertical File, Jimmy Carter Library (hereafter JCL), obtained by Alexander Lanoszka. PRM/NSC 13 is also available at https://www.jimmycarterlibrary.gov/assets/documents/memorandums/prm13.pdf.

[175] William H. Gleysteen, *Massive Entanglement, Marginal Influence: Carter and Korea in Crisis* (Washington, DC: Brookings Institution Press, 1999), p. 17. Gleysteen succeeded Sneider as US ambassador to Seoul on 24 July 1978 and served in that post until 10 June 1981.

[176] "Letter from Jimmy Carter to Park Chung Hee, 15 February 1977," *Carter Chill: US-ROK-DPRK Trilateral Relations* (Washington, DC: Woodrow Wilson International Center for Scholars, 2013), pp. 53–54. The outgoing Ford administration had prepared the FY 1978 request for $275 million in FMS credits.

[177] "Letter from Park Chung Hee to Jimmy Carter, 15 February 1977," Ibid., pp. 60–63.

[178] "Telegram from the American Embassy in Seoul to the Secretary of State, 'Reply to President Carter's Letter,' 26 February 1977," Ibid., pp. 64–68.

are at an all-time low ebb."[179] Yet from the outset, Carter's desire to withdraw the remaining 40,000 US combat troops ran into opposition. Privately, Sneider and General John Vessey Jr., the commander of US Forces in Korea (USFK) and of the United Nations Command in Korea (UNCK), privately expressed reservations about a complete troop withdrawal.[180]

The Interagency Group decided to "slow walk" the president's directive. Gleysteen recalls that Vance, Holbrooke, Secretary of Defense Harold Brown, Deputy Assistant Secretary of Defense Morton Abramowitz, and Michael Armacost, director for East Asia on the NSC Staff, resolved to persuade Carter to endorse an option "that would involve withdrawal of a largely symbolic number of combat forces along with a large number of noncombat forces, followed by a careful review of the situation in Korea, before any further withdrawal."[181]

At an NSC meeting on 14 April 1977, however, Carter overruled Vance and Brown and reaffirmed his intent to withdraw all US combat troops from South Korea over four to five years.[182] Presidential Decision 12 (PD-12) of 5 May 1977 laid out the timetable: one combat brigade (6,000 troops) would depart by December 1978; a second brigade and supporting units (approximately 9,000 troops) would depart by July 1980; and all remaining US ground troops would depart between 1981 and 1982. US air units would remain indefinitely. The final decision on the troop withdrawal sequence would be made in consultation with congressional leaders, as well as the South Korean and Japanese governments.[183]

Carter administration officials were aware that US troop withdrawals would exacerbate Park's abandonment fears.[184] Yet, in April 1977, Sneider wrote that Park and other ROK officials "appeared reconciled to ground troop withdrawal."[185]

---

[179] "Handwritten Note from Jimmy Carter for Zbigniew Brzezinski and Cyrus Vance, 5 March 1977," Ibid., p. 77

[180] See "Memorandum of Conversation with President Carter by General John W. Vessey, 18 February 1977 (Secret)," in Robert A. Wampler, ed., *NSA EBB no. 595* (Washington, DC: National Security Archives, 2017), https://nsarchive2.gwu.edu//dc.html?doc=3696528-Document-01-Memorandum-of-Conversation-with; and "Telegram from the American Embassy in Seoul to the Secretary of State, 'Reply to President Carter's Letter,' 26 February 1977," *Carter Chill: US-ROK-DPRK Trilateral Relations* (Washington, DC: Woodrow Wilson International Center for Scholars, 2013), pp. 64–68. A January 1977 *Washington Post* article did quote Vessey as saying the withdrawal of US troops from South Korea would heighten the risk of war. See John Saar, "US General: GI Pullout Would Heighten Korea War Risk," *Washington Post*, 9 January 1977, p. 20.

[181] Gleysteen, *Massive Entanglement.*, p. 24.

[182] Ibid.

[183] "Presidential Directive 12, US Policy in Korea, 5 May 1977," at https://www.jimmycarterlibrary.gov/assets/documents/directives/pd12.pdf.

[184] "Telegram 1062 from Embassy in Seoul to the Department of State, 7 February 1977," Jimmy Carter, RAC Project Number NLC-26-39-6-3-2, obtained by Alexander Lanoszka.

[185] "Telegram 2723 from Embassy in Seoul to the Department of State, 5 April 1977," Jimmy Carter, RAC Project Number NLC-16-11-1-18-2, obtained by Alexander Lanoszka.

He anticipated the ROK president would "press for satisfactory compensatory actions particularly on timing and availability of weapons." Sneider also noted, "To many, the ground force withdrawal connotes loss of US tripwire and with it [the] loss of US military support in event of [a] North Korean military attack."[186]

Some officials were also concerned the troop withdrawal might prompt Park to reactivate the nuclear weapons program. In winter and spring 1977, however, there was no intelligence to suggest the program had been reactivated. Hong writes that, since the "KNDFI research project closely paralleled the development of South Korea's civilian nuclear energy industry, the United States could not come up with convincing evidence of military intentions to in order to stop KNDFI's research activities."[187]

ROK officials made ambiguous statements about their nuclear intentions in 1977 and 1978. During his annual inspection of the MND in January 1977, Park announced that South Korea "will not go nuclear."[188] Foreign Minister Park Tong Jin told the National Assembly's Foreign Affairs Committee on 29 June: "We have signed the Non-Proliferation Treaty and thus our basic position is that we do not intend to develop nuclear weapons ourselves. But, if it is necessary for national security interests and people's safety, it is possible for Korea as a sovereign state to make its own judgment on the matter."[189] In a June 1977 telegram, Sneider reported, "In response to these suggestions of embracing Korea under US nuclear umbrella, I pointed out that in fact Korea, as any ally, would be covered by US nuclear umbrella and I was surprised that there was any misunderstanding on that point."[190] In August 1977, the CIA warned, "In an obvious attempt to head off complete nuclear withdrawal, the South Korean press has suggested that the Park government would be justified in developing its own nuclear weapons if the US nuclear shield were withdrawn."[191]

Meanwhile, the South Korean missile program continued. In September 1978, ADD successfully test-launched a surface-to-surface missile, the

---

[186] "Telegram from the Embassy in Seoul to the State Department, 19 April 1977," Jimmy Carter, RAC Project Number NLC-10-2-2-23-1, obtained by Alexander Lanoszka.

[187] Hong, "Search for Deterrence," p. 509.

[188] Young-sun Ha, "Nuclearization of Small States and World Order: The Case of Korea," *Asian Survey*, Vol. 18, No. 11 (1978), p. 1142.

[189] "Minister: ROK Could Develop Nuclear Weapons If Necessary," *Seoul Hanguk Ilbo*, FBIS-APA-77-126, *Daily Report: Asia & Pacific*, 30 June 1977, p. E5; and "Minister on Nuclear Weapons, Mutual Defense Treaty," *Seoul Haptong*, FBIS-APA-77-126, *Daily Report: Asia & Pacific*, 30 June 1977, pp. E1, E2, at infoweb.newsbank.com.

[190] "Telegram from Embassy in Seoul to the Department of State, 13 June 1977," Jimmy Carter, RAC Project Number NLC-16-11-2-17-2, obtained by Alexander Lanoszka.

[191] Regional and Political Analysis Memo, *The Implications of Withdrawing Nuclear Weapons from Korea*, Central Intelligence Agency, 11 August 1977, RPM 77-10210, http://nautilus.org/wp-content/uploads/2011/09/CIA_Withdrawing_ROK_NWs.pdf (accessed 15 July 2018).

Paekkom (White Bear). A 1976 agreement restricted South Korean missiles to a range of 180 kilometers, while the multilateral Missile Technology Control Regime (MTCR) imposed range limits of 300 kilometers for military purposes and up to 500 kilometers for research purchases.[192] Park encouraged ADD scientists and engineers to have a long-term objective of developing ballistic missiles with a range of 2,000 kilometers, as well as rockets to launch intelligence satellites.[193]

"Park should be told that any move to produce nuclear weapons would terminate our security relationship," Carter stated on 21 May 1977.[194] His remark was ironic: after all, Nixon's withdrawal of the US Seventh Infantry Division was one of the catalysts for Park to authorize Project 890. There is, however, no evidence in the declassified documents to suggest Carter or senior officials in his administration communicated an unambiguous threat to terminate the US-ROK Mutual Defense Treaty.

"The US 2nd Division . . . has more of an anti-tank capability than the entire ROK army," according to a CIA report from April–May 1977. The report also suggested that South Korean anxieties about US troop withdrawals might lead to a renewal of Park's nuclear weapons and long-range missile programs.[195] Another CIA report concluded that "[T]he Korean nuclear research community believe that, even while bowing to US preferences on the line of work they pursue, certain activities can and should be undertaken to keep Seoul's nuclear option open."[196]

Deputy Secretary of State Warren Christopher wrote to Carter on 19 May to recommend a military assistance "compensation" package of between $500 and $600 million, in addition to the $275 million in FMS credit offered in February 1977. He also recommended accepting a proposal from Park and his defense minister, Suh Jyong-chul, for a combined US-ROK command to replace the UNCK, but with the proviso that a US military officer retain operational control of the ROK armed forces.[197]

---

[192] Hong, "Search for Deterrence," p. 570.

[193] Kim, "Security, Nationalism, and the Pursuit of Nuclear Weapons."

[194] "Memorandum of Conversation (p. 3), 21 May 1977," 5/16-23/77, National Security Affairs, Staff Material: Far East, JCL, obtained by Charles Kraus.

[195] "CIA and National Intelligence Reports on Ground Troop Withdrawals, April–May 1977," *Carter Chill: US-ROK-DPRK Trilateral Relations* (Washington, DC: Woodrow Wilson International Center for Scholars, 2013), pp. 105–116.

[196] CIA National Foreign Assessment Center, "South Korea: Nuclear Development and Strategic Decisionmaking," p. 2.

[197] Memorandum for Jimmy Carter from Warren Christopher, "US Policy in Korea: Withdrawal of Ground Combat Forces, 19 May 1977," *Carter Chill: US-ROK-DPRK Trilateral Relations* (Washington, DC: Woodrow Wilson International Center for Scholars, 2013), pp. 122–130.

Philip C. Habib, the undersecretary of state for political affairs, and General George S. Brown, the chairman of the JCS, arrived in Seoul on 24 May to "consult" with Park and other senior ROK officials about the withdrawal timetable. Park expressed "resigned acceptance" that the troop withdrawal was "publicly announced without consultation with the ROKG."[198] Habib explained that Carter's decision came after an extensive review of the situation on the Korean peninsula, as well as the overall regional context and Park's own efforts to establish military self-reliance. He also said the decision reflected "an assessment of the American domestic political situation."[199]

In late May 1977, Prime Minister Fukuda Takeo of Japan told Habib and Brown that while his government would prefer maintaining current US troop levels in South Korea, he accepted Carter's decision. Fukuda stressed the importance of reassuring friendly East Asian countries of the continued US security commitment to the region.[200] In a report to Brzezinski about his East Asia trip in June 1977, Armacost wrote that "[S]ince no concessions are being sought from [North Korea], most Asians conclude that diplomatic considerations got short shrift."[201]

"The Chinese leaders do not desire further US pullbacks from bases in the Far East," the CIA reported in March 1977.[202] A June 1977 CIA assessment concluded, in part, "The Chinese tacitly have supported a US military presence in South Korea not only as a deterrent to rash action by Kim Il-song, but as one element of the strategic counterweight to the threat of Soviet military encirclement of China."[203] A month later, a Chinese vice foreign minister told

---

[198] Telegram from the American Embassy in Seoul to the Secretary of State, "US Ground Force Withdrawal: Consultations with President Park, 25 May 1977," *The Carter Chill: US-ROK-DPRK Trilateral Relations, 1976–1979* (Washington, DC: Woodrow Wilson International Center for Scholars, 2013), pp. 137–144

[199] Telegram from the American Embassy in Seoul to the Secretary of State, "US Ground Force Withdrawal Second Meeting with President Park, 26 May 1977," *The Carter Chill: US-ROK-DPRK Trilateral Relations, 1976–1979* (Washington, DC: Woodrow Wilson International Center for Scholars, 2013), pp. 145–148.

[200] Memorandum for Jimmy Carter from David Aaron, "Brown/Habib Report on Korea," *The Carter Chill: US-ROK-DPRK Trilateral Relations, 1976–1979* (Washington, DC: Woodrow Wilson International Center for Scholars, 2013), pp. 152–154.

[201] "Memorandum from Zbigniew Brzezinski to Jimmy Carter (p. 3), 10 June 1977," Jimmy Carter, RAC Project Number NLC-15-125-8-1, obtained by Alexander Lanoszka.

[202] "14. Intelligence Memorandum Prepared in the Central Intelligence Agency, RP 77-10038, The Value of the United States to China's National Security, March 1978," *FRUS, 1977–1980, Vol. XIII: China* (Washington, DC: GPO, 2013) pp. 45–48.

[203] Central Intelligence Agency, "US Ground Force Withdrawal: Korean Stability and Foreign Relations, 7 June 1977," *The Carter Chill: US-ROK-DPRK Trilateral Relations, 1976–1979* (Washington, DC: Woodrow Wilson International Center for Scholars, 2013), pp. 159–166

Australian government officials that "There will be war" if all US troops left South Korea.[204]

Vance traveled to Beijing in late August 1977 to consult Chinese leaders on the normalization of diplomatic relations. Foreign Minister Hua Huang repeated the standard demand for the immediate withdrawal of US ground forces from South Korea on 22 August.[205] The following day, Vance met with Deng, who hinted that he would prefer US ground troops not withdraw, since those forces deter North Korean adventurism. "I have on numerous occasions tried to advise our American friends that they should think earnestly when dealing with issues like this in which whole countries are split in two," Deng said, noting that the divided Korean peninsula is analogous to the divisions of Germany and Vietnam, as well as between China and Taiwan. Nationalist sentiment will eventually lead to Korean reunification, just as it led to Vietnamese reunification.[206]

A July 1977 State-DoD analysis of ROK force requirements recommended $800 million in transfers of US military equipment, on top of the $275 million in FMS credits. "We believe such a security assistance package is militarily essential, of significant economic help to the ROK," Vance and Defense Secretary Brown wrote to Carter, adding that the package would be "big enough to assuage but not satisfy Korean security concerns, and modest enough to make it past congressional critics."[207]

By this point, however, Carter's proposal faced strong bipartisan opposition in Congress. The Senate Foreign Relations Committee called Habib and General Brown to testify on 10 June. After Habib's opening statement, Senator Clifford Case (R-NJ) read notes from a CIA briefing that offered a pessimistic assessment of the Korean military balance and called into question the wisdom of withdrawing all US ground forces.[208] Even Senator Hubert Humphrey (D-MN),

---

[204] "Memorandum, 20 July 1977," Jimmy Carter, RAC Project Number NLC-1-3-2-42-9, obtained by Alexander Lanoszka.

[205] "Memorandum of Conversation with US Secretary of State and PRC Foreign Minster et al., 22 August 1977," *The Carter Chill: US-ROK-DPRK Trilateral Relations, 1976–1979* (Washington, DC: Woodrow Wilson International Center for Scholars, 2013), pp. 232–233.

[206] Memorandum of Conversation Between the US Secretary of State and the PRC Vice Premier et al., 24 August 1977, *The Carter Chill: US-ROK-DPRK Trilateral Relations, 1976–1979* (Washington, DC: Woodrow Wilson International Center for Scholars, 2013), pp. 236–237, also published in *FRUS, 1977–1980, Vol. XIII: China*, pp. 191–207.

[207] Memorandum for Jimmy Carter from Cyrus Vance and Harold Brown, "New Security Assistance Program for South Korea, 13 July 1977," *The Carter Chill: US-ROK-DPRK Trilateral Relations, 1976–1979* (Washington, DC: Woodrow Wilson International Center for Scholars, 2013), pp. 176–187.

[208] The CIA briefing for senators apparently drew upon the findings in Central Intelligence Agency, "US Ground Force Withdrawal: Korean Stability and Foreign Relations, 7 June 1977," *The Carter Chill: US-ROK-DPRK Trilateral Relations, 1976–1979* (Washington, DC: Woodrow Wilson International Center for Scholars, 2013), pp. 159–166.

who supported Carter's withdrawal decision, said the matter was serious and required careful consideration by the committee. The senators wanted to hear DCI Stansfield Turner's assessment of the Korean military balance and the overall security situation in East Asia.[209]

On 16 June, the Senate passed an amendment to the foreign affairs appropriation bill sponsored by the majority leader, Senator Robert C. Byrd (D-WV), requiring the president to consult Congress before withdrawing troops from South Korea.[210] On 29 June, Armacost wrote to Brzezinski about his "astonishment" that the DoD turned over a cache of sensitive JCS messages, including secret and top secret messages to Vessey concerning the troop withdrawal schedule and ROK military assistance requirements, to the House Armed Services Committee, chaired by Representative Samuel Stratton (D-NY).[211] The Senate and House minority leaders, Howard Baker (R-TN) and John Rhodes (R-AZ), writing on behalf of their respective caucuses, wrote an open letter to Carter on 18 July requesting he appoint a special prosecutor to investigate KCIA involvement in US domestic politics.[212]

When Defense Secretary Brown briefed the House and Senate Armed Services and Foreign/International Relations Committees on 20 July 1977 about the Korea troop withdrawals and the administration's request for an $800 million "compensatory" package, he encountered strong resistance. Representatives Stratton and Edward Derwinski (R-Il) and Senators John Tower (R-TX) and John Glenn (D-OH) all expressed concerns about the United States' reputation as a superpower, while Senators Humphrey and Chase complained the troop withdrawals were not conditional on reciprocal North Korean moves. Citing Koreagate and concerns about Park's crackdown on dissent, Senator Charles Percy (R-IL) and Representative George Mahon (D-TX) chastised the administration for seeking a $800 million compensatory package. As Brzezinski told

---

[209] "Memorandum for Jimmy Carter from Zbigniew Brzezinski, 'Korean Troop Withdrawals: Brown/Habib Testimony,' 10 June 1977," *The Carter Chill: US-ROK-DPRK Trilateral Relations, 1976–1979* (Washington, DC: Woodrow Wilson International Center for Scholars, 2013), pp. 167–168.

[210] Graham Hovey, "Senate Bars Support for a Korea Pullout," *New York Times*, 17 June 1977, p. A9.

[211] "Memorandum for Zbigniew Brzezinski from Mike Armacost, 'DoD Transmission to Congress of JCS Recommendations Concerning Troop Withdrawals,' 29 June 1977," *The Carter Chill: US-ROK-DPRK Trilateral Relations, 1976–1979* (Washington, DC: Woodrow Wilson International Center for Scholars, 2013), pp. 169–170.

[212] "Letter to Howard Baker from Jimmy Carter, Release via the Office of the White House Press Secretary, 18 July 1977," *The Carter Chill: US-ROK-DPRK Trilateral Relations, 1976–1979* (Washington, DC: Woodrow Wilson International Center for Scholars, 2013), pp. 188–189.

Carter, "Not one senator or congressman spoke up in support of the troop withdrawal.... It is clear that we face an uphill battle ... with Congress."[213]

Carter wrote to Park on 17 January 1978 to reiterate his pledge to secure congressional approval for compensatory measures as the first phase of US troop withdrawal approached.[214] That same month, Senators Humphrey and Glenn issued a report to the Senate Foreign Relations Committee warning that the decision to withdraw all US combat troops "reduce[ed] the deterrent effect" on North Korea, whose ground forces were deployed in an offensive posture near the DMZ. The report also warned, "each phrase of the US troop withdrawal should be approached more cautiously" and recommended legislation requiring submission of a "detailed presidential report prior to each withdrawal phase."[215]

Holbrooke, Abramowitz, Armacost, and Michael Oksenberg, another NSC staffer, sent a memorandum to Vance, Brown, and Brzezinski on 4 April reminding them that the president needed to make decisions on a set of interrelated issues including: garnering congressional support for the troop reductions and the compensatory assistance package for South Korea; the normalization of US-China diplomatic relations; and weapons sales to Taiwan. Noting that the president had made the troop withdrawal contingent upon congressional approval of generous military assistance and that a congressional defeat would expose "the hollowness of our pledges," Holbrooke et al. recommended modifying the withdrawal timetable.[216]

On 21 April 1978, Carter announced that the non-combat elements of the Second Infantry Division (approximately 2,600 personnel) would withdraw by December 1978, but that two combat brigades would remain through the end of 1979. He would ask Congress to approve $275 million in FMS credits

---

[213] "Memorandum for Jimmy Carter from Zbigniew Brzezinski, 'Congressional Reaction to Our Korea Policy,' 21 July 1977," *The Carter Chill: US-ROK-DPRK Trilateral Relations, 1976–1979* (Washington, DC: Woodrow Wilson International Center for Scholars, 2013), pp. 193–194.

[214] "Letter to Park Chung Hee from Jimmy Carter, 17 January 1978," *The Carter Chill: US-ROK-DPRK Trilateral Relations, 1976–1979* (Washington, DC: Woodrow Wilson International Center for Scholars, 2013), pp. 266–267.

[215] Senators H. Humphrey and J. Glenn, *US Troop Withdrawal from the Republic of Korea: A Report to the Committee on Foreign Relations, US Senate*, 9 January 1978 (Washington, DC: GPO), pp. 1–5.

[216] "92. Memorandum from the Assistant Secretary of State for East Asian and Pacific Affairs (Holbrooke), the Deputy Assistant Secretary of Defense for East Asian and Pacific Affairs (Abramowitz), and Michael Armacost and Michel Oksenberg of the National Security Council Staff to Secretary of State Vance, Secretary of Defense Brown, and the President's Assistant for National Security Affairs (Brzezinski), 4 April 1978," *FRUS, 1977–1980, Vol. XIII: China* (Washington, DC: GPO, 2013), pp. 324–337.

for South Korea in FY 1979 and to "move expeditiously to deal with the $800 million equipment transfer legislation."[217]

In May 1978, the CIA produced a revised estimate of the conventional military balance on the Korean peninsula. Over the previous eight years, North Korea had undertaken a major military buildup, facilitated by large Soviet and Chinese arms transfers, the expansion of its domestic arms industry, and a sustained effort to expand and modernize the KPA. The KPA enjoyed a two-to-one advantage over the ROK army in tanks, armed personnel carriers (APCs), and artillery, which greatly reduced the latter's manpower advantage. CIA analysts expected ROK military capabilities to improve over time, especially if the ROKG increased defense expenditures to 6 or 7 percent of gross domestic product (GDP). But for the next few years, the conventional military balance would favor North Korea.[218]

Carter wrote to Park on 17 May to reaffirm his promise of compensatory measures to improve the ground capabilities of the ROK army and to offset US troop withdrawals.[219] On 20 July, he wrote to the speaker of the House of Representatives, Thomas P. O'Neill (D-MA), to request congressional approval of equipment transfers and arms sales to South Korea. He assured O'Neill that the withdrawal of the Second Infantry Division would not follow a rigid schedule but would instead take into account prevailing circumstances.[220]

In early January 1979, however, a recent CIA and Defense Intelligence Agency (DIA) assessment of the KPA order of battle leaked to *The Army Times*.[221] Stratton and Robin Beard (R-TN), the ranking minority member of the House Armed Services Committee, urged the president to defer any US troop withdrawals.[222] On 22 January, Carter ordered that the phrased withdrawal of

---

[217] "Memorandum for Zbigniew Brzezinski from Mike Armacost, 'Korean Troop Withdrawals' 19 April 1978," *The Carter Chill: US-ROK-DPRK Trilateral Relations, 1976–1979* (Washington, DC: Woodrow Wilson International Center for Scholars, 2013), pp. 306–309; and "Statement of the President, 21 April 1978," Ibid., p. 310.

[218] "Intelligence Memo, 'Military Balance on the Korean Peninsula,' 10 May 1978," *The Carter Chill: US-ROK-DPRK Trilateral Relations, 1976–1979* (Washington, DC: Woodrow Wilson International Center for Scholars, 2013), pp. 315–318.

[219] "Letter from Jimmy Carter to Park Chung Hee, 17 May 1978," *The Carter Chill: US-ROK-DPRK Trilateral Relations, 1976–1979* (Washington, DC: Woodrow Wilson International Center for Scholars, 2013), pp. 330–331.

[220] "Letter to Speaker Tip O'Neill from Jimmy Carter, 20 July 1978," *The Carter Chill: US-ROK-DPRK Trilateral Relations, 1976–1979* (Washington, DC: Woodrow Wilson International Center for Scholars, 2013), pp. 385–386.

[221] Don Oberdorfer, "Estimate of North Korean Army Raised; Estimate of North Korean Ground Forces Increased," *Washington Post*, 4 January 1979, p. A1; and Don Oberdorfer, "North Korea's Army Now Ranked Fifth-Largest in World by US," *Washington Post*, 14 January 1979, p. A9.

[222] "Memorandum for Zbigniew Brzezinski, Through Madeleine Albright, from Nick Platt, 'Troop Withdrawals from the ROK—Congressman Stratton and Beard Letter,' 9 January 1979," The

the Second Infantry Division be held "in abeyance" pending the administration's review of revised estimates of North Korean military strength.[223]

Carter and Park had a tense summit meeting in Seoul on 30 June 1979. At one point, Park asked Carter to freeze US troop levels until "the disparity between North Korea and South Korea is changed and until North Korea changes its policy." Carter declined to make such a promise. Instead, Carter pressed Park to increase ROK defense spending to at least 6 percent of GDP in FY 1980, rescind Emergency Measure 9, release political prisoners, and to support his bid to broker trilateral peace talks on the Korean peninsula. Park reluctantly agreed to Carter's terms.[224]

On 20 July 1979, Brzezinski read a statement in the White House briefing room declaring that President Carter ordered the withdrawal of one I-Hawk air battalion (roughly 800 troops) from South Korea by the end of 1979. The withdrawal of combat elements of the Second Infantry Division would remain in abeyance until 1981, pending further review. He cited revised intelligence estimates of North Korean military strength, the recent agreement Carter and Park reached to work together to reduce tensions on the Korean peninsula, and the recent normalization of US-China diplomatic relations as having contributed to the president's decision.[225]

The assassination of Park Chung-hee by KCIA director Kim Jae-kyu on 26 October 1979 plunged South Korea deeper into political turmoil. Park's death ended direct Blue House support for preserving a nuclear weapons option, but it did not end the activities of the missile development team at ADD or the nuclear fuel fabrication project at KNDFI. Nor did Park's death end the decade-long crisis in the alliance.

Major General Chun Doo-hawn, the commander of the ROK Defense Security Command, charged with overseeing the investigation of a KCIA conspiracy against Park Chung-hee, seized power in a coup on 12 December 1979.[226]

Carter Chill: US-ROK-DPRK Trilateral Relations: 1976–1979—A Critical Oral History Conference (Washington, DC: Woodrow Wilson International Center for Scholars, 2013), pp. 431–434.

[223] "PRM-45, US Policy Toward Korea, 22 January 1979," https://www.jimmycarterlibrary.gov/assets/documents/memorandums/prm45.pdf (accessed 1 July 2018).

[224] "Memoranda of Conversation, President Jimmy Carter, South Korean President Park Chung Hee, et al., 30 June 1979, Secret," in Robert A. Wampler, ed., *NSA EBB no. 595* (Washington, DC: National Security Archives, 2017), https://nsarchive2.gwu.edu//dc.html?doc=3696536-Document-09-Memoranda-of-Conversation-President.

[225] See "Memorandum for Zbigniew Brzezinski from Nick Platt, 'Announcement of Korean Troop Withdrawal Policy (C),' 19 July 1979," in *The Carter Chill: US-ROK-DPRK Trilateral Relations: 1976–1979* (Washington, DC: Woodrow Wilson International Center for Scholars, 2013), pp. 653–655.

[226] "Cable, Seoul 18811, Amembassy Seoul to Secretary of State, Subject: Younger ROK Officers Grab Power Positions, 13 December 1979, Secret," in Robert A. Wampler, ed., *NSA EBB no. 595* (Washington, DC: National Security Archives, 2017), https://nsarchive2.gwu.edu//

Acting President Choi Kyu-hah remained in office, but he was essentially powerless. In August 1980, Chun engineered his election to the presidency by the National Conference on Unification, the electoral college established by Park's *Yushin* Constitution.[227] Throughout 1980, the Carter administration expressed grave concerns about the new Chun government's human rights record, especially its brutal suppression of the Gwangju student protests of 18–27 May, as well as the arrest, conviction, and death sentence of opposition leader Kim Daejung for allegedly fomenting that uprising.[228]

Epilogue: The Reagan administration and "Resetting" the US-ROK alliance, 1981

In the closing months of 1980, the United States confronted unfavorable power distributions and short time horizons for threats to its interests across multiple regions, including the Middle East, South Asia, and East Asia. Updated intelligence estimates in 1978 and 1979 suggested that North Korea had not only built up its conventional military capabilities over the past several years, but that the military balance on the Korean peninsula would tilt in Pyongyang's favor for the next several years.

As part its efforts to contain the growth of Soviet Union's influence in those regions, the incoming Reagan administration sought to strengthen US security commitments to treaty and non-treaty allies. Shortly after taking office in January 1981, President Ronald Reagan invited South Korean president Chun Doo-hwan to make an official visit to the White House.

As Richard V. Allen, the national security adviser, wrote to Reagan, "Whereas President Carter's first message to Asia was his intention to reduce troop strength in Korea, your first signal to the region is that you are cognizant of the

---

dc.html?doc=3696540-Document-13-Cable-Seoul-18811-Amembassy-Seoul-to. For a discussion of the factionalism within the ROK army and Park's use of competing security services to maintain himself in power, see Joo-Hong Kim, "The Armed Forces," in Byung-Kook Kim and Ezra F. Vogel, eds., *The Park Chung Hee Era: The Modernization of South Korea* (Cambridge, MA: Harvard University Press, 2011), pp. 168–199.

[227] For an account of 12 December 1979 coup and the Carter administration's policy responses, see Gleysteen, *Massive Entanglement, Marginal Influence*, pp. 77–98.

[228] "Memorandum of Conversation, National Security Advisor Zbigniew Brzezinski, Blue House Secretary General Kim Kyong Won, et al., 18 November 1980 [with Cover Memorandum], Confidential," in Robert A. Wampler, ed., *NSA EBB no. 595* (Washington, DC: National Security Archives, 2017), https://nsarchive2.gwu.edu//dc.html?doc=3696543-Document-16-Memorandum-of-Conversation-National.

vital interests of the Free World in Asia."[229] Secretary of State Alexander M. Haig expected Chun would seek Reagan's reaffirmation of the United States' security commitment, a pledge not to resume the withdrawal of US ground forces, and expanded FMS credits for ROK force modernization. Haig wrote to Reagan, "We should also utilize Chun's visit at the early phase of his leadership to brief him on our nuclear deployments and review our non-proliferation concerns."[230]

Reagan and Chun, accompanied by their respective national security teams and translators, met in the White House Cabinet Room on 2 February 1981. Reagan said he "wanted to make it plain" that his administration would not withdraw US ground troops from South Korea. Chun responded, "I take your words as a gift, and they will allow me to return home with an easy mind." Reagan said he was aware of the economic burden South Korea carried in order to continue its high level of defense spending. He promised his administration would expedite the transfer of technology and weapons systems to South Korea and work with Congress to increase the FMS credit available. Finally, Reagan said that if Chun wanted to purchase the F-16, his administration would proceed with the necessary notifications to the Congress.[231]

Following the plenary meeting, Haig assured Chun and Foreign Minister Shin Yong-lho that "Korea could rely on the United States as a source of [the] nuclear fuel supplies and technology for Korea's nuclear power program" and that he appreciated "Korea's adherence to a non-proliferation policy."[232] During a 5 February meeting with Shin to finalize the communiqué, Haig stated: "For our part, we would maintain and improve our military forces in Korea, we would retain our nuclear weapons, although—as he had explained to President

---

[229] "Memorandum, Richard Allen to President Reagan, 29 January 1981, Subject: President Chun of Korea, with Attached Cover Memorandum, Donald Gregg to Allen, Same Date," in Robert Wampler, ed., *NSA EBB no. 306* (Washington, DC: National Security Archive, 2010), https://nsarchive2.gwu.edu/NSAEBB/NSAEBB306/doc01.pdf.

[230] "Talking Paper for the Conduct of the Summit Meeting, Ca January 1981," in Robert Wampler, ed., *NSA EBB no. 306* (Washington, DC: National Security Archive, 2010), https://nsarchive2.gwu.edu/NSAEBB/NSAEBB306/doc03.pdf.

[231] "Memorandum of Conversation, Subject: Summary of the President's Meeting with President Chun Doo Hwan of the Republic of Korea, 2 February 1981, 11:20–12:05 P.M., Cabinet Room, with Cover Memorandum, Richard V. Allen to President Reagan, 6 February 1981, Subject: Your Meeting with President Chun of Korea," in Robert Wampler, ed., NSA EBB no. 306 (Washington, DC: National Security Archive, 2010), https://nsarchive2.gwu.edu/NSAEBB/NSAEBB306/doc05.pdf.

[232] "Cable, SECSTATE to Amembassy Seoul, 6 February 1981, Subject: ROK President Chun's Meeting with the Secretary at the State Department," in Robert Wampler, ed., *NSA EBB no. 306* (Washington, DC: National Security Archive, 2010), https://nsarchive2.gwu.edu/NSAEBB/NSAEBB306/doc06a.pdf.

Chun—it was important for the ROK to continue cooperation with our nonproliferation policy."[233]

Over the next year, Chun ordered a major reorganization of the ADD, resulting in the dismissal of 800 employees and the downsizing of the long-range missile development team. The Chun government also abandoned Park's weapons procurement policies, which prioritized building ROK defense industries, choosing instead to purchase high-tech weapons platforms from the United States.[234] The South Korean nuclear power industry's violations of various IAEA safeguards and reporting requirements continued well into the 1980s and 1990s.[235] Nonetheless, the Reagan-Chun summit of February 1981 was significant because it was the first step in repairing the alliance after more than a decade of continual crises.

The Reagan administration's accommodative strategy toward South Korea in winter 1981 is consistent with the neoclassical realist theory hypothesis: When US policymakers perceive an unfavorable regional power distribution and short time horizons for emerging threats to the United States interests in the region, but they only have to overcome low domestic mobilization hurdles, they will pursue an accommodative strategy toward a nuclear-aspiring ally. Reagan and his national security team offered Chun a stronger US military commitment to South Korea—no further withdrawal of US ground troops, no changes in tactical nuclear weapons deployment, the F-16 transfers, and additional FMS credits—and international legitimacy for his regime, in exchange for his nonproliferation pledges.

Unlike its predecessor, the Reagan administration confronted low domestic mobilization hurdles in pursuing its preferred strategies toward South Korea. In the November 1980 elections, the Republicans won a majority in the Senate, although the Democrats retained a sizable majority in the House of Representatives. Furthermore, in the wake of the Soviet invasion of Afghanistan in December 1979, few senators or congressmen would oppose conventional arms transfers and large military assistance packages to vulnerable frontline allies, such as South Korea, even if such allies had authoritarian regimes.

---

[233] "Cable, SECSTATE to Amembassy Seoul, 5 February 1981, Subject: Korea President Chun's Visit—the Secretary's Meeting at Blair House," in Robert Wampler, ed., *NSA EBB no. 306* (Washington, DC: National Security Archive, 2010), https://nsarchive2.gwu.edu/NSAEBB/NSAEBB306/doc04.pdf.

[234] Hong, "Search for Deterrence," p. 510; Kim, "Security, Nationalism, and the Pursuit of Nuclear Weapons," p. 69.

[235] See Paul Kerr, "IAEA: Seoul's Nuclear Sins in Past," *Arms Control Today*, Vol. 34 (December 2004); and Jungmin Kang and H. A. Feiveson, "South Korea's Shifting and Controversial Interest in Spent Fuel Reprocessing," *Nonproliferation Review*, Vol. 8, No. 1 (2001), pp. 70–78.

This chapter juxtaposed hypotheses from neoclassical realist theory against hypotheses from all three alternative theories—nuclear domino theory, security commitment theory, and credible sanctions theory—to explain variation in the types of strategies the United States pursued toward South Korea between 1970 and 1981, with an emphasis on the "critical phase" of the proliferation dispute between March 1974 and January 1976.

Unlike the proliferation disputes with Israel in the 1960s and Pakistan in the late 1970s and 1980s, the risk of containment failure in East Asia remained relatively low for much of the 1970s. Instead of preventing an expansion of Soviet military, economic, and political influence in the region, the overriding objective of the Nixon, Ford, Carter, and Reagan administrations in East Asia was to enlist China as an ally of convenience against the Soviet Union. South Korea's acquisition of reprocessing technology in 1974–1976 put that objective at risk. The risk of containment failure in East Asia only appeared to increase in 1978, when revised intelligence estimates revealed that North Korea, the one Soviet ally in the region, enjoyed a substantial conventional force advantage over South Korea.

Overall, neoclassical realist theory explains the variation in the strategies undertaken by the Nixon, Ford, Carter, and Reagan administrations toward South Korea between 1970 and 1981. The Ford administration's assurances to Park regarding US troop deployments in 1974–1976 were also consistent with security commitment theory. Yet Carter's plan to withdraw the remaining 40,000 US combat troops and tactical nuclear weapons from South Korea, despite residual concerns about Park's nuclear intentions, is an anomaly for security commitment theory.

Nuclear domino theory and credible sanctions theory, however, fared even less well in explaining the Ford administration's strategies to thwart South Korea's acquisition of the French reprocessing plant in 1974–1976. Officials received no intelligence that South Korean nuclear activities increased the likelihood of reactive proliferation by either North Korea or Japan. Although congressional interest in worldwide nonproliferation increased after India's May 1974 PNE, there is no evidence to suggest that pending nonproliferation legislation prompted the Ford administration to adopt a coercive strategy to thwart South Korea's reprocessing plant acquisition.

6

The United States and Taiwan's Nuclear Weapons Program, 1967–1978

Like the proliferation dispute between the United States and South Korea, the proliferation dispute between the United States and the Republic of China on Taiwan (ROC or Taiwan) was the consequence of the Nixon administration's pursuit of three objectives in the early 1970s. The first was to extricate US forces from the Vietnam War. The second was to reduce the US troop presence in East Asia and Southeast Asia. The third was to seek a rapprochement with the People's Republic of China (PRC or China) in the hopes of enlisting it as an ally of convenience against the Soviet Union.

The pursuit of those three objectives had major implications for the military security and the political status of Taiwan. Like Israel, Pakistan, and South Korea, Taiwan faced an existential threat from a more powerful neighbor. Even more than South Korea, Taiwan's nuclear proliferation had major implications for China, and thus, for the prospects of any US-PRC alliance of convenience.

Several books and articles advance various explanations for ROC president Chiang Kai-shek's authorization of a nuclear weapons program in the late 1960s; for the efficacy of threats and inducements by the Ford and Carter administrations in thwarting Taiwanese nuclear proliferation in the 1970s and 1980s; and for Taiwan's nuclear forbearance since its transition from authoritarian to democratic rule in the late 1980s.[1] Instead, this chapter seeks to explain

---

[1] See, for example, Alexander Lanoszka, *Atomic Assurance: The Alliance Politics of Nuclear Proliferation* (Ithaca, NY: Cornell University Press, 2018), pp. 143–147; Nicholas L. Miller, *Stopping the Bomb: The Sources and Effectiveness of US Nonproliferation Policy* (Ithaca, NY: Cornell University Press, 2018), pp. 171–182; Alexandre Debs and Nuno P. Monteiro, *Nuclear Politics: The Strategic Causes of Proliferation* (New York: Cambridge University Press, 2016), pp. 297–325; Eugene B. Kogan, "Coercing Allies: Why Friends Abandon Nuclear Plans" (PhD diss., Brandeis University, 2013), pp. 43–92; Arthur S. Ding, "Will Taiwan Go Nuclear?" in James J. Wirtz and

the shifts in the Nixon, Ford, and Carter administrations' policies toward Taiwan in general, and toward the Taiwanese nuclear weapons program in particular.

Given Taiwan's vulnerability, what prompted the Nixon administration to reduce the frequency of the US Seventh Fleet's Taiwan Strait patrol and to begin reducing the US troop presence on Taiwan in 1969? What compromises did Richard Nixon and Henry Kissinger make regarding the US commitment to Taiwan in order to seek a rapprochement with China in 1971 and 1972? Why did the Ford and Carter administrations employ a mixture of coercive and accommodative strategies to get the government of ROC premier (later president) Chiang Ching-kuo to halt the acquisition of reprocessing technology and unsafeguarded activities at the Taiwan Research Reactor (TRR) between 1975 and 1978?

The shifts in the strategies that the United States pursued toward Taiwan were products of US policymakers' assessments of distributions and time horizons for emerging threats in East Asia. Domestic mobilization hurdles, specifically the degree of congressional support or opposition to the proposed initiatives of the Nixon, Ford, and Carter administrations, however, sometimes skewed the types of policies they ultimately pursued toward Taiwan. The overriding strategic objective of the three administrations in East Asia was to enlist China as an ally of convenience against the Soviet Union. The pursuit of this objective necessitated a dramatic adjustment of the United States' diplomatic and military policies toward Taiwan. The Taiwanese nuclear weapons program, however, was an obstacle to any US-China alliance of convenience.

The Nixon, Ford, and Carter administrations perceived favorable power balances in East Asia and long time horizons for emerging threats to US interests there. Yet domestic mobilization hurdles, in the form of congressional concern about global proliferation threats (mostly by Democrats in the Senate)

Peter R. Lavoy, eds., *Over the Horizon Proliferation Threats* (Stanford, CA: Stanford University Press, 2012), pp. 33–46; Vincent Wei-Cheng Wang, "Taiwan: Conventional Deterrence, Soft Power, and the Nuclear Option," in Muthiah Alagappa, ed., *Long Shadow: Nuclear Weapons and Security in 21st Century Asia* (Stanford, CA: Stanford University Press, 2008), pp. 404–428; Etel Solingen, *Nuclear Logics: Contrasting Paths in East Asia and the Middle East* (Princeton, NJ: Princeton University Press, 2007), pp. 100–118; Rebecca K. C. Hersman and Robert Peters, "Nuclear U-Turns: Learning from South Korean and Taiwanese Rollback," *The Nonproliferation Review*, Vol. 13, No. 3 (2006), pp. 539–553; Derek J. Mitchell, "Taiwan's Hsin Chu Program: Deterrence, Abandonment, and Honor," in Kurt M. Campbell, Richard J. Einhorn, and Mitchell B. Reiss, eds., *The Nuclear Tipping Point: Why States Reconsider Their Nuclear Choices* (Washington, DC: Brookings Institution Press, 2004), pp. 293–316; and David Albright and Corey Gay, "Taiwan: Nuclear Nightmare Averted," *Bulletin of the Atomic Scientists*, Vol. 54, No. 2 (1998), pp. 54–60.

and residual hostility to the PRC and loyalty to the ROC by conservative Republicans in the Senate, led the Ford and Carter administrations to pursue hybrid nonproliferation strategies toward Taiwan. Both administrations combined threats to terminate US-ROC nuclear cooperation with the continued provision of US arms transfers to Taiwan, even as the United States moved ever closer to normalizing relations with China.

The remainder of the chapter is organized chronologically, beginning with the origins of the US-ROC alliance between 1949 and 1954. The "acute" phase of the US-Taiwan proliferation dispute, which lasted from 1975 to 1978, meets the scope conditions for all three of the alternative theories outlined in chapter 2. Nuclear domino theory would expect the Ford and Carter administrations to have pursued coercive strategies to halt Taiwan's nuclear proliferation to the extent officials perceived a highlighted likelihood of reactive proliferation by other East Asian states. Credible sanctions theory would expect comprehensive nonproliferation legislation, specifically the Symington Amendment, to push the two administrations to pursue coercive strategies toward Taiwan. Security commitment theory would expect the Ford and the Carter administrations to pursued accommodative strategies, such as delaying the withdrawal of US military personnel, as an inducement for the ROC government to end the nuclear weapons program.

Chiang's "Abandonment" Fears and the ROC Nuclear Weapons Program, 1966–1969

The United States' alliance with Taiwan was an outgrowth of the Chinese Civil War and the Korean War. In 1949, the Chinese Communist Party (CCP) of Mao Zedong defeated the forces of the Kuomintang (KMT or Chinese Nationalist Party) of Generalissimo Chiang Kai-shek. Mao proclaimed the People's Republic of China on 1 October 1949 and signed a treaty of alliance and friendship with the Soviet Union on 14 February 1950. Meanwhile, Chiang and the KMT fled to Taiwan (Formosa), where they established a government-in-exile, the Republic of China. Neither the PRC nor the ROC recognized the other. Both claimed to be the legitimate government of China. Chiang vowed to retake the Chinese mainland, while Mao claimed that Taiwan and the other islands held by the KMT were merely renegade provinces of China.

The State Department concluded as early as 1947 that little could be done to prevent a CCP victory. In summer 1949, President Harry S. Truman, Secretary of State Dean Acheson, and other officials even considered cutting ties with Chiang and seeking a modus vivendi with Mao and the CCP. However, prominent Republican senators and representatives excoriated the Truman administration for "losing China" to the Communists.² On 5 January 1950, Truman announced that the United States would neither intervene in the Taiwan Strait nor provide military assistance or advice to Chinese Nationalist forces on Formosa (Taiwan).³

North Korea's invasion of South Korea on 25 June 1950 prompted a reversal of this nonintervention policy. On 27 June, Truman dispatched four US army divisions to halt the North Korean advance.⁴ He also ordered the US Seventh Fleet to "neutralize" the Taiwan Strait as part of a pivotal deterrence strategy: an effort to simultaneously deter a CCP attack on Taiwan and a KMT effort to retake the Chinese mainland.⁵ Declining Chiang's offer to send troops to fight in Korea, Truman called upon the Chinese Nationalists to "cease all air and sea operations against the mainland ... the future status of Formosa must await the restoration of security in the Pacific."⁶ In February 1951, four months after China directly intervened in the Korean War, the Truman administration announced a Mutual Defense Assistance (MDA) agreement to provide arms to Taiwan, with the stipulation that Chiang's regime would only use the arms for maintaining "internal security" or "legitimate self-defense."⁷

On 4 December 1955, the Eisenhower administration and Chiang's government signed the US-ROC Mutual Defense Treaty, which obligated the parties to develop their "individual and collective capacity to resist armed attack and communist subversive activities directed from without" against their respective territories in the Western Pacific. The treaty granted the United States the right to station "land, air and sea forces in and about Taiwan and the Pescadores as may be required for their defense, as determined by mutual agreement." Finally,

---

² Thomas J. Christensen, *Useful Adversaries: Grand Strategy, Domestic Mobilization, and Sino-American Conflict, 1947–1958* (Princeton, NJ: Princeton University Press, 1996), pp. 59–100.

³ See "387. Memorandum by the Executive Secretary of the National Security Council (Souers) to the National Security Council, Enclosing NSC 48/2, 'Position of the United States with Respect to Asia,' 30 December 1949," *FRUS, 1949, Vol. VII: The Far East and Australasia, Part 2* (Washington, DC: GPO, 1976), pp. 1219–1220. Also see "President Truman's Statement on the Status of Formosa, 5 January 1950," and "Dean Acheson's Speech at the National Press Club. 12 January 1950," in Roderick MacFarquhar, ed., *Sino-American Relations, 1949–71* (New York: Praeger, 1972), pp. 70–72.

⁴ For an analysis of the Truman administration's decision to intervene in the Korean War (25–30 June 1950) and to neutralize the Taiwan Strait, see Jeffrey W. Taliaferro, *Balancing Risks: Great Power Intervention in the Periphery* (Ithaca, NY: Cornell University Press, 2004), pp. 140–147.

⁵ See Timothy W. Crawford, *Pivotal Deterrence: Third-Party Statecraft and the Pursuit of Peace* (Ithaca, NY: Cornell University Press, 2003), p. 187. Also see Bruce A. Elleman, *High Seas Buffer: The Taiwan Patrol Force, 1950–1979* (Newport, RI: Naval War College Press, 2012).

⁶ "109. Telegram from the Secretary of State to the Embassy in the United Kingdom, 27 June 1950," and "Statement Issued by the President, 27 June 1950," *FRUS, 1950, Vol. VII: Korea* (Washington, DC: GPO, 1976), pp. 707–710 and pp. 761–764.

⁷ "Mutual Defense Assistance Agreement Between the United States and the Republic China, 9 February 1951," in MacFarquhar, *Sino-American Relations*, p. 99.

the treaty allowed either party to terminate it after giving the other one year's notice.[8]

As with the treaty with South Korea signed the previous year, President Dwight D. Eisenhower and Secretary of State John Foster Dulles sought this treaty primarily to restrain Chiang and the KMT.[9] An exchange of notes between Dulles and the ROC foreign minister George K. C. Yeh (aka Yeh Kung-ch'ao) on 10 December 1954 stated that the use of force against the PRC required "mutual consultation" between Washington and Taipei.[10]

From 1949 onward, the United States overriding objective in East Asia was to prevent the Soviet Union and China from increasing their military, economic, and diplomatic penetration of region. After the bloody stalemate of the Korean War, aiding and abetting a KMT venture to retake all or part of the Chinese mainland was simply not a viable option for most Washington policymakers. There was a sharp disjuncture between Eisenhower and Dulles's public statements in support of "Free China" and their private efforts to restrain Chiang Kai-shek during the 1954–1955 and the 1958 Quemoy-Matsu crises.[11]

During the Vietnam War, Taiwan became a staging area for US air operations throughout Southeast Asia. In the 1960s, the United States transferred large quantities of arms to the ROC including 300 M-48 Patton tanks, more than 100 F-5A fighter aircraft, 65 F-100A fighter aircraft, 18 U-2 reconnaissance aircraft, 12 destroyers, 5 minesweepers, and several dozen Hawk and Nike-Hercules surface-to-air (SAM) missiles.[12]

---

[8] "Mutual Defense Treaty Between the United States of America and the Republic of China, 4 December 1954," *American Foreign Policy, 1950–1955: Basic Documents* (Washington, DC: GPO, 1957), pp. 945–947.

[9] Victor D. Cha, *Powerplay: The Origins of the American Alliance System in Asia* (Princeton, NJ: Princeton University Press, 2016), pp. 80–86. Also see Hsiao-Ting Lin, "U.S.-Taiwan Military Diplomacy Revisited: Chiang Kai-Shek, *Baituan*, and the 1954 Mutual Defense Pact," *Diplomatic History*, Vol. 37, No. 5 (2013), pp. 971–994.

[10] "Exchange of Notes Between the Secretary of State and the Chinese Minister of Foreign Affairs, 10 December 1954," *American Foreign Policy, 1950–1955: Basic Documents* (Washington, DC: GPO, 1957), pp. 947–949.

[11] Nancy Bernkopf Tucker, *Strait Talk: United States–Taiwan Relations and the Crisis with China* (Cambridge, MA: Harvard University Press, 2009), pp. 13–17. Also see Lin, "U.S.-Taiwan Military Diplomacy Revisited," pp. 990–993; and Gordon H. Chang, "To the Nuclear Brink: Eisenhower, Dulles, and the Quemoy-Matsu Crisis," *International Security*, Vol. 12, No. 4 (1988), pp. 96–123.

[12] "Transfers of Major Weapons: Deals with Deliveries or Orders Made for 1955 to 1970, US to ROC," in Stockholm International Peace Research Institute, ed., SIPRI Arms Trade Database (Stockholm, Sweden: 2018), at http://armstrade.sipri.org/armstrade/page/trade_register.php (accessed 27 July 2018).

The US military assistance program (MAP) to the ROC in FY 1964 was $436 million. By FY 1970 it grew to $1.2 billion.[13] There were 19,044 US troops deployed in Taiwan in FY 1958, but that figure declined to 4,402 in FY 1959 and to 3,922 in FY 1963. With the escalation of the Vietnam War, US troop levels on Taiwan increased from 3,802 in FY 1964 to 9,243 in FY 1969.[14] Meanwhile, US foreign economic assistance to the ROC declined from $41 million in FY 1960 to $12 million in FY 1969, before increasing to $26 million in FY 1970.[15]

The ROC's fundamental dilemma was that its one reliable ally was on the other side of the Pacific Ocean. And like Park Chung-hee in Seoul, Chiang Kai-shek and his advisers had a recurrent fear that the United States might not come to their defense in the event of war. But Chiang repeatedly also asked Washington policymakers to support a Nationalist attempt to retake the Chinese mainland.[16]

Developments in the mid-1960s exacerbated Chiang's fear of "abandonment." China detonated its first atomic bomb—a 20 kiloton uranium device—at the Lop Nur testing site on 16 October 1964. The test was not a surprise to officials in Washington or in Taipei. After all, CIA U-2s flown from Taiwan by Chinese Nationalist pilots beginning in 1961 provided early high-resolution imagery of the nuclear complex at Baotou.[17] Nonetheless, the prospect of the PRC developing a nuclear weapon and delivery systems led Chiang to escalate calls for preventive military operations against the mainland.

---

[13] United States Agency for International Development, *US Overseas Loans and Grants: Obligations and Loan Authorizations, July 1, 1945–September 30, 2016* (Washington, DC: GPO, 2016) available at http://pdf.usaid.gov/pdf_docs/pbaah600.pdf (accessed 28 July 2018).

[14] Thomas Kane, *Global U.S. Troop Deployment, 1950–2005, 2006* (Washington, DC: The Heritage Foundation), available at http://thf_media.s3.amazonaws.com/2006/xls/troopMarch2005.xls (accessed 27 July 2018).

[15] United States Agency for International Development, *US Overseas Loans and Grants: Obligations and Loan Authorizations, July 1, 1945–September 30, 2016* (Washington, DC: GPO, 2016), available at http://pdf.usaid.gov/pdf_docs/pbaah600.pdf (accessed 28 July 2018).

[16] See Keren Yarhi-Milo, Alexander Lanoszka, and Zack Cooper, "To Arm or to Ally? The Patron's Dilemma and the Strategic Logic of Arms Transfers and Alliances," *International Security*, Vol. 41, No. 2 (2016), pp. 90–139. Yarhi-Milo, Lanoszka, and Cooper argue that before the PRC and the US normalized diplomatic ties in 1979, the US and ROC had complementary security interests in East Asia: both saw China as a threat. I disagree with them on two points: first, senior officials in the Nixon administration ceased to perceive China as a threat in 1969—two years before US-PRC rapprochement and a full decade before normalization. Second, US and ROC security interests were not complementary in the 1950s, 1960s, and early 1970s, since Chiang Kai-shek never abandoned his (delusional) plans to retake the Chinese mainland.

[17] "Arms Control and Disarmament Agency, 'Summary and Appraisal of Latest Evidence on Chinese Communist Advanced Weapon Capabilities,' 10 July 1963, Top Secret," in William Burr and Jeffrey T. Richelson, eds., *NSA Electronic Briefing Book No. 38* (Washington, DC: National Security Archive, 2001), https://nsarchive2.gwu.edu/NSAEBB/NSAEBB38/document8.pdf.

In September 1963, Chiang's son, Chiang Ching-kuo, traveled to Washington at the invitation of Director of Central Intelligence (DCI) John McCone. The younger Chiang, then the ROC intelligence chief, discussed the possibility of US airstrikes or joint US-Taiwanese commando raids on Chinese nuclear facilities with McCone and Ray Cline, the CIA's deputy director for intelligence (and a former CIA station chief in Taipei), as well as with McGeorge Bundy, President John F. Kennedy's national security adviser. Bundy assured Chiang that the Kennedy administration placed a "high priority on measures to weaken the Chinese Communist regime." However, Bundy warned, the administration had no interest in sponsoring an attack on the Chinese mainland that might negate the recent Sino-Soviet split.[18]

The Generalissimo claimed "no amount of talk of explanation could neutralize the tremendous psychological or moral effect" that China's atomic bomb would have on other East Asian states. He asked the United States to give ROC "the necessary means to destroy CHICOM [Chinese Communist] nuclear installations," adding that US forces would not need to participate.[19] President Lyndon B. Johnson wrote to Chiang in December 1964 that the United States' commitment to defend Taiwan would "in no way be weakened by Chinese Communist development of nuclear weapons." He also tried to restrain Chiang from launching military operations against the Chinese mainland, adding that "successes against the [Chinese] Communists is to be won principally by political means, not by force."[20]

Chiang requested additional Nike-Hercules and Hawk missiles, as well as expedited delivery of items already programmed such as the M 41 tank, F-100 modification kits, and the M113. He also complained that Washington had given insufficient attention to the military assistance program (MAP) to the ROC, which should really be given the highest priority in military aid, next to South Vietnam. US ambassador Jerauld Wright reported, "We have on several previous occasions emphasized to President [Chiang] and his principal supporters that

---

[18] "Memorandum to McGeorge Bundy, Special Assistant to the President, from William E. Colby, for Deputy Director of Plans, Central Intelligence Agency, 'Visit of General Chiang Ching-Kuo,' 19 September 1963, Enclosing, 'Meeting between Mr. McGeorge Bundy and General Chiang Ching-Kuo, 10 September 1963', Secret," in William Burr and Jeffrey T. Richelson, eds., *NSA Electronic Briefing Book No. 38* (Washington, DC: National Security Archive, 2001), https://nsarchive2.gwu.edu/NSAEBB/NSAEBB38/document9.pdf.

[19] "U.S. Embassy, Taipei, Cable Number 347 to Department of State, 24 October 1964, Secret, Excised Copy," in William Burr and Jeffrey T. Richelson, eds., *NSA Electronic Briefing Book No. 38* (Washington, DC: National Security Archive, 2001), https://nsarchive2.gwu.edu/NSAEBB/NSAEBB38/document20.pdf.

[20] "74. Telegram from the Department of State to the Embassy in the Republic of China, 21 December 1964, 9:52 A.M.," *FRUS, 1964–1968, Vol. XXX: China* (Washington, DC: GPO, 1998).

GRC's best air defense is US nuclear deterrent."[21] Wright subsequently assured then ROC defense minister Chiang Ching-kuo that "the entire retaliatory capability of [US] nuclear forces would be equally effective in deterring an attack on Taiwan."[22]

In his 1965 New Year's Message, Chiang pledged to destroy China's nuclear installations before Beijing acquired a delivery system to "speed devastation to all parts of the world."[23] In August, he warned Cline that "the Chinese Communists and their Vietnamese allies are about to engage the US in a long war of attrition we cannot hope to win."[24] Therefore, he argued the Nationalists had a fading window of opportunity to retake the Chinese mainland. As he put it: "It is now or never; the Sino/Soviet dispute assures that the USSR will not intervene, and the Chinese Communists have not yet achieved a sufficient nuclear buildup to deter a Nationalist invasion."[25]

During an official visit to Washington on 20 September 1965, Madame Chiang Kai-shek (Soong Mei-ling) told Secretary of State Dean Rusk and Secretary of Defense Robert S. McNamara that "the only course of action ... was for the United States (to provide the means) to take out the ChiComs nuclear installations now by the employment of conventional forces."[26] Meeting with McNamara at the Pentagon the following day, Chiang Ching-kuo repeated his father's request for US air and naval support for a Nationalist attack on the mainland.[27] However, as Johnson and his advisers escalated US air and ground operations in defense of South Vietnam throughout 1965, they were also at pains to avoid any step that might provoke a full-scale Chinese military intervention on the side of North Vietnam.

In June 1966, the US Embassy in Taipei reported that the Chungshan Institute of Science and Technology (CIST), which handled research and development for the ROC Ministry of National Defense, had started a clandestine

---

[21] "81. Telegram from the Embassy in the Republic of China to the Department of State, 23 March 1965, 4 P.M.," *FRUS, 1964–1968, Vol. XXX: China* (Washington, DC: GPO, 1998).

[22] "95. Memorandum From James C. Thomson, Jr., of the National Security Council Staff and the President's Special Assistant for National Security Affairs (Bundy) to President Johnson, 5 August 1965," *FRUS, 1964–1968, Vol. XXX, China* (Washington, DC: GPO, 1998)..

[23] "Chiang Vows to End Peking Atom Power," *New York Times*, 1 January 1965, p. 17.

[24] "Chiang Vows to End Peking Atom Power," *New York Times*, 1 January 1965, p. 17.

[25] "95. Memorandum from James C. Thomson, Jr., of the National Security Council Staff and the President's Special Assistant for National Security Affairs (Bundy) to President Johnson, 5 August 1965," *FRUS, 1964–1968, Vol. XXX: China* (Washington, DC: GPO, 1998).

[26] "103. Memorandum of Conversation, 20 September 1965," *FRUS, 1964–1968, Vol. XXX: China* (Washington, DC: GPO, 1999).

[27] "104. Memorandum of Conversation, re: Call on the Secretary of Defense by the Chinese Minister of Defense, 22 September 1965, 9:15–11:00 A.M.," *FRUS, 1964–1968, Vol. XXX: China* (Washington, DC: GPO, 1999).

program to develop nuclear weapons and ballistic missiles. Whether or not the elder Chiang personally authorized the program is a matter of dispute. Hsu Cho-yun, a history professor at Taiwan National University and a member of the CIST governing council, told the Embassy that the Generalissimo gave his personal authorization. A cable from the Embassy read in part: "At the direction of President Chiang, the GRC [Government of the Republic of China] Defense Ministry continues to try to develop an atomic weapon and delivery system, according to a source close to the effort. The president has overridden the advice of Lt. General T'ang Chun-pu, vice minister of defense who also heads up the defense scientific program; T'ang believes the attempt impractical and beyond ROC resources."[28]

In an 1988 interview, however, Professor Ta-you Wu, who had been director of the Science Advisory Committee of the ROC National Security Council in the late 1960s, claimed that General Tan Jung-pug, then director of CIST, had persuaded Chiang Ching-kuo to start the program without his father's knowledge.[29] Code named the Hsin Chu Project and jointly overseen by CIST and the Institute for Nuclear Energy Research (INER), the $140 million scheme called for the purchase of a heavy-water reactor, a heavy-water production plant, and a plutonium separation plant from foreign suppliers, in addition to an indigenous effort to develop ballistic missiles.[30]

Taiwan, like South Korea, Pakistan, and Israel, had been a beneficiary of Eisenhower's Atoms for Peace Program in the 1950s. The program built a research reactor at the Tsing Hua University. But, unlike Israel and Pakistan, Taiwan also developed a nuclear power industry in the 1960s.[31] In March 1966, the US embassies in Taipei and Tel Aviv reported that Victor Chung, the INER

---

[28] "US Embassy Taipei, Airgram 1037, 20 June 1966, Indications GRC Continues to Pursue Atomic Weaponry," in William Burr, ed., *NSA Electronic Briefing Book no. 20* (Washington, DC: National Security Archive, 1999), http://nsarchive.gwu.edu/NSAEBB/NSAEBB20/docs/doc18.pdf.

[29] David Albright and Corey Gay, "Taiwan: Nuclear Nightmare Averted," *Bulletin of the Atomic Scientists*, Vol. 54, No. 2 (1998), pp. 54–60, at p. 56.

[30] See Albright and Gay, "Taiwan: Nuclear Nightmare Averted," p. 55. Also see Mitchell, "Taiwan's Hsin Chu Program," p. 296. The project's codename, Hsin Chu, refers to a city just south of the Taiwanese capital, Taipei, where Tsing Hua University is located.

[31] Nicholas L. Miller contends that in South Korea and Taiwan, construction of nuclear power reactors began after the initiation of their respective nuclear weapons programs. See Miller, "Why Nuclear Energy Programs Rarely Lead to Proliferation," *International Security*, Vol. 42, No. 2 (2017), pp. 40–77, at p. 54. This is correct, but in Taiwan and South Korea, government and commercial interest in nuclear power generation predated the initiation of nuclear weapons programs.

director, and his deputy meet with Israeli nuclear scientists, including Mordechai Morahg, the director of the Soreq Nuclear Research Center.[32]

The US Embassy in Bonn reported that other Taiwanese officials made inquiries of the Siemens Corporation about the purchase of two 50 MW natural uranium reactors. International Atomic Energy Agency (IAEA) scientists who conducted a site study for two nuclear power plants in Taiwan reported that a consortium of Tsing Hua University (the site of the Atom for Peace reactor), Taiwan National University, and other "interests" in the GRC, rather than the Taiwan Power Company (Taipower), sought to purchase Siemens reactors.[33]

"Despite comments by secretary-general of GRC Atomic Energy Council," the Taipei Embassy reported in February 1967, "we are not convinced that purpose motivating GRC desire for Siemens reactor is unrelated to interest in nuclear weapons."[34] The State Department, however, chose not to attempt to forestall the sale by approaching the West German government or Siemens. "Approach on the grounds of possible use for weapons research would cast doubt on US confidence in IAEA safeguards; approach on grounds that reactor [on] economic [grounds] would give rise to German suspicions that US attempting displace Siemens sale."[35]

Shortly thereafter, however, the Siemens reactor deal collapsed. Wu later claimed he persuaded Chiang that the CIST's plan was too costly and would risk a direct confrontation with the United States. Wu also claimed he advised the president that the civilian nuclear energy council assume responsibility for nuclear energy development, as was the practice in most other countries.[36] In February 1968, the ROC military formally turned over the nuclear facilities on

---

[32] "US Embassy Tel Aviv, Airgram 793, 19 March 1966, Nationalist Chinese Atomic Experts Visit Israel," in William Burr, ed., *NSA Electronic Briefing Book no. 20* (Washington, DC: National Security Archive, 1999), http://nsarchive.gwu.edu/NSAEBB/NSAEBB20/docs/doc21.pdf.

[33] "US Embassy Taipei, Airgram 813, 8 April 1966, GRC Request to IAEA Team for Advice on Location of Reactor for Possible Use by Military Research Institute," in William Burr, ed., *NSA Electronic Briefing Book no. 20* (Washington, DC: National Security Archive, 1999), http://nsarchive.gwu.edu/NSAEBB/NSAEBB20/docs/doc22.pdf.

[34] "US Embassy Taipei, Airgram 566, 21 February 1967, GRC Plans for Purchase of 50-Megawatt Heavy Water Nuclear Power Plant, with Copy of Agreement Between Union Industrial Research Institute and Siemens Copy Attached," in William Burr, ed., *NSA Electronic Briefing Book no. 20* (Washington, DC: National Security Archive, 1999), http://nsarchive.gwu.edu/NSAEBB/NSAEBB20/docs/doc19.pdf.

[35] "State Department to Embassies Taipei and Bonn, Cable 16187, 20 March 1967," in William Burr, ed., *NSA Electronic Briefing Book no. 20* (Washington, DC: National Security Archive, 1999); "State Department to Embassies Taipei and Bonn, Cable 16187, 20 March 1967," in William Burr, ed., *NSA Electronic Briefing Book no. 20* (Washington, DC: National Security Archive, 1999), http://nsarchive.gwu.edu/NSAEBB/NSAEBB20/docs/doc24.pdf.

[36] Albright and Gray, "Taiwan Nuclear Nightmare Averted," p. 56.

the CIST campus to the Chinese Atomic Energy Council (CAEC). Nonetheless, CIST remained heavily involved and the clandestine effort to obtain plutonium production capabilities continued, albeit with a civilian facade. Henceforth, the INER would seek to purchase nuclear components from various foreign suppliers, ostensibly for research purposes.[37]

Concerns about Taiwanese nuclear intentions continued, as did Chiang's agitation for support for military operation against China. In March 1967, he told Arthur J. Goldberg, the US ambassador to the United Nations (UN), that: "Given the serious split between Moscow and Peking, the drain of Vietnam on Peking's resources, and the serious turmoil on the mainland itself, now is the golden opportunity to rid the mainland of the Communist regime and destroy the Chinese nuclear threat."[38] A CIA analyst warned that "Communist China's nuclear power is growing and the [Generalissimo] feels strongly that the Communists intend using it against Taiwan."[39]

The Drawdown of US Forces on Taiwan and Nixon's Opening to China, 1969–1973

China's atomic bomb test in October 1964, along with fear that the United States might "abandon" Taiwan, appears to have been the primary impetus for the Hsin Chu Project in the late 1960s. However, it was the Nixon administration's East Asian policies in the early 1970s that really set the stage for the "acute" phase of US-Taiwan proliferation dispute later in the decade.

As noted in the previous chapter, Nixon advocated rapprochement with China in a 1967 article in *Foreign Affairs*.[40] By the time he became president in January 1969, Sino-Soviet rivalry had degenerated into open hostility. Chinese leaders were wary about the buildup of Soviet forces along the northern borders

---

[37] "Embassy Taipei to State Department, Chung Shan Nuclear Research Institute, Cable 1197, 24 February 1973," in William Burr, ed., *NSA Electronic Briefing Book No. 20* (Washington, DC: National Security Archive, 1999), http://nsarchive.gwu.edu/NSAEBB/NSAEBB20/docs/doc09.pdf.

[38] "245. Memorandum from the Representative to the United Nations (Goldberg) to President Johnson, re: Report on First Leg of Asian Trip, 9 March 1967," *FRUS, 1964–1968, Vol. XXX: China* (Washington, DC: GPO, 1999).

[39] "278. Memorandum from Donald S. Macdonald of the Bureau of Intelligence and Research to the Director of the Bureau (Hughes), 18 August 1967," *FRUS, 1964–1968, Vol. XXX: China* (Washington, DC: GPO, 1999). CIA and INR analysts, as well as mid-level officials in the Bureau of East Asian and Pacific Affairs (EA), attended this meeting.

[40] Richard M. Nixon, "Asia After Viet-Nam," *Foreign Affairs*, Vol. 46, No. 1 (1967): 111–125.

with the USSR and Outer Mongolia in the late 1960s.[41] By the end of 1968, Mao and the CCP Central Military Commission began the withdrawal of PLA troops from the Vietnam theater, slowed the flow economic aid to Hanoi, and dropped their opposition to direct US-North Vietnamese peace negotiations.[42]

The Sino-Soviet rivalry nearly escalated to war on 2 March 1969. Chinese and Soviet border troops exchanged fire on the disputed Zhenbao (or Damanskii) Island on the Ussuri River.[43] China, which detonated its first thermonuclear device on 17 June 1967, conducted two more thermonuclear tests on 22 and 29 September 1969.[44] The Soviet Union responded by deploying nuclear-capable ballistic missiles near the Sino-Soviet border and conducting offensive military exercises targeting Chinese nuclear facilities. "Throughout the 1970s," PLA units "undertook extensive defensive exercises targeted toward a potential Soviet attack."[45] During a face-to-face meeting at the Beijing airport in mid-September 1969, Zhou warned Soviet premier Alexei Kosygin that if Soviet jets bombed Chinese nuclear facilities, "this would be an act of war that China would oppose to the end."[46]

Although US combat forces remained mired in Southeast Asia, Nixon and his national security adviser, Henry Kissinger, saw the power distribution in East Asia was shifting in the United States' favor. In February 1969, Kissinger ordered the National Security Council (NSC) to undertake a comprehensive study of the United States' relations with the PRC and the ROC, including "the nature of the Chinese Communist threat and intentions in Asia."[47] As part of that review, the CIA reported there was no evidence China planned "to expand beyond it borders or use armed force to pursue its objectives, except for the possibility of a military move against Taiwan."[48]

---

[41] See Wang Zhongchun, "The Soviet Factor in Sino-American Normalization, 1969–1979," in William C. Kirby, Robert S. Ross, and Gong Li, eds., *Normalization of US-China Relations: An International History* (Cambridge, MA: Harvard University Press, 2005), pp. 150–151.

[42] Christensen, *Worse Than a Monolith*, pp. 202–203.

[43] See Viktor M. Gobarev, "Soviet Policy Toward China: Developing Nuclear Weapons 1949–1969," *Journal of Slavic Military Studies*, Vol. 12, No. 4 (1999), pp. 1–53; Yang Kuisong, "The Sino-Soviet Border Clash of 1969: From Zhenbao Island to Sino-American Rapprochement," *Cold War History*, Vol. 1, No. 1 (2000), pp. 21–52; and William Burr, "Sino-American Relations, 1969: The Sino-Soviet Border War and Steps Towards Rapprochement," *Cold War History*, Vol. 1, No. 3 (2001), pp. 73–112.

[44] John Wilson Lewis and Litai Xue, *China Builds the Bomb* (Stanford, CA: Stanford University Press, 1988), p. 244.

[45] Zhongchun, "The Soviet Factor in Sino-American Normalization," p. 153.

[46] Quoted in Ibid., 152.

[47] "4. National Security Study Memorandum 14, 5 February 1969," *FRUS, 1969–1976, Vol. XVII: China, 1969–1972* (Washington, DC: GPO, 2006).

[48] "12. Summary of the CIA Response to NSSM 14, Undated," *FRUS, 1969–1976, Vol. XVII: China, 1969–1972* (Washington, DC: GPO, 2006).

Undersecretary of State Elliot Richardson informed the Taipei Embassy and the commander of the US Taiwan Defense Command (COMUSTDC) on 24 September 1969 that Nixon decided to reduce the frequency of the Seventh Fleet's Taiwan Strait patrol. Richardson wrote the reduction was "part of over 100 ship reduction in worldwide US naval deployment, made pursuant to recent $3.0 billion reduction in defense expenditures," but added the move had no implications for the 1954 Mutual Defense Treaty or the Seventh Fleet's ability to defend Taiwan.[49]

Chiang renewed his request for F-4 Phantoms and submarines, as well as an immediate review of Plan Rochester—the US plan for the defense of Taiwan and the Pescadores from a Chinese attack. Kissinger advised Nixon to decline Chiang's request for submarines, which would be ineffective in defending Taiwan. He noted that administration did plan to sell additional F-104 aircraft to Taipei, thus enabling the ROK air force to phase out of the older F-86. Kissinger opposed selling Taiwan the F-4s, which were capable of delivering nuclear payloads. Nixon sent a noncommittal reply to Chiang on 16 December 1969, which read in part, "If your defense authorities believe that some modifications of plan 'Rochester' are required, the officers in the Taiwan Defense Command will be interested in hearing your views."[50]

The Nixon administration announced a sharp reduction in the FY 1972 MAP to the ROC in October 1970. Vice President Spiro Agnew had mentioned a possible reduction in the MAP during an official visit to Taipei in August. However, Vice Premier Chiang Ching-kuo said he and his colleagues had not anticipated the level would go below $15 million. Chiang told US ambassador Walter McConaughey, "confidence in US consistency and dependability had been seriously diluted in all sectors of his government" and that he did not see how the Nixon administration's decision "could be reconciled with the requirements of alliance and friendship." In reply, McConaughey pointed out, "the absence of any apparent immediate aggressive intent against Taiwan by the ChiComs and the impressive economic progress of the GRC were necessarily taken into account in Washington when the painful decisions had to be made."[51]

---

[49] "34. Telegram from the Department of State to the Embassy in the Republic of China and Commander, US Taiwan Defense Command, Washington, 23 September 1969," *FRUS 1969–1976, Vol. XVII: China, 1969–1972* (Washington, DC: GPO, 2006).

[50] "50. Memorandum from the President's Assistant for National Security Affairs (Kissinger) to President Nixon, Washington, 6 December 1969," *FRUS 1969–1976, Vol. XVII: China, 1969–1972* (Washington, DC: GPO, 2006). The full text of Nixon's 16 December 1969 letter to Chiang Kai-shek is in State Department telegram 208044 to Taipei, 16 December 1969 (National Archives, RG 59, Central Files 1967–69, DEF 6-2 US).

[51] "92. Telegram from the Embassy in the Republic of China to the Department of State, Taipei, 22 October 1970," *FRUS 1969–1976, Vol. XVII: China, 1969–1972* (Washington, DC: GPO, 2006).

Although the secret Warsaw talks between US ambassador Walter Stroessel and the PRC chargé d'affairs, Lei Yang, resumed in January 1970—after a hiatus of two years—Nixon and Kissinger began to pursue rapprochement with Beijing in earnest in autumn 1970.[52] They maintained strict secrecy, bypassing the State Department and relying on Pakistan's president, General Muhammad Yahya Khan, to establish a backchannel to Zhou.[53] Contrary to the claim in Kissinger's memoir that Taiwan was not a "primary concern," declassified documents reveal that Taiwan's status and the US military presence on the island were the major issue in the negotiations leading to Nixon's trip to Beijing in February 1972.[54]

On 12 December 1970, Zhou told the Romanian deputy premier Gheorghe Radulescu, "Between China and the US, there is one main issue—the issue of Taiwan."[55] "With respect to the US military presence in Taiwan," Kissinger wrote in a 16 December 1970 letter to Zhou (sent via Yahya Khan): "You should know that the policy of the United States Government is to reduce progressively its military presence in the region of East Asia and the Pacific as tensions in the region diminish."[56] In a 29 May 1971 message to Nixon, Zhou wrote: "It goes without saying the first question to be settled . . . is the question of the concrete

---

[52] For an argument that the reactivated Warsaw talks played a role in the evolution of Nixon and Kissinger's strategy on the Taiwan issue in 1971, see Robert Accinelli, "In Pursuit of a Modus Vivendi: The Taiwan Issue and Sino-American Rapprochement, 1969–1972," in William C. Kirby, Robert S. Ross, and Li Gong, eds., *Normalization of U.S.-China Relations: An International History* (Cambridge, MA: Harvard University Press, 2005), pp. 13–17.

[53] "Memcon, Meeting Between the President and Pakistan President Yahya, 25 October 1970, Top Secret/Sensitive," in William Burr, ed., *NSA Electronic Briefing Book no. 66* (Washington, DC: National Security Archive, 2002), http://nsarchive2.gwu.edu/NSAEBB/NSAEBB66/ch-03.pdf; and "Kissinger to Nixon, 'Chinese Communist Initiative,' c. 10 December 1970, Enclosing Draft Note Verbal and Message from Zhou Enlai, as Conveyed by Hilaly, with Comments by Yahya, Top Secret/Sensitive," in William Burr, ed., *NSA Electronic Briefing Book no. 66* (Washington, DC: National Security Archive, 2002), http://nsarchive2.gwu.edu/NSAEBB/NSAEBB66/ch-06.pdf.

[54] Henry Kissinger, *White House Years* (Boston: Little, Brown, 1979), p. 703.

[55] "Memorandum of Conversation Between Romanian Deputy Premier Gheorghe Radulescu and Zhou Enlai, 12 December 1970," *Cold War International History Project Bulletin*, Vol. 16 (2007), pp. 438–441, at p. 439. Zhou and other PRC officials discussed the status of Taiwan and the US military presence on the island in meetings with their Romanian counterparts in 1969. See "Telegram from Romanian Ambassador in Beijing Aurel Duma to Foreign Minister Corneliu Manescu Regarding Conversations with Representatives of the PRC Ministries of Trade, Foreign Affairs, and Defense, May 13, 1969," Ibid., pp. 411–412; and "Minutes of Conversation Between Ion Gheorghe Maurer, Paul Niculescu Mizil, Zhou Enlai, and Li Xiannian, 7 September 1969," Ibid., pp. 418–426.

[56] "Memo of Record by Col. Richard T. Kennedy, 16 December 1970, Enclosing Response to PRC via Hilaly and Yahya, Top Secret/Sensitive, Delivered in Beijing on 5 January 1971," in William Burr, ed., *NSA Electronic Briefing Book no. 69* (Washington, DC: National Security Archive, 2002), http://nsarchive2.gwu.edu/NSAEBB/NSAEBB66/ch-08.pdf.

way for the withdrawal of US armed forces from Taiwan and the Taiwan Strait area."⁵⁷

Kissinger secretly met with Zhou in Beijing from 9 to 11 July 1971. From the outset, Zhou insisted that the United States would have to recognize the PRC as the sole legitimate government of China, withdraw its military forces and installations on Taiwan "within a limited period," and terminate its alliance treaty with the Chiang regime. Kissinger noted the Nixon administration had already taken certain symbolic steps, such as ending the Taiwan Strait Patrol, withdrawing a squadron of air tankers from Taiwan, and ordering a 20 percent reduction of the US military advisory group.⁵⁸

Zhou repeatedly raised concerns about a Taiwanese independence movement and whether the United States supported a "two Chinas" or "a one China, one Taiwan" formula. Kissinger assured him that that United States opposed all three and would never support a KMT military operation against mainland China. He also pledged the Nixon administration would "withdraw that part of our force which its related to the war in Vietnam," or approximately two-thirds of US troops on Taiwan over the next year. As US-PRC relations improved, Kissinger said, the administration would continue to withdraw US forces from Taiwan.⁵⁹

Nixon's brief televised announcement on 15 July 1971 about Kissinger's secret talks with Zhou and his own planned visit to Beijing shocked the world.⁶⁰ None of the three US treaty allies in East Asia—South Korea, Japan, or Taiwan—had been consulted beforehand.

On 27 July, James C. H. Shen, the ROC ambassador in Washington, asked Kissinger whether he discussed the question of "two Chinas" and the United

---

⁵⁷ "Message from Zhou to Nixon, 29 May 1971, with Commentary, Conveyed by Hilaly to White House," in William Burr, ed., *NSA Electronic Briefing Book no. 66* (Washington, DC: National Security Archive, 2002), http://nsarchive2.gwu.edu/NSAEBB/NSAEBB66/ch-26.pdf.

⁵⁸ "Memcon, Kissinger, and Zhou, 9 July 1971, 4:35–11:20 P.M., Top Secret / Sensitive / Exclusively Eyes Only, with Cover Memo by Lord, 29 July 1971," in William Burr, ed., *NSA Electronic Briefing Book no. 66* (Washington, DC: National Security Archive 2002), http://nsarchive2.gwu.edu/NSAEBB/NSAEBB66/ch-34.pdf.

⁵⁹ "Memcon, Kissinger and Zhou, 10 July 1971, Afternoon (12:10 PM–6:00 P.M.), Top Secret/Sensitive/Exclusively Eyes Only, with Cover Memo by Lord, 6 August 1971," in William Burr, ed., *NSA Electronic Briefing Book no. 66* (Washington, DC: National Security Archive, 2002), http://nsarchive2.gwu.edu/NSAEBB/NSAEBB66/ch-35.pdf; and also "Memcon, Kissinger and Zhou, 10 July 1971, Evening (11:20–11:50 P.M.), Top Secret /Sensitive / Exclusively Eyes Only, with Cover Memo by Lord, 12 August 1971," Ibid., http://nsarchive2.gwu.edu/NSAEBB/NSAEBB66/ch-36.pdf.

⁶⁰ "Remarks to the Nation Announcing Acceptance of an Invitation to Visit the People's Republic of China," 15 July 1971, *Public Papers of the Presidents of the United States: Richard Nixon, 1971* (Washington, DC: GPO, 1972), pp. 819–820.

States' position on the China seat in the UN with Zhou. Kissinger said he reiterated the long-stated US position that it would not oppose a peaceful resolution of the PRC-ROC dispute, that the United States had a mutual defense treaty with the ROC, and that the Nixon administration hoped the PRC would not use force against Taiwan. When Shen expressed concerns about the items Nixon planned to discuss in Beijing, Kissinger replied he assumed the president would not make any concessions on Taiwan.[61]

Preparations for Nixon's Beijing visit occurred alongside a debate over China's admission to the UN. On 15 October 1971, the General Assembly narrowly approved a resolution (sponsored by Albania) to expel the ROC and to admit the representatives of the PRC, which was yet another blow to Taiwan's international standing.[62] The vote overlapped with Kissinger second (and publicized) trip to Beijing to prepare for Nixon's forthcoming visit.[63]

Nixon's week-long trip to China between 21 and 27 February 1972 began with a courtesy call to the ailing Mao at his residence. Nixon then had eight extended meetings with Zhou in which the two discussed a variety of topics.[64] "There is one China, and Taiwan is a part of China," Nixon told Zhou in their second meeting. He added, "There will be no more statements made—if I can control our bureaucracy—to the effect that the status of Taiwan is undetermined."[65]

The Shanghai Communiqué of 27 February 1972 was a masterpiece of constructive ambiguity.[66] The United States acknowledged, "All Chinese on either

---

[61] "152. Memorandum of Conversation, 27 July 1971, 12:05–12:31 P.M.," *FRUS, 1969–1976, Vol. XVII: China, 1969–1972* (Washington, DC: GPO, 2006).

[62] UN General Assembly Resolution 2758, "Restoration of the Lawful Rights of the People's Republic of China in the United Nations," 25 October 1971, http://www.un.org/ga/search/view_doc.asp?symbol=A/RES/2758(XXVI) (accessed 1 August 2018).

[63] See "Conversation Between President Nixon and National Security Adviser Kissinger, Followed by Conversation Among Nixon, Kissinger, and UN Ambassador George Bush, 30 September 1971," in William Burr, Sharon Chamberlain, Gao Bei, and Zhao Han, eds., *NSA Electronic Briefing Book No. 70* (Washington, DC: National Security Archive, 2002), https://nsarchive2.gwu.edu/NSAEBB/NSAEBB70/doc6.pdf.

[64] "194. Memorandum of Conversation, Beijing, 21 February 1972, 2:50–3:55 P.M.," *FRUS, 1969–1976, Vol. XVII: China, 1969–1972* (Washington, DC: GPO, 2006).

[65] "196. Memorandum of Conversation, Beijing, 22 February 1972, 2:10–6 P.M.," *FRUS, 1969–1976, Vol. XVII: China, 1969–1972* (Washington, DC: GPO, 2006).

[66] Detailed studies of the 1971–1972 negotiations that produced the Shanghai Communiqué include: Harry Harding, *A Fragile Relationship: The United States and China Since 1972* (Washington, DC: Brookings Institution, 1992), chapters 1–2; Robert S. Ross, *Negotiating Cooperation: The United States and China, 1969–1989* (Stanford, CA: Stanford University Press, 1995), chapters 1–3; and Alan D. Romberg, *Rein in at the Brink of the Precipice: American Policy Toward Taiwan and US-PRC Relations* (Washington, DC: Henry L. Stimson Center, 2003), chapters 1–3. On the concept of "constructive ambiguity," see Crawford, *Pivotal Deterrence*, p. 189; Christopher Honeyman, "In Defense of Ambiguity," *Negotiation Journal*, Vol. 3, No. 1 (1987), pp. 81–86; Raymond Cohen, *International*

side of the Taiwan Strait maintain there is one China and that Taiwan is a part of China" and "reaffirms its interest a peaceful settlement of the Taiwan question by the Chinese themselves." Nixon also agreed to "the ultimate objective of the withdrawal of all US forces and military installations from Taiwan." The communiqué further stated that neither China nor the United States should seek hegemony in the Asia-Pacific region and that "each is opposed to efforts by any other country or group of countries to establish such hegemony."[67] The last phrase was a reference to the Soviet Union, as well as reflective of PRC leaders' concerns that Japan might attempt to fill a power vacuum resulting from the departure of US forces from Taiwan.[68]

The "one China" concept was primarily intended to allow the United States and China to each do as they wished with respect to Taiwan's legal status, while respecting the status quo in the Taiwan Strait. More important, the "one China" concept was an implicit warning to the ROC government about the limits of US support. "The deterrent threat would remain dormant," Timothy M. Crawford writes, "so long as Taipei remained wedded to the idea of 'one China' (under KMT rule) and therefore also opposed to separate independence."[69]

In order to enlist China as an ally of convenience against the Soviet Union, therefore, the United States would need to readjust its diplomatic and security relationship with Taiwan.[70] What that readjustment might entail and the time frame in which it might happen had yet to be determined in February 1972. To forestall a potential backlash from conservatives in the Republican Party, such as Senator Barry Goldwater (AZ) and former California governor Ronald Reagan, Nixon and Kissinger stated they had made no "secret deals" in Beijing

---

Politics: The Rules of the Game (London: Longman, 1981), p. 33; and Fred Charles Iklé, *How Nations Negotiate* (New York: Harper & Row, 1964), p. 33.

[67] "203. Joint Statement Following Discussions with Leaders of the People's Republic of China, 27 February 1972," *FRUS, 1969–1976, Vol. XVII: China, 1969–1972* (Washington, DC: GPO, 2003).

[68] In briefing Nixon in preparation for the February 1972 summit with Zhou, Kissinger wrote, "They [the Chinese] don't want us out of Taiwan precipitously only to see the Japanese move in. They don't want us to withdraw from Asia generally and leave the field to Moscow." "Kissinger to Nixon, 'Your Encounter with the Chinese,' 5 February 1972, Top Secret/Sensitive/Exclusively Eyes Only," in William Burr, Sharon Chamberlain, Gao Bei, and Zhao Han, eds., *NSA Electronic Briefing Book No. 70* (Washington, DC: National Security Archive, 2002), https://nsarchive2.gwu.edu/NSAEBB/NSAEBB70/doc27.pdf.

[69] Crawford, *Pivotal Deterrence*, p. 189.

[70] For detailed analysis see Evan Resnick, *Allies of Convenience: A Theory of Bargaining in US Foreign Policy* (New York: Columbia University Press, 2019), chapter 3; Wang Zhongchun, "The Soviet Factor in Sino-American Normalization, 1969–1979," pp. 158–163; Evelyn Goh, "Nixon, Kissinger, and the 'Soviet Card' in the US Opening to China, 1971–1974," *Diplomatic History*, Vol. 29, No. 3 (2005), pp. 475–502; and Goh, *Constructing the U.S. Rapprochement with China, 1961–1974: From "Red Menace" to "Tacit Ally"* (New York Cambridge University Press, 2004), pp. 222–254.

or sacrificed the United States' treaty commitment to Taiwan.[71] Separately or together, the two stressed the benefits of the new US-China relationship in briefings for congressional leaders, cabinet members, the White House staff, and journalists, along with assurances about Taiwan.[72] The reaction to Nixon's trip to Beijing and the Shanghai Communiqué among the Congress, as well as among the media and the public, was largely positive.[73]

Nixon sent Marshall Green, the assistant secretary of state for East Asian Affairs, and John Holdridge, a senior member of the NSC staff, to brief allies in East Asia and Southeast Asia about the Beijing summit. Green and Holdridge flew to Taipei where they briefed Chiang Ching-kuo, as well as the vice president, Yen Chia-ken, and the foreign minister, Chow Shu-kai. Holdridge cabled Kissinger and Haig: "All were concerned particularly over need for continued US support for Taiwan's economic development.... Our relationship with them will continue, because they have nowhere else to go."[74] Upon returning to Washington in early March 1972, Nixon and Kissinger met with Shen to persuade him that Taiwan's interests had not been sacrificed.[75]

In October 1972, Nixon approved the sale of two World War II-era submarines to Taiwan, but with the proviso that the ROC navy only use them for antisubmarine warfare training.[76] US troop levels on Taiwan decreased from 8,568 in FY 1971 to 8,289 in FY 1972.[77] The Nixon administration temporarily deployed two F-4 Phantom squadrons to Taiwan, in exchange for the ROC's transfer of 45 F-5A aircraft to the South Vietnamese air force. This temporary

---

[71] This began with Richard Nixon: "Remarks at Andrews Air Force Base on Returning from the People's Republic of China.," 28 February 1972. Online by Gerhard Peters and John T. Woolley, *The American Presidency Project*, http://www.presidency.ucsb.edu/ws/?pid=3756.

[72] Accinelli, "In Pursuit of a Modus Vivendi," pp. 50.

[73] Ibid., p. 50.

[74] "215. Memorandum for the President's File by John H. Holdridge of the National Security Council Staff, 23 March 1972," *FRUS, 1969–1976, Vol. XVII: China, 1969–1972* (Washington, DC: GPO, 2006), fn. 5. Green and Holdridge also briefed senior officials in Japan, South Korea, South Vietnam, the Philippines, Indonesia, Thailand, Australia, and New Zealand.

[75] "207. Conversation Among President Nixon, His Assistant for National Security Affairs (Kissinger), and the Ambassador of the Republic of China (Shen), 6 March 1972, 4–5:04 P.M.," *FRUS, 1969–1976, Vol. XVII: China, 1969–1972* (Washington, DC: GPO, 2006).

[76] On the submarine transfer see "224. Memorandum from John H. Holdridge of the National Security Council Staff to the President's Assistant for National Security Affairs (Kissinger), 28 April 1972," and "255. Memorandum from John H. Holdridge of the National Security Council Staff to the President's Assistant for National Security Affairs (Kissinger), 6 October 1972," *FRUS, 1969–1976, Vol. XVII: China, 1969–1972* (Washington, DC: GPO, 2006).

[77] Kane, *Global U.S. Troop Deployment, 1950–2006*, available at http://thf_media.s3.amazonaws.com/2006/xls/troopMarch2005.xls (accessed 27 July 2018).

deployment was part of Enhance Plus, the massive US military resupply program for South Vietnam before the 1973 Paris Peace Accords came into effect.[78]

In March 1973, Nixon ordered the withdrawal of the two F-4 squadrons from Taiwan by July 1974. However, he also ordered that F-5As would be used to meet the obligation to replace the 48 F-5As borrowed from the ROC air force under Enhance Plus. The remaining F-4 squadrons would leave Taiwan by 30 May 1975. Nixon further decided the United States and Taiwan would eventually co-produce F-5Es. In the meantime, F-5Es intended for South Korea would be diverted to Taiwan.[79]

While Nixon and Kissinger orchestrated the rapprochement with China and the drawdown of US forces from Vietnam between 1970 and 1973, Taiwan's nuclear programs continued. Publicly, the ROC pledged to maintain its status as a non-nuclear weapons state. Taiwan, at the time recognized by the UN as the Republic of China, signed the Nuclear Nonproliferation Treaty (NPT) when it opened for signatures on 1 June 1968. The ROC National Assembly ratified the treaty in 1970.[80] That same year, the ROC government started negotiations with the IAEA on a safeguard agreement for its nuclear facilities.[81]

The expulsion of the ROC from the UN in October 1971 terminated Taiwan's membership in the IAEA and nullified its signature on the NPT. The ROC, the United States, and the IAEA agreed that an existing trilateral agreement dating from the 1950s would form the basis of safeguards on the ROC nuclear programs. According to that agreement, any nuclear materials Taiwan acquired "would be treated as if they came from the United States and thus, would be subject to restrictions on their applications under US law. The United States, therefore, became the ultimate guarantor of Taiwan's nonnuclear status—backed by IAEA inspections."[82]

The US Export-Import Bank approved a $79.7 million loan to Taipower to build its first nuclear power plant, whose main contractors were Westinghouse Electric Corporation and General Electric (GE), in June 1969. The bank then approved $83.4 million in loans and guarantees for Taipower to build a second

---

[78] "256. Telegram from the Department of State to the Embassy in the Republic of China, 20 October 1972," *FRUS, 1969–1976, Vol. XVII: China, 1969–1972* (Washington, DC: GPO, 2006). Also see Accinelli, *In Pursuit of a Modus Vivendi*, p. 51.

[79] "74. National Security Decision Memorandum 248, 14 March 1973," *FRUS, 1969–1977, Vol. XVIII: China, 1973–1976* (Washington, DC: GPO, 2006).

[80] "No. 10485. Multilateral: Treaty on the Non-Proliferation of Nuclear Weapons, Opened for Signature at London, Moscow, and Washington on 1 July 1968," *Treaty Series: Treaties and International Agreements Registered or Filed and Recorded with the Secretariat of the United Nations*, Vol. 729 (New York: United Nations, 1974), p. 246.

[81] Albright and Gay, "Taiwan: Nuclear Nightmare Averted," p. 58.

[82] Mitchell, "Taiwan's Hsin Chu Program," pp. 297–298.

power plant (also supplied by Westinghouse and GE) in June 1971.[83] Meanwhile, INER sought to purchase a small heavy-water research reactor from Canada. Work began on the Canadian-supplied Taiwan Research Reactor (TRR) on the INER campus in September 1969 and the reactor began operations in April 1973.[84]

A June 1972 *Washington Post* article reported that the Canadian-supplied reactor would be capable of producing twenty-two pounds of plutonium per year, which was more than enough to fuel a nuclear weapon.[85] This was the same type of NRX reactor that India would use to obtain the plutonium necessary for its peaceful nuclear explosion (PNE) in May 1974.[86] The INER also began operating a fuel fabrication plant and purchased approximately 100 metric tons of natural uranium from South Africa, which was far more uranium than needed to operate a research reactor.[87]

"While the nuclear umbrella of the US is still implied by the Mutual Defense Treaty, some on Taiwan may be questioning how long they can count on all-out US support," according to Special National Intelligence Estimate (SNIE) 43-1-72 released in November 1972. "In this perspective, a nuclear weapon option may be seen by the GRC as one of the few feasible deterrents to communist attack in an uncertain future."[88] The State Department's Bureau of Intelligence and Research (INR) concluded in April 1973: "We do not exclude the possibility that a decision to proceed with nuclear weapons development might be taken at some future date, depending on the political climate and Taipei's perception of its military situation."[89] At that point, Taiwan had only one working reactor, the Canadian-built 40 MW research reactor. If ROC scientists intended to acquire

---

[83] "Export-Import Bank Approves $93.4 Million for Taiwan Atom Plant," *Wall Street Journal*, 23 June 1971, p. 26.

[84] "Embassy Taipei to State Department, Chung Shan Nuclear Research Institute, Cable 1197, 24 February 1973," in William Burr, ed., *NSA Electronic Briefing Book No. 20* (Washington, DC: National Security Archive, 1999), http://nsarchive.gwu.edu/NSAEBB/NSAEBB20/docs/doc09.pdf.

[85] Thomas O'Toole, "Canada Building Bomb-Capable Nuclear Reactor on Taiwan," *The Washington Post*, 20 July 1972, p. A23.

[86] Albright and Gay, "Taiwan: Nuclear Nightmare Averted," p. 57.

[87] Mitchell, "Taiwan's Hsin-Chun Program," p. 298.

[88] "Special National Intelligence Estimate 43-1-72, Taipei's Capabilities and Intentions Regarding Nuclear Weapons Development, 16 (?) November 1972, Secret," in William Burr, ed., *NSA Electronic Briefing Book No. 221* (Washington, DC: National Security Archive, 2007), http://nsarchive.gwu.edu/nukevault/ebb221/T-1a.pdf.

[89] "State Department Memorandum of Conversation, ROC Nuclear Intentions, 5 April 1973, with Intelligence and Research (INR) Report on Nuclear Weapons Intentions of the Republic of China Attached," in William Burr, ed., *NSA Electronic Briefing Book No. 20* (Washington, DC: National Security Archive, 1999), http://nsarchive.gwu.edu/NSAEBB/NSAEBB20/docs/doc10.pdf.

plutonium, they would have to run that reactor at full capacity and frequently remove the fuel cores for reprocessing.[90]

CIST representatives approached several foreign suppliers to acquire nuclear technologies that might support a weapons program. In January and February 1973, McConaughey met several times with Foreign Minister Shen Chang-hun to convey the Nixon administration's opposition to the CIST's planned purchase of a reprocessing equipment from a West German firm, the Uhde-Lurgi Group.[91] The State Department learned the plant could reprocess 50 tons of spent nuclear fuel per year.[92]

This reprocessing capacity contradicted assurances that Victor Cheng (aka Cheng Chen-hua), the secretary-general of CAEC, had made in December 1972. Cheng told US officials that Taiwan only sought a small laboratory-sized reprocessing facility.[93] Initially, McConaughey was "reasonably encouraged" that his forceful presentation to Shen had forced the GROC to "think hard before trying to go ahead in the face of explicit US opposition to the reprocessing plant."[94] State Department officials, however, expressed concern about reports from Bonn that CIST representatives had already signed the contract with Uhde-Lurgi.[95]

---

[90] "Memorandum to Mr. [Richard] Sneider from Mary E. McDonnell, US Department of State, Office of Republic of China Affairs, Reported ROC Nuclear Weapons Development Program, 7 April 1973," in William Burr, ed., *NSA Electronic Briefing Book No. 20* (Washington, DC: National Security Archive, 1999), http://nsarchive.gwu.edu/NSAEBB/NSAEBB20/docs/doc11.pdf.

[91] "Embassy Taipei to State Department, Proposed ROC Reprocessing Plant, Cable 685, 31 January 1973," in William Burr, ed., *NSA Electronic Briefing Book No. 20* (Washington, DC: National Security Archive, 1999), http://nsarchive.gwu.edu/NSAEBB/NSAEBB20/docs/doc05.pdf; and "Embassy Taipei to State Department, ROC Decides Against Purchase of Nuclear Reprocessing Plant, Cable 828, 8 February 1973," Ibid., http://nsarchive.gwu.edu/NSAEBB/NSAEBB20/docs/doc06.pdf.

[92] "State Department to Embassies in Bonn, Brussels, and Taipei, Proposed Reprocessing Plant for Republic of China, Cable 2051, 4 January 1973," in William Burr, ed., *NSA Electronic Briefing Book No. 20* (Washington, DC: National Security Archive, 1999), http://nsarchive.gwu.edu/NSAEBB/NSAEBB20/docs/doc01.pdf.

[93] "Memorandum from Leo J. Moser, Office of Republic of China Affairs, to Assistant Secretary for East Asian and Pacific Affairs Marshall Green, Nuclear Materials Reprocessing Plant for ROC, 14 December 1972," in William Burr, ed., *NSA Electronic Briefing Book no. 20* (Washington, DC: National Security Archive, 1999), http://nsarchive.gwu.edu/NSAEBB/NSAEBB20/docs/doc17.pdf.

[94] "Embassy Taipei to State Department, 'Proposed Reprocessing Plant for Republic of China,' Cable 0338, 16 January 1973," in William Burr, ed., *NSA Electronic Briefing Book no. 20* (Washington, DC: National Security Archive, 1999), https://nsarchive2.gwu.edu/NSAEBB/NSAEBB20/docs/doc02.pdf.

[95] "State Department to Embassies in Bonn, Brussels, and Taipei, 'Proposed Reprocessing Plant for Republic of China,' Cable 12137, 20 January 1973," in William Burr, ed., *NSA Electronic Briefing Book no. 20* (Washington, DC: National Security Archive, 1999), https://nsarchive2.gwu.edu/NSAEBB/NSAEBB20/docs/doc03.pdf.

McConaughey met again with Shen on 30 January 1973 to convey opposition to the West German contract. The foreign minister assured McConaughey that the ROC had "neither the intent nor the ability to acquire nuclear weapons." McConaughey questioned whether the ROC wished to proceed acquire a reprocessing plant from a West German supplier at the risk of jeopardizing the plans to acquire four large nuclear power plants from US suppliers, since the latter would seem to be of far greater consequence for the Taiwanese economy.[96]

Meanwhile, Martin Hillenbrand, the US ambassador to Bonn, raised similar concerns about Taiwan's reprocessing plant purchase with the FRG Foreign Office, which, in turn, persuaded Uhde-Lurgi to cancel the contract on 7 February.[97] A few weeks later, McConaughey reported that the CIST director, Chien Chi-peng, had initiated the plan to purchase a German reprocessing plant with a capacity of 50 tons per year. Furthermore, the president of Taipower, L. J. Chien, had no interest in reprocessing technology and claimed that he was unaware that CIST planned to reprocess nuclear fuel for his company.[98]

Cheng traveled to Washington in late March 1973 and met with Richard Sneider, then deputy assistant secretary of state for East Asian Affairs. Claiming to have learned about the West German negotiations only when US officials raised the topic in December, Cheng said that Taiwan did not "keep any nuclear secrets from it friends." When Sneider suggested sending a team of US nuclear experts to Taiwan for the ostensible purpose of discussing civil nuclear cooperation, Cheng seemed amenable.[99]

In September 1973, Arthur W. Hummel Jr., the assistant secretary of state for East Asian Affairs, told Cheng that a reprocessing plant would not be economical relative to the scale of Taiwan's energy needs. Furthermore, Hummel argued that acquisition of such a plant could "cause some countries to be concerned about applications to which ROC intends to put its nuclear program."[100] The

---

[96] "Embassy Taipei to State Department, Proposed ROC Reprocessing Plant, Cable 685, 31 January 1973," in William Burr, ed., *NSA Electronic Briefing Book No. 20* (Washington, DC: National Security Archive, 1999), http://nsarchive.gwu.edu/NSAEBB/NSAEBB20/docs/doc05.pdf.

[97] "Embassy Taipei to State Department, ROC Decides Against Purchase of Nuclear Reprocessing Plant, Cable 828, 8 February 1973," in William Burr, ed., *NSA Electronic Briefing Book No. 20* (Washington, DC: National Security Archive, 1999), http://nsarchive.gwu.edu/NSAEBB/NSAEBB20/docs/doc06.pdf.

[98] "Embassy Taipei to State Department, Chung Shan Nuclear Research Institute, Cable 1197, 24 February 1973," in William Burr, ed., *NSA Electronic Briefing Book No. 20* (Washington, DC: National Security Archive, 1999), http://nsarchive.gwu.edu/NSAEBB/NSAEBB20/docs/doc09.pdf.

[99] "State Department to Embassies in Taipei and Tokyo, ROC Nuclear Research, Cable 51747, 21 March 1973," in William Burr, ed., *NSA Electronic Briefing Book No. 20* (Washington, DC: National Security Archive, 1999), http://nsarchive.gwu.edu/NSAEBB/NSAEBB20/docs/doc29.pdf.

[100] "State Department Cable 174889 to US Embassy Taiwan, Call on Assistant Secretary Hummel by Victor Cheng, 4 September 1973, Secret," in William Burr, ed., *NSA Electronic Briefing Book No. 221*

following month, the Dutch engineering firm Comprimo informed the State Department that the reprocessing project was still alive and that Saint-Gobain Nucléaire had been chosen as the project architect. The department proposed sending a study group comprised officials from the Atomic Energy Commission (AEC), the Arms Control and Disarmament Agency (ACADA), the Bureau of International Scientific and Technological Affairs (SCI) at the State Department, and the Embassy Taipei, to tour nuclear facilities at CAEC headquarters and the CIST and INER campuses, and to discuss issues surrounding the Taiwanese nuclear program with Shen and Cheng.[101]

A November 1973 State Department cable stated the study team's goal "is to underscore our concern that ROC may intend to develop nuclear weapons and seriousness with which we regard this matter."[102] The study team toured the facilities and urged Taiwanese officials to observe "even stricter standards than other countries and to go out of its way to remove any ambiguity" about their nuclear intentions. They also mentioned the United States would be willing to facilitate Taiwan's civilian nuclear program, as long as there was no indication of a weapons program. Shen told the team that the ROC government had "definitely dropped" the reprocessing plant purchase.[103] Still, William Gleysteen, then deputy chief of mission in Taipei and a member of the study team, warned, "We cannot guarantee that certain people will not continue to nudge the ROC into activities associated with a nuclear weapons program."[104]

In September 1974 the CIA concluded, "Taipei conducts its small nuclear program with a nuclear option in mind, and it will be in a position to fabricate a

(Washington, DC: National Security Archive, 2007), http://nsarchive.gwu.edu/nukevault/ebb221/T-2a.pdf.

[101] The study group comprised: Abraham Friedman, director of international energy programs, AEC; Nelson Sievering, deputy director of SCI; Franck Helfrich of ACADA; and William Gleysteen, then deputy chief of mission in the US Embassy in Taipei. See "Roger Sullivan to Assistant Secretary of State for Far East and Pacific Affairs Arthur W. Hummel, Jr., Nuclear Study Group Visit to Taiwan, 29 October 1973, Secret," in William Burr, ed., *NSA Electronic Briefing Book No. 221* (Washington, DC: National Security Archive, 2007).

[102] "State Department Cable 223116 to US Embassy Taiwan, Atomic Energy Study Team Visit to Taiwan, 14 November 1973," in William Burr, ed., *NSA Electronic Briefing Book No. 221* (Washington, DC: National Security Archive, 2007), http://nsarchive.gwu.edu/nukevault/ebb221/T-3a.pdf.

[103] "US Embassy Taiwan Cable 7051 to State Department, Fonmin Reaffirms ROC Decision to Refrain from Acquiring Nuclear Reprocessing Plant, 23 November 1973," in William Burr, ed., *NSA Electronic Briefing Book No. 221* (Washington, DC: National Security Archive, 2007), http://nsarchive.gwu.edu/nukevault/ebb221/T-3b.pdf.

[104] "Letter, William Gleysteen, Deputy Chief of Mission, Taiwan, to Thomas Bleha, Deputy Director, Republic of China Affairs, 23 November 1973, Secret," in William Burr, ed., *NSA Electronic Briefing Book No. 221* (Washington, DC: National Security Archive, 2007), http://nsarchive.gwu.edu/nukevault/ebb221/T-3c.pdf.

nuclear device within five years or so."[105] Likewise, according to the November 1974 report from the Interdepartmental Regional Group for East Asia and the Pacific: "the ROC has not abandoned its covert military nuclear energy research program and it probably possesses most of the technological know-how for the development of a nuclear device." It also noted, "ROC access to US military equipment is a major element in Taiwan's sense of security," and that the United States would need to maintain some type of military supply relationship with Taiwan post-normalization.[106]

The Ford Administration's Démarche over Taiwanese Reprocessing, 1975–1976

The start of the acute phase of the proliferation dispute coincided with the impending collapse of the United States' strategic position in Southeast Asia. By the end of April 1975, the North Vietnamese army and the Viet Cong had captured the South Vietnam's capital, Saigon, while the Khmer Rouge had captured Cambodia's capital, Phnom Penh.

Nonetheless, in East Asia, the distribution of capabilities among the major states (China, Japan, the two Koreas, and Taiwan) appeared favorable to the United States' interests in 1975 and 1976. Although relations between the Soviet Union and China had improved since March 1969, the two viewed continued to each other as adversaries. According to a July 1974 CIA report: "China will attempt to use US influence to deter the USSR from attacking China and to offset Soviet efforts to encircle or contain China."[107] The report also put the likelihood of a Soviet conventional or nuclear strike against Chinese territory as no greater than one-in-five, at least for the next decade.[108]

The time horizons for threats to US interests in East Asia appeared long to Washington policymakers. The near-term likelihood of a Chinese attack on

---

[105] "Director of Central Intelligence, Memorandum, Prospects for Further Proliferation of Nuclear Weapons, 4 September 1974, Secret," in Jeffrey Richelson, ed., *NSA Electronic Briefing Book No. 181* (Washington, DC: National Security Archive, 2006), https://nsarchive2.gwu.edu/NSAEBB/NSAEBB181/sa08.pdf.

[106] "90. Study Prepared by the Ad Hoc Interdepartmental Regional Group for East Asia and the Pacific, Washington, 12 November 1974," *FRUS 1969–1976, Vol. XVIII: China, 1973–1976* (Washington, DC: GPO, 2006). This study was prepared pursuit to NSSM 212, "US Security Assistance to the Republic of China," 8 October 1974, at https://www.fordlibrarymuseum.gov/library/document/0310/nssm212.pdf.

[107] "84. Paper Prepared in the Central Intelligence Agency, July 1974," *FRUS, 1969–1976, Vol. XVIII: China, 1973–1976* (Washington, DC: GPO, 2006).

[108] Ibid.

Taiwan appeared low. In June 1976, the PLA did stage large amphibious military exercises off the coast of Fujian, directly opposite Taiwan. While these exercises did include offensive weapons and a simulated amphibious assault on Taiwan, the CIA concluded they were not threatening and probably reflected Chinese leaders' irritation over the slow pace of US-PRC normalization.[109] CIA identified several factors that made a Chinese attack on Taiwan unlikely in the near term, including a "reluctance to alter the delicately balanced Sino-US-Soviet triangle," a "fear of further growth of Soviet influence in Southeast Asia," and an "inability to mount amphibious operations on a large scale."[110]

During his November 1973 meeting with Zhou in Beijing, Kissinger reaffirmed the "one China" formula as well as the Nixon administration's determination to continue withdrawing US troops and military aircraft from Taiwan. He also confirmed the president's personal intent to normalize relations with China before the end of his second term in January 1977, most likely in mid-1976.[111] Normalization stalled after the opening of liaison offices in Washington and Beijing in May 1973. The Watergate scandal, which led to Nixon's resignation on 9 August 1974 in the face of almost certain impeachment, completely upended the normalization timetable.

The withdrawal of US troops and weapons from Taiwan continued. David Bruce, the deputy chief of mission the Taipei Embassy, reported in May 1974 that while Chiang Ching-kuo "in effect gave us a green light to withdraw nuclear weapons in accordance with the planned schedule," he attempted to postpone the withdrawal of the F-4 squadrons.[112] In May 1974, the Nixon administration announced the withdrawal of all US combat aircraft from Taiwan. The process was complete in June 1975 when the second of the two F-4 squadrons departed. By that time, the US troop contingent had declined to about 4,000,

---

[109] Ross, *Negotiating Cooperation*, p. 33. Also see "Cable from Department of State to US Liaison Office–Beijing, US Embassy Taipei, and US Consulate General Hong Kong, re: Developments in Taiwan Strait, 21 July 1976, Secret," *DNSA Collection: China and US Intelligence, 1945–2010* (Ann Arbor, MI: ProQuest, 2016), https://proquest.com/docview/1679089371.

[110] Eastern Forces Division, Office of Strategic Research, Central Intelligence Agency, *Memo EF-7509: PRC Military Options in the Taiwan Strait and the South China Sea in 1976*, Secret, 1 September 1975 (Washington, DC: Central Intelligence Agency), p. 32, https://www.cia.gov/library/readingroom/docs/CIA-RDP86T00608R000700100001-4.pdf.

[111] "56. Memorandum of Conversation, Beijing, 11 November 1973, 3:15–7:00 P.M.," *FRUS, 1969–1976, Vol. XVIII: China, 1973–1976* (Washington, DC: GPO, 2006).

[112] "Telegram from US Embassy Taipei to Department of State, re: Conversation with CCK Regarding Redeployments, 14 March 1974, Top Secret," *DNSA Collection: China and U.S. Intelligence, 1945–2010* (Ann Arbor, MI: ProQuest, 2016), p. 4, https://search.proquest.com/docview/1679090047.

with another 1,200 military personnel scheduled to depart by the end of July.[113]

The Ford administration sought to cultivate China as an ally of convenience against the Soviet Union. On 18 August 1974, Secretary of State Henry Kissinger wrote to the new president, Gerald R. Ford, that: "our defense treaty with Taiwan cannot survive in any legal sense once we have recognized Peking and acknowledged 'One China.'" Post-normalization, Taiwan's security "will probably have to rest chiefly on declarations rather than any formal instrument."[114] However, in the aftermath of Watergate and with a presidential election looming, Ford concluded it simply too politically costly to establish full diplomatic relations with Beijing and to severing official ties with Taipei by mid-1976.

Conservative Republicans, notably Senators Goldwater, Jesse Helms (NC), and Strom Thurmond (SC), who had been critical of Nixon's opening to China in 1972, threatened to back Reagan's challenge to Ford for the 1976 Republican presidential nomination.[115] The former California governor did mount a primary challenge, during which he strongly criticized the Ford and Kissinger for cozying up to "Red China" and abandoning "Free China" on the campaign trail.[116] Thus, in 1975 and 1976, Ford and Kissinger faced the delicate balancing act of maintaining momentum for an alliance of convenience with China, while also not moving too quickly to establish full diplomatic relations with Beijing and sever diplomatic ties with Taipei.

Taiwan continued to be an obstacle for any US-China alliance of convenience for several reasons. First, Chinese leaders insisted that the United States break diplomatic relations with the ROC and end military assistance as a precondition for full diplomatic relations. In November 1974, Kissinger returned to Beijing hoping to obtain Chinese leaders' commitment to a peaceful resolution of the Taiwan issue and their agreement to the United States maintaining a liaison office

---

[113] See Leslie H. Gelb, "US Will Pull Out Planes on Taiwan," *New York Times*, 19 May 1974, p. 8; and Bernard S. Gwertzman, "US Has Removed Combat Aircraft Based on Taiwan," *New York Times*, 8 June 1975, p. 1.

[114] "People's Republic of China [Briefing Paper for President Ford], 14 August 1974, Top Secret, Nodis," *DNSA Collection: China, 1960–1998* (Ann Arbor, MI: ProQuest, 2016), p. 12, https://search.proquest.com/docview/1679040577.

[115] See Ross, *Negotiating Cooperation*, pp. 80–81. For Goldwater's Senate floor remarks on "Free China" see 18 February 1975, 121 *Congressional Record*, Vol. 1, Part 3 (Washington, DC: GPO, 1975), pp. 3110–3111. For Helm's floor remarks on the same see Ibid., 5 February 1975, p. 2567. For Thurmond's remarks on the same see Ibid., Part 10, p. 12904. Also see Leslie H. Gelb, "A Shift on Taiwan by US Is Opposed," *New York Times*, 10 May 1975, p. 11.

[116] See James M. Nordheimer, "Reagan Says US Must Continue Its Support of Taiwan Regime," *New York Times*, 14 February 1976, p. 22; "Kissinger, in Rebutting Reagan, Calls Charges 'False Inventions,'" *New York Times*, 2 April 1976, p. 8; and Ronald Reagan, "Expanding Our Ties with China," *New York Times*, 28 July 1976, p. 24.

in Taipei after normalization with Beijing. Vice Premier Deng Xiaoping, then deputizing for the ill Zhou, told Kissinger such an arrangement would merely be a "variation of one China and one Taiwan" and that if the United States wanted full diplomatic relations with China "then the treaty you have with Taiwan must be done away with."[117]

Meeting in New York City on 28 October 1975, Kissinger candidly told the Chinese foreign minister, Qiao Guanhua, that it would be "domestically impossible" for Ford to announce the normalization of US-PRC relations and the severance of diplomatic ties with Taiwan during the president's planned December 1975 visit to Beijing.[118] During that visit, Ford again raised the prospect of some type of official US representation on Taiwan after normalization.[119] Deng replied that normalization between Beijing and Washington could only be realized with "the abolishing of the so-called US–Chiang Kai-shek defense treaty, and the withdrawal of United States troops from Taiwan, and the severing of diplomatic relations with the Chiang Kai-shek government."[120]

Second, Taiwan's efforts to acquire uranium processing technology from foreign suppliers would likely be seen as a provocation by Chinese leaders. Kissinger had assured Zhou in November 1973 that the United States would withdraw its nuclear weapons from Taiwan, along with its troops and conventional weapons.[121] Mao told Kissinger: "I say that we can do without Taiwan for the time being, and let it come after one hundred years," adding "It is only such an island with a population of a dozen or more million."[122]

Deng told Kissinger and later Ford that China had no intention of attacking Taiwan in the near term, although like them he declined to repudiate the threat of force.[123] Yet if Taiwan developed a nuclear weapon capability, then it might be able to deter Chinese military operations against the island and thus call into question the "one China" formula. As SNIE 43-1-72 had warned, China would

---

[117] "94. Memorandum of Conversation, Beijing, 26 November 1974, 3:40–5:00 P.M.," *FRUS, 1969–1976, Vol. XVIII: China, 1973–1976* (Washington, DC: GPO, 2006).

[118] "119. Memorandum of Conversation, New York City, 28 September 1975, 8:10–11:55 P.M.," *FRUS, 1969–1976, Vol. XVIII: China, 1973–1976* (Washington, DC: GPO, 2006).

[119] In mid-October 1975, Goldwater gave a public speech urging Ford to drop plans to visit Beijing and visit Taipei instead. See "Goldwater Urges Ford to Visit Taipei," *New York Times*, 16 October 1975, p. 10.

[120] "137. Memorandum of Conversation, Beijing, 4 December 1975," *FRUS 1969–1976, Vol. XVIII: China, 1973–1976* (Washington, DC: GPO, 2006).

[121] "56. Memorandum of Conversation, Beijing, 11 November 1973, 3:15–7:00 P.M.," *FRUS, 1969–1976, Vol. XVIII: China, 1973–1976* (Washington, DC: GPO, 2006).

[122] "58. Memorandum of Conversation, Beijing, 12 November 1973, 5:40–8:25 P.M.," *FRUS, 1969–1976, Vol. XVIII: China, 1973–1976* (Washington, DC: GPO, 2006).

[123] On this point, see "94. Memorandum of Conversation, Beijing, 26 November 1974, 3:40–5:00 P.M.," *FRUS, 1969–1976, Vol. XVIII: China, 1973–1976* (Washington, DC: GPO, 2006).

likely treat evidence of a Taiwanese nuclear weapons capability as a threat to peace and stability in East Asia.[124]

Third, although Ford administration officials realized that the US-ROC Mutual Defense Treaty would have to end, they also sought to maintain a stable military balance across the Taiwan Strait. The Interdepartmental Regional Group for East Asia concluded: "Severely reduced access to US equipment leading to an unmistakable deterioration of ROC military capabilities would risk the danger of setting off a train of developments on Taiwan seriously harmful to our (and possibly PRC) interests."[125]

A May 1976 joint CIA and Defense Intelligence Agency (DIA) report stated that the ROC had "little prospect of becoming self-sufficient in arms production in the next decade" because it "never developed the high technologies and skills necessary for manufacturing arms and military supplies on a commercial basis."[126] Therefore to avoid further complications in US-PRC normalization, in June 1976, Lt. Gen. Brent Scowcroft, the national security adviser, recommended Ford approve an arms transfer policy of "limited ROC access to new weapons," that is, the transfer of arms that "were essentially defensive in nature" and "did not contribute to the ROC's nuclear, long-range/intermediate-range missile, or chemical warfare development programs."[127]

Finally, the INER's efforts to acquire reprocessing technology occurred against the backdrop of a US presidential election and increased congressional attention to nuclear proliferation. Congressional Democrats, as well as some Republicans, were critical of the Nixon administration's handling of nonproliferation issues, especially after India's atomic bomb test in May 1974.

In December 1975, the Senate passed a resolution sponsored by Senators Alan Cranston (D-CA), Charles Mathias (R-MD), and Bill Brock (R-TN) calling upon the administration to impose tighter export restrictions on nuclear

---

[124] "Special National Intelligence Estimate 43-1-72, Taipei's Capabilities and Intentions Regarding Nuclear Weapons Development, 16 (?) November 1972, Secret," in William Burr, ed., *NSA Electronic Briefing Book No. 221* (Washington, DC: National Security Archive, 2007), http://nsarchive.gwu.edu/nukevault/ebb221/T-1a.pdf.

[125] "90. Study Prepared by the Ad Hoc Interdepartmental Regional Group for East Asia and the Pacific, Washington, 12 November 1974," *FRUS 1969–1976, Vol. XVIII: China, 1973–1976* (Washington, DC: GPO, 2006).

[126] "Central Intelligence Agency and Defense Intelligence Agency, Secret, Interagency Intelligence Memorandum (IIM 76-020): Prospects for Arms Production and Development in the Republic of China, May 1976," *DNSA Collection: China and US Intelligence, 1945–2010* (Ann Arbor, MI: ProQuest, 2016), p. 14, https://search.proquest.com/docview/1679090839.

[127] "Memorandum for the President from Brent Scowcroft, re: US Security Assistance to the Republic of China, NSSM 212, June 1976, Top Secret," *DNSA Collection: China, 1960–1998* (Ann Arbor, MI: ProQuest, 2016), p. 6, https://search.proquest.com/docview/1679041057.

technology.¹²⁸ Senator Stuart Symington (D-MO) proposed an amendment to the 1961 Foreign Assistance Act that would require the president to suspend foreign military and most economic assistance to states whose nuclear energy programs did not comply with IAEA safeguards. The Symington Amendment passed both houses of Congress in June 1976, but it did not go into effect until April 1977.¹²⁹

Concerns about Taiwanese contacts with French, Belgian, and Dutch suppliers in summer 1976 prompted the Ford administration to issue a démarche to Chiang. Specifically, the administration threatened to terminate US-ROC nuclear cooperation, unless the ROC government ceased acquisition efforts or if it failed to adhere to IAEA guidelines regarding the disposition of spent nuclear fuel.

Yet, even as the proliferation dispute unfolded, Ford administration officials continued with plans for a $250 million arms package for Taiwan, including a $34 million air defense system, upgrades to the ROC's existing battalion of 24 Hawk anti-aircraft missiles and the sale of a new Hawk battalion, and 60 additional F-5E interceptor aircraft.¹³⁰ The ROC government had already signed a $95 million contract with Northrop Corporation to purchase 120 F-5E interceptors, with the proviso that Taiwan would be licensed to produce and assemble parts. US arms transfers to Taiwan totaled $196 million in FY 1974, then $215 million in FY 1975 and $293 million in FY 1976.¹³¹ Thus, the strategies the Ford administration pursued vis-à-vis the ROC in summer and autumn 1976 were a hybrid of coercion (threats to suspend nuclear cooperation) and accommodation (arms transfers).

In July 1976, the US Embassy in the Hague reported that Dutch officials learned about negotiations between the Taiwanese and the Dutch energy company Comprimo. An executive with Comprimo had discussed the issue with the Ministry of Foreign Affairs, saying that "He had the impression there was a real

---

¹²⁸ S. Res. 221, reprinted in Joint Committee on Atomic Energy, "S. 1439 Export Reorganization Act of 1976: Hearing Before the Joint Committee on Atomic Energy, Congress of the United States, 94th Congress, Second Session, 22 June 1976," *Joint Committee on Atomic Energy Digital Archive* (Stanford, CA: Stanford University Press, 1976), pp. 198–201.

¹²⁹ Defense Security Cooperation Agency, 2017. Chapter 1: Security Cooperation Overview and Relationships. In *Security Assistance Management Manual*, Defense Security Cooperation Agency, http://samm.dsca.mil/chapter/chapter-1#C1.2 (accessed 10 January 2017).

¹³⁰ "Memorandum for the Assistant to the President for National Security Affairs (Brent Scowcroft) from the Deputy Secretary of Defense (William P. Clement), re: US Security Assistance to the Republic of China: NSSM 212, 12 April 1976, Top Secret," *DNSA Collection: Presidential Directives, Part II* (Ann Arbor, MI: ProQuest, 2016), p. 7, https://search.proquest.com/docview/1679050966.

¹³¹ Leslie H. Gelb, "US Arming Taiwan Against an Attack," *New York Times*, 4 August 1976, p. 69.

effort in the ROC to gain knowledge and understanding of the entire nuclear cycle." The ministry told the Comprimo official that they would "look with disfavor even on the passing abroad of technical know-how."[132]

On 30 July, Kissinger informed the Taipei Embassy that he was considering another démarche to the ROC on reprocessing, and would request an assessment and recommendation "as soon as they are available."[133] In mid-August, US ambassador Leonard Unger presented Frederick F. Chien (aka Chien Fu), the ROC vice minister of foreign affairs, with a file on nuclear reprocessing efforts the United States was monitoring around the world to "underline continuing concern the US government has about this nuclear proliferation problem wherever it may arise in the world." Unger stated Chien "well understood" the United States' concerns and that Ford administration officials "need have no worries here."[134]

Over the next few weeks, administration officials confronted two other worrying developments. First, they received intelligence that Taiwanese agents had also made inquiries of Belgo Nucléaire (BN), a Belgian nuclear firm, about the purchase of reprocessing components; BN declined the request.[135] Second, the *New York Times* and the *Washington Post* published articles about Taiwan's secret reprocessing efforts, citing unnamed sources from the IAEA, as well from the ACADA and the Energy Development Research Administration (EDRA).[136]

On 31 August, Shen summoned Unger to discuss the *Washington Post* article. "The ROC is unchanging in its position not to make nuclear weapons," as Chiang Ching-kuo had previous expressed, the foreign minister claimed. He added that the ROC would continue to abide by IAEA safeguards and its NPT

---

[132] "US Embassy Netherlands Cable 8502 to State Department, Nuclear Fuel Processing Plant, 7 July 1976, Secret Limdis," in William Burr, ed., *NSA Electronic Briefing Book No. 221* (Washington, DC: National Security Archive, 2007), http://nsarchive.gwu.edu/nukevault/ebb221/T-4a.pdf.

[133] "State Department Cable 188617 to US Embassy Taiwan, Nuclear Reprocessing, 30 July 1976, Secret Limdis," in William Burr, ed., *NSA Electronic Briefing Book No. 221* (Washington, DC: National Security Archive, 2007), http://nsarchive.gwu.edu/nukevault/ebb221/T-4c.pdf.

[134] "US Embassy Taiwan Cable 5536 to State Department, Nuclear Fuel Reprocessing Plant, 16 August 1976, Secret Exdis," in William Burr, ed., *NSA Electronic Briefing Book No. 221* (Washington, DC: National Security Archive, 2007), http://nsarchive.gwu.edu/nukevault/ebb221/T-4b.pdf.

[135] "US Embassy Belgium Cable 8149 to State Department, Nuclear Processing in ROC, 20 August 1976, Secret Limdis," in William Burr, ed., *NSA Electronic Briefing Book No. 221* (Washington, DC: National Security Archive, 2007), http://nsarchive.gwu.edu/nukevault/ebb221/T-4e.pdf.

[136] See Edward Schumacher, "Taiwan Seen Reprocessing Nuclear Fuel," *Washington Post*, 29 August 1976, p. 1; and Fox Butterfield, "Taiwan Denying Atomic Operation," *New York Times*, 5 September 1976, p. 5. EDRA was the successor agency to the Atomic Energy Commission (AEC). Also see "US Mission IAEA Cable 6195 to State Department, Fuel Reprocessing Pilot Plant in Taiwan, 19 August 1976, Confidential," in William Burr, ed., *NSA Electronic Briefing Book No. 221* (Washington, DC: National Security Archive, 2007), http://nsarchive.gwu.edu/nukevault/ebb221/T-4d.pdf.

obligations. Furthermore, the nuclear program was solely "for peaceful purposes which are important to the island's economic development and which depend on the supply of fuel from the US."[137]

Kissinger sent a cable to Unger on 4 September instructing him to deliver a formal démarche to Shen and Chiang that: "No repeat no reprocessing shall take place on Taiwan." Citing intelligence about INER's "clandestine efforts to acquire reprocessing technology and equipment from Comprimo," Kissinger wrote that the Ford administration did not accept the claim that a reprocessing plant was necessary to support the Taiwanese nuclear power program. Consequently, any further effort by the GROC or its subsidiaries acquire reprocessing technology would jeopardize future US-Taiwan nuclear cooperation.[138]

Unger, accompanied by Gleysteen, meet with Chiang and Shen on 14 September. Chiang claimed that Shen's reply to the 7 September démarche "should have left no question about the GROC's nuclear research policy." He also stated that "We do not deny that we made some progress in nuclear research, but this process is not toward weapons." To avoid any further misunderstanding, the premier stated that the GROC had stopped research inquiries into the reprocessing facility and would invite US government experts as "resident, long-term advisers" to the INER, CIST, and AEC facilities. In his cable to the State Department, Unger wrote: "I could not escape the impression that the premier had hoped to be able to obfuscate or skirt the principal cause of our current concern namely, GROC interest in acquiring a pilot reprocessing facility."[139]

Two days after this meeting, the English-language newspaper *The China Post* and Chinese-language newspapers in Taiwan printed stories about Chiang's emphatic declaration at the 16 September Executive Yuan (cabinet) meeting that the ROC had never intended to develop nuclear weapons. The Executive Yuan also released a public statement: "The GROC has no intention whatsoever to use its human and natural resources for the development of nuclear weapons or

---

[137] "US Embassy Taiwan Cable 5965 to State Department, Ambassador Meets with Foreign Minister Shen to Discuss Recent Press Reports Concerning Reprocessing on Taiwan, 31 August 1976, Confidential," in William Burr, ed., *NSA Electronic Briefing Book No. 221* (Washington, DC: National Security Archive, 2007), http://nsarchive.gwu.edu/nukevault/ebb221/T-5a.pdf.

[138] "State Department Cable 91733 to Embassy Taiwan, Roc's Nuclear Intentions, 4 September 1976, Secret Exdis," in William Burr, ed., *NSA Electronic Briefing Book No. 221* (Washington, DC: National Security Archive, 2007), http://nsarchive.gwu.edu/nukevault/ebb221/T-6a.pdf.

[139] "US Embassy Taiwan Cable 6272 to State Department, ROC's Nuclear Intentions: Conversation with Premier Chiang Ching-Kuo, 15 September 1976, Secret Nodis," in William Burr, ed., *NSA Electronic Briefing Book no. 221* (Washington, DC: National Security Archive, 2007), http://nsarchive.gwu.edu/nukevault/ebb221/T-7a.pdf.

to obtain equipment for reprocessing spent nuclear fuel" and promising to open nuclear facilities to IAEA inspections.[140]

Neoclassical realist theory would expect the Ford administration to pursue a coercive strategy to thwart Taiwan's renewed efforts to acquire reprocessing technology. Recall, the theory holds that US policymakers will likely pursue a coercive strategy toward an ally's nuclear weapons program, when they perceive a favorable regional power distribution and long time horizons for threats, but who also confront low domestic mobilization hurdles. The domestic mobilization hurdles for a coercive strategy to thwart continuing Taiwanese efforts to acquire reprocessing technology were relatively low for the Ford administration in 1976.

Senior and mid-level administration officials threatened to curtail future US-ROC civil nuclear cooperation if Chiang Ching-kuo's government did not cease efforts to acquire reprocessing technology from foreign suppliers. There was opposition among the conservative wing of the Republican Party to the normalization of US-PRC relations and severing diplomatic relations with Taiwan. There was, however, congressional support for tighter nuclear export controls and stricter conditions for nuclear cooperation overall. Furthermore, Ford administration officials did not threaten to curtail US foreign military assistance to Taiwan. On the contrary, officials continued with plans to transfer defensive weapons systems to Taipei, including 60 additional F-5E interceptors and the Hawk battalion. And since the United States remained Taiwan's only arms supplier, Washington would retain a great deal of leverage over Taipei.

Nuclear domino theory would expect the Ford administration to have pursued a coercive strategy to halt Taiwan's acquisition of reprocessing technology if administration officials perceived an increased likelihood of reactive proliferation by neighboring states. Yet, there is little documentary evidence to suggest that administration officials saw any links between the South Korean and Taiwanese nuclear weapons programs at this point. And, as noted in the previous chapter, there is little evidence that the Ford administration perceived an increased likelihood of Japanese nuclear proliferation in 1975 and 1976.

Credible sanctions theory would expect the comprehensive nonproliferation legislation enacted by the Congress in June 1976 to have pushed the Ford administration to adopt a more coercive strategy toward Taiwan's nuclear activities than it otherwise might. The evidence is, at best, mixed in this regard. India's nuclear detonation in May 1974 did have a catalyzing effect on how members of

---

[140] "US Embassy Taiwan Cable 6301 to State Department, ROC's Nuclear Intentions, 17 September 1976, Unclassified," in William Burr, ed., *NSA Electronic Briefing Book No. 221* (Washington, DC: National Security Archive, 2007), http://nsarchive.gwu.edu/nukevault/ebb221/T-7b.pdf.

Congress and administration officials thought about global risks of nuclear proliferation. Influential senators and representatives from both parties supported tighter export controls on nuclear technology and making US foreign military and economic assistance conditional on compliance with the NPT and IAEA safeguards.

That said, it is difficult to establish a causal link between the nonproliferation legislation and the strategy the Ford administration actually pursued in summer and autumn 1976. The Symington Amendment did not come into force until April 1977. Although Kissinger did instruct Unger to invoke the threat of sanctions, he and other senior administration officials had actually decided upon the coercive part of their strategy months before the legislation passed Congress.[141] Furthermore, the administration never explicitly or implicitly threatened to cut off US military assistance to Taiwan; instead the State Department merely warned that any further efforts by the ROC government or its agencies to acquire reprocessing technology would jeopardize future civil nuclear cooperation.

Finally, security commitment theory suggests that the Ford administration would pursue an accommodative strategy to dissuade Chiang and his advisers from continuing their quest for reprocessing technology. An offer to postpone withdrawing US troops and weapons systems as an inducement for the ROC to foreswear unsafeguarded reprocessing technology might be consistent with this hypothesis. Ford administration officials, however, never considered revising the troop withdrawal schedule. The number of US troops deployed on Taiwan had dropped precipitously from slightly over 10,000 in January 1969 to approximately 3,800 by August 1975. Offering to postpone the scheduled withdrawal of the remaining US troops would have been politically and strategically untenable. In March 1976, a State Department spokesperson confirmed troop withdrawals would continue.[142] On 20 September 1976, Ford ordered a further reduction of DoD personnel on Taiwan to 1,400 by 31 December.[143]

Ford lost the 1976 presidential election to the Democratic nominee, former Georgia governor Jimmy Carter. Negotiations between the US Embassy Taipei and the ROC Ministry of Foreign Affairs over the US nuclear expert team's visit to Taiwan continued while the presidential transition began in Washington. "We

---

[141] "State Department Cable 91733 to Embassy Taiwan, ROC's Nuclear Intentions, 4 September 1976, Secret Exdis," in William Burr, ed., *NSA Electronic Briefing Book No. 221* (Washington, DC: National Security Archive, 2007), http://nsarchive.gwu.edu/nukevault/ebb221/T-6a.pdf.

[142] "US Says It Intends to Continue Cutting Forces on Taiwan," *New York Times*, 12 March 1976, p. 5.

[143] NSDM 339, "US Force Reductions on Taiwan," 20 September 1976, at https://www.fordlibrarymuseum.gov/library/document/0310/nsdm339.pdf.

have compelling evidence that in spite of solemn and public assurances given by GROC and personally by Premier Chiang, the [Nationalist] Chinese may not have given up their intentions of acquiring a capability for reprocessing nuclear fuels," Unger cabled the State Department in late December.[144]

On 8 January 1977, Kissinger cabled Unger to say he was "encouraged" that the government of the Netherlands had pressured the Dutch engineering firm Comprimo to "suspend" contacts with the INER. Nonetheless, he believed there was a need "to take steps on the Taiwan end as well as to assure the ROC connection with Comprimo has been terminated" and to convey that the United States would remain vigilant in pressing the nuclear issue with Taiwan.[145]

The Carter Administration: US-PRC Normalization and Démarche over TRR, 1977–1978

Like the outgoing Ford administration, the incoming Carter administration sought China as an ally of convenience. To achieve this objective, the new president and his national security team would need to move expeditiously on the long-delayed process of normalizing diplomatic relations with Beijing. Administration officials recognized a sudden termination of US military assistance to Taipei would harm the strategic interests of Washington, and arguably those of Beijing as well. However, Taiwan's unsafeguarded reprocessing of nuclear fuel, conflicting statements by ROC officials (including Chiang) about their nuclear intentions, and the discovery of a secret uranium enrichment program had the potential to derail progress of the US-China normalization.

In 1977 and 1978, the United States continued to face a favorable power distribution in East Asia, as well as long time horizons for threats to US interests in that region. The Soviet Union and China continued to view each other as adversaries. The distribution of military capabilities among the region's major states appeared to be stable. Furthermore, the near-term likelihood of armed conflict in the region's two main flash points—the Demilitarized Zone (DMZ) on the Korean peninsula and the Taiwan Strait—appeared low.

---

[144] "US Embassy Taiwan Cable 8654 to State Department, US Nuclear Team Visit, 30 December 1976, Secret Exdis," in William Burr, ed., *NSA Electronic Briefing Book No. 221* (Washington, DC: National Security Archive, 2007), http://nsarchive.gwu.edu/nukevault/ebb221/T-10a.pdf.

[145] "State Department Cable 4532 to Embassy Taiwan, Taiwan's Continued Interest in Reprocessing, 8 January 1977, Secret Exdis," in William Burr, ed., *NSA Electronic Briefing Book No. 221* (Washington, DC: National Security Archive, 2007), http://nsarchive.gwu.edu/nukevault/ebb221/T-10b.pdf.

Prior to the arrival of the US nuclear team in Taipei in mid-January 1977, Gleysteen presented Chien with evidence of recent contacts between Comprimo and INER representatives. Chien appeared "bewildered" by his presentation and wondered aloud if there were some misunderstanding about the time frame of the alleged contacts. When Gleysteen reiterated that INER had been in contact with Comprimo after Chiang's 17 September 1976 declaration, Chien promised to look into the matter and raise it with the AEC.[146]

The seven-member US nuclear team, led by Burton Levin, the director of the Office of ROC Affairs in the State Department, arrived on 19 January and met with Chien, Admiral Feng Chi-tsung, the vice minister of defense, Chien Szu-liang, the chairman of the AEC, and other ROC officials. Over the next two days, Levin's team also met Chi-peng, the director of INER, and Lt. Gen. T'ang Chun-po, the president of CIST, and their respective staffs. According to Unger, "Levin explicitly and forcefully made clear that our concern was beyond reprocessing" and stated, "any ROC research involving the use of weapons-usable material could not be justified sole on the grounds peaceful application."[147]

The team's final report submitted in mid-February 1977 concluded that the only way to thwart the GROC's intention to develop a nuclear weapon capability would be for the Carter administration to take a strong position on the entire Taiwanese nuclear research and development (R&D) program. Possible actions might include shutting down the TRR on the INER campus, terminating all plutonium handling activities related to fuel reprocessing R&D, and redirecting funds and efforts into areas more consistent with the peaceful uses of nuclear energy.[148] Unger met again with Chien in mid-February. Although the ambassador avoided a detailed discussion of the US nuclear team's report, he stressed the Carter administration's nonproliferation efforts in South Korea, Pakistan, and Brazil. According to Unger, Chien said, "any intention to go ahead with nuclear weapons is 'suicidal.'"[149]

---

[146] "US Embassy Taiwan Cable 209 to State Department, Taiwan's Continued Interest in Reprocessing, 8 January 1977, Secret Exdis," in William Burr, ed., NSA Electronic Briefing Book No. 221 (Washington, DC: National Security Archive, 2007), http://nsarchive.gwu.edu/nukevault/ebb221/T-10c.pdf.

[147] "US Embassy Taiwan Cable 332 to State Department, US Nuclear Team Visit to ROC—Calls, 19 January 1977, Confidential," in William Burr, ed., NSA Electronic Briefing Book No. 221 (Washington, DC: National Security Archive, 2007), http://nsarchive.gwu.edu/nukevault/ebb221/T-10e.pdf.

[148] "US Embassy Taiwan Cable 332 to State Department, US Nuclear Team Conclusions and Recommendations, 17 February 1977, Secret Nodis," in William Burr, ed., NSA Electronic Briefing Book No. 221 (Washington, DC: National Security Archive, 2007), http://nsarchive.gwu.edu/nukevault/ebb221/T-10g.pdf.

[149] "11. Telegram from the Embassy in the Republic of China to the Department of State, 16 February 1977 (8:30)," FRUS, 1977–1980, Vol. XIII: China (Washington, DC: GPO, 2013).

Deputy Secretary of State Warren Christopher raised the subject of proliferation during a private luncheon with Chou Shu-kai, a ROC minister-without-portfolio, on 3 March. Chou mentioned a 27 February *Washington Post* article about Taiwan's nuclear program and said he did not understand why it made no mention of the US nuclear team's recent visit the island.[150] Christopher raised Chiang's recent statements about Taiwan having a nuclear weapon capability, even though the GROC did not intended to produce a nuclear weapon. He told Chou, "it would be desirable for emphasis to be on the latter point and that it could be damaging to the position of the ROC to be proclaiming publicly its possession of a nuclear capability."[151]

An IAEA inspector discovered an unsafeguarded exit port at the TRR in early March 1977 but did not find any nuclear fuel had been diverted. The inspector concluded the "disclosure of circumstances at TRR reflect on lack of ROC cooperation rather than lack of IAEA safeguard effectiveness."[152] Secretary of State Cyrus Vance directed Unger to deliver another warning to Chiang: "The US is convinced that much of INER's current activities have far greater relevance to a nuclear explosive research program than to the ROC's nuclear power program." Vance further instructed Unger to say the US nuclear team had found serious problems and that without significant changes to the nuclear program, the United States would no longer cooperate with Taiwan on nuclear energy matters. These changes included: suspending operations at the TRR and notifying the IAEA; terminating all fuel cycle activities; and avoiding activities involving the "development of a nuclear explosive capability."[153]

On 12 April, the Taipei Embassy received a note from Chien about the "full GROC acceptance [of the proposals] put forward by USG with minor exception regarding notification to IAEA suspension operation of TRR."[154] A week later, National Security Adviser Zbigniew Brzezinski told Carter that US diplomatic pressure achieved its desired results: "It is now quite clear that the Taiwanese Institute of Nuclear Energy Research has been ordered to terminate its heavy

---

[150] Melinda Liu, "Taiwan Develops Nuclear Industry, Weapons Capacity," *Washington Post*, 27 February 1977, p. A21.

[151] "US Embassy Taiwan Cable 1354 to State Department, 11 March 1977, Secret Nodis," in William Burr, ed., *NSA Electronic Briefing Book no. 221* (Washington, DC: National Security Archive, 2007), http://nsarchive.gwu.edu/nukevault/ebb221/T-11b.pdf.

[152] "US Embassy in Japan Cable 3212 to State Department, ROC/IAEA Safeguards, 8 March 1977, Secret Nodis," in William Burr, ed., *NSA Electronic Briefing Book no. 221* (Washington, DC: National Security Archives, 2007), http://nsarchive.gwu.edu/nukevault/ebb221/T-12.pdf.

[153] "State Department Cable 67316 to Embassy in Taiwan, Nuclear Representation to the ROC, 26 March 1977, Secret Nodis," in William Burr, ed., *NSA Electronic Briefing Book no. 221* (Washington, DC: National Security Archives, 2007), http://nsarchive.gwu.edu/nukevault/ebb221/T-13a.pdf.

[154] "23. Editorial Note," *FRUS, 1977–1980, Vol. XIII: China* (Washington, DC: GPO, 2013).

water reactor and close the hot laboratory."¹⁵⁵ A second team of US nuclear experts, led any Gerald Helfrich of ERDA, visited Taiwan in late May. The team made recommendations to reorient the Taiwanese nuclear program away from weapons-related work. Those recommendations included the temporary shutdown of the TRR and the transfer of spent nuclear fuel to Canada.[156]

The Carter administration did not threaten to cut off US military assistance to Taiwan. Instead, officials merely threatened consequences for civil nuclear cooperation. In fact, the controversy over unsafeguarded activities at TRR and uranium enrichment occurred alongside the administration's review of East Asian policies, including Carter's (abortive) bid to withdraw the remaining 40,000 US troops from South Korea, the timing of US-PRC normalization, and the future US diplomatic and military supply relationship with Taiwan after normalization.

Vance wrote to Carter in April 1977 that Taiwan was the only obstacle to US-PRC normalization. He observed, "Continuing Sino-Soviet rivalry is an important and tangible benefit to the United States strategically" and that "placing our relations with the PRC on the best possible footing would help position us to deal effectively with any changes in the Moscow-Peking leg of the triangular relationship." Noting that China would not be capable of taking Taiwan for force for several years (except at a very high cost), Vance advised "maintaining substantial support for ROC military capabilities." He concluded, "continuing government-level ties, however disguised, will be critical to our ability to help sustain Taiwan's prosperity and stability through trade and investment and cooperation with—and control over—their nuclear power program."[157]

There was consensus among Carter's national security team to move toward normalization with China, while continuing to withdraw US troops from Taiwan.[158] As Secretary of Defense Harold Brown argued, "To the extent our opening to China reduces the chances of Sino-Soviet détente, we gain enormously," adding that "The Chinese tie down a significant portion of Soviet military effort." However, Taiwan remained the main obstacle to US-PRC normalization for several reasons. First, the Carter administration sought both private assurances and a public declaration from China that it would not use force

---

[155] "Zbigniew Brzezinski to President Carter, Weekly National Security Report #11, 29 April 1977, Top Secret," in William Burr, ed., *NSA Electronic Briefing Book no. 221* (Washington, DC: National Security Archives, 2007), http://nsarchive.gwu.edu/nukevault/ebb221/T-14.pdf.

[156] "US Embassy Taiwan Cable 3158 to State Department, U.S. Technical Team Visit, 31 May 1977, Secret Limdis," in William Burr, ed., *NSA Electronic Briefing Book no. 221* (Washington, DC: National Security Archives, 2007), http://nsarchive.gwu.edu/nukevault/ebb221/T-16a.pdf.

[157] "26. Memorandum from Secretary of State Vance to President Carter, 15 April 1977," *FRUS, 1977–1980, Vol. XIII: China* (Washington, DC: GPO, 2013).

[158] Presidential Review Memorandum/NSC 24: People's Republic of China, 5 April 1977, https://www.jimmycarterlibrary.gov/assets/documents/memorandums/prm24.pdf.

to reunify Taiwan with the mainland. During a 30 July NSC meeting, Assistant Secretary of State for East Asian Affairs Richard C. Holbrooke remarked, "The Chinese will have to understand that they cannot talk publicly about the right to liberate Taiwan by force."[159]

Carter administration officials, however, wanted to maintain some level of US military assistance to and official representation on Taiwan after normalization with China. On this point, Vance observed in an NSC meeting on 30 July 1977, "The issue of continued arm sales to Taiwan in the post-normalization era has never been raised with the Chinese." Michel Oksenberg, an NSC staff member responsible for East Asia, added, "We also have to remember that our continued presence on Taiwan is a plus to the Chinese. We keep Taiwan from going nuclear, from developing relations with the Soviet Union, or from going independent."[160]

Persuading Congress was essential because, as Vance noted, a "combination of conservatives with ties to Taiwan and liberals concerned about human rights in the PRC" opposed normalization.[161] On 29 July, Brzezinski wrote Carter: "The Taiwan Lobby does not constitute a major obstacle to normalization," but he added, the "real issue concerns our willingness to grasp this thorny issue at a time that is strategically and politically advantageous to us."[162] On 27 June, the NSC's Policy Review Committee concluded, "The Hill problem means the issue cannot be absorbed domestically until sometime in 1978 at the earliest."[163]

Vance traveled to Beijing in August 1977 to present the Carter administration's timetable for normalization and its "maximum position" on Taiwan.[164] When Vance first raised the issue of official US representation on Taiwan after normalization, Foreign Minister Huang Hua replied: "The views and ideas you put forward with respect to the normalization of relations between our two countries can only give us the impression that you want to continue to maintain the right to interfere in the internal affairs of China."[165] Vance also raised the issue with Deng, who replied: "No matter what you call it by name or whether you can fly

---

[159] "41. Memorandum of Conversation, 30 July 1977, 9:30–11:15 A.M.," *FRUS, 1977–1980, Vol. XIII: China* (Washington, DC: GPO, 2013).

[160] "41. Memorandum of Conversation, 30 July 1977, 9:30–11:15 A.M.," *FRUS, 1977–1980, Vol. XIII: China* (Washington, DC: GPO, 2013).

[161] "34. Summary of Conclusions of a Policy Review Committee Meeting, Washington, 27 June 1977, 3–4:30 P.M.," *FRUS, 1977–1980, Vol. XIII: China* (Washington, DC: GPO, 2013).

[162] "40. Memorandum from the President's Assistant for National Security Affairs (Brzezinski) to President Carter, 29 July 1977," *FRUS, 1977–1980, Vol. XIII: China* (Washington, DC: GPO, 2013).

[163] "34. Summary of Conclusions of a Policy Review Committee Meeting, Washington, 27 June 1977, 3–4:30 P.M.," *FRUS, 1977–1980, Vol. XIII: China* (Washington, DC: GPO, 2013).

[164] Cyrus R. Vance, *Hard Choices: Critical Years in America's Foreign Policy* (New York: Simon and Schuster, 1983), p. 79.

[165] "49. Memorandum of Conversation, Beijing, 24 August 1977, 9:30 A.M.–12:20 P.M.," *FRUS, 1977–1980, Vol. XIII: China* (Washington, DC: GPO, 2013).

your flag on it—in the final analysis it is the reversal of the existing Liaison Office, switching the Liaison Office to Taiwan."[166] While Deng said that China was prepared to "seek peaceful means to settling [the Taiwan Strait] issue without the participation of the United States," he would not "exclude the forceful liberation of Taiwan under military means."[167]

Normalization remained at an impasse for the rest of 1977, as did the administration's arms transfer policy toward Taiwan. Some officials also had lingering suspicions about the Taiwanese nuclear program, especially after the ROC government requested permission to restart the TRR in December 1977.[168] Gerald Smith, ambassador-at-large for nonproliferation issues, warned in March 1978 that some weapons-related activities may have continued, but that it was not clear those activities were actually geared toward weapons production.[169] During the first half of 1978, however, the Carter administration focused on arms transfers to Taiwan, the timing of establishing full diplomatic relations with China, and plans for post-normalization cultural and economic ties with Taiwan.

In February 1978, a joint State-DoD study argued that while the PRC leadership found continued US arms transfers to the ROC "distasteful," they were also pragmatic. "Pending normalization, there are some indications that Peking views our existing relationship to Taiwan as a deterrent to Taipei's looking elsewhere for support or seeking unilaterally to alter the island's status." Furthermore, the "maintenance of a credible military deterrent in the ROC not only works to preserve military stability in the area but also provides the sense of psychological confidence on Taiwan." The study recommended the Carter administration consider ROC military equipment requests on a case-by-case basis and avoid replicating the Nixon administration's "Enhance Plus," especially as normalization with China approached.[170]

---

[166] "50. Memorandum of Conversation, Beijing, 24 August 1977, 3–5:40 P.M.," *FRUS, 1977–1980, Vol. XIII: China* (Washington, DC: GPO, 2013).

[167] Ibid.

[168] "State Department Cable 305275 to Embassy Taiwan, the Taiwan Research Reactor, 22 December 1977, Secret Nodis," in William Burr, ed., *NSA Electronic Briefing Book no. 221* (Washington, DC: National Security Archives, 2007), http://nsarchive.gwu.edu/nukevault/ebb221/T-18a.pdf; and "Memo from Ronald J. Better to Mr. Oxmand et al., Taiwan Memo on Nuclear Issues, 22 December 1978, Enclosing Memorandum, Nuclear Agreements with the ROC, 22 December 1978, Confidential," Ibid., http://nsarchive.gwu.edu/nukevault/ebb221/T-24.pdf.

[169] "Memorandum, Gerard Smith to Allen, 10 March [1978?], with Response by Al, Unclassified," in William Burr, ed., *NSA Electronic Briefing Book no. 221* (Washington, DC: National Security Archives, 2007), http://nsarchive.gwu.edu/nukevault/ebb221/T-19.pdf.

[170] "78. Memorandum from the Executive Secretary of the Department of State (Tarnoff) to the President's Assistant for National Security Affairs (Brzezinski), 8 February 1978," *FRUS, 1977–1980, Vol. XIII: China* (Washington, DC: GPO, 2013).

Increasingly alarmed about the Soviet Union's support of proxies in sub-Saharan Africa, South Asia, and Southeast Asia in early 1978, Carter and his advisers redoubled efforts to enlist China as an ally of convenience.[171] Carter recognized that Chinese leaders were quite wary about expansion of Soviet influence in Southeast Asia (in particular Vietnam). He dispatched Brzezinski to Beijing in mid-May 1978 with specific instructions to "share with the Chinese my view of the Soviet threat."[172] Six days before Brzezinski's departure for Beijing, Carter ordered lowering the ceiling of all DoD military and civilian personnel on Taiwan to 660 by 1 October 1978.[173]

Brzezinski arrived in Beijing on 20 May. At a banquet hosted by Hua, he announced that the United States "had made up its mind" to move toward full diplomatic relations with China.[174] In their private meeting, Hua reiterated China's three conditions for normalization: the severance of US-ROC diplomatic ties; the withdrawal of all US forces and military installations from Taiwan; and the "abrogation" of the US-ROK Mutual Defense Treaty.[175]

Brzezinski told Deng that "In our relationships we will remain guided by the Shanghai Communique, by the principle that there is only one China and that the resolution of the issue of Taiwan is your problem." Deng, who had previous rejected proposals by Vance in August 1977 (and by Kissinger in November 1974) that the United States maintain retain a liaison office in Taipei after normalization with Beijing, was now amenable to the so-called Japanese formula—an arrangement whereby Japan maintained non-governmental and commercial contacts with Taiwan after it established full diplomatic relations with China in September 1972.[176] He suggested the United States might do the same. In a cable to Carter and Vance, Brzezinski reported telling Deng about "our need to make a unilateral statement expressing our hopes for a peaceful resolution of the Taiwan

---

[171] Ross, *Negotiating Cooperation*, pp. 120–128.

[172] Carter's letter of instruction to Brzezinski for the May 1978 mission to Beijing appears in Zbigniew Brzezinski, *Power and Principle: Memoirs of the National Security Adviser, 1977–1981* (New York: Farrar, Straus & Giroux, 1983), pp. 551–555, annex 1.

[173] "103. Memorandum from the President's Assistant for National Affairs (Brzezinski) to Secretary of Defense Brown, 12 May 1978," *FRUS, 1977–1980, Vol. XIII: China* (Washington, DC: GPO, 2013).

[174] See Fox Butterfield, "Brzezinski, in China, Calls Goal Full Ties," *New York Times*, 21 May 1978, p. 8; and "US Set to Normalize Ties, Brzezinski Says in Peking," *Washington Post*, 21 May 1978, p. 1.

[175] "109. Memorandum of Conversation, re: Summary of Dr. Brzezinski's Meeting with Foreign Minister Huang Hua, Beijing, May 21, 1978, 9:52 A.M.–1:20 P.M.," *FRUS, 1977–1980, Vol. XIII: China* (Washington, DC: GPO, 2013).

[176] "110. Memorandum of Conversation, re: Meeting with Vice Premier Teng Hsiao P'ing, Beijing, May 21, 1978, 4:05–6:30 P.M.," *FRUS, 1977–1980, Vol. XIII: China* (Washington, DC: GPO, 2013).

issue that will not be contradicted by the Chinese side." But he added that "We did not talk about arms sales directly."[177]

Upon Brzezinski's return to Washington, Carter authorized Ambassador Leonard Woodcock, the chief of the US Liaison Office in Beijing, to begin negotiations with Deng, Hua, and other PRC officials on normalization. Carter set a deadline of 15 December 1978 for the agreement. He also swore Woodcock to complete secrecy, telling him "I don't trust (1) Congress, (2) White House, (3) State, or (4) Defense to keep a secret."[178]

On 1 November 1978, Carter proposed a $119 million Foreign Military Sales (FMS) for Taiwan that included: the long-promised co-production of an additional 48 F-5E aircrafts, the sale of 72 Harpoon missiles and 12 launchers, 400 laser-guided bomb kits, and 500 Maverick missiles.[179] As Brzezinski noted, the extension of the current co-production arrangement, as well as approving the F-5E sale, would assure Congress and the ROC that the Carter administration planned to continue defense ties with Taiwan, regardless of US-China relations.[180] Carter, however, decided not to sell the more advanced F-5G aircraft to the ROC, because that move might provoke China.[181]

The Carter administration's deliberations about the FY 1979 military assistance package (MAP) is significant because it occurred alongside renewed confrontation over the Taiwanese nuclear program. In late July 1978, the US technical nuclear team met with CIST Director Tang, along with Vice Foreign Minister Chien, CAEC secretary-general Cheng, and Taipower president Chu. Suspicions that CIST had a secret uranium enrichment program—parallel to the INER's efforts to purchase reprocessing technology from foreign suppliers—triggered this meeting.[182]

---

[177] Ibid., footnote 1. The cable is Backchannel message 7 from Beijing to the White House Situation Room, May 21; Carter Library, National Security Affairs, Staff Material, Far East, Oksenberg Subject File, Box 56, Policy Process: 5/16–31/78.

[178] Brzezinski, *Power and Principle*, p. 274.

[179] "148. Memorandum from the President's Assistant for National Security Affairs (Brzezinski) to Secretary of State Vance and Secretary of Defense Brown, 1 November 1978," *FRUS, 1977–1980, Vol. XIII: China* (Washington, DC: GPO, 2013).

[180] "147. Memorandum from the President's Assistant for National Security Affairs (Brzezinski) to President Carter, 26 October 1978," *FRUS, 1977–1980, Vol. XIII: China* (Washington, DC: GPO, 2013).

[181] Bernard Gwertzman, "US Modifies Taiwan's Request for Advanced Planes," *New York Times*, 7 November 1978, p. A9.

[182] "Taiwan Embassy Cable 4988 to State Department, Nuclear Team Visit: Initial Calls: Discussion with CIST Director Tang, 31 July 1978, Secrete Exdis," in William Burr, ed., *NSA Electronic Briefing Book no. 221* (Washington, DC: National Security Archives, 2007), http://nsarchive.gwu.edu/nukevault/ebb221/T-20a.pdf.

The technical team stressed the importance of the ROC's strict adherence to prior agreements in the nuclear field. Noncompliance with those agreements, they warned, would trigger the suspension of nuclear exports from the United States under Section 307 of the Nuclear Nonproliferation Act (NNPA) that Congress passed, and Carter signed into law in March 1978. According to Unger, ROC officials "predictably" expressed a commitment to abide by the existing bilateral agreements with the United States and the IAEA. Chien also reiterated Chiang's offer to invite US nuclear scientists to reside at ROC nuclear facilities at his government's expense.[183]

Unger met with Chiang, Chien, and presidential secretary James Soong on 8 September to discuss the US technical team's visit. He also delivered a letter from Vance to Chiang about uranium enrichment. The State Department had instructed Unger to deliver an oral message about the unsafeguarded storage of spent nuclear fuel on the CIST campus. Chiang expressed frustration, outlining how Taiwan had cooperated with the United States in the nuclear field more than any other country. Unger told the State Department that Chiang "was more obviously annoyed and disturbed than I have ever seen." Chiang believed the ROC's "extreme vulnerability" and "unique relationship" with the United States allowed the latter to "treat this government in a manner few other countries would tolerate."[184]

However, within a week of that meeting, Chiang replied to Vance's letter. He wrote, "The Republic of China has no intention whatsoever to develop nuclear weapons" or to "engage in any activities related to reprocessing purposes."[185] Chang reiterated his invitation for US nuclear scientists to work along their Taiwanese counterparts on a long-term basis to prevent any further "misunderstanding" about the ROC nuclear program.[186]

The timing of Chiang's reply to Vance is significant for two reasons. First, Chiang was aware that the Carter administration would normalize diplomatic

---

[183] Ibid.

[184] Unger writes that he personally delivered Vance's letter to Chiang on 8 September in "US Embassy Taiwan Cable 6065 to State Department, Follow-up to Nuclear Team Visit: Demarche to President Chiang, 8 September 1978, Secret Nodis," in William Burr, ed., *NSA Electronic Briefing Book no. 221* (Washington, DC: National Security Archive, 2007), http://nsarchive.gwu.edu/nukevault/ebb221/T-21a.pdf.

[185] "US Embassy Taiwan Cable 6279 to State Department, President Chiang's Reply to Secretary Vance's Letter on Nuclear Matters, 14 September 1978, Secret Nodis," in William Burr, ed., *NSA Electronic Briefing Book no. 221* (Washington, DC: National Security Archive, 2007), http://nsarchive.gwu.edu/nukevault/ebb221/T-21d.pdf.

[186] "US Embassy Taiwan Cable 6351 to State Department, 'Proposed Assignment of U.S. Nuclear Scientists to ROC,' 18 September 1978, Secret Nodis, Excised Copy," in William Burr, ed., *NSA Electronic Briefing Book no. 221* (Washington, DC: National Security Archive, 2007), http://nsarchive.gwu.edu/nukevault/ebb221/T-21e.pdf.

relations with Beijing, and thus sever official ties with Taipei, within the next several months. On 30 May, Unger briefed Chiang on the substance of Brzezinski's meetings with Deng, Huang, and Hua in Beijing.[187] Despite Carter swearing Woodcock to secrecy, throughout summer 1978, the *New York Times, Washington Post*, and other newspapers reported that the United States and China would soon normalize ties and that the US-ROC Mutual Defense Treaty would be collateral damage.[188]

On 19 September, Carter told Ambassador Chai Zemin, the chief of the PRC Liaison Office in Washington, that his administration "was prepared after a relatively brief interim period to end all official representation on Taiwan." The president added, "As you know, the people of Taiwan have the scientific capability for the development of atomic weapons, and we feel some relations with us are important to prevent this dangerous development."[189]

Second, Chiang's government had been in negotiations with the Carter administration over the FY 1979 MAP, which would likely be the last significant cache of advanced weapons systems and equipment Taiwan could acquire under the mutual defense treaty. In particular, Chiang and his advisers were eager to renew the co-production of the F-5E aircraft. The aircraft would be vital in defending Taiwan and the Taiwan Strait from incursions by the PLAN air force.

Deng and Woodcock finalized the terms of a communiqué on 13 December 1978. The United States pledged to withdraw all remaining DoD military and civilian personnel (approximately 660 at that point) and close the US Embassy in Taipei within four months of establishing full relations with Beijing on 1 January 1979. At that point, the US Liaison Office in Beijing and the PRC Liaison Office in Washington, DC, would be upgraded to embassies, while the US Embassy in Taipei would close. Deng agreed to compromise proposal whereby "the people of The United States will maintain cultural, commercial and other unofficial relations with the people of Taiwan." Carter extended an invitation for Deng to make an official visit to Washington in February 1979.[190]

---

[187] "114. Telegram from the Embassy in the Republic of China to the Department of State, 30 May 1978," *FRUS, 1977–1980, Vol. XIII: China* (Washington, DC: GPO, 2013).

[188] See, for example, Bernard Gwertzman, "US Reported Acting to Strengthen Ties with Peking Regime," *New York Times*, 25 June 1978, p. 1; "China Accuses Taiwan of Seeking to Disrupt Relations with US," *Washington Post*, 19 July 1978, p. 1; and Dusko Doder, "Kremlin Showing Alarm as Sino-U.S. Ties Grow," *Washington Post*, 24 August 1978, p. 1.

[189] "135. Memorandum of Conversation, re: Summary of the President's Meeting with Ambassador Ch'ai Tse-Min, 19 September 1978, 11:35 A.M.–12:12 P.M.," *FRUS, 1977–1980, Vol. XIII: China* (Washington, DC: GPO, 2013).

[190] "166. Backchannel Message from the Chief of the Liaison Office in China (Woodcock) to Secretary of State Vance and the President's Assistant for National Security Affairs (Brzezinski), Beijing, 13 December 1978," *FRUS, 1977–1980, Vol. XIII: China* (Washington, DC: GPO, 2013).

Finally, the Carter administration insisted that it would terminate the US-ROC Mutual Defense Treaty in accordance with the terms of that treaty—that is, after giving the ROC one year's notice—rather than "abrogate" it as Chinese leaders had demanded since 1971. In exchange the Carter administration agreed to Deng's request for a one-year moratorium on new arms sales to Taiwan.[191] Congress would need to pass new legislation governing future US arms supplies to Taiwan, as well as a mechanism for containing US economic, cultural, and people-to-people ties with Taiwan. The Carter administration, however, planned to submit such legislation to Congress after the normalization of relations with Beijing.[192]

On 15 December 1978, Vance and Brzezinski informed Unger that Carter planned to make a televised address that evening announcing establishment of full diplomatic relations with China effective on 1 January and the concurrent termination of diplomatic relations with Taiwan.[193] Unger delivered the message to Chiang, Chien, and Soon on 15 December.[194] A few days later, Christopher instructed Unger to inform the ROC government on 1 January 1979 of the termination of the mutual defense treaty in exactly one year's time.[195]

The Carter administration's nonproliferation strategies toward the ROC in 1977 and 1978 were consistent with the neoclassical realist theory hypotheses. The core objective of Carter's national security team was to solidify an alliance of convenience with China. In order to do that, however, policymakers needed

---

[191] "169. Backchannel Message from the Chief of the Liaison Office in China (Woodcock) to the President's Assistant for National Security Affairs (Brzezinski), 15 December 1978," *FRUS, 1977–1980, Vol. XIII: China* (Washington, DC: GPO, 2013).

[192] See "174. Summary of Conclusions of a Special Cooperation Committee Ad Hoc Group on China Meeting, 18 December 1978, 10–11:40 A.M.," *FRUS, 1977–1980, Vol. XIII: China* (Washington, DC: GPO, 2013). The battle between the Carter administration and Congress over the Taiwan Relations Act (PL 96-8, 93 Stat. 4, 10 April 1979) is outside the scope of this chapter. For a recent analysis, see Resnick, *Dealing with Devils*, chapter 3. For documentation on the legislative history, see "Legislative History of the Taiwan Relations Act: P.L. 96-8: 93 Stat. 14: April 10, 1979" (Washington, DC: Covington & Burling, 1979).

[193] "171. Backchannel Message from Secretary of State Vance and the President's Assistant for National Security Affairs (Brzezinski) to the Ambassador to the Republic of China (Unger), 15 December 1978 (15:18)," *FRUS, 1977–1980, Vol. XIII: China* (Washington, DC: GPO, 2013).

[194] See "173. Backchannel Message from the Ambassador to the Republic of China (Unger) to Secretary of State Vance and the President's Assistant for National Security Affairs (Brzezinski), 15 December 1978," *FRUS, 1977–1980, Vol. XIII: China* (Washington, DC: GPO, 2013). For the text of Carter's televised address, in which he read a unilateral statement and the joint communiqué, see: "Address to the Nation on Diplomatic Relations Between the United States and the People's Republic of China," 15 December 1978, *Public Papers of the President of the United States: Jimmy Carter, 1978* (Washington, DC: GPO, 1979), pp. 2264–2268.

[195] "180. Telegram from the Department of State to the Embassy in the Republic of China, 23 December 1978 (21:10 P.M.)," *FRUS, 1977–1980, Vol. XIII: China* (Washington, DC: GPO, 2013).

to rapidly normalize diplomatic ties between Washington and Beijing. However, Taiwan's nuclear weapons program, specifically concerns about unsafeguarded activities at the TRR and the clandestine uranium enrichment activities, was an obstacle to normalization with China.

In spring and summer 1978, Carter administration officials still perceived a stable overall power distribution in East Asia. In May 1978, the CIA did produce a revised estimate of the conventional military balance on the Korean peninsula. That intelligence about North Korea's numerical and firepower advantage vis-à-vis South Korea contributed to the demise of Carter's plan to withdraw the Second Infantry Division. Nonetheless, the overall power distribution in East Asia remained favorable to the United States in 1977 and 1978.

Officials also perceived long time horizons for emerging threats to the United States' interest in East Asia. The near-term likelihood of increased Soviet penetration of that region was low, especially compared to other regions. China and the Soviet Union still viewed each other as adversaries. The near-term likelihood of armed conflict in either of the region's two flashpoints—the DMZ on the Korean peninsula and the Taiwan Strait—were low.

The Carter administration had to overcome high domestic mobilization hurdles in pursuing strategies toward China and Taiwan in general, and toward the unsafeguarded activities at the TRR and uranium enrichment activities in particular. There were still members of Congress, especially conservative Republicans, who were opposed to efforts to normalize US-PRC relations and terminate the US-ROC Mutual Defense Treaty. As Brzezinski told Carter in July 1977, the allies of the Taiwan Lobby in Congress—principally Senators Goldwater, Helms, Thurmond, John Tower (R-TX), Robert Dole (R-KS), and Richard Stone (D-FL) and Representative Clement Zablocki (D-WI)—were not a major barrier to normalization with Beijing.[196] Nonetheless, the Carter administration did not pursue a coercive nonproliferation strategy. Instead, in 1977 and 1978, officials pursued a hybrid strategy toward Taipei.

Vance, Unger, and other officials threatened to cut off civil-nuclear cooperation if the unsafeguarded activities at the TRR and later the parallel uranium enrichment activities did not cease. As the same time, the Carter administration continued to transfer advanced weapons to the ROC, including the co-production of 48 F-5E aircraft and the sale of 72 Harpoon missiles and 12 launchers. Officials never explicitly threatened to withhold the co-production of the F-5Es or the sale of any weapon system if the GROC failed to comply with demands on reprocessing and uranium enrichment. Vance's September 1978

---

[196] "40. Memorandum from the President's Assistant for National Security Affairs (Brzezinski) to President Carter, 29 July 1977," *FRUS, 1977–1980, Vol. XIII: China* (Washington, DC: GPO, 2013).

démarche only threatened consequences for nuclear cooperation. Nonetheless, the fact that the administration pursued both initiatives concurrently—the provision of the FY 1979 $119 million arms package and the threat to terminate civil nuclear cooperation—suggests an implicit linkage.

Nuclear domino theory would expect the Carter administration to have pursued a coercive nonproliferation toward Taiwan to the extent US policymakers perceived Taiwanese nuclear activity as provoking reactive proliferation by neighboring states. Like the Ford administration, Carter administration officials did not perceive an increased likelihood of Japanese nuclear proliferation in 1977 and 1978. As examined in the previous chapter, Park Chung-hee had terminated much of South Korea's clandestine nuclear weapons program, Project 890, in December 1976. North Korea did not become a proliferation concern for the United States until 1985.

Neither the credible sanctions theory hypothesis nor the security commitment theory hypothesis explains the Carter administration's nonproliferation strategies toward Taiwan in 1977 and 1978. The former would expect administration officials to pursue a purely coercive nonproliferation strategy toward Taiwan, particularly threats to invoke Symington Amendment sanctions and thus a termination of US military assistance. Administration officials did not make those threats.

Likewise, the security commitment theory hypothesis finds little empirical support in this period. By the time Carter took office in January 1977, approximately 1,400 US military personnel remained on Taiwan. Carter ordered a further reduction to 660 by the end of 1978. There was never any discussion of reversing or even pausing the decade-long withdrawal of US troops from Taiwan as a means to secure the ROC's compliance with nonproliferation demands.

Epilogue: The Reagan Administration and the Démarche to Lee Tung-wei, 1987

Ronald Reagan, the Republican nominee, defeated Carter in the November 1980 presidential election. Initially, there were deep divisions within the Reagan administration over China and Taiwan. Reagan, Secretary of Defense Caspar Weinberger, and Richard V. Allen, Reagan's national security adviser, favored continued arms sales to Taiwan. Other officials, must notably Secretary of State Alexander M. Haig, favored a strategic partnership with China to contain the Soviet Union. The Reagan administration's consideration of selling the advanced FX fighter jet to Taiwan in 1981 strained US-PRC relations. The proposed FX transfer exposed the limits the agreements Carter administration had reached with Deng in 1978.[197]

Following Haig's resignation in June 1982, Reagan decided not to sell the FX jet to Taiwan, but to instead renew the co-production of the F-5E.[198] As the September deadline to notify Congress about the F-5E renewal approached, Hummel, then US ambassador to Beijing, negotiated a joint statement with Huang and Deng regarding arms transfers to Taiwan. While reaffirming the "one China" formula, the 17 August 1982 statement pledged that the United States: "does not seek to carry out a long-term policy of arms sales to Taiwan" and that "it intends to reduce gradually its sales of arms to Taiwan, leading over a period of time to a final resolution." The statement referenced the PRC government's past statements on the peaceful reunification of Taiwan with the mainland.[199] Robert S. Ross observes, "Although it continued to reject linkage, the PRC thus acquiesced to US linkage of US arms sales to Taiwan and Chinese policy on peaceful resolution of the Taiwan issue."[200] In effect, by late summer 1982, the Reagan administration adopted a strategy of limited arms sales to Taiwan (in accordance with the 1979 Taiwan Relations Act) while continuing the alliance of convenience with China.

While the acute phase of the US-ROC proliferation dispute ended in 1978, Taiwan's clandestine nuclear activities continued. In 1987 the INER began building hot cell facilities in which scientists could conduct reprocessing experiments, in violation of the agreements reached with the United States and the IAEA in 1976.[201]

In December 1987, Colonel Chang Hsien-yi, the deputy director of the INER, defected the United States, along with his family. Chang, who had been a CIA human source since his days as an army cadet in the 1960s, provided classified documents on Taiwanese nuclear activities.[202] In February 1988, the State Department dispatched yet another team of nuclear inspectors to Taiwan. The team confronted ROC officials with satellite images of the hot cell facilities and demanded their immediate shutdown. The following month, the ROC told the

---

[197] Ross, *Negotiating Cooperation*, pp. 195–197. See also Jaw-ling Joanne Chang, "Negotiation of the 17 August 1982 US-PRC Arms Communiqué: Beijing's Negotiating Tactics," *The China Quarterly*, No. 125 (1991), pp. 33–54.

[198] Chang, "Negotiation of the 17 August 1982 US-PRC Arms Communiqué," pp. 41–43.

[199] "Text of the US-China Communique on Taiwan," *New York Times*, 18 August 1982, p. A12.

[200] Ross, *Negotiating Cooperation*, p. 198.

[201] Albright and Gay, "Taiwan: Nuclear Nightmare Averted," p. 59; Paul Kerr, "IAEA Investigating Egypt and Taiwan," *Arms Control Today*, Vol. 35, No. 1 (2005); and Richelson, *Spying on the Bomb*, pp. 367–368.

[202] Tim Weiner, "How a Spy Left Taiwan in the Cold," *New York Times*, 20 December 1997, p. A7.

IAEA that it would shut the TRR, in order to convert it to a light-water reactor.[203] Reagan administration officials also reportedly demanded that Lee Teng-hui, who became ROC president after Chiang Ching-kuo's death in January 1988, sign a memorandum renouncing all nuclear weapons research.[204]

This chapter tested hypotheses from neoclassical realist theory against hypotheses from all three alternative theories—nuclear domino theory, security commitment theory, and credible sanctions theory—to explain variation in the types of strategies the Ford and the Carter administrations pursued toward Taiwan's nuclear weapons program. Overall, the strategies adopted by both administrations were consistent with neoclassical realist theory. The hypotheses from nuclear domino theory, credible sanctions, and security commitment theory found little empirical support.

---

[203] Stephen Engleberg and Michael R. Gordon, "Taipei Halts Work on Secret Plant to Make Nuclear Bomb Ingredient," *New York Times*, 23 March 1988, pp. A1 and A15; and R. Jeffrey Smith and Don Oberdorfer, "Taiwan to Close Nuclear Reactor," *Washington Post*, 24 March 1988, p. 1.

[204] See Albright and Gay, "Taiwan: Nuclear Nightmare Averted," p. 59; and Mitchell, "Taiwan's Hsin Chu Program," pp. 300–301.

7

Conclusions

This book began by questioning whether preventing the proliferation of nuclear weapons, even to strategically vulnerable allies, has actually been a co-equal pillar of the United States' grand strategies for the past seventy years, along with the containment of great power adversaries and the promotion of economic openness.[1] I argued that the United States' dedication to preventing the proliferation of nuclear weapons varied over time and across regions.

Previous chapters tested hypotheses from neoclassical realist theory against alternative hypotheses from nuclear domino theory (chapters 3, 4, 5, and 6), security commitment theory (chapters 5 and 6), and credible sanctions theory (chapters 4, 5, and 6) to explain variation in the types of nonproliferation strategies the United States pursued toward four Cold War frenemies, Israel, Pakistan, South Korea, and Taiwan.

South Korea, Taiwan, Israel, and Pakistan had or established long-term bilateral security relationships with the United States despite the existence of diverging security interests and political objectives. Each of them displayed patterns of manipulation, deception, evasion, and sometimes obstruction of the expressed interests of its superpower patron. Their leaders not only engaged in such behaviors to hamper the United States' efforts to uncover and thwart their nuclear weapons programs, but also in other areas of their bilateral relations. Forging and maintaining alliance ties with the United States was a means to obtain security guarantees and material assistance against their local adversary. By contrast, for US policymakers, alliance ties with Israel, Pakistan, South Korea, and Taiwan were a means to deny the Soviet Union access to the Middle East, South Asia, and East Asia, respectively. From Washington's perspective, these weaker allies were pawns in a global chess match.

In this concluding chapter, I undertake three tasks. First, I summarize the core theoretical argument and the empirical support for the neoclassical realist

---

[1] Francis J. Gavin, "Strategies of Inhibition: U.S. Grand Strategy, the Nuclear Revolution, and Nonproliferation," *International Security*, Vol. 40, No. 1 (2015), pp. 9–46.

theory, nuclear domino theory, credible sanctions theory, and security commitment theory hypotheses found in the previous four chapters. Second, I highlight several theoretical implications of my argument and avenues for future research. Third, I briefly consider what my neoclassical realist theory would suggest for some dilemmas in contemporary US foreign policy.

The Core Argument and Evidence Revisited

The takeaway of this book is that during latter half of the Cold War, Washington policymakers' assessments of regional power dynamics and emerging threats drove how the United States responded to nuclear proliferation by allies in volatile regions. In some instances, presidential administrations pursued overtly coercive strategies such as insisting upon inspections of nuclear facilities and threats to terminate foreign military and economic assistance programs. In other instances, they pursued accommodative strategies, offering tangible inducements such as conventional arms transfers and explicit security guarantees in exchange for the ally's nuclear forbearance. Yet, in a few other instances, administrations pursued strategies combining elements of coercion and accommodation toward nuclear-aspiring allies due to the height of domestic mobilization hurdles in Congress. The result was variation in the types of nonproliferation strategies that the United States pursued toward allies in different regions and that the United States sometimes pursued toward the same ally over time.

During the Cold War, the overriding strategic objective of successive US presidential administrations in the Middle East and South Asia was to prevent containment failure, which officials defined as any increase in the Soviet Union's military, economic, or political penetration of those regions. As the regional power distributions and time horizons shifted, so did Washington policymakers' willingness to adopt coercive or accommodative nonproliferation strategies toward Israel and Pakistan.

In the early 1960s, the Kennedy administration perceived a favorable power distribution in the Middle East and long time horizons for threats to US interests. Administration officials, however, feared that Israel's development of a nuclear weapon capability might prompt the Soviet Union to increase conventional arms transfers to Egypt and Syria. President John F. Kennedy and other officials pressured Israeli prime minister David Ben-Gurion into allowing US scientists to conduct periodic inspections of the Dimona complex.

The Soviet Union accelerated transfers of conventional weapons to Syria and Egypt in the mid-1960s. As the regional power distribution grew more unfavorable and as time horizons for threats grew shorter, officials in Washington became less inclined to pursue coercive strategies to halt Israel's clandestine nuclear program. Instead, they forged a de facto alliance with Israel. By the late 1960s, the Johnson administration, and later the Nixon administration, acquiesced to the Israeli nuclear weapons program and offered inducements in the form of conventional arms sales (e.g., A-4 Skyhawks and the F-4 Phantoms) and conditional security guarantees to bolster Israel as a bulwark against further Soviet penetration in the Middle East. At the same time, high domestic mobilization hurdles, namely increased congressional support for arms sales to Israel beginning in the mid-1960s, made it difficult for the Johnson and Nixon administrations to link arms sales to Israeli concessions on the nuclear issue.

President Richard Nixon and Israeli prime minister Golda Meir reached a special understanding in September 1969, whereby the United States both acquiesced to Israel's possession of a nuclear arsenal and agreed to become its principal conventional arms supplier, in exchange for an Israeli pledge not to "introduce" nuclear weapons into the Middle East (e.g., no public declarations about its nuclear status, no nuclear weapons tests, and no use of US-supplied aircraft to deliver nuclear payloads). That special understanding nearly unraveled during the closing days of the October 1973 War, when the Israel Defense Forces (IDF) task force encircled the Egyptian Third Army in the Suez Canal Zone and General-Secretary Leonid Brezhnev threatened to deploy Soviet troops to enforce a United Nations Security Council ceasefire resolution. The crisis was only resolved after Secretary of State Henry Kissinger privately threatened to "abandon" Israel in the Security Council if the IDF task force failed to observe the ceasefire.

In South Asia, the United States' nonproliferation policies toward Pakistan oscillated from accommodation to coercion and back in the 1975–1990 period. In the mid-1970s, US officials perceived a stable, although not necessarily favorable, distribution of power in South Asia. The Carter administration pursued a coercive strategy, invoking the Symington Amendment, which cut off US military and economic aid to Pakistan in April 1979. The December 1979 Soviet invasion of Afghanistan, however, dramatically shifted the power distribution and shortened the time horizon for threats in South Asia.

In the 1980s, the Reagan administration needed Pakistan as a frontline ally and conduit for covert military aid to the Afghan insurgents. Officials extracted pledges from Pakistan's president, General Muhammad Zia-ul-Haq, that the nuclear weapons program would not cross certain "red lines." In exchange, Pakistan received billions of dollars of US conventional arms and economic assistance. When Pakistan flagrantly crossed two of those red lines (specifically, prohibitions on nuclear technology transfers and uranium enrichment over the 5 percent level), Reagan administration officials circumvented nonproliferation legislation in order to continue the flow of US military assistance to Zia's government, and by extension the flow of arms to the Afghan insurgents. Once Soviet forces withdrew from Afghanistan in spring 1989, however, the George H. W. Bush administration declined to certify that Pakistan was not in possession of a nuclear weapon (as required by the 1986 Pressler Amendment).

The overriding strategic objective of the Nixon, Ford, and Carter administrations in East Asia throughout the 1970s was to enlist China as an ally of convenience against the Soviet Union. Compared to the Middle East and South Asia, the threat of containment failure in East Asia was low. Instead, the Nixon administration and its successors sought to exploit the Sino-Soviet rivalry. South Korea and Taiwan embarked upon nuclear weapons programs because their respective leaders feared the United Sates might "abandon" them in the wake of the Vietnam War. However, their nuclear weapons programs complicated the United States' efforts to forge ties with China.

Despite the collapse of South Vietnam and Cambodia in spring 1975, US policymakers perceived a favorable power distribution in East Asia and long time horizons for the emergence of threats to US strategic interests in that region. High domestic mobilization hurdles, however, made it difficult for the Ford and Carter administrations to pursue overly coercive strategies toward South Korea and Taiwan. The Ford administration pursued a hybrid strategy to thwart South Korea's acquisition of a French-designed reprocessing plant. Specifically, officials threatened to withhold an Export-Import Bank loan for a nuclear power reactor and to suspend civil nuclear cooperation, while concurrently promising a moratorium on US troop reductions and the sale of advanced combat aircraft.

Likewise, the Ford and Carter administrations pursued hybrid strategies to thwart Taiwan's acquisition of reprocessing technology from European suppliers and to halt unsafeguarded activities at the Taiwan Research Reactor (TRR). Both administrations combined threats to terminate civil nuclear cooperation with inducements, namely continued arms transfers to Taiwan, even as the United States moved closer to normalizing relations with China.

Table 7.1 summarizes the empirical support the neoclassical realist, nuclear domino, credible sanctions, and security commitment hypotheses in chapters 3 through 6.

In general, neoclassical realist theory found empirical support across all four proliferation disputes. There was one major anomaly, however. In 1975 and 1976, the Ford administration pursued an accommodative nonproliferation strategy toward Pakistan. Specifically, President Gerald R. Ford and Kissinger offered to sell advanced weapons systems (including 100 A-7 aircraft) in exchange for Prime Minister Zulfikar Ali Bhutto's canceling a contract to purchase a French-designed uranium enrichment plant.

The neoclassical realist hypothesis would expect the Ford administration to have pursued a coercive strategy to thwart Pakistan's acquisition of reprocessing

Table 7.1 **Empirical Support for Alternative Hypotheses**

	Neoclassical Realist Hypotheses	Nuclear Domino Hypotheses	Security Commitment Hypotheses	Credible Sanctions Hypotheses
US and Israeli nuclear weapons program (1960–1973)	Confirmed	Partially confirmed (1961–1963)	NA	NA
US and Pakistani nuclear weapons program (1975–1990)	Confirmed (1979–1990) Anomaly (1975–1976)	Disconfirmed	NA	Partially confirmed (1979)
US and South Korean nuclear weapons program (1970–1982)	Confirmed	Disconfirmed	Disconfirmed	Disconfirmed
US and Taiwanese nuclear weapons program (1967–1978)	Confirmed	Disconfirmed	Disconfirmed	Disconfirmed

technology, since US policymakers perceived a favorable power distribution in South Asia and long time horizons for emerging threats in that region during the 1975–1976 period. Furthermore, administration officials would have faced low domestic mobilization hurdles to pursuing a coercive strategy, given mounting concern in Congress about nuclear proliferation.

The nuclear domino theory hypothesis only finds partial support in the early stages of the US-Israel proliferation dispute. Some officials in the Kennedy administration did worry that Israel's clandestine activities at Dimona might prompt a reactive proliferation by Egypt in the early 1960s. Kennedy warned Ben-Gurion, both during their first meeting in May 1961 and in writing, that suspicion of Israeli efforts to develop a nuclear weapon might prompt Egypt to follow suit. By the mid-1960s, however, concerns about reactive proliferation by Egypt largely disappear from the documentary record.

There is no empirical support for the nuclear domino theory hypothesis in the three other proliferation disputes. For example, there was no evidence to suggest that the risk that India might weaponize its nuclear capability prompted the Carter administration to impose Symington Amendment sanctions on Pakistan in April 1979. Similarly, there is no evidence to suggest that the increased likelihood of reactive proliferation in East Asia drove the Ford administration's nonproliferation strategies toward South Korea or the Ford and Carter administrations' nonproliferation strategies toward Taiwan.

The case studies of the United States' proliferation disputes with South Korea and Taiwan largely disconfirm the hypotheses from security commitment theory. The Nixon administration began the withdrawal of US troops from Taiwan and South Korea in the 1969–1971 period. One might argue that the Ford administration's pledge to maintain US troop levels in South Korea in 1975–1976 offers some support for the security commitment hypothesis. At the same time, however, officials combined pledges to maintain troop levels with threats to terminate civil nuclear cooperation if President Park Chung-hee did not cancel the French reprocessing plant contract. Similarly, intelligence about the Taiwan's clandestine nuclear activities and efforts to acquire reprocessing technology from foreign suppliers did not prompt the Ford or the Carter administrations to halt (or least slow) the withdrawal of US troops, despite pleas from Premier (later President) Chiang Ching-kuo.

The credible sanctions theory hypotheses find no support in the case studies of the United States' proliferation disputes with South Korea and Taiwan. As noted earlier, both proliferation disputes straddle the passage of the Symington Amendment in summer 1976. The hypothesis would have expected the Carter administration's nonproliferation strategies toward Seoul and Taipei to be coercive, since the legislation came into force in April 1977. Carter and other administration officials never seriously contemplated, let alone directly threatened, to impose Symington Amendment sanctions on South Korea.

The credible sanctions theory hypothesis, however, does receive some empirical support in the US-Pakistan proliferation dispute. In March 1979, Deputy Secretary of State Warren Christopher personally warned Zia that unsafeguarded uranium enrichment would trigger the imposition of Symington Amendment sanctions. President Jimmy Carter imposed sanctions the following month, suspending all US military assistance and most economic assistance to Pakistan. Following the Soviet invasion of Afghanistan six months later, however, Carter administration officials scrambled, albeit unsuccessfully, to develop an emergency aid package for Pakistan and to secure congressional approval for a Symington Amendment waiver.

In 1981, the Reagan administration succeeded in getting Congress to approve a Symington Amendment waiver, along with a $3.4 billion package of economic and military assistance for Pakistan. For the next six years, administration officials circumvented various nonproliferation laws (e.g., the Glenn, Solarz, and Pressler amendments) in order to continue the flow of military assistance to Zia government, despite two high-profile nuclear smuggling cases and intelligence about Pakistani uranium enrichment. The Bush administration only reimposed nonproliferation sanctions in October 1990, more than a year after Soviet troops withdrew from Afghanistan.

Theoretical Implications and Avenues for Additional Research

The neoclassical realist theory developed and tested in the previous chapters purports to explain variation in the types of nonproliferation strategies that the United States pursued toward particular allies in the latter part of the Cold War. For the past twenty-eight years, the global distribution of power in the international system has been unipolar, not bipolar. The only states that accelerated their nuclear weapons and long-range ballistic missile programs since the end of the Cold War have been North Korea and Iran, both long time regional adversaries of the United States.[2] Since the 1970s, no ally of the United States has initiated a nuclear weapons program, although some non-nuclear allies, including Japan, South Korea, and the Federal Republic of Germany, allegedly maintain a latent nuclear capacity.[3] Nonetheless, neoclassical realist theory has a number of broader theoretical implications and suggests several avenues for new research.

The first concerns how the foreign policy executives (FPEs) of states, especially those of the great powers or hegemons, make power assessments. Proponents of structural realism and neoclassical realism have long argued that power (which they generally define as material capabilities) comes in various forms or categories. These include, but are not limited to, latent power versus mobilized power, land power versus maritime power, state power versus

---

[2] The Iranian and the North Korean nuclear weapons programs both predated the end of the Cold War in November 1989 and the collapse of the Soviet Union in December 1991.

[3] Classic works on nuclear latency include: George H. Quester, "Some Conceptual Problems in Nuclear Proliferation," *The American Political Science Review*, Vol. 66, No. 2 (1972), pp. 490–497; Albert J. Wohlstetter, *Swords from Plowshare: The Military Potential of Civilian Nuclear Energy* (Chicago: University of Chicago Press, 1979); Stephen M. Meyer, *The Dynamics of Nuclear Proliferation* (Chicago: Chicago: University of Chicago Press, 1984); and Ariel E. Levite, "Never Say Never Again: Nuclear Reversal Revisited," *International Security*, Vol. 27, No. 3 (2002), pp. 59–88. More recent works on the political implications of nuclear latency include: Scott D. Sagan, "Nuclear Latency

national power (or national political power), potential power versus economic power and military power, etc.[4] Policymakers' assessment of relative power and power trends is highly complex and frequently contested.[5] Recent work by Evan Braden Montgomery and Steven E. Lobell suggests that policymakers do not give equal weight to all components of other states' material capabilities, but instead give greater weight to the components they perceive (or correctly or incorrectly) as more threatening to their own state's survival or strategic interests.[6]

The members of a hegemon's FPE will not just be concerned with assessing the current distribution of power between their own state and a rising great power, but also the current distribution of power within a contested region and across different regions.[7] After all, rising great powers are more likely to assert their influence and to challenge the United States in regions closer to their own homelands. Therefore, the hegemon's senior policymakers would need to be

---

and Nuclear Proliferation," in William C. Potter and Gaukhar Mukhatzhanova, eds., *Forecasting Nuclear Proliferation in the 21st Century, Vol. 1: The Role of Theory* (Stanford, CA: Stanford University Press, 2010), pp. 80–101; Matthew Fuhrmann and Benjamin Tkach, "Almost Nuclear: Introducing the Nuclear Latency Dataset," *Conflict Management and Peace Science*, Vol. 32, No. 4 (2015), pp. 443–461; Vipin Narang, "Strategies of Nuclear Proliferation: How States Pursue the Bomb," *International Security*, Vol. 41, No. 3 (2017), pp. 110–150; and Nicholas L. Miller, "Why Nuclear Energy Programs Rarely Lead to Proliferation," *International Security*, Vol. 42, No. 2 (2017), pp. 40–77. For a recent study that examines whether South Korea, Japan, and North Korea were able to use varying degrees of nuclear latency to compel the United States in disputes between 1957 and 2007, see Tristan A. Volpe, "Atomic Leverage: Compellence with Nuclear Latency," *Security Studies*, Vol. 26, No. 3 (2017), pp. 517–544.

[4] For discussions of these various categories of power see Thomas J. Christensen, *Useful Adversaries: Grand Strategy, Domestic Mobilization, and Sino-American Conflict, 1947–1958* (Princeton, NJ: Princeton University Press, 1996); Fareed Zakaria, *From Wealth to Power: The Unusual Origins of America's World Role* (Princeton, NJ: Princeton University Press, 1998); Dale C. Copeland, *The Origins of Major War* (Ithaca, NY: Cornell University Press, 2000); John J. Mearsheimer, *The Tragedy of Great Power Politics* (New York: W. W. Norton & Company, 2014); and Stephen G. Brooks and William C. Wohlforth, *America Abroad: The United States' Global Role in the 21st Century* (New York: Oxford University Press, 2016).

[5] See Aaron L. Friedberg, *The Weary Titan: Britain and the Experience of Relative Decline, 1895–1905* (Princeton, NJ: Princeton University Press, 1988), chapter 6. On the difficulties of assessing military power in particular see Stephen D. Biddle, *Military Power: Explaining Victory and Defeat in Modern Battle* (Princeton, NJ: Princeton University Press, 2004); Risa Brooks and Elizabeth A. Stanley, eds., *Creating Military Power: The Sources of Military Effectiveness* (Stanford, CA: Stanford University Press, 2007); and Ashley J. Tellis, *Measuring National Power in the Postindustrial Age* (Santa Monica, CA: RAND, 2000).

[6] On this point see Evan Braden Montgomery, *In the Hegemon's Shadow: Leading States and the Rise of Regional Powers* (Ithaca, NY: Cornell University Press, 2016), esp. chapter 1; and Steven E. Lobell, "A Granular Theory of Balancing," *International Studies Quarterly*, Vol. 62, No. 3 (2018), pp. 593–605.

[7] For a discussion of the bilateral (US-China) bias in extant studies of the East Asian military balance, see Michael Beckley, "The Emerging Military Balance in East Asia: How China's Neighbors Can Check Chinese Naval Expansion," *International Security*, Vol. 42, No. 2 (2017), pp. 78–119, at p. 80, n. 8.

attuned to both the current distribution of capabilities among regional actors and the extent to which a rival great power's penetration of that region might shift the power balance. Furthermore, policymakers will tend to give greater weight to shifts in the components of regional power distributions they perceive (whether correctly or incorrectly) as more threatening to their states' strategic interests.

A second pertains to time horizons. Neoclassical realist theory posits that policymakers are not only making subjective assessments about current power balances within a region, but also calculations about when threats to their state's interests will materialize. On the one hand, if policymakers expect those threats to materialize or become acute over the span of several years or decades, they face greater uncertainty in the present. Exogenous factors and unanticipated developments may dissipate or exacerbate that threat over time. Policymakers have more time and presumably a great range of potential options to redress the threat. Nonetheless, not acting in the present, whether in order to conserve resources or to gather more intelligence, may entail paying a dramatically higher price to redress the threat in the future.[8]

On the other hand, if policymakers anticipate the threat will materialize over the span of weeks, months, or a year, they may face less uncertainty. There is less time for the capabilities of the relevant actors—whether a local state or a rival great power—to shift. However, the range of potential options to redress the threat will be narrower. Furthermore, when policymakers see threats as temporally proximate, they are also more likely to suffer from "false certainty" about outcomes.[9] Consequently, when policymakers perceive less uncertainty, they may be less receptive to new intelligence and more inclined to select options that seem to offer an immediate redress to the threat, even if those options entail high costs.

A third involves the theory's intervening variable, the height of the domestic mobilization hurdles an administration must overcome in the pursuit of its preferred strategy toward an ally. In the present book, I operationalized this variable in terms of the anticipated degree of congressional support or congressional opposition to the administration's preferred policies. Congressional opposition

---

[8] See David M. Edelstein, *Over the Horizon: Time, Uncertainty, and the Rise of Great Powers* (Ithaca, NY: Cornell University Press, 2017).

[9] On false or misplaced certainty, see Jennifer Mitzen and Randall L. Schweller, "Knowing the Unknown Unknowns: Misplaced Certainty and the Onset of War," *Security Studies*, Vol. 20, No. 1 (2011), pp. 2–35. There is some overlap with the pseudo certainty effect of prospect theory, the tendency to treat high likely, but uncertain, outcomes as if they were in fact certain. See Jack S. Levy, "Prospect Theory and International Relations: Theoretical Applications and Analytical Problems," in Barbara Farnham, ed., *Avoiding Losses/Taking Risks: Prospect Theory and International Conflict* (Ann Arbor: University of Michigan Press, 1994) pp. 119–146.

may lead an administration to pursue a hybrid strategy toward an ally's nuclear weapons program, even when administration officials perceive a favorable power distribution and long time horizons for threats in the ally's region. This dynamic occurred during the proliferation disputes with South Korea and Taiwan in the mid-1970s.

Two aspects about Congress's role in the proliferation disputes with Israel, Pakistan, South Korea, and Taiwan are worth noting. First, even during periods of divided government in the United States, there was still a great deal of bipartisanship on national security issues, including nuclear proliferation and alliance management.[10] For example, Carter's proposal to withdraw the remaining 40,000 US troops (the Second Infantry Division) from South Korea in 1977 and 1978 faced bipartisan opposition in Congress. Democratic senators like Robert Byrd, Sam Nunn, Hubert Humphrey, and John Glenn were some of the more vocal critics of Carter's plan. Nine years earlier, Nixon decided not to link the F-4 Phantom sale to the Meir government's commitment to sign the NPT because he (and Kissinger) recognized such linkage would face strong opposition from Democrats, as well as from Republicans. The most vocal critics of Nixon's 1972 rapprochement with China and Ford's initial moves to normalize diplomatic ties with China in 1975 and 1976 were conservative Republicans like Senators Barry Goldwater, Jesse Helms, and Strom Thurmond, and former California governor (and future president) Ronald Reagan.

Second, because of the technical nature of nuclear proliferation, only a small number of senators and representatives in both parties took an active interest in these issues. These legislators tended to have seniority and to occupy formal or informal leadership roles on the appropriate oversight committees in either chamber (e.g., Armed Services or Foreign Relations/Foreign Affairs). Thus presidents, secretaries of state and defense, and other administration officials only had to bargain with a relatively small group of representatives and senators.

In chapter 2, I acknowledged that domestic mobilizations hurdles are not completely endogenous and that some hurdles may be the residue of prior international stimuli or domestic political dynamics. In the cases examined in chapters 3 through 6, that prior international stimulus was the Cold War competition with the Soviet Union. Similarly, the degree of congressional skepticism and sometimes opposition

---

[10] The periods of divided government during the cases examined were: (1) January 1969 to January 1977, when the Democrats had majorities in both houses of Congress and Republicans Richard N. Nixon and Gerald R. Ford held the presidency; (2) January 1981 to January 1987, when the Democrats had the majority in the House of Representatives, the Republicans had a majority in the Senate, and Republican Ronald Reagan was president; and (3) January 1987 to October 1991, when the Democrats held majorities in both houses of Congress while Reagan and George H. W. Bush occupied the White House.

to administrations' foreign policy initiatives varied over time. In the wake of the Vietnam War and the Watergate scandal, the Ford and the Carter administrations had to contend with greater congressional pushback on foreign and defense policy issues in general (and thus higher mobilization hurdles), than did the Kennedy and the Johnson administrations in the 1960s. How the decline in bipartisanship in Congress (especially in Senate) and the demise of the senior system for committee chairmanships in the Senate and the House over the past quarter century may affect the types of domestic mobilization hurdles for presidential administration's foreign policies is an avenue for more research.

Frenemies (along with other types of allies) were and are not passive partners of the United States. Instead, these weaker allies actively tried to shape US foreign and defense policies in directions they deemed conducive to their own strategic interests. One tactic for doing so involved the mobilization of supporters in the United States, such as sympathetic members of Congress, lobbyists, and members of their diaspora communities, to modify, slow, or thwart an administration's policy initiatives.

Israel, South Korea, and Taiwan each pursued this tactic with varying degrees of "success" in their respective proliferation disputes with the United States. By the mid-1960s, the Eshkol government became adept at mobilizing congressional support for US arms transfers to Israel. The Park Chung-hee government "overplayed its hand" in trying to forestall additional US troop withdrawals in the mid-1970s. The revelations that South Korean lobbyist Park Tung-sin and his associates made illegal gifts and cash donations to ninety members of Congress, as well as congressional staffers, over the course of seven years led to a sharp deterioration in bilateral relations. By the time the proliferation dispute between the Ford administration and Chiang Ching-kuo's government began in earnest in 1975, the influence of the so-called Taiwan lobby in Congress had greatly diminished.

This book did not explicitly address variation in weaker allies' ability to penetrate the US political system, thereby raising the domestic mobilization hurdles a presidential administration would need to overcome.[11] Explaining variation in weaker allies' ability to raise domestic mobilization hurdles for the FPEs of the

---

[11] Two other books in the neoclassical realist literature that briefly address weaker allies' penetration of the US political system are Jeremy Pressman, *Warring Friends: Alliance Restraint in International Politics* (Ithaca, NY: Cornell University Press, 2008); and Evan Resnick, *Allies of Convenience: A Theory of Bargaining in US Foreign Policy* (New York: Columbia University Press, 2019). On "domestic" political penetration of a stronger ally by a weaker ally, see Stephen M. Walt, *Taming American Power: The Global Response to US Primacy* (New York: Norton, 2005), pp. 194–217.
Also see John J. Mearsheimer and Stephen M. Walt, *The Israel Lobby and US Foreign Policy* (New York: Farrar, Straus & Giroux, 2007); and Tony Smith, *Foreign Attachments: The Power of Ethnic Groups in the Making of American Foreign Policy* (Cambridge, MA: Harvard University Press, 2000).

United States and other great powers might become an explicit topic of future neoclassical realist research.[12]

Another potential advance for research concerns the concept of alliance abandonment. Glenn Snyder, who introduced the concept of an alliance security dilemma thirty years ago, stated that abandonment could take several forms: abrogation of the alliance; de-alignment; a failure to fulfill specific commitments; or a failure to "provide support in contingencies when support is expected."[13] In two of the cases examined in this book (Taiwan and South Korea), leaders authorized clandestine nuclear weapons and/or missile programs in large part because they feared the United States might not fulfill a treaty commitment to defend their territory against a local adversary (namely China and North Korea). In two other cases (Israel and Pakistan), leaders authorized nuclear weapons programs at a time when the United States had no formal or implied obligation to come to the defense against local adversaries (Egypt and Syria and India, respectively).

Several scholars claim that the United States explicitly or at least implicitly threatened to "abandon" various Cold War allies, including West Germany, Taiwan, South Korea, Pakistan, and Israel, if they did not cease and desist their efforts to develop nuclear weapons or acquire dual-use components.[14] At various points, US policymakers and diplomats did threaten to suspend arms transfers, economic assistance, and civil nuclear assistance to Israel, Pakistan, South Korea, and Taiwan. However, none of the seven administrations (John F. Kennedy through George H. W. Bush) implicitly or explicitly threatened to terminate alliance ties with these states altogether.

The Carter administration did terminate the US-ROK Mutual Defense Treaty, effective 1 January 1980, but that move had long been anticipated by Chiang

---

[12] There is a large literature on asymmetric conflict and the paradoxical bargaining advantages of weaker parties, but none of it from the perspective of neoclassical realism. Seminal works include: Robert O. Keohane, "The Big Influence of Small Allies," *Foreign Policy*, No. 2 (1971), pp. 161–182; A. J. R. Mack, "Why Big Nations Lose Small Wars: The Politics of Asymmetric Conflict," *World Politics*, Vol. 27, No. 2 (1975), pp. 175–200; T. V. Paul, *Asymmetric Conflicts: War Initiation by Weaker Powers* (Cambridge: Cambridge University Press, 1994); Gil Merom, *How Democracies Lose Small Wars: State, Society, and the Failures of France in Algeria, Israel in Lebanon, and the United States in Vietnam* (Cambridge: Cambridge University Press, 2003); and Ivan Arreguín-Toft, *How the Weak Win Wars: A Theory of Asymmetric Conflict* (New York: Cambridge University Press, 2005).

[13] Glenn H. Snyder, "The Security Dilemma in Alliance Politics," *World Politics*, Vol. 36, No. 4 (1984), pp. 461–495, at p. 466.

[14] See, for example, Gavin, "Strategies of Inhibition," pp. 7, 19, and 21; Gene Gerzhoy, "Alliance Coercion and Nuclear Restraint: How the United States Thwarted West Germany's Nuclear Ambitions," *International Security*, Vol. 39, No. 4 (2015), pp. 91–129, esp. pp. 121–124; and Alexandre Debs and Nuno P. Monteiro, *Nuclear Politics: The Strategic Causes of Proliferation* (New York: Cambridge University Press, 2016).

Ching-kuo's government. Neither the Ford nor the Carter administration threatened to terminate the 1954 treaty as a coercive strategy in the proliferation dispute with Taiwan. More important, the Nixon, Ford, Carter, and Reagan administrations continued to sell defensive weapons to Taiwan, first under the 1954 alliance treaty and then, after 1981, under the terms of the Taiwan Relations Act (TRA), despite vigorous protests from China.

From the standpoint of US policymakers, explicit or implicit threats to terminate alliance ties, even ties with frenemies, would have been self-defeating, especially in the context of the Cold War. The United States, after all, maintained alliances with these states as a means to avert containment failure and preserve its own access to various regions. Terminating those ties entirely would mean losing all leverage over the weaker ally, as well as potentially ceding that region to a great power rival. As quarrelsome and contentious as Washington's bilateral relations with Jerusalem, Islamabad, Seoul, and Taipei became during the proliferation disputes examined in this book, US policymakers never considered severing ties entirely.

Nonetheless, from the standpoint of weaker allies, potential "abandonment" by the United States loomed large. For these states, any reduction in US military and economic assistance programs or diplomatic support would constitute being abandoned by Washington. Exactly what constitutes "abandonment" by a superpower ally and the broader issue of credibility may be far more subjective and driven by the weaker ally's perceptions and strategic circumstances than the extant alliance literature acknowledges.

A final avenue for additional research involves the evolution of asymmetric alliances over time. I argued that frenemies are just one among several types of asymmetric alliances that great powers contract and maintain with weaker states. The other categories include alliances of convenience, ambivalent alliances, and special relationship alliances. The differences among these categories lie in the degree of convergence (or divergence) in the strategic interests and the ideologies of the two partners.[15]

I acknowledged that frenemies might evolve into special relationships over time, but that explaining when, why, and under circumstances that evolution might occur lay outside the scope of the present book. Future research might explicitly address this question. Neoclassical realist theory suggests a two-step process. The first step would be a convergence in the strategic interests of the great power and its weaker ally due to shifts in regional power distributions and shared time horizons for threats. The second step might involve the weaker ally's ability to raise the domestic mobilization hurdles for the great power's FPE. Once the

---

[15] See Evan N. Resnick, "Strange Bedfellows: US Bargaining Behavior with Allies of Convenience," *International Security*, Vol. 35, No. 3 (2010), pp. 144–184; Resnick, *Dealing with Devils*, chapter 1.

weaker ally has penetrated the domestic political system of its great power patron, then we might expect to see (over time) increasing ideological convergence between the two allied governments and their societies.[16]

Policy Implications

During the historical period studied in chapters 5 and 6 (roughly 1967 to 1981), the Soviet Union and China viewed each other as adversaries and the United States sought to exploit their rivalry. Today, Russia and China have identified the United States as their primary adversary. As the 2018 *National Defense Strategy* puts it, "The central challenge to US prosperity and security is the reemergence of long-term, strategic competition.... It is increasingly clear that China and Russia want to shape a world consistent with their authoritarian model—gaining veto authority over other nations' economic, diplomatic, and security decisions."[17]

In September 2018, Russia staged its largest military exercises since the end of the Cold War in eastern Siberia, involving some 300,000 Russian military personnel using 1,000 military aircraft and 36,000 pieces of military equipment. Three hundred twenty-thousand Chinese People's Liberation Army (PLA) troops using 900 pieces of equipment and 30 aircraft also participated in the Vostok-2018 exercises. To be clear, China and Russia have not yet forged a full-fledged alliance.[18] Nor are China and Russia presently global competitors of the United States. The former is a potential superpower, while the latter is a former superpower that lags well behind the United States in most categories of material capabilities.[19] Yet, both of them pose serious challenges to US hegemony in various regions—Russia, principally in Europe and the Middle East, and China,

---

[16] This hypothesized two-step process for alliance evolution would be akin to the causal mechanism Norrin M. Ripsman identifies by which peace treaties between regional rivals evolve into stable peace settlements. See Ripsman, *Peacemaking from Above, Peace from Below: Ending Conflict Between Regional Rivals* (Ithaca, NY: Cornell University Press, 2016).

[17] United States Department of Defense, *Summary of the 2018 National Defense Strategy of the United States of America: Sharpening America's Competitive Edge* (Washington, DC: GPO, 2018), p. 2. Available at https://dod.defense.gov/Portals/1/Documents/pubs/2018-National-Defense-Strategy-Summary.pdf.

[18] See Dmitry Gorenburg, "Five Things to Know About Russia's Vostok-2018" *Washington Post*, 13 September 2018. Also see Vasily Kashin, "Current State of Russian-Chinese Defense Cooperation," *CNA Occasional Paper* (Arlington, VA: Center for Naval Analyses, 2018), https://www.cna.org/CNA_files/PDF/DOP-2018-U-018184-Final.pdf.

[19] See Stephen G. Brooks and William C. Wohlforth, "The Rise and Fall of the Great Powers in the Twenty-First Century: China's Rise and the Fate of America's Global Position," *International Security*, Vol. 40, No. 3 (2016), pp. 7–53; and Stephen G. Brooks and William C. Wohlforth, *America*

principally in East Asia and Southeast Asia, including its maritime peripheries in the South China Sea and increasingly in the Indian Ocean, as well.[20]

In the past five years, President Vladimir Putin of Russia has authorized the use of hybrid warfare strategies to annex Crimea and to support pro-Russian separatists in eastern Ukraine; deployed air and ground forces to decisively turn the tide of the Syrian Civil War in favor of President Bashar al-Assad's regime, forging a tacit alliance with Iran toward that end; and authorized the use of cyber espionage and disinformation campaigns on social media to stoke political divisions and influence elections in the United States and several Western European states.[21] In the Middle East, Putin has sought reassert Russian influence by filling the power vacuum created by the Syrian Civil War and the emergence of the so-called Islamic State or Daesh, which in turn, were some of the unintended consequences of the George W. Bush administration's invasion of Iraq in 2003 and the mismanagement of the Iraqi occupation.[22]

Meanwhile, President Xi Jinping of China has authorized the construction and the militarization of artificial islands in disputed waters in the South China Sea; continued the modernization of Chinese air and naval capabilities to pursue an anti-access and area denial (A2/AD) strategy against US naval forces in the western Pacific; circumvented sanctions on North Korea imposed by the UN Security Council; and invested in infrastructure and energy projects throughout Central Asia, South Asia, Southeast Asia, and the Middle East as part of the Belt and Road Initiative.[23]

Abroad: The United States' Global Role in the 21st Century (New York: Oxford University Press, 2016), pp. 48–72. Also see Michael Beckley, *Unrivaled: Why America Will Remain the World's Sole Superpower* (Ithaca, NY: Cornell University Press, 2018).

[20] Robert Sutter, "China-Russia Relations: Strategic Implications and US Policy Options," *NBR Special Report # 23* (Seattle: National Bureau of Asian Research, 2018), https://www.nbr.org/wp-content/uploads/pdfs/publications/special_report_73_china-russia_cooperation_sep2018.pdf.

[21] See Alexander Korolev, "Theories of Non-Balancing and Russia's Foreign Policy," *Journal of Strategic Studies*, Vol. 41, No. 6 (2018), pp. 887–912; Andrew S. Bowen, "Coercive Diplomacy and the Donbas: Explaining Russian Strategy in Eastern Ukraine," *Journal of Strategic Studies* (2017), pp. 1–32; Alexander Lanoszka, "Russian Hybrid Warfare and Extended Deterrence in Eastern Europe," *International Affairs*, Vol. 92, No. 1 (2016), pp. 175–195; and Tor Bukkvoll, "Military Innovation Under Authoritarian Government—the Case of Russian Special Operations Forces," *Journal of Strategic Studies*, Vol. 38, No. 5 (2015), pp. 602–625.

[22] See Samuel Charap, "Is Russia an Outside Power in the Gulf?" *Survival*, Vol. 57, No. 1 (2015), pp. 153–170; and Hal Brands and Peter Feaver, "Was the Rise of ISIS Inevitable?" *Survival*, Vol. 59, No. 3 (2017), pp. 7–54.

[23] Some recent entries in the scholarly debates about the strategic implications of China's naval modernization, activities in the South China Sea, and the Belt and Road Initiative, etc. include: Beckley, "Emerging Military Balance in East Asia"; David Shambaugh, "US-China Rivalry in Southeast

There is a disconnect between President Donald J. Trump's refusal to acknowledge the scope of Russian election interference in support of his candidacy in 2016, his lavish praise of Putin, and his public berating of NATO allies to increase their defense spending, on the one hand, and the actions his administration has taken to counter Russian influence, on the other hand.[24] These actions include the imposition of economic sanctions against Russian government officials and business with ties to Putin; the expulsion of Russian diplomats from the United States; and the continuation of the Obama administration's efforts to bolster the US military commitment to NATO's Eastern European member states.[25] Likewise, there is a contradiction between Trump's initiation of a trade war with China and the increased US naval presence in the western Pacific, on the one hand, and his praise of Xi and reliance on the Chinese president's to help facilitate the "denuclearization" of North Korea, on the other hand.[26]

Asia: Power Shift or Competitive Coexistence?" *International Security*, Vol. 42, No. 4 (2018), pp. 85–127; Eric Heginbotham and Richard J. Samuels, "Active Denial: Redesigning Japan's Response to China's Military Challenge," *International Security*, Vol. 42, No. 4 (2018), pp. 128–169; Jennifer Lind and Daryl G. Press, "Markets or Mercantilism? How China Secures Its Energy Supplies," *International Security*, Vol. 42, No. 04 (2018), pp. 170–204; Jean-Marc F. Blanchard and Colin Flint, "The Geopolitics of China's Maritime Silk Road Initiative," *Geopolitics*, Vol. 22, No. 2 (2017), pp. 223–245; Scott L. Kastner, "Is the Taiwan Strait Still a Flash Point? Rethinking the Prospects for Armed Conflict Between China and Taiwan," *International Security*, Vol. 40, No. 3 (2016), pp. 54–92; and Stephen Biddle and Ivan Oelrich, "Future Warfare in the Western Pacific: Chinese Anti Access/Area Denial, US Air Sea Battle, and Command of the Commons in East Asia," *International Security*, Vol. 41, No. 1 (2016), pp. 7–48.

[24] See, for example, Remarks by President Trump and President Putin of the Russian Federation in Joint Press Conference, Presidential Palace, Helsinki, Finland, 16 July 2018, https://www.whitehouse.gov/briefings-statements/remarks-president-trump-president-putin-russian-federation-joint-press-conference/?utm_source=link (accessed 1 October 2018); and Remarks by President Trump at Press Conference after NATO Summit, Brussels, Belgium, 12 July 2018, https://www.whitehouse.gov/briefings-statements/remarks-president-trump-press-conference-nato-summit-brussels-belgium/?utm_source=link (accessed 2 October 2018).

[25] See Joshua Shifrinson, "Sound and Fury, Signifying Something? NATO and the Trump Administration's Second Year," *H-Diplo, ISSF POLICY Series: America and the World—2017 and Beyond-Diplo*, 15 July 2018, http://issforum.org/roundtables/policy/1-5BI-NATO (accessed 1 October 2018); and Paul K. Macdonald, "America First? Explaining Continuity and Change in Trump's Foreign Policy," *Political Science Quarterly*, Vol. 133, No. 3 (2018), pp. 401–434.

[26] Remarks by President Trump and President Xi of China in Joint Press Statement, Beijing, China, 9 November 2017, https://www.whitehouse.gov/briefings-statements/remarks-president-trump-president-xi-china-joint-press-statement-beijing-china/?utm_source=link (accessed 5 October 2018); Remarks by President Trump at Business Event with President Xi of China, Beijing, China, 9 November 2017, https://www.whitehouse.gov/briefings-statements/remarks-president-trump-business-event-president-xi-china-beijing-china/?utm_source=link (accessed 5 October 2018); and Statement from the President Regarding Trade with China, 18 June 2018, https://www.whitehouse.gov/briefings-statements/statement-president-regarding-trade-china-2/?utm_source=link (accessed 5 October 2018).

If the United States is to maintain (or at least prolong) its preponderant position in the international system, then it will have to redouble efforts to contain Russia and China. The neoclassical realist theory developed in this book suggests that policymakers in the Trump administration, like its Cold War predecessors, should be concerned with averting containment failure in key regions, such as the Middle East, East Asia, and Southeast Asia, as well as preserving the United States' own access to those regions. Consequently, regional power distributions and time horizons for emerging threats should loom large in the calculations of US policymakers. This implies that US policymakers ought to approach proliferation disputes with Iran and North Korea with those grand strategic objectives in mind.

INDEX

access denial
  causes of increasing risk, 56–57
  limited U.S. risks in Africa, 28
  Montgomery's description, 8
  nuclear proliferation's risks of, 10–11
  risk factors, 7–8, 13, 41, 46–47, 56–57
  in southern Africa, 28
accommodation
  coercion in combination with, 14, 48–49, 116, 179, 192, 260
  neoclassical realist theory and, 192
  by Nixon administration, 3, 108
  by Reagan administration, 138
  Reagan's pursuit of, with Pakistan, 138
  U.S. nonproliferation strategies, 1–2, 14
  U.S. occasional pursuit of, 17
Acheson, Dean, 40
Adelman, Kenneth, 144, 149, 151, 153
aerial and satellite reconnaissance, 45, 46n30, 114–15, 154–55, 167–68, 199–200, 215, 257–58
Afghan Interim Government (AIM), 153–54
Afghanistan
  Carter's offer of limited assistance, 133n80
  PDPA's coup against Khan, 124
  Reagan's/Casey's funding of covert operations, 139
  Soviet invasion of, 116–17, 133–35, 158, 209, 261, 264
  Soviet withdrawal from, 153–54, 157
Ahmed, Aziz, 117–18
Allen, Richard V., 140, 256–57
alliances
  alliance coercion theory, 14n35, 14
  alliances of convenience, 18–20
  asymmetric alliances, 18, 19f, 271
  bilateral alliances, 8n15, 18n42
  definition, 17
  eschewing of, by India, 31
  frenemies as ambivalent alliances, 21–22
  origins/purposes of, 20
  regional power distributions and, 6
  special-relationship alliances, 22
  as tools of restraint, 20n46
  of U.S., types of, 4–5, 7–8, 17, 20, 271
Allon, Yigal, 81
Al-Qaeda, 159
"ambivalent alliances," frenemies comparison, 21–22
Amin, Hazifullah, 130–31, 133–34
Arab-Israeli conflicts, 3–4, 25, 65, 66, 74, 75, 77, 79, 86, 92, 94, 96–97, 99, 101, 110
Argentina, nuclear weapons program, 24t
Arif, Khalid, 139–40, 142
Armacost, Michael, 149, 150, 151, 153
  Pakistan-U.S. nonproliferation conflict and, 149, 150, 151, 153
Armed Services Committee (U.S. House of Representatives), 51
Armed Services Committee (U.S. Senate), 51
Arms Control and Disarmament Agency (ACADA), 144
Arms Export Control Act (AECA, 1976), 28–29, 51–53, 144
A-4 Skyhawks
  Israel's interest in purchasing, 68
  Johnson's decision to sell to Israel, 53, 73
  Nixon's sale to Israel, 99–100
Atherton, Alfred, 122
Atomic Energy Commission, Reactor Development Division, 69
Atoms for Peace program, 29, 64, 214–15, 219–20
Atoms for Peace training programs, 29
Australia, SEATO membership, 25n58

Baghdad Pact, 25–26
Baker, James A., III, 40, 43

balance-of-power theories
  hegemonic theory comparison, 7–8
  Waltz's restructuring of, 37
Ball, George, 71
Barbour, Walworth, 68–69, 71, 77
Baruch Plan (1945), 1
Beg, Mirza Aslam, 155
Ben-Gurion, David
  authorization of Israel's secret nuclear program, 64
  Eisenhower's interactions with, 67
  interest in purchasing U.S. anti-aircraft missiles, 67
  invitation to Kennedy to inspect Dimona reactor, 68–69
  Kennedy's efforts at arranging inspections of Dimona reactor, 66–73, 109, 260, 263–64
  Kennedy's rejection of mutual defense treaty request, 71–72, 86–87
  on purpose of Dimona reactor, 69–70
  request of Kennedy to purchase Hawk missiles, 70
  resignation as Israel's prime minister, 71n22, 71
Bennet, Douglas, 122
Bhutto, Benazir, 154
  Khan's clash with, 156
  meeting with Bush, 155
  meeting with U.S. Congress, 155
Bhutto, Zulfikar, 154
  Ford/Kissinger meeting with, 117–18
  Ford's warning letter to, 118–19
  Kissinger's meeting with, 120
  seeking of nuclear weapons capability, 112–13, 115, 146
  Zia's ouster of, 122–23
bilateral asymmetric alliances, 19f
bilateral defense pacts, 2, 259
Bonker, Don, 149–50
Botha, P. W., 27–28
Brazil, nuclear weapons program, 24t
British Empire, global hegemony of, 4–5
Brooks, Stephen, 44
Brown, Harold, 133–34
  role in U.S.-Republic of Korea proliferation dispute, 198, 202, 203–4
Brzezinski, Zbigniew, 134–35, 136
  role in U.S.-Republic of China on Taiwan proliferation dispute, 246–47, 248, 250–51, 252–53, 254, 255
  role in U.S.-Republic of Korea proliferation dispute, 197–98, 201, 203–4, 206
Buckley, James, 140–41, 142
Bundy, McGeorge, 33n92, 68, 75
Bureau of Intelligence and Research (INR, U.S. State Department), 64–65, 94, 99, 141–42, 172, 178, 185–86
Bush, George H. W.

  abandonment of Pakistan, 152–59
  Cold War and, 20
  efforts at halting nuclear proliferation, 59
  on Iraqi occupation of Kuwait, 43
  leadership in 1989 revolutions, 40
  reimposition of Pakistan sanctions, 12
  termination of military/economic assistance to Pakistan, 116
  U.S.-Pakistan dispute and, 116

Carter, Jimmy, 52
  Christopher's letter on Pakistan's uranium reprocessing efforts, 121–22
  efforts at averting containment failure in South Asia, 116–17
  efforts at halting nuclear proliferation, 3–4, 12, 59, 115–16
  offer of limited assistance to Afghanistan, 133n80
  role in U.S. troop withdrawal from Republic of Korea, 194–207
  role in U.S.-Pakistan proliferation dispute, 116–17, 120, 121–38, 158–59
  role in U.S.- Republic of China on Taiwan dispute, 3–4, 211–13, 243–56
Casey, William, 139
Cavanna, Thomas P., 30n78
Central Europe, collapse of Soviet bloc, 40
Central Intelligence Agency (CIA)
  analysis of Pakistan's nuclear program, 154–55, 156
  Cuban Missile Crisis and, 42–43
  identification of India as nuclear proliferator, 29
  on Moscow's pursuit of détente with U.S., 99–100
Central Treaty Organization (CENTO), 25–26, 27
Chiang Ching-kuo, 3–4
  role in U.S.-Republic of China in Taiwan dispute, 217–19, 223, 228, 235–36, 240–41, 242, 257–58
Chiang Kai-shek, 20
  role in U.S.-Republic of China on Taiwan dispute, 211–12, 213–14, 215, 216, 216n16
China
  existential threats by, 25
  first nuclear weapons test, 29
  Kennedy's effort at slowing nuclear programs, 67n4
  nuclear ambitions of, 2
Chinese Atomic Energy Council (CAEC), Taiwan, 220–21, 231, 232–33, 251
Chinese Civil War (1949), 40
Christopher, Warren
  role in U.S.-Pakistan proliferation dispute, 121–22, 123, 127–28, 134–35, 136
Chun Doo-hwan, 161, 207
Chung, Victor, 219–20

INDEX

Chung-hee, 3–4
Chungshan Institute of Science and Technology (CIST, ROC), 218–19, 220–21, 231–33, 241, 245, 251
Clark, Dick, 28–29
Clifford, Clark, 79, 82–84
Clinton, Bill, 30
"Coercing Allies: Why Friends Abandon Nuclear Plans" (Kogan), 25n55
coercion
   with accommodation (hybrid strategy), 14, 48–49, 108, 116, 179, 192, 260
   alliance coercion, 14, 14n35, 32, 56, 61t, 63
   Ford administration and, 179, 192, 239
   Kennedy administration and, 72
   Kogan on, 25n55
   Taiwan Relations Act and, 27
   toward Pakistan, 116, 133, 261
   by U.S. vs. South Africa, 27–28
Cohen, Avner, 71–72
Cold War
   Cuban Missile Crisis (1962), 39–40
   global bipolar system during, 38–39
   importance of South Africa, 28–29
   latter half, policymaker's assessments of regional power dynamics, 260
   structural realism and, 6
   Truman years power distributions, 40
   U.S. nonproliferation strategies, 11, 37
   U.S. strategic objective, 7, 260
   U.S.-Soviet rivalry, 9, 20
   warming of, influence on U.S.-Pakistan dispute, 152
Constable, Peter, 129, 136
containment failure
   causes of increasing risk, 9, 13, 41, 46–47, 56–57, 89
   in East Asia, 210
   Ford/Carter/Reagan, effort at averting in South Asia, 116–17
   Kennedy/Johnson/Nixon's efforts at avoiding in the Middle East, 65–200
   limited U.S. risks in Africa, 28
   in the Middle East, 260
   minimizing risks of, 7–8
   Montgomery's description, 8
   in South Asia, 116–17, 120, 137, 152–53, 157–58, 260
   time horizons and, 47
   U.S. stance on, 11
Cooper, Zack, 53
credible sanctions theory, 16, 25n56
   application to Pakistan-U.S. proliferation dispute, 158
   description, 16, 24–25
   non-applicability to U.S.-Israeli proliferation dispute, 25n56
   security commitment theory comparison, 60

Crimean War (1854), 39
Croach, Jesse, 69
Cuba, support for Mozambique leftist government, 28
Cuban Missile Crisis (1962), 39–40, 42–43

Debs, Alexander, 28, 29
deep engagement strategy, 8n16
Defense Intelligence Agency (DIA, U.S.)
   analysis of Pakistan's nuclear program, 154–55, 156
   assessment of Arab-Israeli balance, 99
   estimates on Soviet forces in Afghanistan, 136
Demilitarized Zone (DMZ), between North and South Korea, 164, 166–67, 181, 184, 204
Deng Xiaoping
   role in U.S.-Republic of China on Taiwan dispute, 236–38, 248–49, 250–51, 252–54
   role in U.S.-Republic of Korea's proliferation dispute, 185, 186, 202
denial and deception (D&D) of nuclear intentions, 45
Desai, Rajiv, 120
Digital National Security Archives (DNSA), 32–33
Dimona reactor (Israel)
   application of nuclear domino/neoclassical realist theories, 85
   Ben-Gurion's comment on purpose of, 69–70
   challenges getting information about, 64–65
   Eisenhower's discovery of, 65
   Kennedy's demands for inspection, 12, 66–67
   Nachal Soreq reactor (Israel), 64
   Soviet reconnaissance sorties over, 46n30
   U.S. scientists visits to, inspections of, 68–73, 74–75, 77–78, 85, 90–91, 93
dominance, definition, 5–6
Dukakis, Michael, 154
Dulles, John Foster, 11–12, 215

East Asia
   drawdown of U.S. military presence, 26, 160
   emerging threats in, 161
   nuclear domino effects in, 60
   U.S. nonproliferation dispute with, 110–11
   U.S. power distribution variability, 39–40
   U.S. security commitments to, 3–4
   Washington's defined geographic boundaries for, 6
Eastern Europe, collapse of Soviet bloc, 40
Eban, Abba, 76, 77, 83
Edelstein, David, 44n20
Egypt. See also Suez Canal Zone
   acquisition of Soviet weapons, 68, 73, 80
   concerns for Israel's nuclear weapons development, 73

INDEX

Egypt *(cont.)*
efforts at slowing nuclear weapons programs in, 75–76
existential threats by, 25
purchase of Soviet jets, 99
Sadat's expulsion of Soviet military advisors, 99–100
Six Day War with Israel, 78–79
U.S. non-treaty security partnership with, 2
War of Attrition *vs.* Israel, 94
Eisenhower, Dwight D., 20
Atoms for Peace program, 29, 64, 214–15, 219–20
discovery of Israel's Dimona complex, 65
efforts in thwarting Israel's nuclear program, 46n28, 67
interactions with Ben-Gurion, 67
role in U.S.-Republic of China on Taiwan, 20, 214–15, 219–20
role in U.S.-Republic of Korea proliferation dispute, 20, 164, 175
equilibrium (balance-of-power) theories, 7–8
Erhard, Ludwig, 74
Eshkol, Levi, 53
Cohen's comment on Eshkol's agreement, 71–72
Johnson's interactions with, 73–74, 86–87
Kennedy's efforts at arranging inspections of Dimona reactor, 67, 71
"no introduction of nuclear weapons" pledge, 77
purchase of U.S. made M-48/M-60 tanks, 73, 74
request to purchase F-4 Phantoms, A-4 Skyhawks, 53, 78–79
signing of MOU agreement, 75, 80
signing the NPT and, 83–84
visit with Johnson, 79–81
Europe
argument in favor of controlled nuclear proliferation, 7n13
collapse of Soviet bloc, 40
protests against Russia's seizure of Crimea, 44
Evron, Ephraim, 80
Executive Committee of the National Security Council (EXCOM), 42–43, 43n15

false certainty problem, 44n22, 44
Farley, Philip, 68–69
Fascell, Dante B., 149–50
Feinberg, Abe, 83
Feldman, Myer "Mike," 70
Fettweis, Christopher, 39n5
F-4 Phantom
Eshkol's request to purchase, 53
Johnson's decision to sell to Israel, 73
Nixon administration's sale to Israel, 85
Rabin's request to purchase, 97

Ford, Gerald R.
Bhutto's meeting with, 117–18
economic assistance to India, 52
efforts at averting containment failure in South Asia, 116–17
efforts at halting nuclear proliferation, 3–4, 12, 115–16, 117–18
reprocessing acquisition dispute with South Korea, 177–94
role in U.S.-Pakistan-U.S. proliferation dispute, 116–21
role in U.S.- Republic of China on Taiwan nonproliferation dispute, 3–4, 211–13, 229, 234–44
uranium fuel reprocessing plant negotiations with Pakistan, 117–21
warning to Bhutto, 118–19
Foreign Affairs (or International Relations) Committee (U.S. House of Representatives), 51
Foreign Assistance Act (FAA, 1961), 51–53, 120–21, 147
Foreign Assistance Act (FAA, 1968), 82
foreign policy executive (FPE), 33–34
Foreign Relations Committee (U.S.), 51, 93
The Foreign Relations of the United States (FRUS) series, 32–33
France
India's nuclear collaboration with, 29n72
nuclear weapons programs, 15f, 23, 24t
participation in the NPT, 9–10
supplying of reactor technology to Israel, 64
uranium reprocessing plant contract with Pakistan, 117–21
weapon sales to Israel, 81–82
frenemies, 17–22
"ambivalent alliances" comparison, 21–22
characteristics of, 21–22
divergent security interests of, 20n45, 20
"ideal types" of, 18n42
primary concerns of, 20–21
term origin/definitions, 17–18
Friedberg, Aaron L., 41–42
F-12 aircraft, 109–10
Fuhrmann, Mathew, 23n53

Gandhi, Indira, 120
Gates, Robert, 156
Gavin, Francis J., 1
Gazit, Mordecai, 68
German Federal Republic, nuclear weapons program, 24t
Germany (Nazi), nuclear weapons program, 24t
Ginor, Isabella, 46n30
Giscard d'Estaing, Valéry, 123–24
Glaspie, April, 43
Glenn, John, 124, 146

Glenn Amendment, 52, 122–23
   U.S.-Pakistan dispute and, 122–23, 124, 147
"global commons" (Posen), 7–8
global hegemons
   emerging threats to regional interests, 42–47
   interests in various geographic regions, 4–5, 13, 38
   Lobell's definition of, 4–5
   strategic interests in varied geographic regions, 3–4
global nuclear nonproliferation regime, origins, 1
Goldberg, Arthur J., 221
Gorbachev, Mikhail, 153–54
Great Britain
   distribution of power in North America (1850s), 39
   hegemonic rule of, 38–39
   nuclear weapons programs, 15f, 23
   U.S. special relationship alliance with, 22

Haig, Alexander, 257
   role in U.S.-Pakistan nonproliferation conflict, 139–40, 141
   WSAG management group membership, 107n195
Harman, Avraham, 68–69, 80
Harriman, W. Averell, 74
Hart, Parker T., 82–83
Hartman, Arthur, 123
Hatfield, Mark, 141
HAWK antimissile batteries, 25, 86–87
hegemony. *See also* global hegemons
   Asia-Pacific region and, 226–27
   balance-of-power theories comparison, 7–8
   causes of, 38–39n5
   definitions of, 4–5, 39n5
   dominance, defined, 5–6
   Kennedy's view on, 67
   Kissinger/Nixon's view on, 98
   polarity comparison, 38–39n5
   polarity *vs.*, 5n5
   region, defined, 6n8, 6
   of the U.S., and nuclear proliferation, 4–12
   of the U.S., through military alliances, 1, 2
Helms, Jesse, 236, 255, 269
Helms, Richard, 87–89, 93, 94, 167
highly enriched uranium (HEU), 44–45, 46n29, 126, 146, 147–48, 156, 193
Hinton, Deane, 144–46
History and Public Policy Program (HAPP), Woodrow Wilson International Center for Scholars, 32–33
Hod, Mordechai, 80
Hsin Chu Project, 218–19, 221
Hsu Cho-yun, 218–19
Hua Goufeng, 131
Hummel, Arthur W., 122–24, 127, 128

Hussein, Saddam, 43
hybrid strategies
   accommodation-coercion (example), 108, 179, 239
   accommodative strategies comparison, 14
   neoclassical realist theory and, 192
   of presidential administrations, policymakers, 2–3, 36, 48–49, 54–56, 162, 192, 212–13, 255, 262, 267–68
   Putin's authorization of, 273

India. *See also* Pakistan-India rivalry
   civil nuclear energy program, 29
   defeat of Pakistan, 1971 war, 112–13
   eschewing of alliances by, 31
   existential threats by, 25
   Ford's economic assistance to, 52
   Nixon's response to nuclear testing, 52
   Non-Alignment Movement leadership, 31
   nuclear weapons program, 24t, 29n74
   peaceful nuclear explosion (PNE), 29n73, 30, 30n75, 115–16, 120–21, 193–94, 210, 230
   U.S.-India rapprochement failure, 31–32
Indian Atomic Energy Commission (IACC), 29
INR. *See* Bureau of Intelligence and Research
Institute for Nuclear Energy Research (INER, ROC), 219
institutionalist theory, 9n21
intelligence failures, 45–46, 64–65
Intelligence Reform and Terrorism Prevention Act (2004), 34n94
International Atomic Energy Agency (IAEA), 45, 52, 59, 73–74, 117–18
international system
   importance of structure, 37
   limits in nuclear weapons program in, 9–10, 10n25
   polarity within, 39n5, 38
   regions within, 6
   role of foreign policy executives (FPEs), 33
   role of hegemony, 1, 4
   structural realism, neoclassical realism, and, 37–56
   Waltz's view on, 6–7
Iran
   nuclear weapons program, 24t
   U.S. efforts at thwarting nuclear development, 2
Iran-Iraq War (1980-1988), 43
Iraq
   invasion of Kuwait (1990), 43
   nuclear weapons program, 24t
   U.S. efforts at thwarting nuclear development, 2, 3
Israel. *See also* Arab-Israeli conflicts; Dimona reactor (Israel)
   acceptance as nuclear state by U.S., 92–93

Israel (cont.)
  Atoms for Peace Program in, 219–20
  efforts at getting Israel to sign the NPT, 81–84, 86–89, 90
  Egypt's War of Attrition vs., 94
  existential threats against, 25
  France's supplying reactor technology, 64–65
  France's weapon sales to, 81–82
  frenemy status with U.S., 23
  Johnson/Nixon, acquiescence to nuclear program, 66
  Johnson's approval of weapon sales to, 53, 77, 80–81
  Kennedy/Johnson/Nixon's efforts at avoiding containment failure, 64–111
  Kennedy's antimissile battery sales to, 25
  Nachal Soreq reactor, 64, 75–76, 219–20
  Nixon's accommodation of, 3, 12
  Norway's supplying of heavy water, 64–65
  nuclear weapons programs, 15f, 23, 24t
  pledge to not introduce nuclear weapons in the Middle East, 84–85
  proliferation disputes, 24–25, 25n56
  purchase of U.S. combat aircraft, 76
  purchase of U.S. made M-48/M-60 tanks, 73, 74, 75
  request to purchase A-4s, 94
  request to purchase F-4 Phantoms, 53, 78–79, 94–95
  Six Day War with Egypt, 78–79
  U.S. coercive diplomacy with, 2
  U.S. efforts at halting nuclear proliferation, 3, 46n28
  U.S. fears of Soviet influence, 65
  U.S. non-treaty security partnership with, 2
  U.S. special relationship alliance with, 22
  U.S.'s supplying of "swimming pool" nuclear reactor, 64
Israeli Air Force (IAF), 78

Japan
  Carter administration and, 196, 201, 250–51, 256
  Ford administration and, 193, 210, 234, 242
  Nixon administration and, 172, 225, 227n67
  normalized relations with Republic of Korea, 165n19, 165–66
  nuclear domino theory and, 256
  reprocessing plant in, 184
  Soviet's loss of ground in, 185–86
  U.S. bilateral defense pact with, 2
  U.S. military presence in, 40, 186
Johnson, Lyndon B.
  acquiescence to Israeli nuclear program, 66
  agreement of MOU compromise language, 86–87
  arms embargo on India and Pakistan, 113–14
  coercive strategies of, 12
  decision to sell weapons to Israel, 53, 77, 80–81
  efforts at avoiding containment failure in the Middle East, 64–111
  efforts at dissuading India's nuclear proliferation, 30
  Eshkol's visit with, 79–81
  meeting with Eban on sale of F-4s, 83
  meeting with Eshkol, 73–74
  role in U.S.-Republic of Korea nuclear proliferation dispute, 165–67, 173n62
  role in U.S.-Republic of Republic of China on Taiwan nonproliferation dispute, 217, 218
  sale of weapons to Israel, 53
  signing of Foreign Assistance Act (1968), 82
Jones, Lewis, 68–69

Kamal, Babrak, 133–34, 152–53
Katzenbach, Nicholas, 77–78, 79
Kennedy, John F., 3
  arranging of inspections of Israel's Dimona reactor, 66–73
  coercive strategies of, 12
  criticism of NATO, 67
  Cuban Missile Crisis (1962), 39–40, 42–43
  declining of Ben-Gurion's defense treaty request, 86–87
  effort at enlisting India against China, 31
  effort at halting Israel's nuclear weapons program, 3, 64–111
  efforts at arranging of inspections of Israel's Dimona reactor, 66–73, 109, 260, 263–64
  efforts at avoiding containment failure in the Middle East, 3, 64–111
  efforts at dissuading India's nuclear proliferation, 30
  efforts at slowing China's nuclear program, 67n4
  HAWK missile sales to Israel, 25, 86
  Israel's nuclear program and, 11n28
  on Middle East power distribution, 260
  signing of National Security Action Memorandum 231, 70
  stymied efforts in thwarting Israel's nuclear program, 46n28
Khan, A. Q., 155
Khan, Ghulam Ishaq, 154
Khan, Mohammed Daoud, 124
Khan, Munir, 142, 146
Khan, Sahabzada Yaqub, 118–20, 124, 139–40, 142
Khan, Shahyar, 157
Khan Junejo, Muhammad, 148
Kim Il-sung, 163–64, 166n24, 166–67
Kissinger, Henry A.
  acceptance of Israel as nuclear state, 92–93
  Bhutto's meeting with, 117–18
  concerns of Israel's nuclear problem, 89, 92–93

efforts at getting Israel to sign NPT, 88–89
efforts at halting Pakistan's nuclear proliferation, 115–16, 117–18, 119–20
efforts at Israel-Egypt peacekeeping, 66
initiation of NSSM 81 and 82, 93
Khan's meeting with, 118–20
Rabin's communications with, 91
role as Nixon's national security advisor, 33n92
role in U.S.- Republic of China on Taiwan proliferation dispute, 212, 219n31, 222, 223, 224–26, 227n67, 227–28, 228n75, 229, 235, 236–, 240, 243, 244, 250–51
role in U.S.- Republic of Korea proliferation dispute, 167n32, 169, 171, 173–74, 178, 179n95, 181–82, 184, 185–87, 188–90, 191
seeking of rapprochement with China, 31–32
skepticism about the NPT, 85n98, 85, 91–92
on Soviet's Near East hegemony, 98
Koenig, Matthew, 11
Kogan, Eugene B., 25n55
Komer, Robert, 74, 75
Korean People's Army (KPA), 164
Korea Worker's Party, 163–64
Kuwait, Iraq's invasion of (1990), 43

Laird, Melvin P., 87–88, 92–93, 95–96, 97, 169–70, 171, 172–73
Lake, UU, 131
Lanoszka, Alexander, 53, 58, 62n59
Leach, Jim, 149–50
Lee, Ming Young, 165–66
Libya
   nuclear weapons program, 24t
   U.S. efforts at thwarting nuclear development, 2
Lobell, Steven E., 4–5
Long, Austin, 64–65

McMahon, John N., 143–44
McNamara, Robert S., 76, 80
Meir, Golda
   agreement to purchase Hawk missiles, 70
   Nixon's understanding with, 3–4, 66, 85–101
   request to purchase electronic jamming equipment, 97
   testing of Nixon's understanding with, 101–9
Memorandum of Understanding (MOU) agreement, 74, 75, 80, 86–87
Middle East. *See also* Arab-Israeli conflicts; Israel
   balance of power issues, 3–4
   Carter administration and, 194n163
   CENTO's role in protecting, 25–26
   effort at avoiding containment failure in, 65, 89
   effort at avoiding polarization in, 76, 79
   Johnson administration and, 65, 74
   Kennedy administration and, 65, 260
   Nixon administration and, 92, 100
   potential U.S.-USSR confrontation, 92–93

power distribution variability, 39–40, 72, 85, 109, 207
prioritizing containment *vs.* nonproliferation, 109–11
Soviet influence in, 65, 78–79, 95, 98, 113, 259
varied nuclear proliferation strategies in, 61–62
Washington's defined geographic boundaries for, 6
military assistance program (MAP, U.S.)
   reduction of, in Republic of China on Taiwan, 216, 217–18, 223, 225, 243, 251, 253, 256
   reduction of, in South Korea, 170–71, 172–73, 176–77, 186–87, 220
Miller, Nicholas L.
   coining of "nuclear domino theory" term, 8
   credible sanctions theory, 16n38
   on effects of China/India nuclear tests on U.S., 60
   on Nixon's view of Israeli nuclear program, 91–92
   "The Secret Success of Nonproliferation Sanctions," 35n96
   Stopping the Bomb, 16, 30n75, 59–60n55, 60n56
   "Why Nuclear Energy Programs Rarely Lead to Proliferation," 42–43
Missile Technology Control Regime (MTCR), 30
Monteiro, Nuno, 28, 29
Montgomery, Evan Brandon, 8. *See also* access denial
Morahg, Mordechai, 219–20
M-48 tanks, Johnson's decision to sell to Israel, 53
Multilateral Nuclear Force (MLF, NATO), 67
multilateral treaty alliances, 2. *See also* specific treaty alliances
Murphy, Robert, 149–50
Muskie, Edmund, 136
Mutual Defense Assistance (MDA) agreement, U.S.-Taiwan, 214
Mutual Defense Treaty, U.S. and Republic of China on Taiwan, 214–15, 215n9, 230–31, 238, 250, 252–53, 254, 255
Mutual Defense Treaty, U.S. and Republic of Korea, 27, 173–74, 200

Nachal Soreq reactor (Israel), 64, 75–76, 219–20
Naik, Naiz, 146
Najibullah, Mohammad, 152–54
Nance, John, 140
Napoleonic Wars, 39
Nasser, Gamal Abdel, 73
National Archives and Records Administration (NARA) II, 32–33
National Intelligence Estimate (NIE), 143–44
   intelligence on Pakistan, 143–44
National Security Action Memorandum (NSAM) 231, 70

INDEX

National Security Agency (NSA)
  assessment of Pakistan's nuclear program, 154–55, 156
  identification of India as nuclear proliferator, 29
National Security Archive (NSA) Electronic Briefing Books, 32–33
National Security Council (NSC), 34n94, 40n8, 74, 88–89
National Security Planning Group (NSPG), 145
National Security Study Memorandum 27 (NSSM 27), 173n62
National Security Study Memorandum 40 (NSSM 40), 87–88, 89n111, 92n130
National Security Study Memorandum 81 (NSSM 81), 93
National Security Study Memorandum 82 (NSSM 82), 93
National Security Study Memorandum 212 (NSSM 212), 234n105
neoclassical realism (neoclassical realist theory), 3, 13–16
  application to U.S.-Israel conflict, 65, 72, 85
  application to U.S.-Pakistan conflict, 120, 137, 157–58
  application to U.S.-ROC nonproliferation dispute, 254–55, 258
  argument on forms of power, 43–44
  assumptions of, 13–14
  on causal path linking independent-intervening variables, 54
  claims about domestic-level processes, 49
  credible sanctions theory alternative, 16
  global hegemons and, 13
  international system and, 37–56
  main hypotheses of, 36
  nuclear domino theory alternative, 16
  nuclear domino theory comparison, 57
  observations on foreign policy executives (FPEs), 16
  ongoing relevance of, 3–4
  relation to structural realism, 13
  security commitment theory alternative, 16
  on a state's strategic (security) environment, 38
  on Trump, 275
Netanyahu, Benjamin, 22
Newsom David, 123–25
New Zealand, SEATO membership, 25n58
9/11 terrorist attacks, 159
Nixon, Richard M.
  acceptance of Israel as nuclear state, 92–93
  accommodation to nuclear-armed Israel, 3, 12
  acquiescence to Israeli nuclear program, 66
  efforts at avoiding containment failure in the Middle East, 3, 64–111
  efforts at dissuading India's nuclear proliferation, 30
  efforts at halting nuclear proliferation, 3
  efforts at rapprochement with China, 26
  F-4 sales to Israel/understanding with Meir, 85–101
  Meir's understanding with, 3–4, 66, 85–101, 129
  objectives in East Asia, Southeast Asia, 160–61
  response to India's nuclear test, 52
  role in U.S.-Republic of China on Taiwan proliferation dispute, 212, 216n16, 221–34
  role in U.S.-Republic of Korea proliferation dispute, 160, 161–63, 167–73, 186, 200, 210
  skepticism of the NPT, 85n98, 85, 91–92
  "special understanding" with Meir, 3–4, 66
  testing of Meir's understanding with, 101–9
  Watergate scandal, 117–18, 196–97, 235, 236, 268–69
  withdrawal of combat troops from South Korea, 161
  withholding of F-4s/A-4s sales to Israel, 98
Nixon Doctrine, U.S.-Republic of Korea proliferation dispute, 26, 91–92, 163–77
Non-Alignment Movement leadership (India), 31
nonproliferation strategies. See also specific strategies
  accommodation strategies, 1–2
  Gavin on, 1
  influence of international forces, domestic politics, 2–3
  Middle East/containment over nonproliferation, 109–10
  neoclassical realism and, 3
  Nuclear Nonproliferation Treaty (1971), 9
  as post-1945 U.S. strategy, 36
  security commitment theory and, 16
  U.S. development of, 2–3
  U.S. hegemony and, 1
  U.S. initiatives, 30–34
  U.S. presidential interests in, 3–4
  variations on types of, 14
non-treaty security partnerships, 2
North Atlantic Treaty Organization (NATO), 2, 67
North Korea (Democratic People's Republic of Korea), Demilitarized Zone (DMZ) with South Korea, 164, 166–67, 181, 184, 204
"now-or-later" dilemma of policymakers, 42
nuclear breakout, definition, 44–45
nuclear domino theory (Miller)
  application to U.S.-Israel conflict, 65, 66, 72, 85
  application to U.S.-ROC conflict, 258
  description, 8–9, 11–12, 16, 24–25, 25n56, 56–57
  on Ford's/Carter's/Reagan's efforts in South Asia, 117
  independent variables posited by, 24–25
  Koenig on the logic of, 11
  Miller's coining of term, 8

INDEX

neoclassical realist theory comparison, 57
Pakistan-India rivalry and, 117
regional arms races and, 9
security commitment theory/credible sanctions theory comparison, 25n56, 34–35
as structural realism strand, 6
and U.S. responses to nuclear programs of allies, 12
nuclear latency dataset codes, 23n53
Nuclear Nonproliferation Act (U.S., 1978), 30
Nuclear Nonproliferation Treaty (NPT)
Article IX, Section 3, 9–10n22
efforts at getting Israel to sign, 81–84, 86–89, 90
negotiation stage, 77
Nixon's skepticism of, 85n98, 85, 91–92
nuclear weapons states recognized by, 9–10
Symington Amendment, 52
nuclear proliferation optimism, 6n10, 6–7
Nuclear Supplier's Group (NSG), 30
nuclear weapons proliferation. *See also* specific nuclear proliferation disputes
as access denial risk to the U.S., 10
application of neoclassical realism, 13–14
denial and deception (D&D) by states, 45
disputes/resolutions between allies, 50
Europe's controlled proliferation, 7n13
highly enriched uranium (HEU), 44–45, 46n29, 146, 147–48, 156, 193
Koenig on, 11
nuclear breakout, definition, 44–45
reactive nuclear proliferation, 9, 110
technical barriers to development, 45n24
as threat to international status hierarchy, 9–10
time horizon for unfolding, 11–12
U.S. efforts at halting, 2, 3–4
U.S. hegemony and problem of, 4–12
U.S. structural realist baselines, 6–12
nuclear weapons states (NWSs), 9–10, 23, 24t *See also* specific states (countries)
Nunn, Sam, 146

Oakley, Robert, 156
O'Neill, Thomas P., 152
Ottoman Empire, 39
Owen, Henry, 86

Packard, David, 87–90, 97
Pakistan. *See also* United States (U.S.)-Pakistan proliferation dispute
Atoms for Peace Program in, 219–20
CENTO membership, 26n60
defensive strategic objective of, 113
frenemy status with U.S., 23–25
Glenn Amendment and, 122–23, 124, 147
nuclear smuggling case plea deal, 52–53
nuclear weapons programs, 15f, 23, 24t, 116
proliferation disputes outcomes, 24–25

Reagan's economic, military assistance to, 139
SEATO membership, 25n58, 26n60
secret contract with France for reprocessing plant, 118–19
treaty alliance with U.S., 25–26
uranium processing efforts, 121–22
U.S. bilateral security relationship with, 259
U.S. coercive diplomacy with, 2
U.S. economic, military assistance to, 139, 140
U.S. efforts at thwarting nuclear development, 3, 12
U.S. non-treaty security partnership with, 2
view of Bush's termination of military, economic assistance, 116
Pakistan Atomic Energy Commission (PAEC), 112n2, 142, 146
Pakistan-India rivalry
Johnson's arms embargo, 113–14
1990, brink of war, 156
1965 war, 113–14
1971 war, 112–13, 114–15
nuclear domino theory and, 117
Pakistan Institute of Nuclear Science and Technology (PINSTECH), 154–55
Pakistan Muslim League-N, 157
Pakistan People's Party (PPP), 122–23, 154
Park Chung-hee (ROK president). *See also* United States (U.S.)-Republic of Korea (ROK) proliferation dispute
ascendance to presidency, 165
assassination by Kim Jae-kyu, 206
effort at forestalling U.S. troop withdrawals, 269
Ford's/Carter's, nonproliferation efforts with, 3–4
KCIA conspiracy against, 206–7
pursuit of nuclear weapons, 160–61
termination of Project 890, 256
Paul, T. V., 9, 25n57, 26n59
peaceful nuclear explosion (PNE), India (1974), 29n73, 30n75, 30, 115–16, 120–21, 193–94, 210, 230
People's Democratic Party of Afghanistan (PDPA), 124
People's Movement for the Liberation of Angola (MPLA), 28
People's Republic of China
Nixon's seeking of rapprochement with, 26
nuclear weapons program, 24t
participation in the NPT, 9–10
Pervez, Arshed, 148–50, 151
Philippines
SEATO membership, 25n58
U.S. bilateral defense pact with, 2
Pickering, UU, 131
plutonium (PU), 44–45, 46n29
Porter, William J., 165–67
Posen, Barry, 7–8

Pressler, Larry, 147
Pressler Amendment, U.S.-Pakistan proliferation dispute and, 147n133, 147–48, 157
Project 890, U.S.-ROK proliferation dispute, 163–77
Putin, Vladimir
  authorization of hybrid strategies, 273
  move to annex Crimea, 43–44
  Trump's praise of, 274

Rabin, Yitzhak, 83
  Kissinger's communications with, 91
  request to purchase F-4s, A-4s, 97
  Richardson's meetings with, 90
  signing of MOU agreement, 84–85, 86
  Warnke's meetings, 84
Rafael, Gideon, 77
Raphel, Arnold, 154
reactive nuclear proliferation (nuclear domino effects), 9, 110
Reagan, Ronald
  "constructive engagement" toward South Africa, 28–29
  economic/military assistance to Pakistan, 139, 140
  efforts at halting nuclear proliferation, 59, 115–16
  establishment of nuclear "red line" with Pakistan, 3–4, 138
  funding of covert operations to Afghan *mujahidin*, 139, 153
  invocation of the Solarz Amendment for Pakistan, 152
  nonproliferation objectives in South Asia, 116–17, 138
  pursuit of accommodative strategies with Pakistan, 138
  red lines for Pakistan's nuclear program, 3–4, 138–53
  request for Symington Amendment waiver for Pakistan, 140–41
  role in U.S.- Republic of China on Taiwan dispute, 256–58
  strategy against Pakistan's nuclear development, 3
reconnaissance, aerial and satellite, 45, 46n30, 167–68, 215
regional power distributions
  assessments of, 40–42, 54
  during Cold War/Truman years, 40
  defined, 38
  favorable *vs.* unfavorable, 40–41, 55–56
  global hegemons and, 13
  methods for altering, 6, 38
  in the Middle East, 66, 72–73
  neoclassical realist theory and, 3, 57, 108, 158
  offering of inducements, 47–48

South Asia/U.S.-Pakistan proliferation dispute, 116–17, 120–21, 131–32, 137, 152–53, 157, 158
U.S.-Republic of China (ROC) on Taiwan proliferation dispute, 222, 242, 244, 255
U.S.-Republic of Korea (ROK) proliferation dispute, 000, 161, 162, 172, 185–86, 192, 194, 195, 207, 209
regional security complexes (RSCs), 6n8
regions
  access denial, containment failure, and, 7–8, 11, 28
  definition, 6
  global hegemons' interests in, 4–5, 13
  power distribution assessments, 41–42
  power dynamics, x
  time horizon for emerging threats, 42–47
  U.S. alliances, 2
  U.S. attempted influence in, 20
  U.S. power distribution in, 34–35, 47–56
Reid, Ogden, 67
Remez, Gideon, 46n30
Republic of China (ROC) on Taiwan. *See also* United States (U.S.)-Republic of China (ROC) on Taiwan proliferation dispute
  bilateral alliance with U.S., 27
  Chiang Kai-shek's presidency, 211–12
  existential threat for Taiwan, 211
  Mutual Defense Assistance (MDA) agreement, 214
  transition from authoritarian to democratic rule, 211–12
  U.S. bilateral alliance with, 27
  U.S. bilateral security relationship with, 259
  U.S. efforts at nuclear nonproliferation, 3–4
Republic of Korea (ROK)(South Korea). *See also* Park Chung-hee; United States (U.S.)-Republic of Korea (ROK) proliferation dispute
  bilateral alliance treaties with U.S., 27
  Chun Doo-hwan's leadership, 161
  Demilitarized Zone (DMZ) with North Korea, 164, 166–67, 181, 184, 204
  Eisenhower's alliance treaty with, 20
  existential threats against, 25
  fear of abandonment by U.S., 26
  frenemy status with U.S., 23–25
  Nixon's withdrawal of U.S. combat troops, 161
  nuclear weapons programs, 15f, 23, 24t
  Park's ascendance to presidency, 25
  transition to democratic rule (1980s), 161
  U.S. bilateral defense pact with, 2, 27
  U.S. bilateral security relationship with, 259
  U.S. coercive diplomacy with, 2, 3–4
Resnick, Evan, 18, 21, 21–22n49, 160n1
Rogers, William P., 86, 87–88, 94, 96–97, 98–99, 170, 173–74

Rostow, Walt. W., 33n92, 79, 80, 83
Rusk, Dean, 67, 68, 76, 77, 83, 84

Sadat, Anwar al-, 97, 98–99, 101–2, 106–8
satellite reconnaissance, 45, 114–15, 154–55, 199–200, 257–58
Saudi Arabia, U.S. non-treaty security partnership with, 2
Science Advisory Committee of the ROC National Security Council, 219
sea lanes of communication (SLOCs), 40–41
security commitment theory
   applicability to U.S.-Taiwan, U.S.-South Korea disputes, 25n56
   credible sanctions theory comparison, 60
   description, 16, 57–59, 62
   independent variables posited by, 24–25
   nuclear domino-/neoclassical realist theory comparison, 25n56, 59
Senate Governmental Operations Committee (U.S.), 154–55
Senior Review Group (SRG) of the NSC, 88–89
September 11, 2011 terrorist attacks, 159
Shahi, Agha, 123–24, 125, 127–28, 130–31, 135, 139–40
Sharif, Nawaz, 157
Shifrinson, Joshua, 64–65
Shultz, George P., 144, 145, 150, 151–52, 153
Sino-Indian War (1962), 31
Sisto, Joseph J., 87, 118–19
Six Day War (Israel-Egypt), 78–79
SNIE. *See* Special National Intelligence Estimate
Solarz, Stephen A., 147, 148
Solarz Amendment, Pakistan-U.S. proliferation dispute and, 147–48, 149–50, 151
Solarz Amendment to the FAA, 52–53
South Africa
   military/economic advantages of, 28
   nuclear weapons program, 24t, 27–29
   Reagan's "constructive engagement" toward, 28–29
   risks of Soviet invasions, 28
South Asia
   containment failure threat levels, 120, 137, 152–53, 157–58
   nuclear domino effects in, 60
   Reagan's long-term nonproliferation objectives in, 116–17, 138
   regional power distributions, 116–17, 120–21, 131–32, 137, 152–53, 157, 158
   U.S. nonproliferation dispute with, 110–11
   U.S. power distribution variability, 39–40
   Washington's defined geographic boundaries for, 6
Southeast Asia
   drawn of U.S. deployments, 160
   Nixon's objectives in, 160
   U.S. power distribution variability, 39–40
South East Asia Treaty Organization (SEATO), 25n58
Soviet Union/Russia
   collapse in Eastern-Central Europe, 40
   Cuban Missile Crisis (1962), 39–40, 42–43
   decline of, 153–54
   global hegemony by, 4–5
   identification as Cold War adversary, 20
   invasion of Afghanistan (1979), 116–17, 133–35, 158, 209, 261, 264
   MiG 32 renaissance over Dimona nuclear reactor, 46n30
   nuclear ambitions of, 2
   nuclear proliferation optimism and, 7
   nuclear weapons program, 24t
   offer to sell weapons to Jordan, 73–74
   participation in the NPT, 9–10
   sale of weapons to Egypt, 68, 73
   seizure of Crimea from Ukraine (2014), 43–44
   supply of jets to Egypt, 99
   threats against Pretoria, 28
   withdrawal from Afghanistan, 153–54, 157
Spanish Empire, global hegemony of, 4–5
Special National Intelligence Estimate (SNIE), 115–16, 141–42
Staebler, Ulysses, 69
Strategic Arms Limitation Treaty II (SALT II), 132–33
structural realism (Waltz), 5–6, 13n34, 37, 265–66. *See also* nuclear domino theory; nuclear proliferation optimism
   argument on forms of power, 43–44
   baselines for U.S. nuclear proliferation, 6–13
   dual strands of, 6, 7–8
   international system and, 37–56
   international system's relation to, 37
   nuclear proliferation optimism strand, 6
   relation to neoclassical realist theory, 13
Suez Canal Zone, 94, 261
   Brezhnev's U.S.-Soviet deployment proposal, 106
   Egypt's offensive into, 101–2, 106, 261
   Rogers-Sadat talks about, 98–99
   Soviet weapons/military advisors in, 96–97, 100
Symington, Stuart, 93
Symington Amendment (to the Foreign Assistance Act), 30, 52–53
   Carter administration and sanctions, 121–38
   Congressional passage of, 120–21
   description, 134
   Pakistan-U.S. nonproliferation conflict and, 117, 119–20, 121–38, 139–41, 148–49, 151, 152, 158
Syngman Rhee, 20
Syria, existential threats by, 25

Taiwan. *See also* United States (U.S.)-Republic of China (ROC) on Taiwan proliferation dispute
   Eisenhower's alliance treaty with, 20
   existential threats against, 25
   fear of abandonment by U.S., 26
   frenemy status with U.S., 23–25
   nuclear weapons program, 24t
   nuclear weapons programs, 15f, 23, 26
   proliferation disputes outcomes, 24–25
   U.S. coercive diplomacy with, 2
Taiwan Relations Act (TRA, U.S., 1979), 27, 254n191, 257, 270–71
T'ang Chun-pu, 218–19
Tan Jung-pug, 219
Taraki, Nur Muhammad, 123–24
Ta-you Wu, 218–19
Thailand, SEATO membership, 25n58
time horizons for emerging threats
   containment failure and, 47
   description, 42
   U.S.-Pakistan proliferation dispute, 116–17, 120–21, 131–32, 137, 152–53, 157, 158
   U.S.-Republic of China (ROC) on Taiwan proliferation dispute, 212–13, 234–35, 242, 244, 255
   U.S.-Republic of Korea (ROK) proliferation dispute, 161, 162, 172, 185, 192, 194, 195, 207
Tkach, Benjamin, 23n53
Treaty of Friendship, Cooperation, and Mutual Assistance between the Union of Soviet Socialist Republics and the Democratic People's Republic of Korea, 164n8
Truman, Harry S.
   Cold War and, 20, 40
   Mutual Defense Assistance (MDA) agreement with Taiwan, 214
Trump, Donald J.
   neoclassical realist theory on, 275
   praise of Putin, berating of NATO allies, 274
   remarks at Chinese Business Event, 275n26
Turner, Stansfield, 132–33, 136, 202–3

United Kingdom (UK)
   hegemonic rule of, 38–39
   nuclear weapons program, 24t
   participation in the NPT, 9–10
   SEATO membership, 25n58
United Nations (UN) Security Council, 14
United States Forces in Korea (USFK), 164
United States (U.S.). *See also* United States (U.S.)-Pakistan proliferation dispute; United States (U.S.)-Republic of China (ROC) on Taiwan proliferation dispute; United States (U.S.)-Republic of Korea (ROK) proliferation dispute
   acceptance of Israel as nuclear state, 92–93
   access denial/containment failure risks, 13
   accommodative nonproliferation strategies, 1–2
   bilateral defense pacts, 2, 27
   Britain's distribution of power (1850s), 39
   Cold War strategic objective, 7
   Congressional oversight leverage, 51
   development of nonproliferation strategies, 2–3
   dual core interests in a region, 47
   East Asian security commitments, 3–4
   economic/military assistance to Pakistan, 139
   failure to anticipate India's PNE, 120–21
   fears of Soviet influence in Israel, 65
   global hegemony by, 4–5
   hegemonic rule of, 38–39
   hegemony through military alliances by, 2
   identification of Soviet Union as Cold War adversary, 20
   independent variables in power distribution, 47n32, 47–49, 48t
   inspections of Israel's Dimona reactor, 68–73
   intervening variables in power distribution, 49n34, 49–56
   leadership in 1989 revolutions, 40
   nonproliferation initiatives, 30–34
   non-treaty security partnerships, 2
   and nuclear proliferation, structural realist baselines, 6–12
   nuclear weapons program, 24t
   participation in the NPT, 9–10
   proliferation disputes with South Korea, Taiwan, 25n56
   rapprochement failure with India, 31–32
   scientists' visit to Dimona reactor, 68–73, 74–75, 77–78, 85, 90–91, 93
   SEATO membership, 25n58
   special relationship alliances with Britain and Israel, 22
   tracking of India's nuclear weapons program, 29n73
   treaty alliance with Pakistan, 25–26
   troop withdrawal from Republic of Korea, 3–4, 161, 162, 194–207
United States (U.S.)-Pakistan proliferation dispute, 27, 62n61, 62–63, 112–59
   Afghan *mujahidin* and, 139, 153
   Armacost's role, 149, 150, 151, 153
   Atherton's/Bennet's warning on Pakistan's nuclear efforts, 122
   Bush, George H. W., abandonment of Pakistan, 152–59
   Carter administration's role, 116–17, 120, 121–38, 158–59
   Christopher's role, 121–22, 123, 127–28, 134–35, 136
   CIA/DIA/NSA analysis of Pakistan's nuclear program, 154–55, 156
   containment failure threat levels, South Asia, 120, 137, 152–53, 157–58

credible sanctions theory and, 158
Ford administration's uranium fuel reprocessing plant contract, 116–21
France's uranium reprocessing plant contract with Pakistan, 117–21, 123–24, 125
Geneva Accords between Najibullah government and Afghan insurgents, 153–54
INR's warning on Pakistan, 27, 62n61, 62–63
National Security Planning Group analysis, 145
neoclassical realist theory and, 120, 137, 157–58
nuclear domino theory and, 117, 137–38, 158
Pakistan's smuggling nuclear components from Germany, 155–56
presidential waiver of Symington Amendment for, 140–41
Pressler Amendment and, 147n133, 147–48, 157
Reagan's red lines, 3–4, 138–53, 156
Shultz's role, 144, 145, 150, 151–52, 153
SNIE warning on Pakistan, 115–16, 141–42
Solarz Amendment and, 147–48, 149–50, 151
South Asia regional power distributions and, 116–17, 120–21, 131–32, 137, 152–53, 157, 158
South Asia time horizons of emerging threats and, 116–17, 120–21, 131–32, 137, 152–53, 157, 158
Soviet invasion of Afghanistan and, 117, 133–35, 158
Special National Intelligence Estimate (1974), 115–16
State Department's recommendations, 144
Symington Amendment and, 117, 119–20, 121–38, 139–41, 148–49, 151, 152, 158
time horizons for emerging threats, 116–17, 120–21, 131–32, 137, 152–53, 157, 158
U.S. congressional concerns, meetings, 124
Vance's role, 122, 123–24, 125–26, 130–31, 133–34
Walters meetings in Pakistan, 142–43
warming of Cold War's influence on, 152
Zia's role, 116–17, 122–23, 125–26, 127–28, 129, 131, 134–35, 139, 140–41, 142–46, 148, 150, 154
United States (U.S.)-Republic of China (ROC) on Taiwan proliferation dispute, 211–58
Atoms for Peace Program in, 219–20
Brzezinski's role, 246–47, 248, 250–51, 252–53, 254, 255
Carter administration's role, 3–4, 211–13, 243–56
Chiang Ching-kuo's role, 217–19, 223, 228, 235–36, 240–41, 242, 257–58
Chiang Kai-shek's role, 211–12, 213–14, 215, 216n16, 216, 221, 223, 225, 237, 241–42, 243–44, 245, 246, 252–53

Chinese Atomic Energy Council and, 220–21, 231, 232–33, 251
Chungshan Institute of Science and Technology's role, 218–19, 220–21, 231–33, 241, 245, 251
CIST's clandestine nuclear weapons program, 218–19
Deng Xiaoping's role, 236–38, 248–49, 250–51, 252–54
Dulles's role, 11–12, 215
Eisenhower administration's role, 214–15, 219–20
Ford administration's role, 3–4, 211–13, 229, 234–44
foreign military assistance, 238, 242–43, 251
GRC Atomic Energy Council and, 218–19, 220, 223, 230–31
Hsin Chu Project, 218–19, 221
Johnson administration's role, 217, 218
Kissinger's role, 212, 219n31, 222, 223, 224–26, 227n67, 227–28, 228n75, 229, 235, 236–, 240, 243, 244, 250–51
neoclassical realist theory and, 254–55, 258
Nixon Doctrine and, 211, 212, 216n16, 221–34
one China formula, 225, 226–27, 235, 236–38, 250–51, 257
Reagan administration's role, 256–58
reduction of U.S. military assistance program (MAP), 216, 217–18, 223, 225, 243, 251, 253, 256
regional power distributions, 222, 242, 244, 255
Siemens Corporation reactor deal, 220–21
Taiwan Relations Act (1979), 27, 254n191, 257, 270–71
time horizons of emerging threats, 212–13, 234–35, 242, 244, 255
"two Chinas" question, 225–26
U.S-China normalization, 216n16, 234–35, 236–37, 238, 242, 244, 247–51, 254
U.S.-ROC Mutual Defense Treaty, 214–15, 215n9, 230–31, 238, 250, 252–53, 254, 255
Vance's role, 246, 247–49, 250–51, 252–53, 254, 255–56
United States (U.S.)-Republic of Korea (ROK) proliferation dispute, 24–25, 25n56, 160–210
alliances, China and Soviet Union, 163–64, 164n8
alliances, U.S.-ROK, 000, 160–61, 162–63, 165–66, 168, 176, 196–97, 206, 207
Brown's role, 198, 202, 203–4
Brzezinski's role, 197–98, 201, 203–4, 206
Carter and U.S. troop withdrawal, 3–4, 161, 162, 194–207
Deng Xiaoping's role, 185, 186, 202
Department of Defense policy paper, 163

United States (U.S.)-Republic of Korea (ROK) proliferation dispute (*cont.*)
    Eisenhower's deployment of nuclear weapons to ROK, 164
    Ford administration's role, 3–4, 161, 162, 176–94
    Johnson administration's role, 165–67, 173n62
    Kissinger's role, 167n32, 169, 171, 173–74, 178, 179n95, 181–82, 184, 185–87, 188–90, 191
    military assistance, foreign, 170–71
    military assistance, U.S., 162, 164–65, 168, 169, 171, 177, 181–82, 186–87, 195, 200, 203, 204
    Nixon administration's role, Nixon Doctrine, 160, 161–63, 167–73, 186, 200, 210
    Park Chung-hee's role, 3–4, 160–210
    Park's fear of abandonment by the U.S., 163–77
    Project 890, 163–77
    Reagan administration's role, 161, 162–63, 207
    regional power distributions, 161, 162, 172, 185–86, 192, 194, 195, 207, 209
    time horizons for emerging threats, 161, 162, 172, 185, 192, 194, 195, 207
    U.S. troop reductions, 161, 162, 168, 169–70, 171, 172–73, 174–75, 181–82, 183, 195–96, 197, 198–99, 200, 202–3–, 205–6, 207–8
    U.S.-China normalization and, 202, 204, 206
    U.S.-ROK Mutual Defense Treaty, 27, 173–74, 200
    U.S.-ROK Mutual Security Treaty, 173–74
    Vance's role, 167, 197–98, 202, 204
U.S. Army Reserves, 51
U.S. Declassified Documents Online (USDDO), 32–33
U.S. Intelligence Community, 34n94
    concerns about North Korea, 192–93
    detection of nuclear proliferation behavior, 45
    divided attention of, 46n27
    tracking of India's nuclear weapons program, 29n73
U.S. National Guard, 51
U.S.-ROK Mutual Defense Treaty, 27

Vaid, Nazir Ahmed, 146–47
Vance, Cyrus, 122
    role in U.S.-Pakistan proliferation dispute, 122, 123–24, 125–26, 130–31, 133–34
    role in U.S.-Republic of China on Taiwan proliferation dispute, 246, 247–49, 250–51, 252–53, 254, 255–56
    role in U.S.-Republic of South Korea proliferation dispute, 167, 197–98, 202, 204
Vietnam War, 94, 160, 162, 165–66, 168, 172, 211, 215–16, 262, 268–69
Vorster, Balthazar Johannes ("John"), 27–28

Walters, Vernon, 142–43
Waltz, Kenneth N., 6–7
    reformulation of balance-of-power theory, 37
    structural realism of, 5–6, 13n34, 37, 265–66
    view of the international system, 6–7
Warnke, Paul, 83–84
    meetings with Rabin, 84
    signing of MOU agreement, 84–85, 86
War of Attrition (Egypt *vs.* Israel), 94
Watergate scandal, 117–18, 196–97, 235, 236, 268–69
Way, Christopher, 23n53
Webster, William, 154–55
Weinberger, Caspar, 143–44, 145, 153, 256–57
Weiss, Leonard, 146
Western Europe, U.S. power distribution variability, 39–40
West Germany, nuclear weapons programs, 15*f*, 23
Wheeler, Earle, 76, 80
Wohlforth, William, 44
Woodcock, Leonard, 251, 252–53

Yanukovych, Viktor, 44
Yarhi-Milo, Keren, 53

Zablocki, Clement, 124
Zia-ul-Haq, Muhammad
    military dictatorship of Pakistan, 116–17, 122–23
    Reagan's establishment of nuclear "red line" with, 3–4
    role in Pakistan-U.S. proliferation dispute, 116–17, 122–23, 125–26, 127–28, 129, 131, 134–35, 139, 140–41, 142–46, 148, 150, 154
    U.S.-Pakistan conflict and, 125